D0725710

Criterion-Referenced Language Testing

THE CAMBRIDGE APPLIED LINGUISTICS SERIES

Series editors: Michael H. Long and Jack C. Richards

This series presents the findings of work in applied linguistics which are of direct relevance to language teaching and learning and of particular interest to applied linguists, researchers, language teachers, and teacher trainers.

Recent publications in this series:

Cognition and Second Language Instruction edited *by Peter Robinson*
Computer Applications in Second Language Acquisition *by Carol A. Chapelle*
Contrastive Rhetoric *by Ulla Connor*
Corpora in Applied Linguistics *by Susan Hunston*
Criterion-Referenced Language Testing *by James Dean Brown and Thom Hudson*
Culture in Second Language Teaching and Learning edited *by Eli Hinkel*
Exploring the Second Language Mental Lexicon *by David Singleton*
Focus on Form in Classroom Second Language Acquisition edited *by Catherine Doughty and Jessica Williams*
Immersion Education: International Perspectives edited *by Robert Keith Johnson and Merrill Swain*
Interfaces Between Second Language Acquisition and Language Testing Research edited *by Lyle F. Bachman and Andrew D. Cohen*
Learning Vocabulary in Another Language *by I.S.P. Nation*
Network-based Language Teaching edited *by Mark Warschauer and Richard Kern*
Pragmatics in Language Teaching edited *by Kenneth R. Rose and Gabriele Kasper*
Research Perspectives on English for Academic Purposes edited *by John Flowerdew and Matthew Peacock*
Researching and Applying Metaphor edited *by Lynne Cameron and Graham Low*
Second Language Vocabulary Acquisition edited *by James Coady and Thomas Huckin*
Sociolinguistics and Language Teaching edited *by Sandra Lee McKay and Nancy H. Hornberger*
Teacher Cognition in Language Teaching *by Devon Woods*
Text, Role, and Context *by Ann M. Johns*

Criterion-referenced Language Testing

James Dean Brown
University of Hawai'i at Manoa

Thom Hudson
University of Hawai'i at Manoa

CAMBRIDGE
UNIVERSITY PRESS

WITHDRAWN

LORETTE WILMOT LIBRARY
NAZARETH COLLEGE

PUBLISHED BY THE PRESS SYNDICATE OF THE UNIVERSITY OF CAMBRIDGE
The Pitt Building, Trumpington Street, Cambridge, United Kingdom

CAMBRIDGE UNIVERSITY PRESS
The Edinburgh Building, Cambridge CB2 2RU, UK
40 West 20th Street, New York, NY 10011–4211, USA
477 Williamstown Road, Port Melbourne, VIC 3207, Australia
Ruiz de Alarcón 13, 28014 Madrid, Spain
Dock House, The Waterfront, Cape Town 8001, South Africa

http://www.cambridge.org

© Cambridge University Press 2002

This book is in copyright. Subject to statutory exception
and to the provisions of relevant collective licensing agreements,
no reproduction of any part may take place without
the written permission of Cambridge University Press.

First published 2002
Reprinted 2003

Printed in the United Kingdom at the University Press, Cambridge

Typeset in Sabon 10.5/12pt   System 3b2   [CE]

A catalogue record for this book is available from the British Library

Library of Congress Cataloguing in Publication data applied for

ISBN 0 521 80628 3 hardback
ISBN 0 521 00083 1 paperback

418.0076
Bro

In memory of our fathers

Dean Brown
Charles Hudson

Contents

Series editors' preface

Given the well-documented washback effects of testing on curriculum and teaching, almost any new book on language testing is potentially important for testing specialists and non-specialists alike. This is especially true of the present volume, however, for it is the first to deal exclusively and comprehensively with what must surely be the future of language testing in many contexts, namely, criterion-referenced language testing.

In so many situations, the goal of assessment is to determine whether any or all individuals can or cannot do something at a level determined by experts to be relevant for future success, not to find out how they compare with one another, as is the case with norm-referenced measurement. In a driving test, for instance, the question is whether John and/or Mary can drive safely, not which one drives better than the other. And so it is with much language testing. Can students understand particular spoken registers of language X well enough to follow a lecture in their field of study delivered in X? Can they speak, read and write at the required levels? Can these individuals make themselves understood well enough in language Y to travel unaccompanied in a country where only Y is spoken? Do these applicants command enough of language Z to take a vocational training course delivered in Z or to perform well in a job using Z?

While criterion-referenced testing (CRT) has come of age in many fields, and while articles about it have occasionally appeared in language teaching journals for some 20 years, there has not until now been a book in language teaching and applied linguistics devoted solely to the topic. J. D. Brown and Thom Hudson, both of the University of Hawai'i's Department of Second Language Studies, are two of the best known and most widely respected experts on CRT, and their new book should remedy the situation most capably. Writing clearly and providing copious examples throughout, Professors Brown and Hudson start by situating CRT within general approaches to language testing. They then cover the role of criterion-referenced measurement in curriculum-related testing, the development and evaluation of CRT items, and the statistical tools required for validating a CRT, as distinct from those familiar with norm-referenced measures, ending with a practical guide to using CRT measures and reporting findings. In an innovative addition to the book, the authors and Cambridge University Press have provided a web-site offering a list of key terms, a set of review questions, and numerous application exercises with answer keys, to accompany each chapter.

Criterion-referenced language testing is a most welcome addition to the *Cambridge Applied Linguistics Series*. It should prove a valuable reference guide for language teachers and testers, curriculum developers, program designers, and graduate students preparing themselves for careers in any of these fields.

Michael H. Long
Jack C. Richards

Acknowledgements

The authors wish to thank many individuals for their contributions and support throughout the development of this book and the ideas behind it. We would like to acknowledge the support of Mike Long and Jack Richards as editors of CALS series. Mike Long has been particularly involved in the development of the text since its inception. We would also like to acknowledge the help and gentle nudging of Mickey Bonin at Cambridge. We also acknowledge the comments and insights by students over the years. We thank especially John Norris, Siwon Park, Youngkyu Kim, Emily Detmer, Bill Bonk, and students in many many testing classes who listened and commented on the role of criterion-referenced measurement. Colleagues whose ideas, insights, and comments have contributed over time, whether they know it or not, are Carol Chapelle, Lyle Bachman, Tim McNamara, Geoffrey Brindley, Fred Davidson, Jean Turner, Frances Butler, and especially Brian Lynch. Finally, very special thanks and appreciation also go to Kimi Kondo-Brown and Shira Smith for their love and support.

The authors and publishers are grateful to those authors, publishers and others who have given permission for the use of copyright material identified in the text. It has not been possible to identify, or trace, sources of all the materials used and in such cases the publishers would welcome information from copyright owners.

Testing in Language Programs, Brown, J.D. 1996 with permission from Pearson Education Inc. *Functional language objectives in a competency based curriculum* by Findlay, C.A., Nathan, L.A., TESOL Quarterly, Vol 14, No2, 1980 , pp 221–231. Reprinted by permission of TESOL Quarterly via the Copyright Clearance Center. *A categorical instrument for scoring second language writing skills*, by Brown, J.D. & Bailey, K.M. Language Learning 34:2, 1984, pp 21–42. Reprinted by permission of Blackwell Publishing. *Statistical tables for biological, agricultural and medical research* by R.A. Fisher and F. Yates 1963. Reprinted by permission of Pearson Education

Limited. *Designing second language performance assessments* by Norris, J.M., Brown, J.D., Hudson, T., Yoshioka, J. 1998. Reprinted by permission of the University of Hawai'i Press. *Reading for Professional Purposes: Studies and practices in native and foreign languages* by Brown, J.D. Reprinted by permission of Heinemann Educational Publishers. *Components of engineering-English reading ability* by Brown, J.D. Reprinted from System, Vol. 16, pp 193–200, 1988, with permission from Elsevier Science.

Preface

In the mainstream educational testing literature, the notion of criterion-referenced testing dates back to Glaser and Klaus (1962), Glaser (1963), and Popham and Husek (1969), and has been steadily gaining acceptance ever since (see Popham (1978 & 1981) and Berk (1980a & 1984) for much more on criterion-referenced testing and its background; for recent examples of work in this area, see almost any recent issue of *Journal of Educational Measurement* or *Applied Psychological Measurement*. The authors of this book were both trained in ESL and Applied Linguistics at UCLA and, as part of that training, studied with such experts in educational measurement as Shavelson, Webb, Muthen, and Popham. Naturally, they were influenced by the work of these experts in criterion-referenced testing. It was therefore with some surprise that both authors realized ten or more years ago that criterion-referenced testing was largely being ignored in language teaching and research. As a result, during the past decade, we have been at the heart of a quiet revolution that has been brewing in language testing circles: steadily, year by year, the concept of criterion-referenced testing has been gaining importance in the language testing literature.

Although the concept of criterion-referenced testing seems to have first entered the language testing literature in 1968 with an article by Cartier in the *TESOL Quarterly*, it did not appear again until the 1980s. Chronologically listed, some of the best examples of work involving criterion-referenced language testing are as follows: Cartier (1968); Cziko (1982; 1983); Brown (1984a); Hudson & Lynch (1984); Delamere (1985); Henning (1987); Brown (1988a); Bachman (1989); Brown (1989a); Hudson (1989 a & b); Bachman (1990); Brown (1990a & b); Cook (1990); Brown (1992; 1993); Griffee (1995); and Brown, (1995a & b; 1996).

What is criterion-referenced testing?

Criterion-referenced testing is most useful to classroom teachers and curriculum developers because criterion-referenced tests are specifically designed to assess how much of the content in a course or program is being learned by the students. With criterion-referenced tests, the primary purpose is not to compare the performances of examinees to one another (as it is with norm-referenced tests), but rather to examine the performance of each individual vis-à-vis a particular set of material or curriculum. Such tests are labeled *criterion-referenced* because the interpretation of the scores is intimately linked to assessing well-defined criteria for what is being taught. This close link to course objectives means that criterion-referenced tests can be used to diagnose the strengths and weaknesses of students vis-à-vis the goals and objectives of a particular course or program. At other times, criterion-referenced tests may be used to assess achievement, in terms of the amount each student has learned. Such information can be useful for grading student performance in a course, or for promotion to the next level, as well as for improving the materials, presentation, and sequencing of teaching points. In short, sound criterion-referenced tests can help the teacher do a better job because the primary purpose is to determine how much of the course content has been learned.

Since we have long been teaching the concepts of criterion-referenced testing in our introductory and intermediate language testing courses in the Department of Second Language Studies at the University of Hawai'i at Manoa and elsewhere, we have constantly been on the lookout for a book that covers the essential concepts of criterion-referenced testing – particularly one that covers the special problems of criterion-referenced language testing. While many books exist on the topic of language testing, none deals exclusively with the topic of criterion-referenced language testing. In fact, most books on language testing do not even mention the concept. Hence, we feel classroom language teachers and curriculum designers desperately need a guide to strategies for developing, analyzing, and revising criterion-referenced tests, particularly for purposes of diagnostic and achievement testing.

Approach

We have attempted to insure that *Criterion-referenced Language Testing* provides realistic and useful criterion-referenced test development tools that will assist language teachers and curriculum developers in their respective jobs. Both groups have a variety of choices to make in selecting or designing tests that are appropriate for the kinds of decisions that they must make. To facilitate such choices, we explore the use of CRTs from a number of perspectives.

Briefly, the content of each chapter will be as follows:

Chapter 1 Alternate paradigms provides background on what criterion-referenced testing is, what it can do, and how it is related to theoretical issues in language testing.

Chapter 2 Curriculum-related testing explores how testing is related to curriculum, with a special emphasis on performance testing and ways that other forms of alternative assessments (portfolios, conferences, diaries, etc.) can be used to promote fit between testing and curriculum.

Chapter 3 Criterion-referenced test items discusses a number of different item types. Strategies are also presented for using instructional objectives and item specifications, as well as for conducting item content and quality analysis.

Chapter 4 Basic descriptive and item statistics for criterion-referenced tests focuses on the statistical analysis of CRT items, including both descriptive and item statistics. Description of score distributions include basic statistics like the mean and standard deviation as well as graphical representations like histograms. The explanation is built step-by-step starting with the simple item facility index, then the difference index, agreement index, and others. The purpose of these various indices is explained and differentiated.

Chapter 5 Reliability, dependability, and unidimensionality explains score dependability as it relates to CRTs. Starting with a brief review of the traditional concept of test reliability, the chapter focuses on threshold-loss and generalizability approaches to criterion-referenced test dependability because of their importance to making decisions based on CRT scores.

Chapter 6 Validity of criterion-referenced tests covers CRT validity from two central perspectives: content validity is discussed in terms of its relationship to planning a test and using expert judgments, and construct validity is discussed in terms of intervention studies, differential-groups studies, and hierarchical-structure analysis. Numerous examples are given of how these validity strategies have been applied in real language programs. Chapter 6 also explains a number of strategies that have been worked out for setting standards, or cut-points, and making decisions on the basis of those standards.

Chapter 7 Administering, giving feedback, and reporting on criterion-referenced tests ends the book with an exploration of the particular problems of administering criterion-referenced tests, giving criterion-referenced feedback, and reporting criterion-referenced results. Again, examples are used to illustrate each issue.

The explanations are designed to be accessible not only to language teachers and curriculum developers, but also to those graduate students who are preparing to become language teaching professionals. As such, we define and explain the theoretical and practical issues in criterion-referenced language testing in digestible chunks. The statistical concepts are covered in a step-by-step manner with many examples and checklists throughout the discussions. In addition, there is a website to accompany each chapter in the book which includes a list of key terms, a set of review questions, and an extensive collection of application exercises (with answer keys provided), all of which are meant to make the language testing concepts more accessible to readers. You can find the website at uk.cambridge.org/elt/crlt/

Conclusion

In short, this book takes a relatively new approach to the issues involved in developing, implementing, and improving language tests: the criterion-referenced approach. For the first time, one book focuses on helping language teachers and curriculum developers with the types of decisions that they must make in their daily work.

1 *Alternate paradigms*

Introduction

The notion of criterion-referenced educational testing is usually traced back to Glaser and Klaus (1962) or to Glaser (1963). While this is relatively recent given the long history of educational measurement, criterion-referenced testing has emerged as an important tool in educational testing circles over the past few decades. Although only a few decades old, the central concepts of criterion-referenced testing have been around implicitly throughout history and pervade the ways humans deal with the world. For instance, in Judges 12: 5–6, fugitives from Ephraim trying to cross the Jordan river were tested by the Gilead guards with the following consequences:

5 . . . The men of Gilead said unto him, Art thou an E'phra-im-ite? If he said, Nay;
6 Then said unto him, Say now Shib-bo-leth: and he said Sib'-bo-leth: for he could not frame to pronounce it right. Then they took him, and slew him at the passages of Jordan: and there fell at that time of the E'phra-im-ites forty and two thousand.

Similarly, though with less serious outcomes, Conway Twitty sings, "Don't call him a cowboy 'till you've seen him ride." Thus, the underlying principles of directly referencing ability to a particular domain of behavior run deep in human interactions. How these principles are applied to language assessment is the focus of this book.

This chapter will explore the competing paradigms that are represented by the norm-referenced testing predominant throughout most of the past hundred years or so, and the relatively more recent development of criterion-referenced testing. To begin, norm-referenced tests and criterion-referenced tests (and closely related variants) will be defined. Then the differences and similarities of norm-referenced and criterion-referenced approaches will be explored by (a) examining how criterion-referenced tests were developed as a response to major problems with norm-referenced tests and (b) discussing how criterion-referenced tests are fundamentally different from norm-referenced tests. Next, the chapter will cover the place of criterion-referenced tests in language testing theory and research by exploring what makes language testing special, what language proficiency is, what communicative competence is, and what problems criterion-referenced language test developers face.

Some useful definitions

As with almost every academic area, the field of criterion-referenced testing has generated a large body of jargon over the years. Consequently, we must devote at least a portion of this chapter to disentangling some of the definitions that are crucial to understanding criterion-referenced testing. The key terms covered here were all formulated in efforts to clarify the differences and similarities of tests with different types of focus: norm-referenced tests, criterion-referenced tests, domain-referenced tests, and objectives-referenced tests.

Norm-referenced tests

For the purposes of this book, a *norm-referenced test* (NRT) will be defined as follows:

Any test that is primarily designed to disperse the performances of students in a normal distribution based on their general abilities, or proficiencies, for purposes of categorizing the students into levels or comparing students' performances to the performances of the others who formed the normative group.

As discussed more specifically in Brown (1989a; 1996), NRTs are appropriate for assessing abstracted language ability traits representing a "broader, more differentiated content range" (Millman & Greene, 1989, p. 341), for example, overall ESL proficiency, lecture listening ability, academic reading comprehension, and so forth. On such a test, the interpretation given an examinee's score is called a *relative decision* because it is understood as that examinee's position relative to the scores of all of the other examinees who took the test. Thus the examinee's score is referenced to his/her position in the normal distribution (also known as the *bell curve*), which is why this type of test is called norm-referenced.

The purpose of an NRT is to disperse examinees such that those with "low" abilities in a general subject area (such as overall ESL proficiency) will be found at one end of the normal distribution, while those with "high" abilities will be found at the other end. In most cases, the majority of individuals will fall somewhere between the "high" and "low" examinees and score fairly close to the average score.

Criterion-referenced tests

A general definition for a criterion-referenced test (CRT) was provided by Glaser (1963):

Criterion-referenced measures indicate the content of the behavioral repertory, and the correspondence between what an individual does and the underlying continuum of achievement. Measures which assess student achievement in terms of a certain criterion standard thus provide information as to the degree of competence attained by a particular student which is independent of reference to the performance of others. (p. 519)

Some confusion has resulted from the fact that the term *criterion* has been used in two ways in the CRT literature. In one sense, *criterion* means the specified knowledge or set of skills and tasks that the test was designed to sample and measure (as in the Glaser quote above). In another sense, *criterion* has been taken to mean the level of performance that is required to pass a test. For example, both meanings are inherent in the following Glaser and Nitko (1971) definition:

A criterion-referenced test is one that is deliberately constructed to yield measurements that are directly interpretable in terms of specified performance standards. Performance standards are generally specified by defining a class or domain of tasks that should be performed by the individual. (p. 653)

Much confusion has also been generated by the different ways that *criterion-referenced* has been used, as well as by the alternative terms that have evolved for different types of tests closely related to criterion-referenced tests. For example, the notion of domain-referenced tests (DRTs) has appeared in the literature. According to Hively, Patterson, and Page (1968), DRTs are based on *item forms* (documents which delineate a domain of student behaviors and content-area material to which test items are then referenced). As a result, such tests are made up of items directly referenced to a detailed description of the particular behavioral domain, skill, or content area involved (Hively, 1974). Osburn (1968) expanded Hively's notion to describe what he called the *universe-defined test*, which referred to any test "constructed and administered in such a way that an examinee's score on the test provides an unbiased estimate of his score on some explicitly defined universe of item content" (p. 96). Further, tests in the CRT family have been designated as *mastery-referenced* tests (Berk, 1980c) – tests that link mastery decisions to specific instructional contexts with specific instructional objectives that are not necessarily related to any external domain of knowledge. The differences among the different CRT applications, then, tend to focus on types of sampling generalizability (i.e., whether generalized to a domain, to an instructional set of objectives, to a mastery decision, etc.).

Another variation of the criterion-referenced test that has arisen is sometimes called the objectives-referenced test (ORT). An *objectives-referenced test* (or objectives-based test) is usually constructed so that subsets of the items measure the specific objectives of a course, program of study, or other clearly delineated subject-matter area. However, as pointed out by Nitko (1984, p. 22), "Objectives-referenced tests can be criterion-referenced tests if (a) objectives are written to define a domain and (b) items are representative samples of behavior from this domain." This term, then, is generally used to describe a specific type and use of CRT.

In short, while the fine distinctions between criterion-referenced, domain-referenced, universe-defined, and objectives-referenced tests are interesting to theoreticians, they may serve only to confuse those practicing teachers and curriculum developers who need to use tests of this general type. To limit such confusion, this book will use criterion-referenced as a cover term generally referring to all testing of this type and use domain-referenced and objectives-referenced only to refer to variant methods of sampling items when developing criterion-referenced tests. *Domain-referenced test* will be used occasionally to refer to special circumstances when a criterion-referenced test is based on a well-established domain that has been clearly defined with items selected from that domain. *Objectives-referenced test* will also occasionally be used to refer to those particular criterion-referenced tests that are developed to assess the specific objectives of a language course or program.

Note, however, that the distinction between the two sampling techniques used to develop criterion-referenced tests blurs if the objectives of a course can be defended as a representative sample of a domain of behavior (as noted by Nitko, 1984). In other words, in such a situation, the resulting objectives-referenced test could also be said to be domain-referenced. In short, the phrase *criterion-*

referenced test will be used to refer to the general family of test development strategies just discussed.

Thus, for the purposes of this book, a *criterion-referenced test* (CRT) will be defined as any test that is primarily designed to describe the performances of examinees in terms of the amount that they know of a specific domain of knowledge or set of objectives. At any rate, the key factor is having a clearly described assessment domain (Popham, 1994). Moreover, as discussed in more detail in Hudson & Lynch (1984), Brown (1989a; 1996), and Popham (1999), the interpretation of CRT scores is termed an *absolute decision* because each examinee's score is meaningful without reference to the scores of the other examinees. An individual's score indicates the amount (percent, number of items, count, or other quantity) of the knowledge or skill that examinee has at the time of the test. In addition, the distribution of scores will not necessarily be normal. Indeed, if all of the examinees have 100% of the knowledge or skill involved, they should all receive the same score of 100% correct (see Chapter 2 for more on this topic).

The early proposal for criterion-referenced testing by Glaser (1963) was situated in a time when much education was concerned with individual learning and systems of programmed learning, and was strongly influenced by the behavioral psychology of B. F. Skinner. Consequently, much early criterion-referenced test development focused on very discrete skills and narrow instances of learned information. This early identification of criterion-referenced measurement with narrowly focused objectives and multiple-choice items is regrettable in that it has caused an over reliance on relatively minor instructional behaviors. Further, this led to a simplification of what was to be tested and "away from the measurement of broader, fuzzier, but more interesting achievements" (Linn, 1994, p. 13). This historical context often created the incorrect impression that CRTs could not set specifications to test broader, yet definable, "integrative skills and communicative language ability" (Lynch & Davidson, 1997, p. 269). However, over time, emphasis has changed to the assessment of achievement that was grounded in theories of knowledge acquisition and dimensions of acquired proficiency (Linn, 1994). Glaser (1994) notes that "Cognitive and developmental psychology now can supply rich meaning to modern day evolutions of criterion-referenced measurement that appear in current notions of the learning of higher order skills, assessing capabilities of thinking and reasoning, and the values of 'authentic assessment'" (p. 11). Current criterion-referenced language testing has thus moved from strict interpretation of behaviors to the underlying constructs of language performance. The focus is generally directed more at developing test instruments that reveal cognitive language processing and sociolinguistic ability.

The next two sections of this chapter will address the roles of CRTs in educational settings and in language research. Both of these areas have unique testing approaches for which traditional NRTs are of limited value and for which CRTs can provide important new types of information.

Differences and similarities between NRTs and CRTs in educational settings

Why were criterion-referenced tests developed?

Historically, CRTs developed in educational circles in response to problems, or weaknesses, that were perceived in the pervasive norm-referenced testing of the day. The problems with NRTs can be classified into the following categories:

1. Teaching/testing mismatches.
2. Lack of instructional sensitivity.
3. Lack of curricular relevance.
4. Restriction to the normal distribution.
5. Restriction to items that discriminate.

We will explore each of these categories in more depth in order to illustrate some of the important ways that CRTs differ from NRTs.

Teaching/testing mismatches. Some educators feel that NRTs create teaching/testing mismatches (Popham, 1978, p. 78). In cases where large-scale, standardized examinations are used, material tested in the examination may not be directly related to the teaching going on at the particular institution involved. Such mismatches may arise because of the general nature of the material that is typically tested on an NRT or simply because the content of the test is not directly related to the curriculum at the institution.

Even when an NRT is developed at and for a specific institution, mismatches may occur between the teaching that is going on in the classrooms and the testing. Brown (1981) provides an example of just such a situation where mismatches between the English as a Second Language Placement Examination (ESLPE) and the course content in the UCLA ESL service courses apparently led to at least two distinct populations of students in each of the upper level classes:

students who had been placed into the courses and students who had been promoted into the courses from lower level courses. The former group was shown by the end of the course to be significantly higher than the latter group in terms of course grades, final examination scores, and cloze test scores.

Lack of instructional sensitivity. NRTs may also lack sensitivity to instruction. Because of their general and abstracted nature and putative global applicability across a variety of instructional settings, NRTs are not suited to measuring the specific learning points and skills developed in a particular program. As a result, NRTs cannot be expected to measure the amount of knowledge or skill that a student has within a well-defined content area. Furthermore, NRTs cannot be expected to be effective for diagnosis of deficiencies with reference to particular courses or programs.

Any teacher who has ever tried to measure instructional gains on an internationally recognized NRT will readily understand this issue. For instance, at the Guangzhou English Language Center (GELC) in the People's Republic of China in the early 1980s, attempts were made to monitor EFL student achievement based on the *Test of English as a Foreign Language* (TOEFL). The TOEFL, which is definitely a large scale NRT, was only sensitive to instruction to the degree that 300 hours of instruction would cause 20 to 25 point gains (on a 200 to 677 scale). Such small gains would have been discouraging if it had not been for the results obtained on objectives-referenced tests that had been developed specifically for that program. These results indicated clearer and proportionally larger learning gains.

In all fairness, however, we must point out that the TOEFL was not designed to measure the types of detailed language points that would be covered in a curriculum like that at GELC; instead, the TOEFL was designed to measure overall English proficiency as a foreign or second language, which was not precisely what was being taught at GELC. Thus the TOEFL was not directly related to the instruction that the students were receiving at GELC.

Lack of curricular relevance. Because they can cause teaching/testing mismatches and generally lack sensitivity to instruction, some educators feel that NRTs are not effective for evaluating the effects of curriculum change on student achievement. Thus, NRTs are not felt to be particularly well suited to assessing the strengths and weaknesses of a given program, or for suggesting useful areas of instructional amelioration in a specific program, or for comparing the relative strengths and weaknesses of different language programs. Tests that are not developed to directly relate to the instructional objectives of a curriculum will only demonstrate curricular relevance on some of the items in a fairly random fashion depending on which program is being examined. Consequently, tests that are not directly related to the instruction are bound to lack direct curriculum relevance (for more on this, see the discussion of *washback* in the next chapter).

Restriction to the normal distribution. NRTs are designed, statistically analyzed, and revised with the purpose of creating a normal distribution of scores. Though all aspects of an NRT depend heavily on the notion of a normal distribution, the elaborate descriptive, reliability, and validity statistics that have been developed over the years generally assume a normal distribution. Thus one of the first issues that must be addressed in analyzing NRT results is the degree to which the distribution of scores is normal.

If, however, a group of students has just completed a 900–hour intensive language program, testing their achievement in the language with a test that is designed to create a normal distribution may not be desirable. In fact, if all of the students know all of the material, a test that reflects that knowledge would be desirable. In other words, a test would be needed on which all students could score 100 percent – if they knew all of the material. On such a test, however, a normal distribution of scores could not reasonably be expected to appear.

Restriction to items that discriminate. To create an NRT, those items are selected that about half of the students cannot answer correctly on average. Thus the focus of the test is on content that the students (or at least 50 percent of them) do not know rather than on what they have learned (as on a CRT). As a result, test designers sometimes have a tendency to select items simply because they discriminate well between high-achieving students and low-achieving students rather than because the items are related to the curriculum or to anything that the students are learning.

Consider again the situation described above in which a group of students has just completed a 900-hour intensive language program. In designing an achievement test for this group, selecting items that discriminate well between students would not be appropriate. A more appropriate strategy would be to select items based on the curriculum that the students have studied. As noted above, if all of the students know all of the material, items that reflect that knowledge would be desirable. In other words, teachers would want items on such a test that all of the students could answer correctly if they knew all the material. From an NRT perspective, such items might not discriminate very well. Indeed, if all students correctly answered each of the items, item discrimination would be zero.

Criterion-referenced tests are different

Fortunately, criterion-referenced tests can be used to circumvent all of the complaints and problems listed in the previous section. In short, criterion-referenced tests can be expected to have the following characteristics:

1. Emphasis on teaching/testing matches.
2. Focus on instructional sensitivity.
3. Curricular relevance.
4. Absence of normal distribution restrictions.
5. No item discrimination restriction.

In order to better understand how these characteristics are possible (as well as other ways that norm-referenced and criterion-referenced tests differ), consider several sets of comparisons that have already been made between these two families of tests.

The first, Hudson and Lynch (1984, p. 175), addresses the differences between NRTs and CRTs in general terms of "relative standing" and "absolute standing" when they point out that ". . . with NRM [norm-referenced measurement], we get a broad, less descriptive indication of *relative* standing, while with CRM [criterion-referenced measurement], we may get gaps in coverage, but the information is more descriptive and provides a measure of *absolute* standing with respect to the instructional goal."

Second, Brown (1996) provides more detail when he compares NRTs and CRTs in terms of six characteristics on which they differ. These six characteristics are listed in column one of Table 1.1. NRTs and CRTs differ in:

1. The way that scores will be interpreted.
2. The kinds of things that they are used to measure.
3. The purpose of testing.
4. The ways that scores will tend to be distributed.
5. The structure of the tests.
6. What students know about the test questions beforehand.

In Table 1.2, Gronlund (1988, p. 14) illustrates the differences between NRTs and CRTs, but he also provides information about the similarities between these two types of tests.

None of the above is meant to suggest that CRTs are in any way better than NRTs. Both types of tests are very important for their particular decision-making processes in any language program, but they serve different purposes.

Table 1.1. *Differences between norm-referenced and criterion-referenced tests*

Characteristic	Norm-referenced	Criterion-referenced
1. Type of interpretation	Relative (a student's performance is compared to that of all other students).	Absolute (a student's performance is compared only to the amount, or percent, of material known).
2. Type of measurement	To measure general language abilities or proficiencies.	To measure a specific domain or objectives-based language points.
3. Purpose of testing	Spread students out along a continuum of general abilities or proficiencies.	To assess the amount of material known, or learned, by each.
4. Distribution of of scores	Normal distribution of scores around a mean.	Varies, often non-normal, students who know all of the material should all score 100%.
5. Test structure	A few relatively long sub-tests with heterogeneous item content.	A series of short, well-defined sub-tests with homogeneous item content.
6. Knowledge of questions	Students have little or no idea what content to expect in questions.	Students know exactly what content to expect in test questions.

(adapted from Brown, 1996)

Fundamental distinctions between CRTs and NRTs

While it is true that in practice the applications of NRT and CRT assessments may fall along a continuum, this does not negate the uniqueness of each type, in contrast to arguments by Davies (1990) and implications by North (2000). Davies challenges the distinct nature, even existence, of CRT assessment through a set of reductionist principles that are easily dismissed through examination:

1. CRTs cannot be constructed in a completely separate way from NRTs without "the usual canons of item discreteness and discrimination" (p. 18).
2. Because teachers are concerned with very small groups of learners what they require is a criterion-referenced use of norm-referenced

Table 1.2. *Comparison of norm-referenced tests (NRTs) and criterion-referenced tests (CRTs)* *

Common Characteristics of NRTs and CRTs:

1. Both require specification of the achievement domain to be measured.
2. Both require a relevant and representative sample of test items.
3. Both use the same types of test items.
4. Both use the same rules for item writing (except for item difficulty).
5. Both are judged by the same qualities of goodness (validity and reliability).
6. Both are useful in educational measurement.

Differences Between NRTs and CRTs (but it is only a matter of emphasis):

1. NRT – Typically covers a *large* domain of learning tasks, with just a few items measuring each specific task.
   CRT – Typically focuses on a *delimited* domain of learning tasks with a relatively large number of items measuring each specific task.
2. NRT – Emphasizes *discrimination* among individuals in terms of relative level of learning.
   CRT – Emphasizes *description* of what learning tasks individuals can and cannot perform.
3. NRT – Favors items of average difficulty and typically omits easy items.
   CRT – Matches item difficulty to learning tasks, without altering item difficulty or omitting easy items.
4. NRT – Used primarily (but not exclusively) for *survey* testing.
   CRT – Used primarily (but not exclusively) for *mastery* testing.
5. NRT – Interpretation requires a clearly defined group.
   CRT – Interpretation requires a clearly defined and delimited achievement domain.

Gronlund (1988, p. 14)
*When each is built to maximize its type of interpretation.

tests, that "does not discriminate greatly among their students but which does establish an adequate dichotomy . . . between plus success and minus success" (p. 18). Further, for every criterion-referenced test there must be a population for whom the tests could be norm-referenced.

3. Criterion-referencing is linked to exercises while norm-referencing is linked to tests. Since, "by my argument, a test is meant (by definition, as it were) to discriminate, to produce a rank order, an exercise is not so intended" (p. 19). Consequently, "it is appropriate to conclude here that testing is particulary suitable for norm referencing while criterion referencing is more easily exhibited in exercises than tests" (p. 20).

The error of the first principle will be more clearly understood after covering the material that is presented in Chapter 4. It is shown there that while CRT items are certainly concerned with discrimination, they are concerned with discriminating between very different features than those in NRT development. Briefly, in a CRT, one is concerned with discrimination between content exposure vs. non-exposure, or between groups identified as having control of a trait vs. groups identified as not having control of the trait, etc. An NRT aims to discriminate among people in a normative manner, regardless of examinee exposure or identified mastery. Davies' concern with item "discreteness" raises larger issues regarding just what is meant by "discrete". These issues are not settled within either CRT or NRT frameworks.

The second principle – the notion that teachers need a criterion-referenced application of a norm-referenced test – is on the face of it an inverse statement of what goes on in classrooms. In instances when teachers are required to use NRTs, they actually would prefer to have CRTs that relate to the domain content that is of interest. The fact that the test may not discriminate greatly among the students in the class reflects precisely what a successful CRT application is designed to accomplish, not, hopefully, the use of an inappropriately normed test with a truncated sample of students. Additionally, it is not clear why, *ipso facto*, every criterion-referenced test must have a population for which the test is norm-referenced. Indeed, the domain may be one in which a particular group is dispersed widely, but this is a statistical artifact of the particular sample of examinees, not a characteristic of the test use and design.

Finally, in the third principle, Davies relegates CRTs to exercises rather than tests. This conclusion is based on an unsubstantiated assertion as to the definition of a test, namely, "by my argument, a test is meant (by definition, as it were) to discriminate, to produce a rank order" (p. 18). We have not found other sources that restrict the notion of test in this way. Definitions of testing tend to be of the sort: "A predetermined set of questions or tasks to which predetermined types of behavioral responses are sought" (Salvia & Ysseldyke, 1991, p. 658); "Any procedure for measuring ability, knowledge or performance" (Richards, Platt, & Weber, 1985, p. 291); "The means by which the presence, quality, or genuineness of anything is determined" (Random House Dictionary, 1980, p. 897); "Test: any instrument or device used to assess an individual along a particular dimension" (Magill, 1996). Further, rank ordering is not assumed to be important in many traditional focuses of testing involving assessment of such diverse areas as brain damage, neuroticism, vocational interest, stuttering, typing accuracy, driving ability, medical expertise, venereal disease, entrepreneurship, burnout, depression, grief, college adjustment, and many other areas of life that are subject to testing but for which rank order is of no importance whatsoever. Obviously if NRTs inherently rank order individuals and CRTs do not, and if a definition of the term *test* is proffered that includes the requirement that tests rank order individuals, as does that of Davies, then CRTs do not fit that particular definition of the term *test*. Rather, they fit some even less well-defined category of *exercise* in Davies' scheme. However, such a definition is not the general definition for *test* in most general and language assessment literature.

A further issue raised in relation to criterion-referenced testing and its distinctive qualities relates to characteristics of scale use. North (2000) notes that:

levels on a scale of proficiency really operate as standards. If the levels have a pragmatic origin in terms of likely stages of attainment, they are also likely to be derived from "norms" for those stages in the sense of what it is responsible to expect. In trialing the system and seeing if the descriptors do describe what is intended (whether the learners "get there"), the same kind of "norming" information may be used to adjust the cut-off. It is just that in this case the cut-off (standard) may be in a formulation of expectations rather than a numerical score. (pp. 138–139)

This set of concerns is related to North's further notion that "common sense indicates that the norm should not be too far away from the norm (average mark) of the group taking the test" (p. 183). These comments refer to the possibility that criterion-referenced assessments may not produce results that are totally independent from norm levels. That is, criterion-referenced tests are generally at a level such that they in fact distinguish between individuals, and hence, there is generally a possibility that some of the examinees will reach the level and others will not (Nuttall & Goldstein, 1986). Because the tests are generally at a level of some relevance to the abilities of the examinee, there may be some "norm" referencing of the criterion-referenced tests since they are in fact generally appropriate to some of the test takers. Our position is not that this indicates that the tests are necessarily norm-referenced. Rather, it indicates that people frequently exhibit good sense and take tests that they might stand a chance of passing. People generally do not take a test of electronics ability unless they have studied electronics and have some chance of doing well. In short, this argument appears to be a discussion of who takes tests rather than any indication of a change in the test construction process of CRTs. It is more likely that the test takers are sensitive to the knowledge-base "norms", or expectations, than that the test score results are sensitive to the examinee distribution norms. In this discussion, then, "norm" has a technical meaning that is not synonymous with simply being at an appropriate level of difficulty.

In conclusion, there are real conceptual and psychometric differences between CRTs and NRTs. Both types of tests serve particular purposes, and one important value of the distinction between the types of tests is that it can help in making sure that the correct type of instrument is used for the correct type of decision.

The place of CRTs in language testing theory and research

The central question in all language testing is *What are language tests measuring?* In order to answer this question, competing hypotheses have surfaced in the recent literature. Two of these have been of major importance: the divisibility of language ability (unitary hypotheses), and the several articulations of communicative competencies (Canale & Swain, 1980; Bachman & Palmer, 1981, 1982; Bachman, 1990; and so forth). In addition, the appropriate methods for developing, statistically analyzing, and evaluating language tests have come to be of increasing interest in second and foreign language testing. Several concerns have fostered this growing interest.

First, measuring functional language ability, communicative competence, or communicative language ability has become the focus of much discussion in language education, a concern which has affected language testing at many levels (Alderson & Hughes, 1981; Hughes & Porter, 1983; Bachman & Savignon, 1986; Bachman, 1990; Bachman and Palmer, 1996; McNamara, 1996; and others). Views of language ability have their bases in how language is used in the world, in the non-measurement environments of the language user's needs. If tests are to be designed that reflect a user's ability to actually function on those tasks, test developers must use approaches which are congruent with the models of language that underlie their decisions.

A second concern is the application of criterion-referenced testing to testing language proficiency (Cartier, 1968; Cziko, 1982, 1983, 1984; Hudson & Lynch, 1984; Delamere, 1985; Brown, 1984a, 1988a, 1989a, 1990a, 1990b, 1992, 1993, 1995a, 1995b, 1996; Henning, 1987; Hudson, 1989a, 1989b; Bachman, 1990). That is, as language testers have attempted to measure more contextualized language ability, earlier rather simplistic views of language ability have been abandoned. Indeed, recent refocusing on performance assessment in language assessment as well as educational evaluation in general has raised new concerns for language testers (Shohamy, 1995; McNamara, 1996). This recent recognition of the role that performance plays in the assessment of language ability has led to increasing grappling with how performance tasks and language ability interact in complex ways that may be troublesome for test interpretation. As a consequence, language testers have grown much more concerned with being able to answer the question *What are language tests measuring?* Just as we noted in the previous section, NRTs may lack curricular relevance. They may also be inappropriate for doing research on particular language components in second language acquisition research.

The issues of communicative competence and criterion-referenced testing are related in that, when functional or communicative language tasks are identified for testing, decisions at each stage of test development will change depending upon the theoretical approach taken for test development and score interpretation. These issues will be dealt with in detail in the chapters that follow.

To further explore the question *What are language tests measuring?*, the remainder of this chapter will consider four sub- questions and the relationship of CRTs to each:

1. What makes language testing special?
2. What is language proficiency?
3. What is communicative language ability?
4. What problems do CRT developers face?

What makes language testing special?

The focus of this book is on criterion-referenced tests as they can function in *language* testing. As such, the concerns will at times depart from some of the more traditional views of CRT applications in the educational literature. This departure is partially due to the fact that language and language acquisition are different in nature from other educational content areas such as mathematics, history, geography, or other language arts, at least as these are typically taught and assessed in western educational traditions. Differences can be seen in the relationships that exist in the nature of language proficiency and communicative competence. Considerations of these relationships will have a direct bearing on how the construct of language knowledge is defined, how language tests are operationalized (that is, how the underlying concepts are finally actualized as test items), and how they are evaluated. Thus, in order to put criterion-referenced language testing into the context of language testing, we must address how differing views of language and language learning affect the types of measurement that are to be employed.

The fact that language is situated and interactional further makes its assessment different from the assessment of content knowledge. A statement like "You're looking thinner today" could be intended and interpreted as a compliment coming from a friend, or could be intended and interpreted as a concern coming from a physician to a patient. The sociolinguistic context of language increases problems in what areas of language are open for testing and has a strong impact on the form that the testing takes. As long as language testing was limited to narrow grammatical concerns or specific language skills in isolation, there was little problem with relying overwhelmingly on discrete item tests adhering to a multiple-choice format. However, as language assessment has become concerned with more complex uses of language, especially its pragmatics and sociolinguistics, there is more and more reliance on performance assessment (more on this is presented in Chapter 3).

What is language proficiency?

Obviously, a comprehensive answer to this question is well beyond the scope of this book. However, it is an issue that must be addressed, if only briefly, in considerations of how criterion-referenced testing fits into language assessment. Much of the discussion concerning language testing centers around the nature of language proficiency. The reason for this emphasis is that the underlying assumptions of proficiency directly relate to whether or not individual language components can be specified and tested validly and meaningfully. Some research has argued that all performance in a second or foreign language can be traced to a single underlying "General Language Proficiency Factor" (Oller, 1976), while others claim that language competence is divisible into subskills (Bachman & Palmer, 1981, 1982), or separate types of language (Canale & Swain, 1979, 1981; Canale, 1983; Bachman, 1990), and not comprised of a single factor.

In terms of this divisibility dichotomy in language testing, Spolsky (1985) has noted that there is a functional approach and a general proficiency approach. He points out that the functional approach assumes "that the nature of language knowledge is best captured by listing the various uses to which language can be put." In so doing, advocates of the functional approach aim to comprehensively list all the functions and notions of language in a taxonomy (for example, see van Ek & Alexander, 1980). The functional approach is thus embodied, in part, in the communicative views of language. On the other hand, the general proficiency approach is based on the belief that individuals differ basically in the measurable amounts of some indivisible body of competence they possess. These two views of language and the nature of language proficiency directly affect who will accept any particular incarnation of a language test as a valid measure of language for some particular defined use.

However, while few still hold the strong unitary hypothesis, agreement is also lacking about what the divisibility of language competence into subskills really means. Although language testers generally agree that language competence is divisible into subskills or components, such consensus does not mean that these testers agree as to what those subskills or components represent. These components can be viewed in two ways: as representative of all knowledge and skills necessary to communicate, or as independent types of knowledge or skills. For example, one tester might consider writing and speaking to be reflections of some underlying production ability, while another tester might consider these to be two separate and independent components. This contrast has important practical implications for testing and instruction. These implications are related to how testing is to be carried out, in the sense of determining what the test instruments will look like, and related to decisions about whether we need to administer tests covering many subskills at all. Because NRTs provide results that disperse examinee's scores, they have some limitations in any decisions designed to assess an examinee's mastery of language subskills or components, regardless of how these are defined.

However, the questioning of language as a unitary or divisible trait does not lie solely at the feet of those who disagree on the unitary hypothesis as opposed to the skill divisibility hypothesis. Additional disagreements that are particularly relevant to language testing, criterion-referenced testing in particular, emerge from recent discussions of how language skills in practice seldom exist in isolation. These points of view (Leki, 1993; Carson, 1993) exist outside the psychological discussions and blend into sociolinguistic concerns. This area of focusing on language use might best be exemplified by examinations of *literacy acts*. Two examples of relevant literacy acts might be synthesis and summary writing in higher educational contexts. Carson (1993) raised the question of whether it is meaningful to draw a distinction between reading and writing for such tasks given the fundamental inseparability of the two in the completion of the product. Basically, the point raised is that the appropriate level of analysis is not the language skill, but the language task (much more will be said about this in the next section of this chapter).

This last set of concerns holds particular relevance for the utility of criterion-referenced approaches to language testing in complex language settings. In past critiques of criterion-referenced testing, a criticism has been leveled that CRT focuses too narrowly on clearly definable low level instructional concerns and is limited in its application to more complex language performances. Throughout this book, it is argued that on the contrary, CRT is very appropriate and useful in the assessment of such clearly definable yet complex language tasks. Clear criteria can be set for the nature and evaluation of such real-world academic tasks (see below). In short, the acknowledgement that language is complex in its instantiations in social interactions does not pose a limitation for CRT applications in assessment any more than it does for NRT applications. In fact, CRT approaches to evaluation of such tasks can elicit more detailed descriptions of the particular task features that are most relevant for evaluation. In most cases, the purpose of such task evaluation would not be to achieve results that disperse examinees' scores in their synthesizing or summarizing abilities; rather, the function would be to assess the language users' language proficiency in carrying out these tasks.

What is communicative language ability?

For at least the past twenty years in language teaching, testing, and research, a primary emphasis has been placed on the role of *communicative competence* and how to assess it. This emphasis on testing communicative competence has grown from the theories of language use and the instructional methodologies that have emerged to address the concepts of communicative competence as a component of language. Communicative competence was proposed by Hymes (1972) and Campbell and Wales (1970) as a broader view of Chomsky's (1965) strong claim that linguistic competence was to be associated solely with knowledge of a spectrum of grammatical rules. Essential to the notion of communicative competence is the important role played by the context of discourse beyond sentential constructions. Thus, frameworks of communicative competence, as noted by Bachman and Savignon (1986), extended the definition of knowledge necessary to use a language beyond that of earlier models. Such frameworks include knowledge of language functions, and knowledge of language contexts, in addition to knowledge of grammar. Language testing methods have naturally begun to take these concerns into account.

This said, however, several models of communicative competence are contending with each other in the literature. These models differ mostly in terms of what they include. For Canale and Swain (1980), communicative competence includes grammatical competence, sociolinguistic competence, and strategic competence. In subsequent models, communicative language ability was seen to include organizational competence (made up of grammatical and textual sub-competencies) and pragmatic competence (made up of illocutionary and sociolinguistic sub-competencies) (Bachman, 1990). A final concept in the notion of communicative competence, as noted above, is that language takes place in a setting and occurs for a purpose.

The differing views of communicative competence and communicative language ability produce differing views of how language tests can best assess the communicative abilities of examinees. In terms of language testing, many of the arguments basically revolve around the question of the authenticity of the test, the authenticity of the language samples used in the test, and the extent to which the test measures "ability to use" (Shohamy, 1995). The underlying assumptions here relate to considerations of the degree to which the test is an assessment of competence or an assessment of performance, in the weak sense that competence refers to knowledge or ability in the language and performance refers to actual language use (Canale & Swain, 1980). In practice, the discussion becomes an epistemological issue concerning just how direct or indirect a measure of communicative competence can validly be.

Mislevy (1991) has used the medical model of assessing disease vs. syndrome vs. symptom as an analogy for some aspects of educational and psychological testing. Levels of acceptable analysis are determined by the eventual treatment. In some instances, symptoms can be tested and treated. Analysis of the symptoms can serve as indirect indications of the underlying problems. At other times, simple symptoms do not reflect some systemic problem. However, a more careful analysis of the syndrome that produces the symptoms can provide sufficient information for treatment. Finally, in some cases, the symptoms cannot be addressed effectively without a diagnosis of the underlying disease. The example applies equally well as an explanation for the level of measurement accepted in language testing. At times, indirect measures will be acceptable as sufficient indicators of underlying proficiency. At other times, information gleaned from direct observation will be viewed as necessary. However, some researchers in language testing will tend to insist on the validity of one level of testing over the others. For example, Morrow (1979) considers that the role of language testing is to provide proof:

of the candidate's ability to actually use the language, to translate the competence (or lack of it) which he [sic] is demonstrating into actual performance 'in ordinary situations', i.e., actually using the language to read, write, speak or listen in ways and contexts which correspond to real life. (p. 149)

Consequently, Morrow asserts that language tests must reflect the following features of language use:

1. Language is used in interaction.
2. Interactions are usually unpredictable.
3. Language has a context.
4. Language is used for a purpose.
5. There is a need to examine performance.
6. Language is authentic, not simplified.
7. Language success is behavior based.

As such, in order for a test of communicative language ability to satisfy Morrow's requirements, it would at least:

1. Be criterion-referenced against the operational performance of a set of language tasks.
2. Be concerned with validating itself against those criteria and be concerned with content, construct and predictive validity, not concurrent validity.
3. Rely on modes of assessment which are not directly quantitative, but which are instead qualitative.
4. Subordinate reliability to face validity.

Canale and Swain (1980), on the other hand, reject the notion that the essential purpose of language is to communicate with others:

There is little reason to view (externally oriented) communication as more essential than other purposes of language such as self-expression, verbal thinking, problem-solving, and creative writing. (p. 23)

As a consequence, this view would accept indirect measures such as paper-and-pencil tests.

In Morrow's view, test results sample behavior, or performance. Alderson (1981) notes that the "authenticity" arguments of Morrow are somewhat "sterile" since they assume that the domains of language teaching and testing are not authentic language settings. Taken to the extreme, the requirement for authentic assessment would disallow testing settings or classroom teaching. According to this perspective, only direct assessment of language performance would be accepted as a valid indication of language proficiency.

As Bachman (1990) indicates, much of this disagreement centers around what constitutes an authentic test. This argument goes back to the basic distinctions first articulated by Carroll (1961) between discrete-point and integrative language tests. Oller (1979) notes that:

> Although the types are not always different for practical purposes, the theoretical bases of the two approaches contrast markedly and the predictions concerning the effects and relative validity of different testing procedures also differ in fundamental ways depending on which of the two approaches one selects. The contrast between these two philosophies, of course, is not limited to language testing per se, but can be seen throughout the whole spectrum of educational endeavor. (p. 37)

Carroll's basic argument is that while discrete-point tests might have a role in such low level skills as knowledge of structure, lexicon, and auditory discrimination, testing is incomplete without:

> An approach requiring an integrated, facile performance on the part of the examinee. It is conceivable that knowledge could exist without facility. If we limit ourselves to testing only one point at time, more time is ordinarily allowed for reflection than would occur in a normal communication situation, no matter how rapidly the discrete items are presented. For this reason I recommend tests in which there is less attention paid to specific structure points or lexicon than to the total communicative effect of an utterance. (p. 318)

This point is the basis for the search for "authenticity" in language assessment. It is the desire to get around Carroll's hypothesized situation "that knowledge could exist without facility" that is the driving force behind the quest for "authentic" testing because a lack of authenticity can cast a shadow over a test result's validity of interpretation.

Bachman (1990) points out that within Carroll's comment we may see the two primary approaches to identifying what is meant by "authentic" within language assessment. The first approach, which Bachman terms the "real-life" approach hangs on concerns with the "normal communication" aspect of Carroll's statement, while the second approach, termed "interactional ability" focuses on the "total communicative effect" aspect. Thus, the first approach focuses on the degree to which a test represents language performance in non-testing situational use. The second is concerned more with the "distinguishing characteristic" (Bachman, p. 302) of communicative language use.

According to Bachman, the real-life approach views proficiency as the ability to perform particular tasks, placing a premium on direct versus indirect testing. This focus is represented by Morrow's concerns mentioned above, and centers on content validity and the representativeness of the test tasks to real-world language encounters. In essence, language proficiency is seen as the ability to carry out non-test situations linguistically. Authenticity represents the degree to which the language testing tasks represent tasks that occur outside of testing situations. One important concern, however, is with the representativeness of any particular test, and this places restrictions on the generalizability of the test results to other contexts and tasks. Representativeness has been a central theme in much criticism of the real-life approach. This concern with authenticity is particularly important when we consider that performance on language tasks will be situation specific and vary across social contexts and environments. Bachman notes other criticisms of the real-life approach, particularly its failure to distinguish language ability from the particular performance. In essence, the real-life approach identifies the particular performance with the trait that is being measured. Because the real-life approach focuses on the direct performance of the examinee, it treats the particular examples of ability as the construct. There is, thus, no means to disentangle the particular task performance from the trait, particularly given that there will be a lack of representativeness of all possible tasks of interest in measuring language ability.

The association of language ability with authenticity of language use and setting raises real issues regarding the relationship of competence and performance, given that competence can only be inferred via some sample of performance (Shohamy, 1995). Further, the growing focus on authentic performance of language fits well with a growing interest in direct performance assessment in general measurement outside of language testing circles. This increasing trend toward performance assessment has led to increasing concern that the tasks set for language users and examinees replicate some real-life non-testing situation. There has been, thus, an interest in predicting how learners would succeed or fail on tasks that might be identified through needs analyses as potential target tasks for the language user outside the language learning context. It should be noted that this is almost iconic to the set of concerns discussed with respect to Morrow, Canale & Swain, Bachman, and others regarding definitions of communicative language ability. However, a concern has grown about the extent to which successful task performance involves non-language abilities (Jones, 1985; Skehan, 1996; McNamara, 1996; Wesche, 1992).

Throughout the discussions relating to language performance assessment, then, a key issue involved is just how to account for the non-linguistic factors that are, in part, responsible for success on differing real-life tasks. This concern was tied to conceptualizations of just what the purpose of authentic tasks was. Bachman (1990) notes several criticisms of the real-life approach as demonstrated in performance tasks. The first criticism is that the approach fails to distinguish between language ability and actual performance. That is, the approach conflates the behavioral manifestation of an ability with the trait itself. He proposes that the focus of task design, in sampling, should be the degree to which the examinee's interaction with the test task, whether or not the task is itself authentic, is the primary determinant of whether the task is fruitful as a generator of an interpretable performance. He also sees this as aiding in the possible drawback of task underrepresentativeness in performance testing. Likewise, Skehan (1996) notes that the criteria for judging a language task cannot simply be success in carrying out the task objectives. For Skehan, there must be concerns of language use included in the evaluaton. After all, there are many ways of carrying out the task of acquiring bread at the market – some involve language and some involve weapons. Simple success at a task may not produce the most useable product for assessing communicative language ability. Finally, McNamara addresses the issue by dividing views of performance into two basic implicit assumptions about what test results represent. The first approach takes what he terms a *work sample* approach, with a view of task success being of paramount importance. His second approach is a more cognitive approach that takes a more explicitly linguistic basis and focuses less on the particular task and more on the qualities of the linguistic execution of the task. These views he designates as "a *strong* and a *weak* sense of the term *second language performance test*" (p. 43).

For McNamara, in the *strong* sense of language performance assessment, the tasks represent real-world tasks and the criteria used to evaluate the performance are primarily those real-world criteria used to assess the fulfillment of the task. Language production features will at most be partial criteria in assessing performance fulfillment. In short, performance of the target task is of primary importance and language is viewed simply as the medium through which the task is carried out: "Adequate second language proficiency is a necessary but not a sufficient condition for success on the performance task" (p. 43). In McNamara's *weak* sense, language performance tests are primarily concerned with the language per-formance evinced through the particular tasks. While test tasks may resemble real-life tasks, in that examinees engage in tasks that may exist outside a language testing situation, the capacity to perform the task *per se* is not the primary focus of assessment. One primary purpose of the task is as a mechanism to elicit a language sample – hopefully a language sample demonstrating some fidelity to the language of the real-life event – which can then be evaluated for its linguistic effectiveness and appropriateness. In practice, most language tests are of the *weak* form, and may be represented somewhere along a continuum running from a relatively *strong* to a relatively *weak* sense of a performance scale.

Thus, the interactional ability approach to language assessment focuses on the critical features of communicative language use rather than trying to capture the totality of a language use situation (Bachman, 1990). Authenticity is viewed as being a function of interaction between the test taker, test task, and testing context. This interactional ability approach rests upon a theoretical framework of features of language use that are important to generalizing test scores to overall proficiency ability. Such a framework may be based on the work in communicative competence that takes into account grammatical competence, pragmatic competence, sociolinguistic competence, etc.

However, given the potential variability in such models, a major question that remains is how to most appropriately evaluate any of the particular models that emerge within the general framework. As has been shown, wide disagreement exists even among those who support the communicative competence approach to language as to the most appropriate methods for evaluation and testing. A basic problem for the general theory is that no adequate model exists for a communicative grammar. A great deal more study of communicative language will be necessary before a generally accepted model becomes available. Yet, assessment must be carried out now. In over twenty years of research, the emergence of solid empirically based models of communicative competence would have seemed possible, yet such research has to date been equivocal in its findings. Cziko (1984) examines several empirically based models of communicative language ability and directly addresses three problematic issues in the development and interpretation of these models.

First, he notes that correlational analyses are problematic. For example, if two skills correlate highly, they might be considered highly related, while if they have a low correlation coefficient, they would more likely be considered relatively independent. However, he notes that a low correlation might also be the result of little within-skill variation on one or both of the skill tests. For instance, examinees might all score high in both skill areas.

Second, he notes that variable language skill exposure in a group may lead to misleading interpretations. For example, examinees may have had varying exposure to specific types of reading skills. Some may have had exposure to many skills over a long period of language training, while others may have had specific-purpose reading skills. However, all examinees may have had similar exposure in speaking situations.

Third, heterogeneous groups of subjects may show high within-skill variance in language proficiency while homogeneous groups may show low within-skill variance. If a heterogeneous group shows high within-skill variance and low between-skill variance, the two skills would appear to be unrelated while in fact they might be related for each group of examinees.

Given these issues, Cziko concludes that traditional methods of analysis are deficient for examining functional test data. He contends that, in order to understand models of communicative competence, research must involve the use of criterion-referenced language tests and appropriate statistical analyses designed to reveal true skill patterns. Thus NRTs have limited value in assessing proficiency within current views of language. CRTs, on the other hand, in essence force testers to define their views of language in order to make statements about acquisition.

What problems do CRT developers face?

Hambleton (1983) notes that scores obtained from a set of items in a test are commonly used for three things:

1. to rank order examinees;
2. to make descriptive statements about examinee performance in relation to well-defined domains of content; and
3. to make mastery/non-mastery decisions in relation to well-defined domains of content (p. 34).

As we will see throughout this book, the norm-referenced testing approach is generally best suited to the first use of ranking examinees relative to each other, while the CRT approach has been most productive in describing performance in particular content or cognitive domains and providing bases for decisions about whether students have or have not mastered a particular content area. As such, the CRT approach addresses itself to questions concerning what the scores on a test mean in terms of an examinee's performance in the referenced domain.

Thus CRTs are particularly important for developing language tests that can be used for the descriptive statements and decisions about content mastery (numbers 2 and 3 above). Naturally, there emerges a set of concerns regarding just what is meant by "well-defined domain", and how restrictive this notion may be in meaningful assessment of complex language use. These concerns are at the heart of perceived potential difficulties facing criterion-referenced language test developers. First, there must be a concerted effort not to define the domains too narrowly. This potential limitation has haunted CRT development back to its early association with such discrete instructional objectives as "ability to multiply two digit numbers". Language assessment is broader and more involved than these very narrow goals, and this needs to be continually incorporated into CRT views of assessment. Second, criterion-referenced testing needs to avoid defining language criteria scales and interpretations in a circular manner (North, 2000). This problem can be seen in the descriptions of the ACTFL/ETS guidelines (ACTFL/ETS, 1986). The ACTFL/ETS guidelines, along with the antecedent basis for these guidelines, the ILR (The US Government's Interagency Language Roundtable) (Lowe, 1998), are frequently viewed as being criterion-referenced (Lowe, 1998; Dandinoli, 1987). However, there is a circularity in the level descriptors given that a text may be defined as a Level Two text, for example, because it can be read by examinees who are at a Level Two ability, and they are at a Level Two ability because they are able to read Level Two texts (Dandinoli, 1987; North, 2000). In this case, it is not clear whether the described criterion text actually reflects the language construct domain it is supposed to reflect (Lee & Musumeci, 1988). Third, CRT development must take into account the potential for underrepresenting the trait as a result of often having a restricted number of sample tasks because of practical constraints involving time and resources necessary for taking the test. The need to adequately sample all specifications places a very clear demand that the tests include only non-trivial items. Finally, there is a need to recognize that CRTs are not always looking at a simple master/non-master division. Hambleton's second use of test scores is a case in point. Many people discussing CRTs tend to focus on the dichotomous nature of test interpretation, yet, the continuum nature of much CRT use is implied in Glaser's initial 1963 introduction to notions of CRT:

Underlying the concept of achievement measurement is the notion of a continuum of knowledge acquisition ranging from no proficiency at all to perfect performance. An individual's achievement level falls at some point on this continuum as indicated by the behaviors he displays during testing. The degree to which his achievement resembles desired performance at any specified level is assessed by criterion-referenced measures of achievement or proficiency. The standard against which a student's performance is compared when measured in this manner is the behavior which defines each point along the achievement continuum. The term "criterion", when used in this way, does not necessarily refer to final end-of-course behavior. Criterion levels can be established at any point in instruction where it is necessary to obtain information as to the adequacy of an individual's performance. (Glaser, 1963, pp. 519–520)

Thus, from its formal inception, criterion-referenced testing has included concerns both for mastery/non-mastery level decisions as well as an acknowledgment that performance and ability may be seen on a continuum represented by a scale, and that points on this scale may be explicitly defined as points on a scale.

However, in serving its many purposes and goals, CRT developers must face several practical questions:

1. How can item analysis be performed when: (a) no comparison group is designated as instructed or uninstructed group; (b) no externally identified masters and non-masters are defined; or (c) when mastery groups are defined and available?
2. How dependable are the decisions made on the basis of the test? How generalizable are the scores and analyses to those of other examinees on other forms of the test?
3. How can a standard, or cut-point, be rationally set?
4. What advantages and disadvantages accrue from application of the statistical approaches provided by NRT or CRT analyses?

The remaining chapters of this book are designed to address these questions and others which may arise in actually trying to implement the ideas of criterion-referenced language testing.

See uk.cambridge.org/elt/crlt/ for chapter summary and exercises.

2 *Curriculum-related testing*

Introduction

As pointed out in the previous chapter, tests are used to make decisions, and these decisions serve useful purposes only insofar as they provide useful information to students, teachers, or institutions. Thus, in one way or another, tests are, or should be, directly related to the language teaching/learning processes. In this chapter, we will explore the idea of curriculum-related testing. To do so, we will cover several issues:

1. The components of language curriculum design.
2. The relationship between objectives and criterion-referenced testing.
3. Fitting assessment to curriculum.

Language curriculum components

As illustrated in Figure 2.1, language curriculum development includes at least six components: (a) analyzing needs; (b) developing goals and objectives; (c) putting appropriate norm-referenced and criterion-referenced tests into place; (d) adopting, adapting, or creating materials; (e) supporting teachers in their efforts; and (f) regularly evaluating all the other five components in a formative manner (and occasionally in a summative matter). Brown (1995a) provides a full chapter of discussion on each of those six curriculum components, so we will not repeat all of that information here. However, we will try to show how testing interacts with each of the other components of curriculum design and serves a central function.

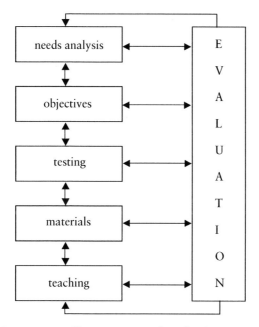

Figure 2.1. Components of language curriculum development (adapted from Brown, 1995a)

Which curriculum components involve testing?

In many respects, testing and the other five curriculum components are integrally interrelated. In fact, testing can, or should be, involved in all phases of curriculum development as we will explain.

Analyzing needs. Needs analysis will be defined here (after Brown 1995a) as "the systematic collection and analysis of all subjective and objective information necessary to define and validate defensible curriculum purposes that satisfy the language learning requirements of students within the context of particular institutions that influence the learning and teaching situation" (p. 36). Brown also lists and describes 24 different procedures that can be used for gathering information in a needs analysis (1995a, pp. 45–51). Four of those procedures are broad categories of tests: proficiency, placement, diagnostic, and achievement. The information provided by all of these types of tests can inform needs analyses in different ways. Unfortunately, published placement, diagnostic, and achievement tests are not widely available for language teaching situations, and those that are available will probably not be appropriate given the very specific levels of ability and learning goals of a particular language program.

However, professionally developed proficiency tests do exist. Examples for English as a second/foreign language include the *Test of English as a Foreign Language* (TOEFL), *Test of Spoken English* (TSE), and *Test of Written English* (TWE) from Educational Testing Service (ETS). Other proficiency tests include the oral proficiency interviews developed on the basis of the *ACTFL Proficiency Guidelines* (see American Council on the Teaching of Foreign Languages, 1986). For example, Liskin-Gasparro (1987) provides guidelines for doing such interviews in ESL/EFL contexts. Many other related proficiency interview procedures have been developed for languages other than English. The following are some examples:

1. ACTFL Japanese Proficiency Guidelines (American Council on the Teaching of Foreign Languages, 1987)
2. Chinese Speaking Test (see Clark & Li, 1986; Center for Applied Linguistics, 1989; or for a review of the CST, see Brown & Hua, 1998)
3. German Speaking Test (Center for Applied Linguistics, 1996)
4. Portuguese Speaking Test (Center for Applied Linguistics, 1988)

In addition, the National Standards in Foreign Language Education Project (1996) shows how and why such guidelines should be directly related to foreign language curriculum.

Such proficiency tests can provide information about students' overall abilities in a particular language, and having such information can save needs analysts considerable work because the scores on such tests describe the range of abilities of the students and by extension the range of their needs in ability terms. Put another way, proficiency tests can help needs analysts determine the outer limits in proficiency terms of the program they are trying to design. Using proficiency test results, the needs analysts can quickly eliminate from consideration many needs that might fall above or below (that is, outside) the range of abilities that they learned about from the proficiency test scores.

Thus testing can and should be an important part of needs analysis.

Developing goals and objectives. In a very real sense, well-designed CRTs can serve to operationalize a set of objectives. In brief, *objectives* are generally defined as statements of what we want our students to be able to do by the end of a course or program. (We will discuss *objectives* in considerably more detail in the next section, "A closer look at objectives and criterion-referenced testing".) To *operationalize* means to define a practical or theoretical concept in observable terms. For instance, researchers and curriculum developers sometimes operationalize the concept of overall English language proficiency in terms of scores on the TOEFL. That is, scores on the TOEFL become an observable (or in this case, measurable) indicator of students' overall English language proficiency levels.[1]

Since criterion-referenced tests, as they are most often used in curriculum development, are designed to measure specific sets of objectives and provide a score indicating the degree to which students have mastered the objectives, criterion-referenced tests can be said to operationalize those objectives. Hence, criterion-referenced tests are directly linked to curriculum objectives, and can be used to evaluate the adequacy of the objectives as a whole, the effectiveness of each objective, and the efficiency of each test item (as we will demonstrate in Chapter 4). Such evaluations of the objectives and their relationships to the criterion-referenced tests can be done from three different perspectives: diagnostic, progress, or achievement.

Criterion-referenced *diagnostic testing* is most often done at the beginning of a term of instruction. The purpose of such testing is usually to determine the strengths and weaknesses of each student so they can focus their energies on their weaknesses where those energies will be most effective and efficient. Similarly, teachers can use overall diagnostic information about the average performances of students on the objectives of a particular course to decide where to focus their teaching energies so students will benefit most from instruction. In curriculum terms, the central question in diagnostic testing is: Do the students need to learn the language material or skills outlined in the course objectives?

Criterion-referenced *progress testing* is usually done as the course progresses rather than at the beginning of instruction; the purpose is to determine the strengths and weaknesses of each student as the learning progresses. Such feedback affords the students the opportunity to refocus their energies on any remaining weaknesses in order to make their learning as effective and efficient as possible. And again, teachers can use the overall progress information about the students in a particular class to decide how to tailor their teaching energies so the students will most benefit from the continuing instruction. In curriculum terms, the central question in progress testing is: How are the students doing in learning the language material or skills outlined in the course objectives?

Criterion-referenced *achievement testing* is usually done at the end of a course of study. The purpose of criterion-referenced achievement

---

[1] Note that we are not necessarily endorsing such an operationalization.

testing is to determine the degree to which the students successfully learned the language material or skills covered in the course, sometimes for feedback purposes but more often for grading purposes, or for deciding if they should be promoted to the next level of study or graduated. In curriculum terms the central question in achievement testing is: How much of the language material or skills outlined in the course objectives did the students learn?

Recall that three curriculum-related questions were posed above:

1. Do the students need to learn the language material or skills outlined in the course objectives?
2. How are the students doing in learning the language material or skills outlined in the course objectives?
3. How much of the language material or skills outlined in the course objectives did the students learn?

By examining the answers to these three curriculum-related questions, teachers or other curriculum developers can study the effectiveness of the course objectives in terms of: (a) whether the students needed to cover them at all, (b) how quickly or slowly the objectives were learned, (c) the degree to which each and every objective was learned. Answering such questions not only makes it possible to study the effectiveness of the course objectives, but also to revise and refine them so they function better in future courses. Thus testing can and should be an important part of setting goals and objectives.

Putting tests in place. Naturally, putting appropriate norm-referenced and criterion-referenced tests into place can help in improving the tests themselves. Whether you are adopting, adapting, or creating tests for a program, their effectiveness should be assessed through analysis of the results. No test – norm-referenced or criterion-referenced – is effective, reliable, and valid unto itself. Tests are effective, reliable, and valid for particular purposes with specific types of students who have a particular range of abilities.

To give a clear example, because we are testing specialists, we have often received calls from ESL professionals in other programs asking for a copy of our ELIPT, a placement test designed specifically for the English Language Institute at our university. For instance, adult education administrators might ask for the test so they could accurately place their students. They had heard that we had a good test, so such a request seemed reasonable to them. Naturally, we had to refuse because using our test (suitable for our English for academic purposes program with our types of students, who are predominantly Chinese speakers and who range from about 500 to 600 on the TOEFL) would be totally inappropriate in a program where the purposes of the language teaching would better be described as English for social or survival purposes and where the students are predominantly Pacific Islanders and South-East Asians with proficiency levels well below 500 on the TOEFL. Our test would not fit that program at all. The students would probably score very low on each and every item. Thus, the test would not spread them out and would be useless for making placement decisions. The same would be true if the test were too easy. In fact, it is a matter of degrees, but any placement test that does not fit the particular program in question cannot be expected to function well for making placement decisions. The same would be even more true for a criterion-referenced test because of the way criterion-referenced tests must match a particular curriculum objective by objective in terms of the purpose of the objectives, the types of students, and the ability range of the students.

Hence, any test (whether adopted or adapted from an outside source or specifically designed for the language program in question) should be constantly monitored to insure that it effectively fits the purposes of the program and the types of students, especially in terms of their range of abilities. The topics covered in the rest of this book will help you examine the effectiveness, dependability, and validity of your criterion-referenced tests. For more information on examining norm-referenced tests in the same way, see Brown (1996). Thus the testing in a language program can and should be viewed as a way of improving the tests themselves.

Adopting, adapting, or creating materials. Teachers often ask why materials come after testing in the model shown in Figure 2.1. To many teachers, testing is something that you do after you have done your teaching, at the end of a course. In contrast, our view is that it is much safer to consider implementing materials in a curriculum only after criterion-referenced tests have verified that the objectives actually fit the students. Certainly, if those objectives are based on thorough needs analysis, they should fit the students in the program in question reasonably well. But do they always do so?

In the English Language Institute at the University of Hawai'i at Manoa, we had an experience that indicated that it is much safer to develop the tests before putting too many resources into implementing materials. We developed the criterion-referenced test for our reading course in 1986. We chose to do the reading course first because the objectives were already in reasonably good shape. We developed the reading criterion-referenced test in two forms so we could administer the test at the beginning and end of the course without giving any student exactly the same test. The results of the test administration at the beginning of the course were to be used for diagnostic and curriculum development purposes; the administration at the end of the course was to be used for achievement and curriculum development purposes, as well as for grading and promotion decisions. The teachers all pitched in and helped to write items, and the tests were ready to use in the first week of classes.

We actually administered the tests during the first class of the second week of classes. Eager to analyze the results, we soon discovered that we had a curriculum disaster on our hands. The students had scored very high on average for every objective. In short, our curriculum, as expressed in our objectives, was underestimating what our students could do in reading. And, it had been doing so for years. The students had not complained, probably because the course was so easy for them, and the teachers were happy because the students were doing so well on the final exams. Little did the teachers know that the students could have done just as well on the finals during the first or second week of class.

The point is that we learned something valuable from implementing our tests as diagnostic pre-tests: our course objectives were not at the appropriate level of difficulty. We immediately adjusted the situation, not by changing the objectives themselves, but rather by changing the readability levels of the reading passages to which those objectives would be applied from 8th to 12th grade readability to the more appropriate 13th to 17th grade level (using the Fry readability scale – Fry, 1985). We had to start over again on the tests, which was a waste of time and energy, but imagine the waste if we had already developed a complete set of materials for the course before verifying, through the use of our diagnostic beginning-of-course test, the appropriateness of the objectives upon which the materials were based.

In addition, once materials are put into place, criterion-referenced achievement testing at the end of the course can be used to examine the effectiveness of the materials in terms of how well the students learned the objectives. Further comparison of the students' pre-test and post-test results can be used to study or evaluate the overall amount of gain made, as well as the more detailed objective-by-objective gains. In this way, the effectiveness of the materials can be examined in terms of how students actually perform.

Thus criterion-referenced testing is an important part of determining the appropriateness of the objectives before investing the energy and resources necessary to adopt, adapt, or create materials because such tests can verify that the objectives actually fit the needs of the students and by extension can help insure that the materials will also do so.

Supporting teachers in their efforts. Teachers often find that testing is the most onerous task they have to perform (second perhaps to useless paperwork). We believe they feel this way, in part, because they frequently lack the specific expertise to do testing well. That is why Brown (1995a, 1996) advocates that curriculum developers should provide teachers with technical help in developing classroom-level criterion-referenced tests. Administrators can take at least four steps to help teachers:

1. Get those teaching a particular course to work together on a common set of tests to be used at the beginning and end of the course.
2. Provide staff to handle the logistics of duplication, distribution, and collection of the tests.
3. Furnish the expertise and resources necessary for scoring and analyzing the results.
4. Give immediate and timely feedback to teachers and students.

If teachers feel that curriculum supports them rather than hampers or constrains them, they are much more likely to cooperate. Once they realize that they benefit substantially from such a test development project, teachers will quite naturally *want* to cooperate.

Regularly evaluating all the other five components. Program evaluation as we view it entails regularly evaluating all the other five elements in the curriculum in a formative manner (and, again, occasionally in a summative manner). The pre-test and post-test evaluation built into the test development process (for each test, and indeed, as we will explain in Chapter 3, built into the analysis of each item) is one way of evaluating the effectiveness of teaching/learning in the curriculum as a whole.

However, on a continuing basis, sound criterion-referenced testing can provide more detailed evaluative information about:

1. The degree to which our views of the students' *needs* are accurate with regard to what they can actually learn within the constraints of time, energy, resources, etc. of the given language program.
2. The appropriateness of the existing course *objectives* and the degree to which each is being achieved.
3. The effectiveness of the criterion-referenced *tests* themselves in terms of dependability, validity, and practicality.
4. The degree to which the classroom *materials* fit each course's objectives, and in turn, fit the needs of the students.
5. The effectiveness of the *teaching* within the program, especially with regard to what is going well and what could be improved.

In addition, as mentioned above, comparing students' performances on the objectives at the beginning of the course (on the diagnostic tests) with their performances at the end of the course (on the achievement tests) promotes the overall *evaluation* of the program in terms of the degree to which learning is going on, the efficiency of that learning, and ways to improve that learning process.

Central role of testing. The arrows in Figure 2.1 point in all directions, indicating that all of the components of curriculum development are interrelated in one way or another. Indeed, in previous sections, we illustrated how testing is related to all six curriculum components. In a very real sense, sound CRTs provide the glue connecting the components of curriculum development to one another. However, for test developers, the key relationship is between objectives (which describe what the language program wants the students to be able to do at the end of the course) and the CRTs that are designed to measure those outcomes. Based on such tests, then, rational curriculum revision decisions (for revising the program's view of students' needs, the goals and objectives, the tests, the materials, and the teaching strategies) can be made on the basis of what students are able to do at the beginning and end of the course.

A closer look at objectives and criterion-referenced testing

As pointed out in Brown (1984a), educational objectives are (or should be) at the heart of most program level criterion-referenced testing. *Educational objectives* will be defined here as any set of statements that describe what teachers expect students (a) to be able to do at the end of a particular language course or program, or (b) be able to do in a specific domain of knowledge, skills, or abilities.

The relationship between objectives and criterion-referenced tests is often a direct one. Particularly for objectives-based tests, educational objectives should serve as the basis for development of the item specifications (described in detail in the next chapter) that will then be used to develop criterion-referenced test items. However, even for domain-referenced tests, one sound way to define the domain would be to list a set of objectives that describes the domain, then, develop item specifications from those objectives, and create items based on the item specifications.

Subjective reactions to objectives

Before developing objectives, item specifications, and criterion-referenced tests, however, test developers may have to overcome certain psychological and political barriers that arise because some language professionals have very negative, knee-jerk reactions to educational objectives (for example, see Valdman, 1975, or Tumposky, 1984). We feel that, in part, such negative attitudes are caused by association in some teachers' minds between educational objectives and the narrow types of stimulus/response objectives that might arise out of operant conditioning in instructional psychology. Consider a tongue-in-cheek example objective: *By the end of the course, the students will salivate when they hear a bell.* Such a narrowly defined objective obviously has limited utility and appeal. Why then would anyone think that language curriculum designers and language testers are so naïve that they would exclusively use such objectives? Nonetheless, that is precisely what Valdman (1975) and Tumposky (1984) imply.

What such language educators fail to recognize is that objectives can take many different forms. Terms like *behavioral objectives*, *educational objectives*, *instructional objectives*, and *performance objectives* have been used interchangeably and have been defined rather loosely. For purposes of this discussion, we would like to restrict their usage and define them more clearly. *Educational objectives* will be the phrase that we use to refer to all kinds of objectives. Within this general category, objectives can range from extremely narrow objectives which we will call *instructional objectives*[2] to more general *performance objectives* to even broader *experiential objectives*. Each of these types will be defined more clearly in the three sections that follow.

In all cases, objectives are and should remain flexible, not rigid, and should be allowed to take many shapes and forms from simple lists to elaborate descriptions. In addition, they should serve as the basis for developing classroom tests, materials, teaching strategies, evaluation procedures, and other curriculum elements.

Instructional objectives

We will use the term *instructional objectives* to refer only to the sorts of narrowly defined objectives that Mager (1975) characterized as including the following types of precise descriptions:

1. *performance* (what the learner is expected to be able to do by the end of the term);

---

[2] They are also known as behavioral objectives, but we prefer to avoid the term *behavioral* because of its unfortunate and erroneous association with behavioral psychology.

2. *conditions* (important conditions under which the performance will occur);
3. *criterion level* (the level at which learners are expected to perform in order to pass).

Such carefully defined instructional objectives may be appropriate for some language courses, or parts of courses. For instance, courses organized around structural syllabuses may benefit greatly from clearly listing the structures that the students are expected to understand or use by the end of the course. However, many different types of activities can serve as the basis for organizing a set of instructional objectives. As Valette and Disick (1972) put it,

> . . . the outcome of certain types of activities may be specified very precisely: recitation of memorized materials, counting, directed dialogs, conjugations of verbs, declensions of nouns, naming objects in the FL [foreign language], manipulation of sentence patterns, and so on. These types of goals, which represent the simpler or more elementary aspects of language learning lend themselves readily to the mold of the formal [instructional] objective. (p. 4)

Structural objectives might turn out to simply be a list of structures, or they might be stated in clearer terms like the following:

By the end of the term, the students will be able to:

1. Distinguish between simple present, simple future, and simple past tenses in regular verbs in a written passage of about 5th grade reading level on an academic topic with 80 percent accuracy.
2. Correctly write the simple present, future, and past tense regular verbs in obligatory contexts with 60 percent accuracy.
etc.

Similarly, courses organized around reading skills like skimming, scanning, getting the main idea, understanding facts, understanding inferences, understanding vocabulary from context, using prefixes, stems, and suffixes to understand vocabulary, etc. seem to lend themselves to clearly stated instructional objectives. Consider the following objectives:

By the end of the term, the learners will be able to:

1. Correctly answer 3 out of 4 multiple-choice fact questions based on a 500-word academic text on a topic of interest to most educated adults at the 8th grade readability level.
2. Correctly identify the main idea of a 300-word paragraph on an

academic topic of interest to most educated adults at the 8th grade readability level with 80 percent accuracy.

etc.

Objectives focused on the receptive skills (listening and reading), as well as on narrowly defined grammar knowledge can often be stated in the precise manner described above, and once stated, they are relatively easy to measure on a paper-and-pencil test.

From the criterion-referenced test developers' standpoint, one striking advantage to such clearly defined instructional objectives, when they are appropriate and available, is that very little modification will be necessary to create clear item specifications, that is, item specifications may be created by simply adding a bit more information to the instructional objectives.

Performance objectives

As mentioned above, much of the complexity involved in what we are trying to accomplish in current language teaching practices cannot adequately be described by narrow instructional objectives. Language teachers have recently come to understand many new aspects of language learning that have changed the ways they teach. As such, teachers may find themselves needing to test communicative language learning, functional syllabuses, or task-based curriculum, and these trends force us to think in broader terms about performance testing and performance objectives. We will use the phrase *performance objectives* to describe objectives that delineate students' abilities to perform in the language or use it to accomplish something. This definition will lend itself to looking at objectives that will be useful in performance and other more individualized types of tests, where we are actually trying to find out what the students can do with the language. The only necessary requirements for most performance objectives are that they be stated in terms of what the students will be able to do with the language at the end of the course and that the stated performance must be observable in some way or other.

The performance objectives for a particular course might be as simple as a list of functions that the students should be able to use effectively by the end of the course, as in the list provided by van Ek and Alexander (1980), or as elaborate as those formulated by Findley and Nathan (1980), which we will discuss in more detail below.

An abbreviated list of the functions provided by van Ek and Alexander (1980) follows:

1.0 Imparting and seeking factual information
   1.1 Identifying
   1.2 Reporting (including describing and narrating)
   1.3 Correcting
   1.4 Asking
2.0 Expressing and finding out intellectual attitudes
   2.1 Expressing agreement or disagreement
   2.2 Inquiring about agreement or disagreement
   2.3 Denying something
   etc.

A total of 68 functions are listed by van Ek and Alexander under a total of six macro-categories, including the following four additional macro-categories:

3.0 Expressing and finding out emotional attitudes
4.0 Expressing and finding out moral attitudes
5.0 Getting things done (suasion)
6.0 Socializing

These objectives are far less detailed, yet none the less, they state what the students will be expected to be able to do by the end of the course. With such objectives, creating item specifications may be difficult, especially creating item specifications that will be adequate for observing the degree to which students can accomplish those objectives.

A typical example of a CRT based on functions would be the B level (intermediate) speaking test that was developed when Brown (one of the authors of this book) was teaching EFL at the Guangzhou English Language Center (GELC) in the People's Republic of China from 1980 to 1982 (see Brown, 1995a, for a further description of this program). The underlying purposes of this test were to foster learning by giving the students diagnostic and progress feedback at the beginning and middle of the course, respectively. The test was also to be used for assessing their overall achievement at the end of the course. One other hidden purpose was to convince students who were more comfortable with traditional grammar/translation teaching that they should participate in role play, pair-work, and other communicative activities that they thought were odd and useless.

Our course objectives were that the students should to be able to effectively use 15 of the functions covered in the Gambits series (Keller & Warner, 1979) by the end of the term. Naturally, the content of the test was determined to a large extent by the specific objectives that we had chosen for our course. We were trying to develop a performance test, in this case a test of the students' abilities to perform the 15 functions that we were teaching. But many details remained to be clarified. How was the test to be arranged logistically? And how would the language samples be scored? The objectives provided a useful framework for developing the test but, unlike instructional objectives, they did not provide enough detail to easily develop a test based on the objectives alone.

Ultimately, the GELC teachers decided collectively that the test would take the form of a taped interview to be set up in advance as a role play, where each student was to play the role of a student in the United States and the teacher was in the role of a professor in their field of study. We wanted the interviews to last no longer than five minutes each, so to save time, we asked each student to choose three cards from among fifteen (one for each objective), and the interview proceeded. Each card had a number of questions and/or situations that would elicit the function that was being tested by that card. The interviewers used each card until they felt that the students had been given ample opportunity to show what they could (or could not) do with the function in question, then moved on to the next card. No scoring was done while the interview was in progress. However, the interviews were tape-recorded so that scoring could be done later.

At different times during the program, various schemes were used to score these interviews, but the clearest scheme asked two teachers (the student's own teacher and one other) to give the students separate ratings for fluency, content, effectiveness in communicating their meaning, correctness of the exponents chosen to accomplish the function, and stress/intonation (see Figure 2.2). Each of these five categories was accorded five points for a total of 25 points. Each of the five categories was further divided into descriptors for one point, two points, three points, four points, and five points. A grid was then created with the five categories across the top and the five possible points down the left-hand side as shown in Figure 2.2. Descriptors were then written in each of the squares of the grid. For instance, in the square at the top under *Fluency*, a description was created for what it meant to get 5 points in fluency, that is, what it meant to be a very fluent speaker. Similar descriptions were provided in each of the squares, and these obviously became a part of our item specifications. The students' total scores were the sum of the five scores that they received in the five categories (total possible = 25) multiplied by 4 so that we could interpret them in something resembling percentage terms, as is often typical on CRTs. We did not give the tests back to the students, but we did provide them with

Score	Fluency	Content	Meaning	Exponents	Stress/ Intonation
1					
2					
3					
4					
5					

Figure 2.2. GELC scoring grid

feedback (just after the diagnostic and progress tests) in teacher conferences, where we played their tape for them and discussed their performance.

That is how one group of teachers chose to handle performance objectives for a function-based curriculum. In effect, the teachers recognized the inadequacy of the descriptions provided in their list of performance objectives so they unwittingly created item specifications by describing how the interview would be conducted, and by creating a clear scoring grid.

Findley and Nathan (1980) describe another approach that was taken to develop detailed and explicit objectives describing the functions for a curriculum (see Figure 2.3). One example that they give of an objective that would express a function (finding written numerical information) is as follows:

Given the first and last names of 10 persons, 5 with Spanish surnames and 5 with English surnames from a local telephone directory, the learner will locate and write down the telephone numbers in 15 minutes with 90% accuracy. (Findley & Nathan, 1980)

This example shows that with a little imagination some functions of the language can be stated in fairly clear and observable terms while not sacrificing the complexity that may necessarily be involved. Notice that their approach to the problem of stating objectives for more complex functions involves a statement of the performance

Competency Based Curriculum
APPENDIX A
GLOBAL OBJECTIVE: Getting Things Done
TASK (competency): 2.0 Request Others To Do Something

PRIMARY TASK OBJECTIVE	INSTRUCTIONAL METHODS
Given a list of 10 tasks to be accomplished, learner, who is blindfolded or out of view of the "pool of potential laborers," will state 1 talent needed to perform the task and ask person to perform it. Learner must express him/herself with 90% accuracy for both the talent description and the task request.	• Set up a mini-community in classroom by dividing it into service areas; for example, gas station, library, retail store, bank, etc. Have students circulate and request services. Prompt students by giving them cue cards, e.g. "you need a dress cleaned." • Show videotape of persons doing the above at different places around community. Have students identify different styles of asking for service. • Give students a community based exercise in which they must accomplish certain goals by asking others, in school or outside school, to do something. Then they bring the results to class and report their activities in writing or before the group.

EVALUATION
Learner is presented with these tasks: (1) building a stone wall, (2) baking a cake, (3) typing a letter, (4) repairing a car, (6) clothes need ironing, (7) dog needs walking, (8) cow needs milking, (9) pipe needs welding, and (10) man needs a haircut. An instructor monitors a small group. Learner being evaluated may be blindfolded or located in an adjacent room and use intercom. All learners not being evaluated are encouraged to offer their talents as potential laborers. Learner is instructed to state in one sentence a characteristic or talent needed to perform a task. When a potential worker identifies him/herself, learner names the task and requests the speaker to perform it. Scoring: 20 points total; 1 point for each statement of description of needed characteristic, and 1 point for each grammatically acceptable request to perform. (Criterion: 18 points.)

Figure 2.3. Function-based objective
(adapted from Findley and Nathan (1980))

objective itself, a description of how it can be evaluated, and suggestions for ways to teach the objective. With a little further information, this example could easily become the item specifications for the *requesting others to do something* task within the *getting things done* functional objective.

However, performance objectives are not limited to functional syllabuses and communicative classes. Brown and Bailey (1984), for instance, describe a somewhat different set of performance objectives that were developed in a skills based course. The course at UCLA was the upper level ESL course, and the objectives that we refer to are those for the writing skill only. When the project began, the objectives for the writing component of the course were as follows:

By the end of English 33C a student should be able to:

. . .

8. write a precise, convincing and well-organized expository composition with an introduction, body and conclusion.
9. proofread and revise his/her written work.
10. use connectives correctly within and between paragraphs.
11. prepare a term paper (including footnotes, bibliography, title page, etc.).

etc.

As a new teacher (in 1977), one of the authors of this book (Brown) was grateful for this much guidance for teaching in the writing part of this ESL course. However, after teaching the course, he and other teachers found that they needed more detail, which was provided by an ongoing project (to which many teachers contributed) to develop a scoring grid for ESL compositions. One version of that scoring grid is presented in Figure 2.4.

Notice that Figure 2.4 is designed much like Figure 2.2 was for the speaking course in China, except that here we are looking at a scoring grid for writing which was on a scale of 100 points. Hence, the categories and numbers of points are quite different from Figure 2.2. The categories down the left side include: (a) organization, (b) logical development of ideas, (c) grammar, (d) punctuation, spelling, and mechanics, and (e) style and quality of expression. The total number of points possible in each category is 20, with individual descriptors for score ranges labeled across the top as 1–5, 6–11, 12–14, 15–17, and 18–20.

Of particular note is the fact that the grid shown in Figure 2.4 served as the writing performance objectives for the 33C course. Teachers gave each of their students a copy of the grid at the beginning of the course and told them that students wanting an *A* in writing would need to learn how to write like the descriptors to the left in the grid by the end of the course. Hence the five descriptions on the left side of the grid describe five terminal performance objectives, while the other boxes might be said to contain what could be termed *interim* objectives that the students might be able to achieve along the way.

	20–18 Excellent to Good	17–15 Good to Adequate	14–12 Adequate to Fair	11–6 Unacceptable	5–1 Not college level work
I. ORGANIZATION: Introduction, Body and Conclusion	Appropriate title, effective introductory paragraph, topic is stated, leads to body; transitional expressions used; arrangement of material shows plan (could be outlined by reader); supporting evidence given for generalizations; conclusion logical and complete	Adequate title, introduction and conclusion; body of essay is acceptable but some evidence may be lacking, some ideas aren't fully developed; sequence is logical but transitional expressions may be absent or misused	Mediocre or scant introduction or conclusion; problems with the order of ideas in body; the generalizations may not be fully supported by the evidence given; problems of organization interfere	Shaky or minimally recognizable introduction; organization can barely be seen; severe problems with ordering of ideas; lack of supporting evidence; conclusion weak or illogical; inadequate effort at organization	Absence of introduction or conclusion; no apparent organization of body; severe lack of supporting evidence; writer has not made any effort to organize the composition (could not be outlined by reader)
II. LOGICAL DEVELOPMENT OF IDEAS: Content	Essay addresses the assigned topic; the ideas are concrete and thoroughly developed; no extraneous material; essay reflects thought	Essay addresses the issues, but misses some points; ideas could be more fully developed; some extraneous material is present	Development of ideas not complete or essay is somewhat off the topic; paragraphs aren't divided exactly right	Ideas incomplete; essay does not reflect careful thinking or was hurriedly written; inadequate effort in area of content	Essay is completely inadequate and does not reflect college level work; no apparent effort to consider the topic carefully
III. GRAMMAR	Native-like fluency in English grammar; correct use of relative clauses, prepositions, modals, articles, verb forms, and tense sequencing; no fragments or run-on sentences	Advanced proficiency in English grammar; some grammar problems don't influence communication, although the reader is aware of them; no fragments or run-on sentences	Ideas are getting through to the reader but grammar problems are apparent and have a negative effect on communication; run-on sentences or fragments present	Numerous serious grammar problems interfere with communication of the writer's ideas; grammar review of some areas clearly needed; difficult to read sentences	Severe grammar problems interfere greatly with the message; reader can't understand what the writer was trying to say; unintelligible sentence structure
IV. PUNCTUATION, SPELLING, AND MECHANICS	Correct use of English writing conventions; left and right margins, all needed capitals, paragraphs indented, punctuation and spelling very neat	Some problems with writing conventions or punctuation; occasional spelling errors; left margin correct; paper is neat and legible	Uses general writing conventions but has errors; spelling problems distract reader; punctuation errors interfere with ideas	Serious problems with format of paper; parts of essay not legible; errors in sentence-final punctuation; unacceptable to educated readers	Complete disregard for English writing conventions; paper illegible; obvious capitals missing, no margins, severe spelling problems *(contd.)*

	20–18 Excellent to Good	17–15 Good to Adequate	14–12 Adequate to Fair	11–6 Unacceptable	5–1 Not college level work
V. STYLE AND QUALITY OF EXPRESSION	Precise vocabulary usage; use of parallel structures; concise; register good	Attempts variety; good vocabulary; not wordy; register OK; style fairly concise	Some vocabulary misused; lacks awareness of register; may be too wordy	Poor expression of ideas; problems in vocabulary; lacks variety of structure	Inappropriate use of vocabulary; no concept of register or sentence variety

Figure 2.4. Writing scoring grid (adapted from Brown and Bailey, 1984)

Experiential objectives

In many language teaching situations, teachers may simply want the students to experience certain things. Perhaps one teacher wants students to see five English language movies, while another wants the students to read 15 graded readings in French. In order to include such elements in the curriculum planning and development, they are described in *experiential objectives*, which by definition describe exactly what it is that the teacher wants the students to experience and how that experience will be verified or observed.

For instance, in the Reading B course at the GELC, the teachers had a number of instructional objectives for what they called the intensive reading skills, but some time during the semester the teachers also wanted these English for science and technology students to practice extensive reading by going to the language lab and reading five *Scientific American* articles in their major field of study. A description of this experiential objective might start as follows: By the end of the course, the students will have read five *Scientific American* articles in their major field of study. However, according to the definition given at the beginning of this section, an experiential objective should also describe how the "experience will be verified or observed." In this particular case, the teachers chose to ask the students to write a brief summary of the article in lay terms (since none of the EFL teachers were scientists). Those summaries were graded on a check, check-minus, check-plus basis, mostly to simply insure that the students would accomplish the experiential objective and take it seriously (in a way that teachers could observe). The entire objective might be stated as follows: By the end of the course, the students will have read five *Scientific American* articles in their major field of study and written a one paragraph summary of each article in lay terms. In this case, the experiences were more or less checked off when they were completed to verify and record that they had been accomplished.

To sum up, we have examined three types of objectives here: instructional, performance, and experiential. The purpose of all three types of objectives is to set reasonably precise, attainable, and observable goals that students should be able to achieve by the end of a language course or program. As we pointed out above, objectives are usually stated in terms of observable behaviors that the students should be able to perform by the end of the course. Consequently, objectives can serve as the basis for developing criterion-referenced achievement tests. We also pointed out that objectives can vary considerably in nature. Such variation means that the criterion-referenced tests derived from objectives will also tend to take many different forms – an issue we will discuss in the next section.

Fitting assessment types to curriculum

Testing and curriculum often do not match very well, at least in the language curriculums that we have seen. For instance, Brown (1981) investigated differences in performance between two groups of students: those who had been placed directly into the upper-level 33C ESL course at UCLA and those who had come to the course from lower-level courses. He did so for three successive quarters and found that there were statistically significant differences in performance on the final exam (with an average difference between groups of 9.82 points on a 100 point test), on a 50-item cloze test (with an average difference of 6.71 points), and on the course grades (with an average of .69 difference on a 4 point scale). Brown's study clearly identified a mismatch between the placement decisions and the actual progress made by students as they moved up through the courses after placement. In other words, the students placed into the upper-level course were considerably more advanced than the students being promoted into that same course from the lower-level courses.

To avoid or correct such situations, you might want to consider three sets of issues: the significance of the washback effect, the role of feedback, and the importance of using multiple sources of information.

The significance of the washback effect[3]

In the first section of this chapter, we argued that tests, especially criterion-referenced tests, play a central role in any curriculum.

---

[3] Important Note: Dan Douglas once considerably lightened the mood of a very serious meeting at Educational Testing Service by referring to the *washback effect* as the *bogwash effect.*

While all of the elements of curriculum are interdependent in one way or another, as indicated by the arrows in Figure 2.1, sound criterion-referenced tests are particularly important because they provide the glue that holds all of the other elements of a curriculum together. However, the criterion-referenced tests will only serve to unify a curriculum if they create a positive washback effect.

The *washback effect* is usually used to refer to the effect of testing on the curriculum that leads up to it. Our conception of the washback effect is a bit broader in that we are also concerned about the effects of tests on the entire curriculum. In either case, a washback effect can lead to very negative consequences for a curriculum, or very positive ones – depending on what the effect is and how it is used by the curriculum developers. From our point of view, curriculum developers should view the relationship between objectives and the criterion-referenced tests as a key relationship.

If the tests in a curriculum do not match its objectives, they are bound to create a *negative washback effect* on those objectives and on the curriculum as a whole. For instance, if a program has a set of communicative performance objectives, but tests the students by using multiple-choice grammar tests at the end of the courses, a very strong negative washback effect will be created against the communicative curriculum and its performance objectives. Students soon spread the word if there is such a mismatch, and they will almost always want to study whatever it is that is on the tests, to the detriment of any curriculum that is not directly related to the tests. We have seen this occur in dozens of settings.

A far more constructive strategy is to use the tests to create what has been termed a positive washback effect. This occurs when the tests match the course objectives as closely as possible. For example, if a program has a set of communicative performance objectives, and tests the students using performance tests (role plays, interviews, etc.) and personal-response assessments (like self-assessments, conferences, etc.), a very strong positive washback effect will be created in favor of the communicative curriculum and its performance objectives. A positive washback effect is created because the tests measure the same types of outcomes that are described in the performance objectives.

If the relationship between testing and curriculum is solid and clear, if the objectives do indeed reflect the needs of the students, if the materials are designed to teach the objectives, and if the teachers abide by the curriculum, then, the curriculum should hold together well. And, in such a situation, the tests clearly bind all the other components together.

The information provided in the next chapter about the advantages and disadvantages of selected-response tests (binary-choice, matching, and multiple-choice formats), constructed-response tests (fill-in, short-answer, and performance formats), and personal-response assessments (conference, portfolio, and self-assessment formats) should be used when designing objectives to think ahead to just how those objectives will be measured or observed at the end of the course. Doing so, and then following through by using the testing format that best matches each objective will help to create a strong relationship between the tests and objectives and will therefore help to produce a positive washback effect. (For more information on the washback effect, see Alderson & Wall, 1993a, 1993b; Brown, 1997, 1998; Gates, 1995; Alderson & Hamp-Lyons, 1996; Bailey, 1996; Messick, 1996; Shohamy, Donitsa-Schmidt, & Ferman, 1996; Wall, 1996; Wall & Alderson, 1996; and Watanabe, 1996.)

The role of feedback

Recall that the word *criterion* in criterion-referenced testing has two meanings. It can refer to the criterion level, or pass–fail cut-point, (for example, 70%) used in decision making with criterion-referenced tests, or it can refer to the criteria (or course objectives in many cases) on the basis of which such tests are designed. When the latter sense of *criterion* is applied, criterion-referenced tests take on an advantage that makes them particularly useful for language curriculum development. The advantage is that the scores on criterion-referenced tests have meaning in terms of the objectives of a particular course. Often, that means scores are not simply reported as numbers, for instance "you got a 75%", but rather are reported as numbers related to particular objectives, which can be described verbally. For example, scores might be reported as shown in Figure 2.5, where students were given a separate percent report for each of the objectives in the course.

In such a situation, where a set of scores is clearly related to objectives, those scores can serve as an important source of feedback to the students, teachers, and administrators. A score is not just a number showing the student's position in the total distribution of scores somewhere along a scale from say 200–800 as it is on a norm-referenced test. Instead, a set of scores is reported, each referenced to a particular description of behavior in the form of a course objective.

The meaning of this feedback will differ depending on the situation. For instance, if the scores are from a criterion-referenced test (based on the entire set of course objectives) that is administered at

	Objective:	Your Score:
1.	Skim a 600-word passage for six minutes, then answer multiple choice factual questions (without the passage) with 60% accuracy.	_____
2.	Answer multiple-choice factual questions on a 600-word passage in six minutes with 70% accuracy.	_____
3.	Answer multiple-choice factual questions about a graph, chart, or diagram in three minutes with 70% accuracy.	_____
4.	Take notes in outline format on a 600-word passage including main ideas and subideas (that is, at least two levels) with 70% accuracy.	_____

. . .

9.	Fill in connectors (provided) in the appropriate blanks in a 600-word passage with 70% accuracy.	_____
10.	Write labels for missing elements in a graph, chart, or diagram from information provided in a 600-word passage with 70% accuracy.	_____
11.	Fill in meanings (provided) for the prefixes and stems given in appendix in Allen et al (1980) with 70% accuracy.	_____

. . .

14.	Fill in meanings of unknown words based on sentence level context with 70% accuracy.	_____
15.	Identify sentences which function as examples in a 600-word passage with 70% accuracy.	_____
16.	Identify sentences which function as analogies in a 600-word passage with 70% accuracy.	_____

Figure 2.5.   Example score report for GELC Reading B course*
(adapted from Brown, 1995a)

* All reading passages were on general science topics and were grade 11 reading level, which is equal to junior year (next to last) ability in US high school, or approximately the *red* cards in your 4a SRA reading cards.

the beginning of a course in a *pre-test*, then the meaning of the feedback will be diagnostic in nature. In other words, the scores referenced to the objectives will be interpreted diagnostically. Thus a low score on a particular objective means that the student needs to work hard on the knowledge or skill involved in that particular objective, and a high score on another objective means that the student already has the knowledge or skill involved in that objective so the student might benefit more from focusing on other weaker objectives. Thus, the feedback is interpreted in terms of what the students need to do about each objective.

If, in contrast, the scores are based on the same criterion-referenced test, but it is administered at the end of a course in a *post-test*, then the meaning of the feedback will be achievement related. The scores referenced to the objectives will be interpreted in terms of what the students have achieved in the course. Thus a low score on a particular objective would mean that the student failed to get the knowledge or skill involved in that objective. This may mean that the student will be advised to work hard on this weakness as an individual or may be required to do remedial training on this particular objective. Alternatively, if some students score low on a number of objectives, the decision may be that they should not be promoted to the next level, or that they should be failed in the course and required to take it again. Decisions made with such scores must be a matter of policy in the particular institution involved. If based on criterion-referenced tests, however, the making of those decisions will be directly related to the curriculum in the sense that the feedback from the tests will not be just a number, but rather will provide an indication that the student failed to achieve, say, objectives 1, 6, 7, 9, and 12. Thus, criterion-referenced tests provide feedback to the students in terms of what they accomplished in the course, and provide feedback to the teachers that they can use for grading purposes.

In any situation where both diagnostic pre-tests and achievement post-tests have been administered, the averages and distributions of those scores for each class can also provide feedback to curriculum developers. Such summaries can answer three crucial curriculum questions: Did the students need to learn each of the objectives? (a *yes* being indicated if the students scored low on the pre-test); Did the students learn the knowledge or skill in each objective? (a *yes* being indicated if the students scored high on the post-test); and, How much did the students learn of each objective? (as indicated by *gain scores*, or the post-test average percent minus the pre-test average percent for each objective). Answers to all three questions can help in making decisions about what the students really need to learn, which objectives are appropriate, how the tests are working, which materials are effective, which teaching strategies are working well, and how well the curriculum is working. In short, such feedback can help in many ways to shape and change any language curriculum.

One point we would like to stress is that the tests used within particular language programs to give feedback to students, teachers, and curriculum designers must necessarily be *directly* related to curriculum if that feedback is to be maximally useful. In some programs that we know of, TOEFL or TOEIC test scores are used as pre-tests and post-tests for individual courses as well as to assess gain. In most cases, these tests will ***not*** be appropriate for such purposes. They are norm-referenced tests, which are by definition very general tests (as described in Table 1.1 and the associated discussion), and therefore much of what is being tested on TOEFL or TOEIC will not be directly related to what the students are studying in a particular course. In addition, such norm-referenced tests are global in what they test and are not designed to make the fine distinctions that would be necessary to reflect the amounts and kinds of learning that take place during one term in a particular language course. Furthermore, such norm-referenced tests are not course-related in the sense that the material being tested is generally not at precisely the correct level of difficulty for the particular students involved in the course. Because TOEFL and TOEIC must spread students out along a long continuum of ability levels, they must have items of a wide variety of difficulty levels. Thus, many of the items will be too easy and/or too difficult for the students in a particular course, which probably means that those items are inappropriate for measuring the students' performance in that specific course, or for assessing the learning gains that they make in that particular course.

One concern that teachers often express in relationship to the types of criterion-referenced test scores and feedback that we discussed earlier is that they can be used to compare their students (and by implication, their teaching) with those of other teachers. In other words, such scores can be used to answer the question: Did teacher A's class learn the material better than teacher B's class? Such questions are often threatening to teachers. If such a testing program is to succeed, the responsible parties must make it clear to teachers that no teacher would ever be criticized solely on the basis of the test scores of one class in one term. Such scores only provide information about what is going on in the class, and teachers can benefit from that information by finding new ways to improve their teaching. But such scores are only one source of information. A teacher who did not use that information or a teacher whose students consistently (across several courses and several terms) performed poorly might justifiably be criticized. However, because students differ so considerably from class to class and term to term and because there can be many reasons why students do poorly on a test (weak test items, poorly designed materials, insufficient study time, low motivation, etc.) in addition to teaching, it would be very irresponsible to criticize a teacher because a particular class did not do well on a particular achievement test, or did not produce high gain scores in a particular class.

Clearly, feedback is important in criterion-referenced testing, particularly in classroom-oriented, objectives-based testing (Brown, 1992). Generally, students will want to know how they did on any test and, if that feedback can be couched in terms more meaningful than a single score, like subscores related to written descriptions of objectives, then the feedback becomes an integral part of the learning process. Such integration of assessment and feedback is particularly true of the personal-response types of assessments described in the next chapter. Conferences, portfolios, and self-assessments all provide different forms of feedback to the students, feedback that is integrated into their learning. But it may turn out that some mixture of different types of tests and feedback will prove best in a particular curriculum.

For instance, in the GELC Speaking B course that was described above in the discussion associated with Figure 2.2, in addition to functions of the language, the teachers wanted to cover some aspects of pronunciation that were crucial to Chinese learners of English. Thus we had objectives about pronunciation, and we tested those objectives. In that situation, at the beginning, middle, and end of the course, the students were required to read [into a tape recorder] a special pronunciation passage supplied with Prator and Robinett (1985). The teachers then rated the pronunciation samples for certain aspects of phonology (particularly, word and sentence stress, and intonation, the pronunciation objectives for the course). The students and teachers listened together to the tape during conferences at the students' dormitory, and the students were also given their scores and verbal feedback at that time. Thus, testing and conferences were mixed together in this particular situation to maximize the impact of the feedback given to the students.

The importance of multiple sources of information

Basing any decision on a single source of information is very dangerous. For example, hiring a new teacher on the basis of a single recommendation over the phone would be irresponsible because that phone call might be motivated by friendship with the prospective teacher (or even worse, it might be motivated by a desire to get that teacher out of the caller's program because of the teacher's incompetence). Instinctively, most people recognize that multiple sources of information are more reliable than a single piece of information. That's why administrators typically gather many different types of information on teachers when hiring them, for instance, three letters of recommendation, a résumé, graduate school transcripts, a personally written statement of teaching philosophy, an example lesson

LORETTE WILMOT LIBRARY
NAZARETH COLLEGE

plan, an interview with the director, a teacher portfolio (see Brown, & Wolfe-Quintero, 1997; Wolfe-Quintero, & Brown, 1998), and sometimes (especially for the teachers on the short list) a live demonstration lesson. With all those multiple sources of information in hand, a much more dependable decision can be made. As we will explain momentarily, using multiple sources of information is also important in designing tests and in interpreting the scores that result from those tests.

Using multiple sources of information in designing tests. The literature on educational testing argues repeatedly that tests should be made up of a sufficient number of observations, or bits of information, to increase the chances that they will be dependable in themselves. A one-item multiple-choice test would never be satisfying to any teacher or student. Intuitively, neither party would feel that a one-item test was really doing a good job. That is why tests are usually much longer, made up of 30 to 50 multiple-choice items, meaning the scores are made up of 30 to 50 individual bits of information. When thinking about the advantages and disadvantages of the various testing formats discussed above, especially when thinking about how those different formats should be used in a particular curriculum, language educators must remember that decisions based on multiple observations are more dependable generally than decisions based on a few observations. Hence, a single composition written on one occasion is a single piece of information and is less reliable than, say, a portfolio of writing samples taken over a semester's time. Similarly, a score on a composition rated by one rater is less dependable than a score on a composition rated by three raters. The use of multiple sources of information in designing various kinds of tests is an issue that will necessarily be revisited below, particularly in the chapter on test dependability, because it is a key factor not only in test design, but also in comparing the various available testing formats.

Using multiple sources of information in interpreting test scores. One type of decision that is made using test scores is the important university admissions decision. For instance, a TOEFL score is often used in deciding whether an international student should be admitted to the University of Hawai'i. However, admitting a student on the basis of a single TOEFL score would be highly irresponsible. Consequently, other types of information are also used, such as students' high school grades, former teachers' recommendation letters, statement of purpose essays, and transcripts of high school performance. No responsible educator, least of all the testing professionals at Educational Testing Service, is advocating using a single test score in making any decision, because using multiple sources of information of varying types increases the dependability of that information and of any decisions that may result from interpreting the information. As McNamara and Deane (1995) put it, "Using these complementary assessment tools – traditional measures and student self-assessment information – we have a more complete picture of our students' ability, effort, and progress." (p. 21)

By using multiple assessment instruments, each of which contains sufficient observations to be internally dependable, rational decisions can be made about students' lives and about curriculum revision policies (for revising the program views of students' needs, the goals and objectives, the tests, the materials, the teaching strategies, and the overall course evaluation), especially if those instruments are administered at the beginning and end of the courses or throughout the courses in an ongoing manner.

See uk.cambridge.org/elt/crlt/ for chapter summary and exercises.

3 Criterion-referenced test items

Introduction

In his review of Roid and Haladyna (1982), Nitko (1984) notes that:

Although techniques for creating test items are traditionally covered in measurement textbooks, much of what novice item writers read in these textbooks is "clinical lore": Elder item-writers pass down to novices lists of rules and suggestions which they and their item-writing forefathers have learned through the process of applied art, empirical study and practical experience. (p. 201)

Without accepting the mantle of "elder item-writers", we would venture to propose that a set of general rules, which can be modified to help in writing good tests, has already been suggested for the area of discourse interpretation. These rules, called Grice's Maxims for the Cooperative Principle of Discourse (Grice, 1975), are related to quantity, quality, relation, and manner of general discourse, but they can also be used to cover the cooperative nature of test writing. The maxims can be summarized as follows:

1. Make your contribution as informative as is required but not more informative than required.
2. Be relevant.
3. Avoid ambiguity and obscurity of expression.
4. Be orderly.

Therefore, in writing test items and instructions: do not explain too much; do not use trick questions; provide only the information necessary; avoid ambiguity; and be orderly in test presentation. Remember that the examinees will assume that you are presenting them with all, and only, the relevant information.

Before going any further, several terms and their definitions need to be given.

Some useful definitions

Test item

Osterlind (1989) notes that few, if any, precise definitions exist for the concept of *test item* and finds this surprising because many glossaries define a test as a collection or set of test items. Definitions abound for item analysis, item bias, item difficulty, item discrimination, item characteristic curves, and other test components that focus on the item level, but testing book authors apparently assume that the test item itself has no need for definition. In a paraphrase and expansion of Osterlind's definition, the definition used in this book for a *language test item* will be:

A unit of measurement with a prompt and a prescriptive form for responding, which is intended to yield a response from an examinee from which performance in some language construct may be inferred in order to make some decision.

Understanding the implications of this definition is important since much of the rest of the book assumes a common definition for the idea of a language test item. First, as Osterlind notes, a test item is "a unit of measurement". Hence the results of a test item must be quantifiable in some way, either through objective scoring or subjective evaluation. An item may be scored dichotomously (as either right or wrong) or on a scale of some sort (for example, on a scale of one to four).

Second, a test item involves a "prompt and a prescriptive form for responding . . .". Thus an item causes the examinee to respond in a way prescribed by the item, that is, the examinee is directed to select an answer, write a composition, perform some task, or respond in some other way. If there is ambiguity as to what the examinee is to do, the very definition of an item is violated. Also, it is important to note that an item need not be a question. Thus the term *test question* represents only one type of test item, including only those items that take the interrogative form.

Third, the examinee's performance, the prescribed response, is interpreted such that an inference is made in terms of "performance in some language construct . . .". This construct may be a language skill, achievement on some instructional objective, a grammar point, some sociolinguistic or pragmatic ability, or any other language performance. However, the performance must be specified directly, that is, an item has a purpose. For a criterion-referenced item, if no specific construct can be inferred, then, once again, the definition of an item has been violated.

Finally, the performance, or prescribed response, in the construct leads to an inference "in order to make some decision." The idea of decision making is included in the definition in order to put test items solidly within the framework of test purpose. If a test writer has written an item with no focus in mind, the item is purposeless and violates the very definition of a test item. Such a requirement helps to insure that test items will be used for the types of decisions for which they were originally intended.

It is important to recognize that the decision just mentioned may be made in terms of admissions, placement, diagnosis, selection, achievement, research hypothesis testing, or other educational issues. So the decision can be norm-referenced in purpose or criterion-referenced. However, the purpose of an item will be difficult to determine by simply looking at that item; that is, an item destined for use in a norm-referenced test will be impossible to distinguish from one designed for a criterion-referenced test. None the less, the type of decision must be clear initially so that the content, quality, and statistical analyses (brought to bear in piloting and revising the items) can be properly focused to ultimately create a test that is effective for either the norm-referenced or criterion-referenced decision that was initially intended.

While such a prescriptive definition of a test item may appear on the face of it to constrain educators and researchers, this definition actually broadens traditional concepts of test items by: (a) providing a basis for developing test items that are congruent with the various competing hypotheses discussed in Chapter 1; (b) supplying guidelines for language educators and researchers to develop test items which meet their own particular needs (this chapter); (c) helping educators and researchers focus on the various contributions to measurement error (see Chapter 5) throughout the testing process.

The parts of a test item

As demonstrated above in the definition of a test item, language testing has a technical vocabulary like any other academic specialization, and should be used consistently and precisely. The term *prompt*, which appears in our test item definition, is that portion of a test item to which the students must respond. Prompts can take many forms. In cases where the test item is multiple-choice, the prompt would be the *item stem* (that is, that part of the item, typically at the top, that forms the basis for the choices in a multiple-choice item). Consider, for instance, the following item:

According to the passage, Janet ate a _____.
a. pear
b. banana
c. hamburger
d. steak

The item stem includes the top portion of the item, that is, the words "According to the passage, Janet ate a _____." In this type of item, the stem serves as the prompt.

However, with other types of items such as those found on a composition test, the prompt might include a quote to which the student must respond, or several reading passages that the student must analyze and write about.

Determining the appropriate type of prompt requires a conscious and active decision on the part of the test writer. Such a decision should not be based simply on expedience, aesthetics, or preference.

The "prescriptive form for responding" will generally take the form of a selected response, a constructed response, or a personal response. These three types of responses differ in that the selected response requires the examinee to choose from a set of possible solutions to the test item, while the constructed response requires the students to produce some language (from a relatively limited set of possible answers), and the personal response requires the learners to produce an individual response (which may be different for each and every student).

In more detail, in *selected-response items*, examinees choose the correct response from a set of supplied options. The most common form of this format in language testing is the multiple-choice item. The selected-response category also includes binary-choice (that is, true/false) and matching items. For selected-response items, the possible answers from which the examinee selects are called the *options*, or *alternatives*. The *correct answer* is also sometimes called the *key*, and the incorrect alternatives are called *distractors*.

In *constructed-response items*, the examinee supplies a response. Perhaps the most widely known example of this item type is the short-answer item in which the examinee writes a word or phrase to answer an open-ended question. The constructed-response category also includes fill-in and various types of performance tasks.

In *personal-response items*, students produce different responses according to their own personalities and preferences. For instance, within boundaries established between teacher and student, portfolios give students freedom to create and include whatever they feel best represents their own specific work and abilities, and conferences provide a time when teachers and students can tailor assessment to the students' individual abilities and needs. In addition, self-assessments allow students to make personal judgments on their own abilities or language performances.

As we will explain below, all three of these categories have numerous alternative item forms. Virtually every text on language testing discusses the differences between the first two of these item types. However, most such texts have neglected discussion of personal-response testing. Frequently the discussion in language testing books has assumed that selected-response items lead to one type of test information and constructed-response items lead to some other type of information. For example, some testing textbooks assert that multiple-choice items lend themselves to very detailed and specific information, while essays or short answers require synthesis of information; this difference may be true to some extent, however variations among the alternative approaches within each of these two categories may be greater than the differences among the three families of item types. That is to say, the differences in the types of information gained between a short-answer item and an essay question may be greater than that between a short-answer item and a multiple-choice item. For the present, the distinctions among selected-response, constructed-response, and personal-response items will be used in order to provide a common basis for discussion.

General guidelines for item format analysis

We have shown that a wide variety of different testing formats are used in language testing. This section presents some general item writing rules that may prove helpful in initial stages of test construction. These rules hold true for all types of items and reflect the implications of Grice's (1975) cooperative principles. They are presented here as a means for controlling the types of psychological processing required of the examinee while taking the test. In all cases, these rules are designed to help item writers avoid variability due to linguistic or format confoundings (as described in Table 3.1).

Linguistic confoundings

Item writers frequently, though inadvertently, introduce *linguistic confoundings*, or unintentional language problems, into the task of taking the test. While teachers generally want a test that measures language, they do not want the results to be due to the examinees not being able to process the language of the item itself. To avoid such

Table 3.1. *Linguistic and format confoundings*

Linguistic confoundings
1. Items should be written at the examinees' level of proficiency.
2. Items should not contain negatives or double negatives.
3. Items should be unambiguous.

Format confoundings
1. Items should contain only relevant information.
2. Items should be independent.
3. Items should be clearly organized and formatted.

processing errors, test writers should observe at least the following three rules:

First, avoid writing items whose language is at levels of complexity above the examinees' level of language proficiency. If some of the examinees do not understand the language of the stem, answering correctly or incorrectly may be due to one of two factors: (a) a lack of the knowledge or skill being assessed or (b) an inability to process the information in the stem. Thus the scores will be ambiguous. For example, the following prompt would be inappropriate for an intermediate-level student being asked to write a short auto-biographical paragraph:

Homo sapiens achieve personality integration through a modified chronological incorporation of self and society. In one paragraph, relate this to your own growth experiences.

Second, avoid negative and double negative statements because they are difficult to process and may cause confusion on the part of the examinee. For example, suppose the examinees were required to read a passage about a student whose grade was marked down as a result of continual tardiness, but who did not think tardiness was relevant to grading, and who, in addition, was afraid to talk to the teacher. Now, consider a test item such as "Why did the student not deny lack of punctuality as an inappropriate basis for grading?". Clearly a test item of this sort becomes a problem solving exercise, or riddle, divorced from the information presented in the passage.

Third, avoid ambiguity in test items. The examinees need to know exactly what is required of them. For example, the following item could have two answers: *Family plays an important role in life. It sometimes complicates matters. Explain this.* If the examinees understand *this* to refer to the family's *role in life*, one answer would be produced; if they interpret *this* as referring to the complication involved, quite another answer might result.

Format confoundings

Just as the language used in test items can cause problems, *format confoundings*, or inadvertent confusion due to item appearance or content, may needlessly disorient students. Three rules may help to avoid such confusion.

First, as mentioned in Grice's (1975) cooperative principles, avoid presenting irrelevant information; instructions that are too complicated or verbose place unintended processing demands on the examinees. On the other hand, instructions should not be so terse that the examinees cannot understand what is expected of them. The test directions in Example 1 provide unnecessary and irrelevant information while the directions in Example 2 do not provide enough information:

Example 1:

The following twenty vocabulary items have been selected from the second reading text in Unit 2 of the reading packet. Your teacher discussed each of these words in class during the Wednesday vocabulary lesson. The words are presented in alphabetical order, rather than the order they appeared in the text. Two words come from each paragraph, except paragraph five. Three words come from that paragraph. Select five of the words and write them on a separate piece of paper. Then, select the best definition from the list at the end of this handout. Write that next to each word. Of the remaining fifteen words, select five and show the prefixes, word roots, and suffixes by writing them below the words and definitions listed above. Put a slash "/" between each prefix, root, and suffix (for example, Prefix/Root/Suffix).

Example 2:

Write an essay comparing relationships in two countries.

Second, avoid items which are not independent. Items that violate this rule are produced in two ways. In Example 3, answering a subsequent item is dependent upon correctly answering an earlier item:

Example 3:

1. What is the square root of 100?
2. Multiply this by 7.

In Example 4, one item provides the answer to a subsequent item:

Example 4:

1. Why did Captain Cook go to Hawai'i?
2. What explorer went to Hawai'i?

When items are not independent, interpreting why examinees got an item right or wrong may be difficult or even impossible.

Third, items should be clearly organized and formatted. All parts of an item should appear together, not be physically divided across two pages so that examinees don't answer only the first part of the item without realizing that there is more. Items of like format should be grouped together within sections or subtests so examinees will not be confused by unnecessary shifts in the types of responses they are required to make. Shifting from multiple-choice to short answer to true/false and back to multiple-choice formats can be distracting. Also, sufficient space should be provided for examinees to give a complete response to the item. If students are given five lines to respond to an essay prompt or are provided with half a page to answer a short answer question, they will tend to see the space as providing guidelines for the extent to which they are to answer. Finally, the test should look attractive, with a readable typeface and a layout that is clear, uncluttered, and consistent. This is a frequently overlooked and underestimated factor in test development.

These linguistic and format confoundings are summarized in Table 3.1.

Specific guidelines for item format analysis

As we have discussed elsewhere (Brown & Hudson, 1998), test types can be classified into three basic categories (see Table 3.2):

1. Selected response (including binary-choice, matching, and multiple-choice format).
2. Constructed response (including fill-in, short-answer, and performance format).
3. Personal response (including conference, portfolio, and self-assessment formats).

For examples of many of these item formats, see Brown 1998a. Note that all of these item formats could be used for either norm-referenced or criterion-referenced purposes; it is rather the use to which they are put that distinguishes between the two purposes.

Each of these three response categories has pros and cons, and all

Table 3.2. *Overview of language test types*

Response type	Item format
Selected response	Binary-choice (true/false) Matching Multiple-choice
Constructed response	Fill-in the blank Short answer Performance
Personal response	Conferences Portfolios Self-assessment

have appropriate and inappropriate uses. Some areas of research and teaching call for the types of receptive-language information obtained relatively efficiently and quickly through selected-response items; other areas call for productive-language use and are most appropriately examined through constructed-response formats; and still other areas require the relatively high degree of flexibility and individualization found in personal-response assessments.

Selected-response items

Selected-response items are those in which students choose the correct answer from among a set of options, either by circling it, darkening the correct circle on the answer sheet or a similar selection procedure. In these tests, students do not *create* any language. Hence selected-response items are most appropriate for testing the receptive skills of listening and reading. Within the selected-response format, three types of items will be considered in more detail: binary-choice, matching, and multiple-choice.

The overall advantages and disadvantages of selected-response tests are shown at the top of Table 3.3. Generally speaking, administering and scoring them are relatively easy, and the scoring is objective, but they are relatively difficult for the test writer to create and require no language production on the part of the students. For all selected-response items, guessing should be limited as a factor in the examinees' scores. In our discussions of binary-choice, matching, and multiple-choice, we will discuss strategies for minimizing this. One other overall guideline is that the correct answers should be

Table 3.3. *Advantages, disadvantages, and item writing guidelines for selected-response items*

Overall	*Advantages* – requires a short time to administer; easy to score; scoring is objective. *Disadvantages* – relatively difficult to create; requires no language production on the part of the students. *Overall Guidelines* – limit the effect of guessing as much as possible; correct answers should be randomly dispersed.
A. Binary-choice	*Advantages* – useful for assessing ability to discern between two choices; simple and direct measure of comprehension. *Disadvantages* – tend to be tricky or deceptive; large guessing factor (50%); need large number of items; typically focus on details and facts. *Guidelines* 1. avoid long and complex statements; 2. avoid including more than one concept in each item; 3. avoid *absolutes*.
B. Matching	*Advantages* – requires little space; low guessing factor (10% for 10-item test). *Disadvantages* – restricted to measuring students' abilities to associate one set of facts with another. *Guidelines* 1. restrict matching sets to brief lists; 2. make lists homogeneous in content and form; 3. insure that all options are plausible; 4. create more options than prompts.
C. Multiple-choice	*Advantages* – smaller guessing factor; useful for testing a wide variety of learning points. *Disadvantages* – often overused; sometimes used for inappropriate purposes. *Guidelines* 1. make sure alternatives are grammatically consistent with stem; 2. write alternatives of about the same length; 3. avoid overlapping options; 4. avoid inadvertent clues; 5. avoid options like *none of the above, A and B, but not C*, etc.; 6. avoid excess wordiness.

randomly dispersed in order to avoid a pattern that the students can use to their advantage in guessing. Such randomization can be done in many ways. For example, an item writer can use playing cards. The aces and twos can be used for true/false items, or the aces, twos, threes, and fours can be used for four-option multiple-choice, and so forth. The cards are shuffled and then drawn at random to decide which option will be the correct answer. Another method is to always arrange the options for each item in alphabetical order, or from the longest option to the shortest, or vice versa.

Binary-choice. This format requires students to respond to the language by selecting one of two choices, for instance, between true and false or between correct and incorrect. The most commonly used binary-choice format is the *true/false format*.

Looking at the advantages and disadvantages of binary choice, we see that their primary strength is that they focus on assessing the ability to discern between only two alternatives, thus providing simple and direct indices of whether a particular point has been comprehended or not.

A weakness of binary-choice tests is that test writers may tend to write items that are deceptive (that is, items that turn on the meaning of a single word or phrase, or that depend on some ambiguity) in order to make the items work well. If students' ability to respond to deceptive items is what you want to test then this is not a disadvantage. However, most teachers prefer instead to create straightforward tests wherein students who know the answer get it right and students who do not know the answer get it wrong. In this case, it might be best to avoid binary-choice items altogether, or at least pay careful attention to this issue of trickiness.

As we discussed in the overall guidelines for selected-response items, the other main problem is the *guessing factor*: examinees have a 50% chance of getting the answer correct even if they don't know the answer. However, if there are a large number of carefully designed true/false test items, the overall score should overcome much of the influence of guessing. If a test is one item long, an examinee has a 50% chance of getting a perfect score. If a test is two items long, an examinee has a 25% chance of getting a perfect score. The odds continue to diminish until, on a 25-item test, an examinee has only 3 in 100,000,000 chances of getting a perfect score by guessing alone.

Kreiter and Frisbie (1989) note that a possible alternative to the true/false format is the multiple true–false (MTF) format, where the stem is followed by a series of choices, and the examinee responds to each option as true or false. For example, a multiple-choice item on a listening test might be as follows:

1. When Bob discovered that his car had broken down, he ___.
   a. Called his father
   b. Tried to fix it
   c. Walked home
   d. Called a mechanic

However, suppose that Bob actually did several things after discovering that his car had broken down. The MTF item analog might take the following form:

When Bob discovered that his car had broken down, he _____.
1. Called his father   True   False
2. Tried to fix it   True   False
3. Walked home   True   False
4. Called a mechanic   True   False

According to Kreiter and Frisbie (1989), the advantage here is that MTF tests maximize the number of responses per item and provide information regarding the examinee's knowledge of each option, not simply the keyed response. However, this is a relatively new type of item and needs a great deal more research.

If the material of interest lends itself to binary decisions and a sufficient number of test items can be written, then true–false items may be productively used. However, you may have difficulty finding 25 non-trivial points (in, say, a reading passage or listening selection) that are worth testing.

Table 3.3 gives three *guidelines* for writing binary-choice items. First, long and complex statements should be avoided. Such statements tend to indicate that the content being addressed does not lend itself to true dichotomous interpretations. Second, only one concept should be tested by each item. Such items often represent two binary choices in one item and thus present a 25% chance of being true rather than the 50% chance of being true by guessing. Finally, there are few absolutes in the world, and so test items that contain such *absolutes* as "always", "all", or "never" tend to be false. When absolutes appear in a question, examinees can often use their knowledge of the world to guess correctly even if they do not know the answer.

Matching. In this format, examinees select words or phrases in one list that match words or phrases in another list, that is, they match prompts to options. Matching tests are limited to measuring students' abilities to associate one set of facts with another, or one set of definitions with the words they define. They are typically used for testing vocabulary. The following is an example:

Directions: Put the letter of the best definition in Column B in the blank in front of each word or phrase in Column A.

Column A

Column B

_____ 1. Binary-choice

a. students select words or phrases in one list that match words or phrases in another list

_____ 2. Multiple-choice

b. students encounter language material and respond by choosing the correct answer, usually from a set of three, four, or five options

_____ 3. Matching

c. students examine some language material and then select, from among a set of options, the answer that is correct

_____ 4. Selected response

d. students respond to a sample of language by selecting one of two options

e. students read a prompt and write at least a two-page essay on the topic

As indicated in Table 3.3, the advantages of this format are that it requires little space and has a relatively low guessing factor (e.g. 10% for a 10-item test).

The guidelines in Table 3.3 focus firstly on the need for brief lists (Popham, 1981). To do this, you may have to break the matching test into several subtests. Otherwise, the examinees will be involved in a major processing activity just to keep track of all the items. Second, make sure the lists are homogeneous in content and form. Third, insure that all the options are plausible. Fourth, create more options than prompts (so the elimination of options cannot be used to improve the chances of guessing correctly on the remaining items), and make sure you tell the examinees whether each option may be used only once or more than once.

Multiple-choice format. This format requires students to examine some language material and then select, usually from among three, four, or five options, the answer that best completes a statement or best fills in a blank in the statement. Multiple-choice items reduce the 50% guessing factor found in binary-choice tests to 33%, 25%, or 20% depending on whether three, four, or five options are used. A frequent criticism of teachers is to say that "language is not multiple-choice." Presumably they mean that productive language use does not present options for speakers to select from, so multiple-choice test items are not like real spoken language use. (The same argument could, of course, be used against all selected-response tests.) However, many aspects of language, particularly the receptive skills such as reading, listening, grammar knowledge, and phonemic discrimination, can be efficiently tested using the multiple-choice format. Since these skills are often tested in traditional proficiency and placement tests, multiple-choice tests have come to be overused. They have even been twisted to uses that seem quite inappropriate (e.g., to test writing ability or communicative competence).

Table 3.3, lists the advantages and disadvantages of multiple-choice, as discussed above, and offers item writing guidelines.

These focus on reducing the effects of testwiseness and unintentional clues in the answers, and minimizing the amount of cognitive processing required of the examinee. First, the alternatives for multiple-choice items should be grammatically consistent with the stem. Second, the alternatives should be about the same length. A length problem can be an especially serious issue when the correct answer is radically longer or shorter than the other options. For example, the following type of option set (where D is the correct answer) should be avoided:

a. Bob
b. Sally
c. Karen
d. the man in the green suit

Good test takers know that it pays to give special consideration to exceptionally long or short options when guessing.

Third, overlapping options can provide clues to the testwise examinee. Consider the following item based on a reading passage which describes a child:

The child is less than _____ feet tall.
a. 4
b. 5
c. 6
d. 7

Regardless of what the reading passage may have explicitly indicated, "d" would have to be a correct answer.

Fourth, the item stem should contain no inadvertent clues. If the following item were on a reading test, the answer would be a foregone conclusion (alternative c) because of the grammatical clue, whether the examinee had read the passage or not:

John saw a _____.
a. antelope
b. elk
c. bear
d. ox

Such an item may be rewritten with the article in the options rather than in the stem so as to avoid the unintentional clue:

John saw _____.
a. an antelope
b. an elk
c. a bear
d. an ox

Fifth, options such as *none of the above, A and B, but not C,* or *all of the above* should generally be avoided. If an examinee gets an item correct (or incorrect for that matter), you want to know why. With *none-of-the-above* type options, you will never know if the examinees answered incorrectly because of erroneous processing of the plausibility of A, B, and C together, or because they simply did not know the answer. In essence, the examinee is being required to process and remember at least seven different questions:

1. Is A correct?
2. Is B correct?
3. Is C correct?
4. Is the combination of A and B correct?
5. If the combination of A and B is correct, is C incorrect?
6. Is the combination of A and B and C correct?
7. Is any option incorrect?

Sixth, avoid wordiness in the items. For example, consider the following item:

Mary _____.
a. thought he was a gentleman
b. thought she was a gentleman
c. thought him was a gentleman
d. thought her was a gentleman

To avoid the repetition of *thought* and *was a gentleman*, as much material as possible should be included in the stem:

Mary thought _____ was a gentleman.
a. he
b. she
c. him
d. her

Thus, the goal is to develop multiple-choice items which do not (a) provide clues to the answer or (b) require types of cognitive processing that may confound the results. At the beginning of this discussion, we noted that multiple-choice items are frequently criticized for being used too much and for being used for inappropriate purposes. Another criticism is they do not provide the information desired by the practitioner or researcher. This is because, while they are easy to construct, they are very difficult to construct *well*. Test writers should keep this in mind.

Constructed-response items

Constructed-response items are those in which a student is required to actually produce language by writing, speaking, or acting in some way, rather than simply selecting answers. Therefore, they are the most appropriate method for testing the skills of speaking and writing. Constructed-response tests can also be used for observing and measuring the interaction of receptive and productive skills, as in the interaction of listening and speaking in an oral interview procedure, or the interaction of reading and writing in a performance test where students are required to read two academic articles and write an analysis of the differences and similarities between the two.

In contrast to selected-response tests, constructed-response tests eliminate most of the guessing, but introduce all of the problems associated with subjectivity on the part of raters. Also scoring is time-consuming. Another potential problem is that examinees may be able to bluff. For example, on an essay examination, the examinee may write "around" the topic and take a shotgun approach to the answer in hope of hitting something that will be counted as correct. This is a type of guessing, but it is guessing about what the rater wants to find, or will accept, in the answer (rather than guessing which of the specified options may be correct, as in selected-response tests).

As well as listing their advantages and disadvantages, Table 3.4 also gives overall guidelines to creating constructed-response items. We suggest that the definition of a correct answer should be clear before administering the test. You can make the answers maximally clear by having a key or set of criteria for assigning the scores and making sure that scorers are in agreement about what the key or set of criteria mean. Using the responses of the best students as the key for the test is generally a bad idea. Such a strategy may turn out to be unfair because it creates a tendency to ignore or denigrate the potentially correct answers of some of the weaker students. Remember, scoring constructed-response items is necessarily more subjective than it was for the selected-response items discussed above. Hence, you should make every effort to keep the scoring as fair as possible when using any of the three types of constructed-

Table 3.4. *Advantages, disadvantages, and item writing guidelines for constructed-response items*

Overall	*Advantages* – virtually no guessing factor; allows for testing productive language use; allows for testing the interaction of receptive and productive skills. *Disadvantages* – difficult and time consuming to score; scoring is subjective; bluffing is possible. *Overall Guidelines* – make sure the definition of the correct answer is clear before administering and scoring; remember that the scoring is subjective; try to keep scoring fair.
A. Fill-in	*Advantages* – easy to create; flexible to use; requires a short time to administer. *Disadvantages* – limited to testing a single word or short phrase; may have many possible answers. *Guidelines* 1. provide sufficient context; 2. keep blank length consistent; 3. avoid putting blanks too close together.
B. Short-answer	*Advantages* – easy to create; requires a short time to administer. *Disadvantages* – limited to testing a few phrases or sentences; may have many possible answers; each student may produce a completely unique answer. *Guidelines* 1. word question very specifically; 2. give the students some idea of the shape of the desired answer; 3. use a direct question if possible.
C. Performance	*Advantages* – can be designed to simulate authentic language use; can compensate for negative effects of traditional standardized testing; can provide positive washback effects. *Disadvantages* – difficult to create; takes considerable time to administer; may result in increased costs; causes logistical problems; creates reliability and validity problems; increases the risk of test security breaches. *Guidelines* 1. make sure the student's task is clearly defined; 2. plan in advance how to score the examinees' performances; 3. where suitable, develop a scale for scoring the performances (and decide on whether to use a holistic or analytic scoring); 4. score all of the answers to one task together in one session; 5. score the tests anonymously if at all possible; 6. have at least two (but preferably more) raters score each student's performance; 7. warn raters of the possibility of "bluffing".

response items common in language testing: fill-in, short-answer, and performance items.

Fill-in. This format provides a language context of some sort and then removes part of that context and replaces it with a blank. The student's job is to fill in that blank. Fill-in items take many forms ranging from single word fill-in items and cloze passages to phrase-length responses. As shown in Table 3.4, the advantages of this format are that it is relatively easy to construct, is flexible to use from a test writer's point of view, and requires a short amount of time to administer. In addition, the fill-in format measures the students' ability to actually produce language, albeit a small amount of language, as well as the possibility of testing the interaction of receptive and productive skills (as in listening cloze where students are required to listen to a passage while reading it and fill in the blanks).

One limitation to the fill-in format is that it is generally very narrowly focused on testing a single word or short phrase at most. Another problem is that a fill-in blank may have a number of possible answers. For instance, in the process of conducting one study (Brown, 1980), as many as 28 possible answers were found for a particular cloze test blank. For the most part, the acceptable-answer scoring (based on the responses of 77 native speakers of English) indicated that function word blanks (like articles, conjunctions, prepositions, etc.) tended to have a very small number of possible answers, while content word blanks (like nouns, adjectives, action verbs, adverbs, etc.) tended to have many more possible answers, depending on the context.

Fill-in items have several potential pitfalls that should be avoided. The following item exemplifies all of these pitfalls:

Bob _____ in ___ _____.

The main problem is that insufficient context has been provided for the students to produce a clear correct answer for any one of the blanks. Indeed, an almost infinite number of possible answers exists for the blanks in this item. In addition, the blanks are of different lengths. The length of the blanks should be consistent so they are not providing information to the examinees about the correct answers (that is, about the length of the words) unless the test maker intends to provide such information. Furthermore, an item should generally not have several blanks in a row (or very close together) like the example above because they will tend to become interdependent, that is, answering one blank can become, to some degree, dependent on first correctly answering the other blank.

Short-answer. This format generally requires the students to examine a statement or question and then respond to it with a phrase or two, or a sentence or two, in the space provided. As shown in Table 3.4, the short-answer format is very similar to the fill-in format in its advantages and disadvantages, and it is limited to testing a few phrases or sentences. True, unlike fill-in format (which generally has a narrow focus on very specific language components), short-answer items can be somewhat more general in nature, but none the less, limitations of response length must be considered. As with the fill-in format, short-answer format may have many possible answers for each question. Indeed, with fill-in, each student may produce a completely unique answer. This characteristic can cause enormous problems in terms of fair scoring – problems that will be discussed at more length in the next chapter.

In terms of guidelines, remember, for writing short-answer items, the question should lead directly to the desired answer; such directness can be enhanced by making the question very specific. For example, the following item is poor because it does not constrain the examinee in terms of content:

What was the passage about?

The following item is better because it is more specific and requires a more concise answer:

What three areas of the world were discussed in the passage?

Additionally, the example immediately above gives the students some idea of what the desired response will look like. In such situations, a direct question is usually preferable to an incomplete statement or other format because a direct question is usually less ambiguous.

Performance.[1] This format generally requires students to perform some more-or-less real-life, authentic task using the language, most often either productive types of spoken or written language, but sometimes combining two or more skills, like reading and writing, or listening and speaking. Because of their nature, such language performances must usually be scored by several raters. The performance format can take many forms including essays, problem solving assignments, role-playing, group tests, and communicative tasks. To some extent, all language tests can be said to have some degree of performance included. Even in answering multiple-choice

---

[1] Because the performance format and personal-response formats that follow may be less familiar to readers than the foregoing formats, we will dwell on them a bit more than we have on the earlier ones.

grammar items students tend to construct a real-life context in their minds for the item. Hence the most accurate way to think about the performance aspect of language testing might be as a continuum, which has the least direct, least real-world tasks at the less performance-oriented end and the most direct, most real-world and authentic at the most performance-oriented end.

Language teachers have used certain types of performance testing for many years. We are referring to those types of tests that would fall fairly close to the most direct, most real-world and authentic end of the continuum. For example, teachers have tested writing skills by having students write essays like the ones they might have to write in their university courses. Speaking and listening skills have been tested by using job-interview-like interviews with students. Until now, we have not known exactly what to call these types of tests. Some testing researchers called them *integrative tests* because they integrated, or linked, two or more of the language skills (listening, speaking, reading, and writing), two or more of the linguistic aspects of the language (like grammar, pronunciation, and vocabulary), as well as other less-well-understood aspects of language (like cohesion and coherence, suprasegmentals, paralinguistics, kinesics, proxemics, pragmatics, and culture) in ways that testers did not precisely understand. Integrative tests usually stand in contrast to *discrete-point tests*, which by definition clearly assess distinct and identifiable parts of the phonetic, syntactic, or lexical systems, as in multiple-choice grammar or vocabulary tests.

However, some testers recognized that task-based tests were quite different from the fill-in format used on a cloze test, which were also labeled as inegrative tests (e.g., Brown 1996). Such a task-based test was defined as a test in which students are asked to perform tasks that reflect the real-life situations where they will be expected to use the language in the future.

The above description of a task-based test is strikingly similar to occupational tests in which the candidates are required to perform job-related tasks in a test. For instance, candidates for police work might be required to:

1. interview a citizen in the street who is reporting a crime;
2. find a crime victim in a building full of hostile and innocent pop-up targets (without shooting any innocent bystanders); and
3. complete a typed police report.

A similar EOP (English for Occupational Purposes) test could be developed to assess the English as a second language ability of police candidates who happened to be non-native speakers of English.

Occupational tests like these have been called performance tests for years.

In short, by definition, the performance format has three requirements (after Brown, Hudson, Norris, & Bonk, 2001): (a) examinees are required to perform some sort of task; (b) the tasks must be as authentic as possible; and (c) the performances will typically be scored by qualified raters. These three characteristics not only help to define what performance format is but also help to distinguish those performance tests that are commonly used, such as essays, interviews, extensive reading tasks, and so forth from integrative tests like dictations and cloze tests, none of which have any of the above three characteristics. (For more on performance format in language testing, see Wiggins (1989) or Shohamy (1995).)

As shown in Table 3.4, the advantages of performance format are that it involves virtually no guessing, it facilitates the testing of productive language, and it can involve testing the interactions of receptive and productive skills. Moreover, performance format can be used to simulate authentic language use. Because performance format can come close to eliciting actual, authentic communication, advocates argue that it: (a) assesses students' abilities to respond to real-life language tasks; (b) creates more valid assessments of student's actual abilities than traditional multiple-choice tests; and (c) predicts students' future performance in real-life situations more validly. Performance tests can also compensate for many of the negative aspects of standardized testing like negative washback bias, irrelevant content, etc. This is especially true if the performance test in question provides a strong positive washback effect (see discussion in the previous chapter) in its relationship to the curriculum. (For much more detail on the positive aspects of performance format, see pp. 15–16 in Norris, Brown, Hudson, & Yoshioka, 1998.)

The disadvantages of performance format are that it is difficult and time consuming to score, and the scoring is usually fairly subjective. It is also relatively difficult to create such performance tasks. Additional time is also usually required to administer the performance format, which translates into increases in costs for developing performance tests, administering the tests, training teachers, training raters, conducting rating sessions, reporting scores, educating the public, and so forth. Another disadvantage stems from increased logistical problems: storing large amounts of collected material, providing special equipment and security, planning and conducting rating sessions, and so on. Reliability problems may also arise in the form of rater inconsistencies, task-specific variance, the limited number of observations, and subjectivity in the scoring process.

Validity problems may also occur because of inadequate content coverage, lack of construct generalizability, sensitivity of performance tests (to test method, task type, and scoring criteria), construct under-representation (which in language testing terms, means the problem of generalizing from a few observations of language performance to the broad spectrum of real-life performances), and construct-irrelevant variance (that is, performance characteristics that have little or nothing to do with the students' language abilities). Test security may also pose problems because of the small number of test questions, the difficulty of creating and equating new items each time the test is administered, and the potential effects of teachers "teaching to the test". (For much more detail on problematic aspects of using the performance format, see Educational Testing Service, 1995, or Norris, Brown, Hudson, & Yoshioka, 1998.])

In scoring all performance items, *subjectivity* is an issue. Several guidelines can be used to reduce subjectivity and make the interpretation of performance items clearer.

First, make sure the task is clearly defined for the students. For example, do not set a task like the following:

Write an essay about life.

Second, know in advance how you plan to score the examinees' performances. Third, if appropriate, develop a scale against which you will score the performances. To do so, you will first have to decide whether you want to use *analytic scoring* with separate scores for different aspects of the performance (for instance, separate scores on a composition for grammar, mechanics, vocabulary, content, and organization) or whether you prefer to use *holistic scoring*, in which a single overall score is given. Either way, writing a set of clear descriptors for the scale should be your goal.

In addition, the scorers themselves are a potential source of variability. Our fourth, fifth, and sixth guidelines: in order to reduce the influence of raters on the scores, all of the answers to one task should be scored in a single session, all answers should be scored anonymously, and, if possible, all answers should be scored by at least two (but preferably more) raters. One final rater-related problem is that performance items allow test-taking strategies like *bluffing*, which may cloud the results. For example, in writing an essay, the examinee may try to bluff their way through the essay by writing so much that, regardless of the quality of the writing, the rater finally gives up and awards a higher score than the essay deserves simply in order to get on to the next essay. Raters should be warned of the possibility of bluffing.

The main point to keep in mind when scoring performance items is that the process is necessarily subjective, and therefore every effort must be made to make the scoring relatively fair.

Personal-response items

Personal-response items also require students to produce language but, unlike constructed-response items, they allow for the responses and even the ways the tasks are accomplished to be quite different for each student. In a sense, this is *personal assessment*, or individualized testing, because the students' communication is their own, that is, what they actually want to communicate.

In terms of *overall advantages and disadvantages*, Table 3.5 shows that personal-response assessments have the advantages of providing personal (or individualized) assessment, being directly related to and integrated into the curriculum, and, because of their ongoing nature throughout the term of instruction, being particularly appropriate for assessing learning processes. However, personal-response assessments also have the disadvantages of being relatively difficult to create and structure, and involving subjective scoring, if they are scored at all.

These types of assessments are sometimes called *alternative assessments*. As we have argued elsewhere (Brown & Hudson, 1998), we feel that such a label may be mistaken in that such assessment procedures should be subject to exactly the same concerns, such as reliability and validity, as all the other testing formats discussed in this chapter.

Table 3.5 shows one *overall guideline* for personal-response items: advocates of these types of assessments in language teaching situations generally believe that the assessment procedures, what they cover, and how they are scored should be developed in consultation between the students and teachers. The personal-response assessment types covered here include conferences, portfolios, and self-assessments.

Conferences. This format typically involves the student visiting the teacher's office, usually by appointment, to discuss a particular piece of work or learning process, or both. It differs from other forms of assessment because it focuses directly on the learning processes. For example, conferences can be conducted to discuss the students' work on successive drafts of compositions. Some of the *advantages* of conferences are that they can provide personal assessment, can be directly related to and integrated into the curriculum, and can prove useful for assessing learning processes. According to Genessee and Upshur (1996), conferences help students to address their own concerns and increase their understanding of the learning processes

Table 3.5. *Advantages, disadvantages, and item writing guidelines for personal-response assessments*

Overall	*Advantages* – personal assessment; directly related to and integrated into curriculum; appropriate for assessing learning processes. *Disadvantages* – difficult to create and structure; scoring is subjective. *Overall Guideline* – make sure students have a voice in everything that takes place.
A. Conferences	*Advantages* – can help students understand learning processes and learning strategies; help students develop better self-images; teachers can elicit specific skills or tasks that need review; can be used to inform, observe, mold, and gather information about students. *Disadvantages* – requires a lot of time; difficult to use for grading purposes; typically not scored or rated at all. *Guidelines* 1. insure that students feel in control of conference; 2. hold conferences regularly and frequently; 3. consider scoring and grading conferences by applying C. 1–7 in Table 3.4.
B. Portfolios	*Advantages* – enhances student learning; enhances teacher's role; enhances testing process. *Disadvantages* – design decision problems; logistical problems; interpretation problems; reliability problems; validity problems. *Guidelines* 1. decide with students in advance who will do what; 2. introduce and explain portfolios to the students; 3. have students select and collect *meaningful* work; 4. periodically have students reflect on their portfolios; 5. periodically have students, teachers, outsiders, etc. review the portfolios; 6. consider scoring portfolios by applying C. 1–7 in Table 3.4.
C. Self-assessments	*Advantages* – takes less time; involves students in the assessment process; encourages student autonomy; can increase learner motivation. *Disadvantages* – accuracy varies depending on skill levels and material involved; higher level students may tend to underestimate their abilities; prone to subjective errors; may function differently depending on the consequences. *Guidelines* 1. decide in advance what aspect of their language performance they will be assessing;

Table 3.5. *(contd.)*

2. where suitable, develop a written rating scale for the learners to use in scoring (and decide on whether to use holistic or analytic scoring);
3. plan in advance the logistics of how the students will score themselves;
4. use directions that give the students descriptions of concrete linguistic situations that they can score in behavioral terms if at all possible;
5. make sure the student's understand the self-scoring they will do;
6. have students score all of the items of one type in one session;
7. consider having students score themselves on two different occasions or have another student (or the teacher) do the same scoring.

and strategies involved in their own performances, as well as to develop better self-images. Teachers can also elicit performances on specific skills or tasks that they think need to be reviewed, or to focus on any number of other process-related issues. Thus, although conferences are time consuming, that time can be justified as they are an effective method for informing students, observing or gathering information about students, and molding students.

Naturally, these advantages of conferences are offset by certain *disadvantages*. Conferences are relatively difficult to create and structure, require a great deal of time, and, as they are difficult and subjective to score, are often not scored or rated, and so are difficult to use for grading purposes. They can, however, serve as a part of the overall curriculum-related assessment.

We offer the following guidelines for personal-response assessments. To begin with, even though teachers should probably provide some structure to their conferences, students must have a voice in what takes place and should feel they are in control during the conference. To be most effective, conferences should be scheduled regularly and frequently. In the view of Genessee and Upshur (1996), conferences should seldom be used for grading purposes. However, under certain circumstances, you may want to score and grade conferences: (a) in situations where scoring and grading are necessary in order to get the students to take the conferences seriously and (b) in situations where students perform tasks within the conference that are designed to make up for deficiencies in performing those same tasks earlier in class. When scoring conferences or certain aspects of conferences, the performance format guidelines (shown under C. 1–7 in Table 3.4) may prove helpful.

Portfolios. For years, painters, models, photographers, architects, and members of other similar occupations have used portfolios to present samples of their work to potential employers or clients in order to show their skills in a fairly convenient and compact format. More recently, portfolios have been used in teaching in general, and more specifically in language teaching in order to encourage students to collect and display their work. Drawing on the portfolio literature, we have tentatively defined the *portfolio format* as a purposeful collection of any aspects of a student's work that tell the story of the efforts, skills, abilities, achievements, and contributions to a given class. However, a variety of definitions exist for this relatively new assessment procedure – or more aptly, for this family of assessment procedures. (For other definitions, see Wolf, 1989; Arter & Spandel, 1992; Camp, 1993; or Shaklee & Viechnicki, 1995.)

Just as with conferences, the portfolio format helps students understand learning processes and learning strategies, develops better self-images, and helps teachers to elicit specific skills or tasks that need review, and to inform, observe, mold, and gather information about students. Portfolios also have specific advantages for student learning, the teacher's role, and the testing process.

If we look first at student learning, we can see that portfolios build and capitalize on the actual work done in the classroom; facilitate practice and revision processes; help to motivate students because portfolio production, if well-designed, involves a series of interesting and meaningful activities; increase student responsibility for the learning processes; encourage collaboration with teachers and other students; provide a way of setting minimum standards for classroom work; promote a holistic view of learning; and encourage the learning of appropriate metalanguage so that teachers and students can talk about language development.

Portfolios enhance the teacher's role in that they give teachers a clearer picture of student development; change the role of classroom teachers from adversaries to coaches (in the students' eyes); and provide insights into each individual student's progress.

In terms of the testing process itself, portfolios enhance teacher and student involvement in assessment; give teachers a chance to observe students engaging in meaningful language use in a variety of authentic tasks, contexts, and situations (so assessment is based on relatively real language use); allow for the multidimensional nature of language learning (processes, responses, and activities) to be incorporated into assessment; provide opportunities for both students and teachers to reflect on and collaborate in evaluating the students' language development; increase the validity of the information collected on students; and make teachers' approaches to assessing work more systematic. (For more on the advantages of the portfolio format, see Wolf, 1989; Valencia, 1990; Chittenden, 1991; Smit et al., 1991; LeMahieu et al., 1992; or Genessee & Upshur, 1996.)

The literature also addresses the numerous *disadvantages* of using portfolio format. In addition to the overall problem with personal-response assessments of being difficult to create and structure and the subjective nature of scoring, the specific disadvantages of portfolios fall into five categories of problems related to: design decisions, logistics, interpretation, reliability, and validity. *Design decision problems* include: determining who should decide judgment criteria, and how the criteria should be determined; determining who should decide what the portfolio should contain and how those decisions should be made; and determining the extent of daily authentic classroom activities that should be accounted for in portfolios. *Logistical problems* include: finding the increased resources, time, and money necessary to support portfolio assessment; having to rely on the abilities and training of teachers for implementation of portfolio assessment; and finding the time for teachers to read and rate portfolios on repeated occasions during the school term, while simultaneously helping students to develop their portfolios. *Interpretation problems* include: grading and comparing student performances; interpreting the resulting portfolio information in a manner fair to all students; training teachers to make such interpretations; and reporting portfolio assessment results appropriately for all interested audiences (parents, administrators, politicians, etc.). *Reliability problems* include: getting sufficiently high reliability for portfolio assessments across raters and occasions when ratings occur; insuring objectivity; avoiding mechanical errors that can cause problems in pass/fail decisions; assuring standardization in the reading and rating processes; and guaranteeing equal access to resources for all students. *Validity problems* include: establishing the validity of portfolios for making inferences about individual students as well as groups of students; determining how well portfolios represent students' work, ability, and growth; identifying and controlling (to the degree possible) for intervening conditions that may affect performance; and sorting out which abilities lead to which performance characteristics in what amounts. (For more details on the disadvantages of the portfolio format, see Smit et al., (1991); Valencia & Calfee (1991); Arter & Spandel (1992); or Camp (1993).)

Probably the first of the *guidelines* we can offer is that it is wise to decide in advance who will do what with regard to the portfolios. For instance, who will select the kinds of material that go into the portfolio? Who will own, store, and have access to the portfolio? Who will be responsible for creating and designing the portfolio procedures? Are students responsible for and active in the learning process?

Portfolios may be a new concept to the students. Hence, it may be necessary to introduce and clearly explain portfolios to them. When doing so, consider explaining the goals and purposes of this type of assessment, the roles of teachers and students, and whatever assessment scoring and feedback procedures you will use. The portfolio development process itself should probably require that students select and collect a variety of kinds of *meaningful* work including successive revisions of their work to show the underlying processes and any other appropriate indications of learning and metacognition. However, students should only include information and materials they are willing to make public.

At certain points in the process, students may need time to reflect on their perceptions and interpretations of their own work, as well as on their overall strategies for learning. Such reflections might profitably be based on criteria created by the class for checking, editing, and reviewing their own portfolio materials. It may also be necessary to conduct periodic reviews by the students themselves (or by their teachers, outsiders, or others) of the materials in the portfolios. Such reviews should probably be controlled by the students themselves. Finally, whenever scoring portfolios or certain aspects of portfolios, the performance format guidelines listed in C. 1–7 of Table 3.4 may prove helpful.

Self-assessments. This format will be defined here as any assessment that requires students to rate their own language, whether through performance-ability self-assessments, comprehension self-assessments, or observation self-assessments. The *performance-ability self-assessments* require learners to read a situation and then judge how well they think they would respond in that particular situation (on perhaps a scale of 1 to 5). Recent examples of performance-ability self-assessments can be found in Hudson, Detmer, & Brown (1992, 1995), Yamashita (1996), and Brown (1998). *Comprehension self-assessments* also require the students to read a situation and then judge how well they comprehend that particular situation. Examples of comprehension self-assessments are shown in Bergman and Kasper (1993) and Shimamura (1993). *Observation self-assessments* involve learners listening to audio cassette recordings or watching video tapes of their own language behavior (usually in natural situations or in role-play activities) and judging how well they performed. Recent examples of observation self-assessments can be found in Hudson, Detmer, and Brown (1995), Yamashita (1996), and Brown (1998).

As shown in Table 3.5, adherents of the self-assessment format claim that it has a number of *advantages*. In addition to the general personal-response item advantages of being personal assessments, directly related to and integrated into the curriculum, and useful for assessing learning processes, self-assessments can be designed to take very little time. Self-assessments also involve students in the assessment process, which in turn encourages another advantage: student autonomy, or the students' understanding of what it means to learn a language autonomously. Both the student involvement in assessment and their greater understanding of autonomous language learning can substantially increase their motivation to learn the language involved. (For much more information about designing self-assessments, see Oskarsson, 1978; Blanche, 1988; Blanche & Merino, 1989; Oscarson, 1989; McNamara & Deane, 1995; Hudson, Detmer, & Brown, 1992, 1995; and Gardner, 1996.)

The literature also raises some disadvantages to the use of self-assessment format in addition to the general personal-response item disadvantages of being difficult to create and structure and involving subjective scoring. Blanche (1988), after an extensive review of the literature, concluded that, "the accuracy of most students' self-estimates often varies depending on the linguistic skills and materials involved in the evaluations" (p. 81). Both Blanche (1988) and Yamashita (1996) found that the more proficient students tended to underestimate their linguistic abilities. Blanche (1988) also noted that "self-assessed scores may often be affected by subjective errors due to past academic records, career aspirations, peer-group or parental expectations, lack of training in self study, etc." (p. 81). Some of these problems can be overcome if the descriptions that students are referring to in rating themselves are stated in terms of clear and concrete linguistic situations and in terms of exact and precise behaviors that the students are to rate.

However, the "subjective errors" issue may be difficult to overcome because the consequences of a particular self-assessment will become an integral part of that measurement. In one situation, for instance, a self-assessment format might be used successfully in a research project and turn out to be reliable and valid in that particular situation for the intended purposes. That does not mean, however, that the same self-assessment format will function similarly in a higher stakes setting where students are assessing themselves for placement purposes (say into levels of study). Clearly, students who have a vested interest in being exempted from study would tend to rate themselves much higher in the placement setting. (For examples of self-assessment formats used in actual testing and research settings, see Bachman & Palmer, 1981; Davidson & Henning, 1985; LeBlanc & Painchaud, 1985; Heilenman, 1990; Bergman & Kasper, 1993; Hudson, Detmer, & Brown, 1995)

We offer a number of *guidelines* for developing self-assessment procedures. To begin with, it is important to begin by deciding what aspect or aspects of their language performance the students will be assessing. It may also be useful to develop a written rating scale for scoring the performances. Such a scale can be holistic or analytic and can be on many possible scales. For example, scales can range from 1 to 5 like the analytic scale shown in Figure 2.2 in the previous chapter or 1 to 20 like the analytic scale shown in Figure 2.4 in the previous chapter. Naturally, the scale will function better if it is developed in advance, and even better if it has previously been piloted, analyzed, and revised.

You may also want to plan in advance the logistics of how students will evaluate themselves. A place must be found for conducting the self-assessments. Students must be scheduled and notified of when they are to do the self-assessments. And, if students are to view video tapes of themselves or hear audio cassettes, arrangements will have to be made to procure equipment. Copies of the directions must be made and distributed, either in advance or at the time of the self-assessment, as you see fit.

As for the nature of the directions, they must be clear and concise. In foreign language situations where all of the students are likely to speak the same first language, these characteristics might best be achieved by giving the directions in that first language (for instance, in Japanese in an EFL situation in Japan). In second language situations where the students are likely to speak a number of different first languages, you may find it more efficient to use simple, clear, and concise directions in the second language (for instance, English language directions in an ESL situation).

In either case, the directions and the self-assessments themselves should probably give the students descriptions of concrete linguistic situations that they can score in behavioral terms if at all possible. However, because no set of directions is ever 100 percent effective, at the beginning of the self-assessment process you may want to verify that the students understand the self-scoring they are about to do. You can do so by simply asking them, or by having them do a sample self-assessment item and visually checking their work.

Several other policies may help to make self-assessment procedures more reliable. You might want to consider having the students score all of the items of one type together in one session. So, if there are some performance-ability self-assessment types of items and some comprehension self-assessment types, make sure that they are grouped together so the students do not constantly end up shifting gears back and forth in terms of what they are being asked to do. You might also want to consider having students score themselves on two different occasions so you can assess the consistency of their work. Or, you might want to consider having a peer, in the form of another student (or the teacher), do the same scoring in order to add a different perspective and different type of feedback to the student.

Criterion-referenced item format analysis

The item types discussed above are not unique to either criterion-referenced or norm-referenced approaches to language testing. However, in the criterion-referenced approaches, the particular item form that is selected will be directly linked to the course objectives or domain of interest. Thus, if the objective is to make sure students can "decode grammar in reading", selected-response items may be appropriate. Similarly, if the objective of interest is "ability to respond to business correspondence", constructed-response prompts eliciting the use of commercial correspondence conventions will be appropriate. Furthermore, if the domain of interest is "ability to recognize and respond to business correspondence", a teacher might want to employ a selected-response type of item which requires the examinee to identify the particular type of correspondence in tandem with a constructed response that prompts the examinee to write a letter in answer. Of primary importance is the fact that the item type selected is in essence determined by the identified domain and the specificity of its definition. The following section addresses the specific ways criterion-referenced tests are developed.

Criterion-referenced test development

One goal in writing and administering any test is to reduce ambiguity in the minds of the students taking the test. In other words, examinees should not be losing points because of unclear items, vague instructions, or confusing administration procedures; they should be losing points only because they do not know the answer. Unfortunately, eliminating all ambiguity is impossible. First, we do not know everything there is to know about language. Second, we do not know everything about human psychology. Third, we do not know everything about the social and cultural settings in which people are involved. Fourth, no matter how hard we try, test writing is not an exact science; there are definite elements of art involved. However, even though ambiguity cannot be completely expunged, reducing it as much as possible remains a priority.

Test and item specifications are often used to minimize ambiguity, particularly in criterion-referenced tests. The creation of test and item specifications must be viewed as iterative processes in test construction, that is, we do not initially write test specifications which are cast in cement. We begin by writing test specifications for the domain of behaviors that are of interest, and then we write item specifications and items which attempt to measure that domain. In this process, we will frequently find things that we want to revise in the test specifications. Then we administer the items, eliminate some of the items entirely, revise the item specifications again, and go back to change some of the test specifications. All of this may in turn cause us to revise the item specifications in some ways. Regardless of the interrelated nature of all of these processes, in order to make the explanations as clear as possible, the two types of specifications will be described here as though they are separate entities.

Test specifications

The first stage in writing a criterion-referenced test is the construction of test specifications. These provide a set of guidelines as to what the test is designed to measure and what language content or skills will be covered in the test. Additionally, test specifications can be used later for communicating the test writers' intentions to the users of the test. One useful format for test specifications might include an overall test descriptor and specific test descriptors, each of which are carefully characterized in turn.

Overall test descriptor. This communicates what the test is designed to do: the general test objectives and the test format. In essence, the overall test descriptor is an abstract of what the test looks like.

An example, overall test descriptor is shown in Table 3.6. The heading at the top indicates that the overall purpose of the test is to measure competency in academic English. The more detailed descrip-

Table 3.6. *Example of general descriptors*

<table>
<tr><td>

General Test Descriptor:
Test of English Academic Competency

The test is a paper-and-pencil test designed to evaluate mastery of the basic English required for success in a North American university without the need for supplemental ESL instruction. Those examinees mastering this test are capable of taking a full course of studies in the university as well as capable of contributing to the university community and taking advantage of opportunities afforded by the university outside of classroom settings. The test covers the English language skill areas of grammar, writing, reading, and listening. Examinees who demonstrate mastery minimally meet the following profiles:

> The examinee demonstrates mastery of academic: 1) reading abilities, such as utilizing text for study purposes, extensive reading comprehension, library resource use, computer search, and vocabulary in context; 2) listening abilities, such as understanding academic lectures, indicating main ideas and supporting details, organizing main ideas and supporting details, summarizing lectures from notes, and responding to group discussions; and 3) writing skills, such as summarizing authentic text, synthesizing multiple texts, expository composition, and use of bibliographic conventions.

</td></tr>
</table>

tors that follow in the table include areas of emphasis on the test. The descriptors explain what a student at the appropriate level (that is, one who will succeed on the test) can do in each of these categories.

Specific test descriptors. The general descriptors should also be accompanied by specific descriptors. These indicate what areas are included in each of the components. For example, if the test includes grammar, writing, reading, and listening, the particular areas to be included and the levels of achievement or proficiency would be detailed. The components might be listed like those shown in Table 3.7 for grammar, writing, reading, and listening.

Item specifications

Once test specifications have been worked out, cogent item specifica-tions should be written. In Popham's (1981) terms, item specifications are clear item descriptions that include a general description, a sample item, stimulus attributes, response attributes, and specifica-tion supplements. Each of these sections of item specifications will be defined as shown in Table 3.8 (adapting liberally from Popham,

Table 3.7. *Example components for specific test descriptors*

Skill Area Descriptions:

Grammar: A person who masters this area is required to demonstrate understanding of advanced grammatical structures in two to four sentence contexts. Structures tested include:

    embedded forms:
        embedded wh-questions
        restrictive relative clauses
    nominals:
        gerunds
        infinitives
    conditionals:
        present and past unreal
        present real
    modals:
        hypothesis
        hedging
    verb form:
        present perfect
        passive – simple present, simple past, and present perfect, and the
            passive with *It* in subject position
    articles:
        count & non-count
        first mention

Writing: A person who masters this area is required to demonstrate understanding of advanced academic writing skills. Tasks in this area:

    summarizing unsimplified text:
        within academic discipline
        general interest academic and non-academic
    synthesizing multiple texts:
        within academic discipline
        general interest academic and non-academic
    expository composition:
        300–600 word (3–6 paragraphs) essay based on a topic presented in
            reading passage or videotaped lecture segment
    bibliographic conventions

Reading: A person who masters this area is required to demonstrate ability to comprehend advanced academic reading texts and skills. Tasks included for this area include:

    library resource use:
        utilizing library on-line reference search
        Cambridge Language Abstracts

Table 3.7. *(contd)*

> Voyager Library Catalogue
> CD-ROM journal reference
>   ERIC document search
>   Silver Platter search
>
> utilizing text for study purposes:
>   skimming for main idea
>   scanning for specific information
>
> vocabulary in context:
>   field specific
>   academic genre
>
> extensive reading comprehension:
>   synthesis of multiple texts
>   summary of a single text

Listening: A person who masters this area is required to demonstrate ability to comprehend advanced academic lectures and discussions. Tasks in this area:

> understanding academic lectures:
>   indicating main ideas and supporting details
>   outlining main ideas and supporting details
>   understanding clarifications by lecturer
>
> summarizing lectures from notes:
>   discipline specific lecture topics
>   general interest topic lectures
>
> responding to group discussions:
>   lab discussion summary
>   small group discussion

1981, pp. 121–122). (Notice that we are using the phrase *prompt attributes* in place of what Popham calls *stimulus attributes*. We do this in order to be consistent with the discussion above and to avoid any confusion with stimulus-response behavioral psychology.) Example sets of item specifications are shown in Tables 3.9a and b. Let us now turn to a brief discussion of the five elements that make up item specifications: general description, sample item, prompt attributes, response attributes, and specification supplement.

General description. This is a simple one or two sentence description, in general terms, of the behavior being examined and how that behavior will be assessed. Thus the general item description does not differ markedly from a general test descriptor except that it is applied

Table 3.8. *Definitions for elements of item specifications*

1. *General description*: A brief general description of the knowledge or skills being measured by the item.
2. *Sample item*: An example item that demonstrates the desirable item characteristics (further delimited by the prompt and response attributes below).
3. *Prompt attributes*: A clear description of the prompt material, that is, the material that will be encountered by the student, or the material to which they will be expected to react through the response attributes below.
4. *Response attributes*: A clear description of the types of (a) options from which students will be expected to select their receptive language choices (responses), or (b) standards by which their productive language responses will be judged.
5. *Specification supplement*: For some items, it will be necessary to list supplemental material that is needed to clarify the four previous elements, for example, a list of vocabulary items from which the item writer can draw, or lists of grammatical forms, or language functions, and so forth.

(adapted from Popham, 1981)

Table 3.9a. *Example item specification*

Summarizing Unsimplified Text

General description:
> When presented with a short, unsimplified text, the student will summarize the information by re-expressing the main ideas in a paragraph.

Sample item:
> *Directions*: Read the following text carefully and then *summarize* it. Re-express the main ideas and supporting details using *your own words*. Write the summary in the space provided on your answer sheet.

> What we call a symbol is a term, a name, or even a picture that may be familiar in daily life, yet that possesses specific connotations in addition to its conventional and obvious meaning. It implies something vague, unknown, or hidden from us. Many Cretan monuments, for instance, are marked with the design of the double adze. This is an object that we know, but we do not know its symbolic implications. For another example, take the case of the Indian who, after a visit to England, told his friends at home that the English worship animals, because he had found eagles, lions, and oxen in old churches. He was not aware (nor are many Christians) that these animals are symbols of the Evangelists and are derived from the vision of Ezekial, and that this in turn has an analogy to the Egyptian sun god Horus and his four sons. There are, moreover, such objects as the wheel and the cross that are known all over the world, yet that have a symbolic significance under certain conditions. Precisely what they symbolize is still a matter for controversial speculation. (C.G. Jung, "The importance of dreams").

Prompt attributes:
1. Each item will consist of a 100 to 150 word text which is description, survey/experiment, or theoretical argument.
2. The passage will consist of unsimplified text at a college textbook level, and will include details and asides which would not be appropriate to include in the summary.

Response attributes:
1. The student will summarize the passage in the space provided on the answer sheet.
2. The correct response will be a summary which:
   a. condenses the essential information (that is, 50% the original length).
      2 points: Mastery – Summary is 25 to 50% the length of the original, while transmitting the entire general message of the original.
      1 point: Semi-Mastery – Summary is just under 25% or over 50%, while transmitting the whole general message, OR the summary is of an appropriate length, but misses a small portion of the general message.
      0 points: No Mastery – Summary is equivalent to the original in length, or is too short to transmit any of the original.
   b. replaces key words with synonyms:
      2 points: Mastery – More original content words in context are synonyms in the summary than are NOT, roughly 75% synonyms, 25% not, (minimum) or greater.
      1 point: Semi-Mastery – More original content words than synonyms: roughly 50% synonyms, 50% original.
      0 points: No Mastery – Virtually all summary content words match the original.
   c. changes the grammatical structure when possible.
      2 points: Mastery – As with (b) above but for grammar.
      1 point: Semi-Mastery – As with (b) above but for grammar.
      0 points: No Mastery – As with (b) above but for grammar.
   d. uses only main ideas, and deletes explanatory information and examples.
      2 points: Mastery – This summary gives only the main idea and a clear majority of the main supports.
      1 point: Semi-Mastery – A portion of the main idea supports are there, yet without becoming too long. The summary has too many details also. Main idea not readily clear.
      0 points: No Mastery – Either too long by virtue of having the main idea, main supports AND a lot of details, OR correct length, but at the expense of presenting only details and no main ideas and/or main supports.

Table 3.9b. *Example item specification*

Reading Comprehension

General description:
　　After reading a passage of 800–1000 words, students will answer
　　comprehension questions based on the passage.

Sample item:
　　Directions: Read the following passage. After you have finished reading,
　　answer the questions which follow the passage. Write complete sentences on
　　your answer sheet.

Tying Down or Mooring Aircraft
　　Airport tie-down areas are usually equipped with strong steel rings, hooks,
　　or other devices embedded in concrete for the purpose of attaching tie-
　　down ropes, chains, or cables. It is generally recommended that chains or
　　cables be employed for tie-down because ropes deteriorate when exposed
　　to sun and moisture for an extended period of time. Tie-down devices are
　　often left attached to the fitting in the concrete or other pavement, and it is
　　necessary merely to attach the rope, chain, or cable to the aircraft after
　　parking. If a rope is used, it should be attached to the aircraft with a
　　nonslip know such as bowline or square knot. Examples of these knots are
　　shown in . . . (McKinley, J. L. (1980) *Aircraft Basic Science*, Fifth Edition)

　　1. Why are cables or chains preferred over ropes?

　　　_____

　　　_____

　　　_____

Prompt attributes:
　　1. Each selection will be adapted from a college textbook or technical
　　　 manual in the social sciences, physical sciences, life sciences, or humanities.
　　2. Questions will involve the following:
　　　 a. specific information
　　　 b. main ideas for each paragraph
　　　 c. indicate the intended audience
　　　 d. indicate author's opinion
　　3. Each passage will be 800–1000 words in length and will contain 5–7
　　　 paragraphs.
　　4. Each passage will be definition/description, survey/experimental,
　　　 argument, or a combination of these.
　　5. The passage will present specific information and the information tested
　　　 will be context dependent to the degree possible.

Response attributes:
　　1. The student will write a complete sentence answering the question asked.
　　2. The correct answer will be:
　　　 a. for details: a restatement of the information in the passage being
　　　　 sought. It may be either a paraphrase or a direct quote.
　　　 b. for main ideas: a paraphrase of the topic sentence.

to only one type of item within the test rather than to the test as a whole.

Sample item. This serves as an example test item derived from the test specifications. Such an item should be presented along with any directions that will be given to the students. This information provides the test writers with both an idea of how the item will be displayed and a context for understanding the details that will follow in the item specifications.

Prompt attributes. These provide a series of statements that attempt to delimit the general class of material that the examinee will be responding to when answering the type of item involved. Here, any factors that constrain the item construction process should be defined so the item writer will write items congruent with the item specifications. This section of the specifications attempts to control for variability in the types of items which different test writers might generate. For instance, the prompt attributes section might state how long an item might be, the linguistic level and structure within which the item may be tested, the type of discourse genre that may be utilized, the types of information that may be included in the item, and so forth.

Response attributes. This section either defines the characteristics of the options from which the students select their responses or presents the standards by which students' responses will be evaluated. For example, if the item is designed such that the examinees select from a set of multiple-choice options, then this section gives a precise description of the characteristics of the distractors which may be used.

On the other hand, if the item is a constructed-response item, in which the examinee supplies an answer, this section describes what is and is not considered a correct answer. For example, if the examinees are to write the main idea of a paragraph they have just read, the response attribute section might state that spelling does not count in the scoring of the item, or that it need not be 100 percent grammatically correct as long as the main idea is correctly identified.

The important point to remember about describing the correct response is that the basis, or bases, for evaluating a response should be determined in advance with a rationale for insuring that only one language point is being evaluated at any given time. For instance, if the focus of an item is on identifying the main idea of a paragraph, but half credit is to be taken off for incorrect subject/verb agreement, then each of these aspects (that is, the main idea and the subject/verb agreement aspects) should be described explicitly and separately in the response attributes.

Specification supplement. At times, limits for the content of a particular item may need to be delineated in a specification supplement. For example, when testing gerunds and infinitives, the specification supplement might set out which verbs can be used in writing the items. Or, if the items are designed to test knowledge of abbreviations, the specification supplement might list the abbreviations that can be used in the resulting items. Such lists provide limits for the content that the items can contain.

After the test and item specifications are written, both sets of specifications should be circulated to experts for comments. The specifications, course syllabus, and any other pertinent information might then be given to people familiar with the course, as well as to general language teaching methodologists. The experts should evaluate the specifications using a form (as described in the next section "Item quality and content analysis") which asks whether the specifications were clear and whether they have met the course objectives. This important component of the test development process allows the experts to make general comments as well as to evaluate the specifications in terms of the specific objectives.

Improving the specifications

After receiving the comments from the experts, the specifications should then be revised for clarity and accuracy, and re-evaluated for degree of importance. This stage may involve minor changes in wording, major organizational revision, or deletion of a specification altogether.

The specifications should then be given to item writers to actually write the items that will be used on the examination. These writers should be teachers or other experts who are knowledgeable about the particular language program or area of language research. The items that result should all be based on the test and item specifications. They should also be circulated to at least two or three different reviewers before they are accepted for piloting. Such piloting may involve administering the items to both native and non-native speakers of the language being tested. The results of the pilot testing can then provide further input (based on statistical analyses like those discussed in Chapter 4) about the effectiveness of the test and item specifications. This information may result in further revisions or deletions of individual items or of entire item specifications.

Lynch and Davidson (1994, 2000) addressed the process of item specification generation in practical CRT test development conditions. This process linked curricula, teacher experience, and language tests in an examination of how the process provides potential for positive washback effects. The projects they describe involved the development of test specifications and test items through an iterative process leading to refinement in the notion of the actual test criterion. They note that the process of moving from the item writing stage to elaboration and refinement of the specifications helps provide evidence for determining how well the eventual test items and tasks match what the test is supposed to test. More will be said about this in the Chapter 6 discussion of validity. However, a key advantage of the Lynch and Davidson approach to the development of item specifications is the extent to which it systematically involves the teachers in the process. Providing those who are involved in the test writing process with input into item specification development is an important part of professionalizing the entire testing process.

Although test item specifications are time consuming to produce, they do provide a basis for sound interpretation of criterion-referenced test results. The goal of such item specifications is to provide a clear enough description so that any trained item writer using them will be able to generate items very similar to those written by any other item writer. However, even Popham (1978) admits that "some people using the specifications, particularly busy individuals, may find their need for test description satisfied with the general description statement and the illustrative item alone" (p. 123). Thus specifications should be used in language programs and research only to the degree that they are helpful.

Suitable levels of specificity

Concern has been growing recently in the literature with the level of specificity needed in tests and the effect that specifications may have on the test writing process, teaching, and learning. As Popham (1993) notes, the greatest strength of the detailed item specifications discussed above also became their greatest weakness. The very clarity that allowed the construction of well-targeted test items tended to restrict test construction and teaching.

Some test writers wind up not using the specifications because they are too complex and constraining. The specifications sometimes become too narrow, and item writers essentially begin to base their item construction solely on the *sample item* in the specifications. When all items are based on a single item, the tests may become too narrow and restrictive in terms of how they assess the skill or ability. The whole test writing process can become more tedious than is necessary.

A further potential problem is that teachers sometimes teach only to the specific types of items on the test. When the specifications do not reflect more global and integrated test tasks, they can have the effect of driving out more complex teaching activities. Basically, this negative washback can have the effect of dictating to the teachers what form instruction should take for particular curricular objectives. For example, if a teacher knows that the students' reading abilities will be assessed solely with a paper-and-pencil multiple-choice test, then the teacher may not see that it is beneficial to teach the students to read two passages and synthesize the information. While this narrowness could be addressed by having the overall test specification be more explicit about a balanced approach to assessment, it would require a very large number of specifications for all potential item types.

Finally, such detailed specifications as discussed above can also have a negative effect on curricular change. Writing detailed specifications is a time-consuming task that takes the energy of many different people. As noted above, the specification has to be written, reviewed, and then revised. When a set of item specifications for a course or series of courses is put in place, it is just human nature to want them to be used for some time. However, if changes are proposed for the curriculum, as should happen frequently, the specification writers may be loath to go along with the prospective changes.

Popham (1993, 1994) sees a role for some type of intermediate level of specification that allows several types of items to measure a generalizable level of skill mastery. Such specifications would have a brief discussion of the skill or ability that is being assessed as well as several example item types that could be utilized in assessing the skill area of interest. By including several item types to measure each skill area, a richer variety of items may be included on a test.

For example, a specification (after Popham, 1993, 1994, 1999) describing how listening comprehension is to be assessed might have the following discussion of the skill:

Listening to an academic lecture
Items will assess the examinee's ability to comprehend a segment of an academic lecture. Each item may ask the examinee to select or construct the main idea of the segment. Examinees may be required to summarize the gist of the lecture segment or identify the supporting arguments.

Sample prompts
    Explain the main idea of the passage you have just heard.
    What is the main idea of the listening segment?
    Explain the main idea of the passage by speaking into the microphone.
    Find the statement that indicates the main idea of the listening passage.
    a. Greenhouse gasses are destroying the ozone.

    b. Pollution is not as bad as some scientists have said.
    c. We will soon have the problem of pollution solved.
    d. It is too late to save the environment.

This type of item specification is much less restrictive than the first type discussed above. However, Popham (1999) suggests that for high-stakes tests the items generated from these specifications be vetted by a panel-review process of 10 to 20 qualified judges. The panel gives a series of item-by-item judgments regarding the appropriacy of the items. This can be a time-consuming and complex task. Thus, while the item specification writing process is less cumbersome than with the first type of item specification, the item verification process is more involved. However, this approach may be helpful for teachers who need to write a test directly from clear instructional objectives on a one time only basis.

Item quality and content analyses

The quality of a criterion-referenced test can logically be no better than the items upon which it is based. Since criterion-referenced tests are commonly used for testing achievement and diagnosis, the tests will often be fairly specific to a particular program or research agenda. As a result of the program specificity, the analysis of individual item quality may often prove crucial. *Item quality analysis* for CRTs ultimately involves making judgments about: (a) the degree to which the items are valid for the purposes of the test and (b) the appropriacy of the content of the items within the specific language program or research area. Therefore, the first concern in analyzing CRT items is with their content. A second consideration should be with whether the form of the item allows for accurately assessing the desired content.

    Another consequence of the domain-specific nature of criterion-referenced items is that the whole process of item quality analysis must be much more rigorous than it typically is for norm-referenced tests. In developing or revising a norm-referenced test, the purposes are general and the concern is with finding items that discriminate between students in their overall performances. So, items on tests such as the TOEFL could be rejected solely because of item statistical issues, regardless of how good the item looked on re-reading. Thus, in developing norm-referenced tests, the test writer can rely to some degree on item statistics that will help guide the choices of which items to keep and which to discard. With criterion-referenced tests, the test developer must rely to a lesser degree on statistics and more on close examination of item content, and must maintain the goal of creating a test that measures what the examinees know, or what they can do, with regard to the domain being tested or to the particular program's objectives.

In doing item quality analysis, the first concern should be the degree to which the test items are measuring the desired content. This content may turn out to be narrow, objective, receptive, and discrete-point as on a test of each student's ability to distinguish between phonemes, or may be broad, subjective, productive, and integrative as on a test of the examinees' overall oral proficiency. Such choices (and many others) are the responsibility of the teachers or researchers who are developing and using the test. However, regardless of what is decided, the goal of item content analysis for a criterion-referenced test is to consider the degree to which each item is measuring the content that it was designed to measure, as well as the degree to which that content is worth measuring at all. Such decisions will often be heavily judgmental. In addition, such judgments will entail each teacher in a program or several researchers evaluating the test and having some input into which items should be kept in the revised version of the test and which need to be revised or discarded. In some situations, strategies similar to those advocated by Popham (1981) will be employed. These strategies might include writing item specifications, which are judged by teachers as well as by outside and independent reviewers and even perhaps by examinees.

To facilitate all of this, it may prove useful to devise a rating scale to help in judging item content. A sample rating scale is shown in Table 3.10. Notice how it is broken into two categories: *content congruence* (to help in judging the degree to which an item is measuring what it was designed to measure) and *content applicability* (to help in judging the degree to which the content is appropriate for a given language program).

From a political perspective in teaching settings, asking for the item-quality judgments on item quality of all of the teachers may help to insure that everyone has a vested interest in whatever tests are being developed. If conflicting opinions arise, solutions should be found early (before too much effort goes into test development). Such solutions will typically involve compromises which only partially satisfy all of the parties involved. The overall goal of these activities should be to increase the chances that each item will take a form that makes sense for assessing the specified content and that the content is worth measuring, given the context of language teaching that is going on.

Clearly, item quality and content analyses draw heavily on common sense rather than on statistical analyses. They are none the

Table 3.10. *Item content congruence and applicability*

DIRECTIONS: Look at the test questions and objectives that they are designed to test. For each item, circle the number of the rating (1 = very poor to 5 = very good) that you give for each criterion described at the left.

Criteria for Judgment	Very Poor		Moderate		Very Good

CONTENT CONGRUENCE

Overall match between the item and the objective which it is meant to test. Comment:	1	2	3	4	5
Proficiency level match. Comment:	1	2	3	4	5

CONTENT APPLICABILITY

Match between the objective and related material that you teach. Comment:	1	2	3	4	5
Match between the item and related material that you teach. Comment:	1	2	3	4	5

less important because items which are badly constructed are not likely to be fair, even if they initially appear to measure the appropriate content. In short, clear objectives and sound item specifications, regardless of the particular strategies used, seem to be a precondition for effective criterion-referenced testing of any language area. Several statistics can help in analyzing the effectiveness of items (these are covered in Chapter 4). However, statistics can only be useful insofar as they help in analyzing the effectiveness of the item quality and content. In other words, statistics are not ends in themselves, but rather tools that can help build better language tests.

See uk.cambridge.org/elt/crlt/ for chapter summary and exercises.

4 Basic descriptive and item statistics for criterion-referenced tests

Introduction

In this chapter, we will cover the basic statistics testers use for describing and revising criterion-referenced tests. Although this is a book about CRT, the chapter will include a fairly detailed discussion of NRT statistics as well. This is done in order to provide a foundation against which to compare the differing orientations utilized by each. We feel this is important in order for the reader to put the kinds of issues each approach attempts to accommodate into perspective. The chapter first discusses assumptions that each approach makes about the distributions of test scores, and presents basic concepts of descriptive statistics. It then turns to details of item analysis. This examination should make clear that NRT item analyses are designed to help achieve a test which distributes examinees across a scale whereas the CRT item analyses are more concerned with finding items that distribute examinees into known or predicted categories according to their knowledge of the domain criteria.

Since tests are made up of units called items, the chapter will examine the types of item-related analyses that are used for the two basic families of tests. For NRTs, the techniques described here for developing, analyzing, selecting, and improving items will include item format analysis, item facility, and item discrimination indices, as well as distractor efficiency analysis. For CRTs, some of the same analyses will often be used plus others: a focus on item quality analysis, an index which compares item performance of masters and non-masters (called the difference index), and three statistics that are based on whether students passed or failed the test, called the B-index, agreement statistic, and item phi (ϕ).

The purpose of all of these item analyses is to decide which items to keep in revised and improved versions of a test and which to discard. Such revision processes will be described step-by-step for both the NRT and CRT types of test development projects. Throughout the chapter, the techniques will be described whether the test is being developed as an NRT for proficiency or placement decisions or as a CRT for diagnostic or achievement decisions. We will also briefly discuss the usefulness of item response theory (IRT) for creating equivalent forms and for item banking in CRT development.

The discussion which follows provides information essential to an understanding of the rest of the book. Readers familiar with basic statistics or traditional testing concerns may wish to focus on those sections specific to CRT issues. However, we recommend at least a cursory reading in order to familiarize the reader with the notational conventions used throughout.

Description of CRT score distributions

One key difference between NRTs and CRTs is that each examinee's performance on a CRT is compared to a standard of passing performance called a *criterion level*. For example, a CRT might have a criterion level (percentage of correct answers needed to pass) of 60%; an examinee who answered 67% of the questions correctly would pass the test while an examinee with a score of 55% would fail the test. Such interpretations are common on CRTs.

In contrast, on an NRT, each examinee's performance is compared to the performances of all of the other examinees who belong to the norm group. Consider an examinee who scored in the 61st percentile on an NRT. This examinee's percentile score is better than 61 out of 100 examinees. Thus this examinee's position in the distribution of all scores is clear without reference to the actual number of items correctly answered on the test. Such an interpretation is characteristic of an NRT.

Percentages and Percentiles

Close examination of the preceding two paragraphs will reveal that a key difference between NRT and CRT score distributions is captured in the terms percentage and percentile. On a CRT, the primary information of interest is the amount of knowledge or skill that the examinees possess. As a result, the focus is on the *percentage* of items answered correctly, which hopefully reflects the percentage of material known. In other words, the interpretation centers on the percentage of items answered correctly by each examinee (or the percentage of tasks performed correctly) as those items are related to the knowledge or skills being tested and as the examinee's score relates to the criterion level being used.

The percentage scores can be interpreted directly without any reference to other examinees' scores or to the individual examinee's position in the distribution. A high percentage score may indicate that the examinee has a high degree of knowledge or skill in the area being tested, but such a score must be interpreted carefully. A high score may mean that the examinee knew the material being tested or that the test items were written at too low a level. Similarly, a low percentage score may mean that the examinee has a low degree of knowledge or skill in the content being tested or that the test items were written at too high a level. Nevertheless, in all cases, the primary interest is in the percentage of material or skill that the examinee has been shown to possess rather than in the examinee's performance in relationship to the other examinees.

On an NRT, the purpose and interpretation are quite different: the focus is on how the examinee's performance relates to the scores of all of the other examinees. Hence the examinee's *percentile* score is one important way of interpreting an NRT score. The percentile score indicates the proportion of examinees who scored above and below the examinee. As indicated above, an examinee with a percentile score of 61 performed better than 61 out of 100 examinees, but it also indicates that the performance was worse than 39 out of 100. This percentile score of 61 is something very different from a score of 61 reported in percentage terms (as the percentage of correct answers).

Consider what would happen if another similar NRT with more difficult items were administered to the same group. It would be reasonable to expect the percentage of correct answers to be lower on average for all of the examinees, but it would also be reasonable to expect that their positions relative to each other (in terms of percentile scores) would not change very much. Similarly, if yet another NRT were administered that had easy items on it, the percentage of correct answers should be high for all examinees, but their positions in relation to each other in the distribution of scores (in terms of percentile scores) should be fairly similar.

The foregoing discussion explains in part why CRTs are best used for assessing the amount of material known or skills possessed by individual examinees in percentage terms, whereas NRTs are best used for examining the relationship of each examinee's performance to performances of all other examinees in percentile terms.

Distributions of scores

The distinction between percentage and percentile scores ultimately leads to the development of two distinct types of tests that can be

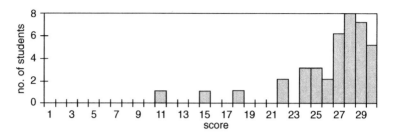

Figure 4.1. Column graph of scores on an effective CRT at the end of a course

expected to produce different types of score distributions. A CRT achievement test in a course where the students all performed reasonably well and learned the material that was being tested might be expected to produce a distribution of scores at the end of the course like that shown in Figure 4.1. Notice that most of the students scored very high, with only a few students not keeping up with the group. Such a distribution is called a negatively skewed distribution because the skewing (or tail) is in the direction of the low scores (that is, in the negative direction).

However, such a distribution can be attained on a CRT by simply making the test relatively easy for the students. In order to assure that the students are learning something and that the test is not simply too easy, it may be a good idea, in addition to testing them at the end of the course with a CRT, to also use the same (or a similar CRT) to test them at the beginning of the course. In an ideal situation, the distribution of scores shown in Figure 4.2 would be obtained at the beginning of the course. Notice that most of the students scored very low on the test indicating that they did not know the material at the outset (that is, they needed to learn it). Naturally, a few students may have prior knowledge related to the course so the resulting distribution might look like the one shown in Figure 4.2. Such a distribution is considered positively skewed because the skewing (or tail) is in the direction of the high scores (that is, in the positive direction).

If both the pre-test and post-test distributions were combined and superimposed on each other, the result would be as shown in Figure 4.3. Note that the pre-test distribution indicates that most of the students did not know the material very well, while the post-test distribution indicates that most of the students had learned the material fairly well by the end of the course.

In a research setting designed to determine some specific language ability, a particular stage of language acquisition for example, similar patterns would be expected to emerge, that is, examinees at a lower

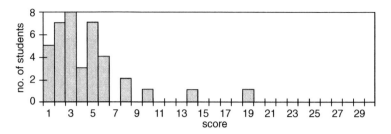

Figure 4.2. Column graph of scores on an effective CRT at the beginning of a course

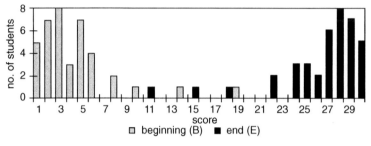

Figure 4.3. Hypothetical CRT

stage of acquisition would be expected to have a distribution like that on the pre-test, while examinees who had reached the particular state of acquisition would produce a distribution such as that shown for the post-test.

Figure 4.4 represents the shape of the normal distribution that would be expected from a well-designed NRT. Note that the shape is symmetrical with the largest number of cases occurring near the middle of the distribution, with decreasing numbers of students at each score as the scores move farther and farther away from the center in both directions. Figure 4.4 represents the approximate expected shape of a normal distribution. Figure 4.5 shows a histogram of a set of scores as they would more likely appear in an actual distribution of NRT scores.

Describing distributions numerically

Any distribution of scores can be described numerically by calculating statistics that represent the central tendency of the scores along with other statistics that represent the dispersion of scores around

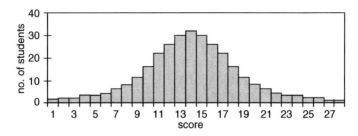

Figure 4.4. Theoretical shape of an NRT distribution of scores

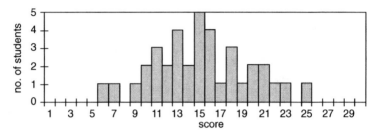

Figure 4.5. Column graph of scores from an actual NRT administration

that central tendency. The measures of central tendency that we will examine indicate the general magnitude of scores in a distribution. They focus on typical scores. The first of these is the *mean*, designated as *M*.

$$M = \frac{\sum X}{N}$$

Where:
M = mean
$\sum$ = sum (or add up)
X = scores
N = number of scores

The mean is calculated by adding up the scores ($\sum X$), and dividing by the number of scores (*N*). These are the same operations anyone does in averaging a set of numbers. For example, using the scores listed in Table 4.1 to illustrate calculation of the mean, it is first necessary to sum, or add up, the scores ($\sum X = 1089$). That sum must be divided by the number of scores (*N* = 35), and the result (*M* = $\sum X$/ *N* = 1089/35 = 31.114286) is the mean, which might be rounded off to two places (*M* $\approx$ 31.11).

Table 4.1. *Calculating the mean for a set of CRT data (from the study described at www.   )*

STUDENT ID	SCORES (B)
72408PREA	39
72202PREA	38
72602PREA	37
72428PREA	37
72416PREA	36
72211PREA	36
72411PREA	36
72418PREA	35
72201PREA	35
72206PREA	35
72216PREA	35
72419PREA	34
72421PREA	34
72212PREA	34
72217PREA	33
72405PREA	33
72219PREA	32
72208PREA	32
72406PREA	31
72203PREA	31
72210PREA	30
72605PREA	30
72401PREA	30
72601PREA	29
72218PREA	29
72209PREA	29
72407PREA	29
72215PREA	28
72205PREA	28
72213PREA	27
72204PREA	25
72220PREA	24
72207PREA	23
72424PREA	20
72214PREA	15
SUM ($\sum X$)	1089
NUMBER (N)	35

$\sum X / N = 1089/35$
$= 31.114286$
≈ 31.11

The mode is simply the point in the distribution that has the most scores. The mode is easiest to determine by looking at a histogram of the distribution and searching for any peak(s). Looking back to Figure 4.5, for instance, the mode is clearly 15 because that is the score in the distribution where the peak occurs (that is, the score with the largest number of Xs). In other situations, the scores themselves can be examined. For example, Table 4.1, it is clear there are two modes because there are two scores that have the largest number of students, that is, two scores (29 and 35) both have four students, which is the largest number found for any of the scores. The distribution shown in Table 4.1 is an example of what is called a bimodal distribution because it has two modes. There are also times when three modes (trimodal) may occur, or even more.

The *median* is that point in the distribution above which half of the scores are found and below which the other half are found. Close examination of the scores shown in Figure 4.5 will reveal that the median is 15. Notice that counting up the students scoring above 15 yields 16 and counting up the scores below 15 also gives 16, the same number. The median does not always turn out to be a nice even number like this, but for the purposes of this book the concept has been adequately illustrated.

The dispersion of a set of scores numerically describes the way the scores vary around the central tendency. The dispersion is most often represented by the range and standard deviation.

The *range* simply represents the distance from the lowest score in the distribution to the highest score. To calculate the range, it is only necessary to subtract the lowest score from the highest score and add 1 as represented in the following formula:

$$Range = High - Low + 1$$

Where:
High = highest score on the test
Low = lowest score on the test

For example, for the scores shown in Table 4.1, the range would be (range = High − Low + 1 = 39 − 15 + 1 = 25). Sometimes, the range is described as the highest score minus the lowest score without adding one. Unfortunately, this approach necessarily leaves out either the high score or the low score. In this book, the range will be calculated by adding one (as is done in most statistics texts) because the range can then be said to include the scores on both ends.

One problem that can arise in using the range as an indication of the dispersion of scores around the central tendency is the fact that one aberrant score can lead to a very distorted picture of the distribution. Such distortion can be caused by one aberrant low score (like one produced by a student who was sick during the test) or one extraordinarily high score (like one produced by a native speaker of French who accidentally took a language placement test in French). Either way, the range would give a distorted picture of how the scores are dispersed around the mean. That is why the standard deviation is most often also used in describing the dispersion of a set of scores. Because it is an averaging process, the standard deviation is less sensitive to aberrant scores like those discussed immediately above when sample sizes are relatively large.

As defined in Brown (1988a), the *standard deviation* is a sort of average of the distances of the scores from the mean. The formula for the standard deviation is as follows:

$$S = \sqrt{\frac{\sum(X - M)^2}{N}}$$

Where:
S = standard deviation
X = scores
M = mean
N = number of students

Table 4.2 shows the calculations for the standard deviation for the set of scores presented in Table 4.1. The standard deviation is calculated by first subtracting the mean from each score $(X - M)$ as shown in Column D of Table 4.2. This subtraction is done in order to find the distance of each score from the mean. The resulting values are then squared as shown in Column E. This squaring is done in order to avoid the fact that without squaring them they will sum (or, add up) to a value very close to zero (0.15 in this case), as shown at the bottom of Column D. Then the squared values are averaged by adding them up and dividing by the number of values involved [$\sum (X - M)^2 / N = 939.54$]. Taking the square root of this last average will bring the result back down from the squared values to the original raw score scale as follows:

$$S = \sqrt{\frac{\sum(X - M)^2}{N}} = \sqrt{\frac{939.54}{35}} = \sqrt{26.84} = 5.18$$

Thus the standard deviation for the scores shown in Table 4.2 is 5.18 – a value that indicates a sort of average of the distance of each student's score from the mean.

Table 4.2. *Calculating the standard deviation for a set of CRT data*

A STUDENT ID	B SCORES (X)	C MEAN (M)	D $= X - M$	E $(X - M)^2$
72408PREA	39	31.11	7.89	62.25
72202PREA	38	31.11	6.89	47.47
72602PREA	37	31.11	5.89	34.69
72428PREA	37	31.11	5.89	34.69
72416PREA	36	31.11	4.89	23.91
72211PREA	36	31.11	4.89	23.91
72411PREA	36	31.11	4.89	23.91
72418PREA	35	31.11	3.89	15.13
72201PREA	35	31.11	3.89	15.13
72206PREA	35	31.11	3.89	15.13
72216PREA	35	31.11	3.89	15.13
72419PREA	34	31.11	2.89	8.35
72421PREA	34	31.11	2.89	8.35
72212PREA	34	31.11	2.89	8.35
72217PREA	33	31.11	1.89	3.57
72405PREA	33	31.11	1.89	3.57
72219PREA	32	31.11	0.89	0.79
72208PREA	32	31.11	0.89	0.79
72406PREA	31	31.11	-0.11	0.01
72203PREA	31	31.11	-0.11	0.01
72210PREA	30	31.11	-1.11	1.23
72605PREA	30	31.11	-1.11	1.23
72401PREA	30	31.11	-1.11	1.23
72601PREA	29	31.11	-2.11	4.45
72218PREA	29	31.11	-2.11	4.45
72209PREA	29	31.11	-2.11	4.45
72407PREA	29	31.11	-2.11	4.45
72215PREA	28	31.11	-3.11	9.67
72205PREA	28	31.11	-3.11	9.67
72213PREA	27	31.11	-4.11	16.89
72204PREA	25	31.11	-6.11	37.33
72220PREA	24	31.11	-7.11	50.55
72207PREA	23	31.11	-8.11	65.77
72424PREA	20	31.11	-11.11	123.43
72214PREA	15	31.11	-16.11	259.53
SUM	1089		0.15	939.54
NUMBER (N)	35			
MEAN	31.114286			$S = 5.18$

Table 4.3. *Descriptive statistics for four ELI reading course CRTs (adapted from Table 1 of the example study described at uk.cambridge.org/elt/crlt/)*

| | TEST | | | |
| | ELI 72 PRE-TEST | | ELI 82 PRE-TEST | |
STATISTIC	FORM A	FORM B	FORM A	FORM B
N	35	29	87	65
k	46	46	34	34
M	31.11	30.90	21.05	21.26
S	5.18	5.47	3.95	3.92
LOW	15	16	13	10
HIGH	39	41	31	30
RANGE	25	26	19	21

Understanding numerical descriptions

Table 4.3 presents the descriptive statistics for four different tests. These numbers can be used to roughly understand the shape of a distribution without reference to a histogram or other graphical depiction of the scores. The tests described in Table 4.3 are for all sections of the ELI 72 intermediate ESL reading course and ELI 82 advanced ESL reading course in the ELI at UHM. The statistics reported are for FORM A and FORM B of each test in the pre-tests administered in Fall semester 1989 (adapted from Table 1 of the example article at uk.cambridge.org/elt/crlt/).

There are a number of things that a set of statistics like those shown in Table 4.3 can reveal to a knowledgeable reader. For instance, notice that there is a considerably smaller number of students (N) who took the ELI 72 pre-tests (which only had N sizes of 35 and 29) than took the ELI 82 pre-tests (resulting in N sizes of 87 and 65). The number of items (k) is also different with 46 items on each form of the ELI 72 test and 34 items on each form of the ELI 82 test. The means indicate that the central tendency for each of these sets of scores are similar for both forms of each test. The two means for the ELI 72 test are 31.11 and 30.90, respectively, and the two for the ELI 82 test are 21.05 and 21.26, respectively. Similarly, the standard deviations indicate that the dispersion for these sets of scores is similar for the two forms of each test, that is, the standard deviations for the ELI 72 test are 5.18 and 5.47, respectively, while

Table 4.4. *Imaginary pre-test/post-test results for two forms of a CRT*

| | TEST | | | |
| | FORM A | | FORM B | |
STATISTIC	PRE	POST	PRE	POST
N	88	79	97	86
k	50	50	50	50
M	30.25	45.79	13.05	41.36
S	4.15	5.10	12.59	5.92
LOW	18	12	3	12
HIGH	42	50	48	49
RANGE	25	39	46	38

those for the ELI 82 test are 3.95 and 3.92, respectively. The same is true when the ranges are compared. In fact, the means, standard deviations, and ranges for these pairs of tests are similar enough within each course for them to be considered nearly parallel.

Table 4.4 shows a set of hypothetical pre-test and post-test results for two forms of a CRT. Notice that between 79 and 97 students took each of the forms with the numbers larger in the pre-test than in the post-test. Perhaps some of the students dropped out of the courses between the two tests. Note also that the number of items on each test is exactly the same, 50. The means indicate that, in general, there was considerable gain between the pre-test and post-test. In other words, the fact that FORM A had a pre-test mean of 30.25 and a post-test mean of 45.79 (with a difference of 15.54 points) may indicate that some learning occurred between the two administrations. Likewise, on FORM B, the contrast between the pre-test mean of 13.05 and post-test mean of 41.36 (and the resulting difference of 28.31 points) appears to support the notion that the students have learned something in the course. In fact, it appears that there was considerably more gain on FORM B than there was on FORM A.

More germane to the discussion at hand, the statistics indicate something about the differences and similarities of the distributions being described. Comparatively speaking, the means indicate that the FORM B pre-test had the lowest central tendency (= 13.05), while the FORM A post-test had the highest value (= 45.79). In terms of dispersion, the standard deviations and ranges show that the FORM B pre-test had the highest amount of dispersion ($S = 12.59$, range = 46), while the FORM A pre-test had the lowest dispersion of scores ($S = 4.15$, range = 25).

Examining the individual distributions of scores reveals additional information about the shapes of the underlying distributions of scores from which these statistics were calculated. It appears that the distribution for the FORM A pre-test scores is normally distributed with a mean (30.25) that is reasonably well centered on the continuum of possible scores (0 to 50). Though the dispersion is not great ($S = 4.15$), there is sufficient space in the range of possible scores for three, or even four, standard deviations above and below the mean. Such relationships are typical of distributions that are approximately normal, and such distributions are not at all unusual on CRT pre-tests.

However, the FORM A post-test results indicate a somewhat different shape for the distribution involved. The mean is very high (45.79 out of 50), and there is only space on the continuum of possible scores (0 to 50) for one standard deviation above the mean (though eight or nine will fit below the mean). Such a set of statistics is typical of a negatively skewed distribution. The results for the pre-test on FORM B are almost exactly the opposite with a low mean of 13.05 and a standard deviation of 12.59. Since only one standard deviation will fit below the mean (while three will fit above it), the scores appear to be typical of a positively skewed distribution.

Item analysis

Item analysis as a whole will be defined here as the systematic statistical evaluation of the effectiveness of individual test items. Item analysis is usually done for purposes of selecting which items will remain on future revised and improved versions of the test. Sometimes, however, item analysis is performed simply to investigate how well the items on a test are working with a particular group of students, or to study which items match the language domain of interest. Item analysis can take numerous forms, but when testing for norm-referenced purposes there are two traditional item statistics that are typically applied: item facility and item discrimination. In developing CRTs, other concerns become particularly important: item quality analysis, the difference index, B-index, agreement statistic, and item phi (ϕ). These will be discussed later in the chapter.

Traditional item statistics

An important part of any approach to test development is the statistical analysis designed to determine whether the test items do what they are supposed to do. The statistics used in traditional NRT item analysis are item facility and item discrimination.

Item facility. *Item facility* goes by many other names: item difficulty, item easiness, *p*-value, or abbreviated simply as IF. Regardless of what it is called, it is a statistic that expresses the percentage of examinees who correctly answer a given item. Thus IF is calculated by adding up the number of examinees who answered a given item correctly and dividing that sum by the total number of examinees who took the test, all of which is expressed in the following formula:

$$IF = \frac{N_{correct}}{N_{total}}$$

Where:
$N_{correct}$ = number of examinees who answered correctly
N_{total} = number of examinees taking the test

This formula is just another way of expressing the same operations that were included in the preceding paragraph. (It is important to note that this formula assumes that items left blank by examinees are wrong.)

Calculating IF will result in values ranging from 0 to 1.00 for each item. These values can be interpreted as the percentage of correct answers for the item in question by simply moving the decimal point two places to the right. For instance, an IF index of .17 would indicate that 17% of the examinees answered the item correctly. This would seem to be a very difficult item because 83% are missing it. An IF of .97 would indicate that 97% of the examinees answered correctly – a very easy item because almost all of the examinees got it right.

The apparently simple information provided by the item facility statistic can prove very useful. Consider the pattern of right and wrong answers shown in Table 4.5. Notice that the data are arranged so they can easily be examined and manipulated. To the left, the examinees' names have been listed. The item numbers for the first ten items and the total scores are labeled across the top. The examinees' responses are recorded as 1s for correct answers and 0s for incorrect answers. Notice that James answered item 10 correctly, as did everyone else except poor Byron, so it must have been a very easy question. However, it was not the easiest item; item 4 was answered correctly by every examinee (as indicated by the 1s straight down that column). It is equally easy to identify that item 9 is the most difficult because no examinee answered it correctly.

Calculating the IF for any item will be done in much the same

Table 4.5. *Item analysis data (first 10 items only)*

STUDENTS	ITEMS											TOTAL
	1	2	3	4	5	6	7	8	9	10	etc ...	%
Shira	1	1	1	1	1	0	1	1	0	1	......	96
Diana	0	1	1	1	1	0	1	0	0	1	......	95
Kathy	0	0	1	1	1	0	1	0	0	1	......	92
Kate	1	0	1	1	1	0	0	0	0	1	......	91
Carolyn	1	1	1	1	0	0	1	0	0	1	......	90
Marsha	1	0	1	1	0	1	1	1	0	1	......	90
Gabi	0	1	1	1	1	0	1	0	0	1	......	88
Sasha	1	0	1	1	0	0	1	0	0	1	......	80
Robert	0	1	1	1	0	1	1	0	0	1	......	79
Eric	0	1	1	1	0	1	0	0	0	1	......	72
Michael	1	0	0	1	1	1	1	1	0	1	......	67
Thom	1	0	0	1	0	1	0	1	0	1	......	66
Graham	1	1	0	1	0	1	0	0	0	1	......	64
James	0	0	0	1	0	1	0	1	0	1	......	64
Byron	0	0	0	1	0	1	1	0	0	0	......	61

manner. For instance, if you count the number of students who answered number 7 correctly, you should get 10. Then count the total number of students, and you should get 15. With those two numbers, you have all the necessary information for calculating the mean with the formula given above:

$$IF = \frac{N_{correct}}{N_{total}}$$

$$IF = \frac{10}{15}$$

$$= .666 \approx .67$$

This IF index of .67 indicates that about 67% of the examinees answered item 7 correctly. Now, try calculating the IF for some of the other items shown in Table 4.5. (The answers are shown in the first row of Table 4.6.)

Arranging the data in a matrix like the one shown in Table 4.5 is very useful in calculating IF values. Other item statistics can also be used for determining different kinds of information and patterns from item analysis data. In calculating these other item statistics, it is sometimes most efficient to sort the data from the highest to lowest total scores as shown in Table 4.5. Notice that the total percent scores in the column furthest to the right range from high to low scores as you scan down the column.

Item discrimination. *Item discrimination* (ID) is an entirely different statistic, which shows the degree to which an item separates the "upper" examinees from the "lower" ones. These groups may also be called the "high" and "low" scorers or the "upper" and "lower" proficiency groups. Once these groups are isolated (usually as the upper third and lower third of the examinees on the whole test), the ID can be calculated. To separate these two groups, it will first be useful to line up the students' names (or identification numbers), their individual item responses (as 1s for correct and 0s for wrong answers), and total scores in descending order. This arrangement, or something very similar, will be necessary to determine which examinees belong in the upper and lower groups.

We indicated above that the upper and lower groups are defined as the upper and lower third, or 33%. However, some language testers will use the upper and lower 27%, while others may use the upper and lower 25% for forming the groups. The decision as to which percent to use is often a straightforward and practical matter. Consider Table 4.5 once more. Notice that there is a blank row between Carolyn and Marsha that separates the upper group from the middle group, and another blank row between Eric and Michael that separates the lower group from the middle one. Thus there are five examinees in the top, middle, and bottom groups (33% each). It is simply convenient given that there are 15 scores. However, if there had been 16 examinees, and the test developer still used the top and bottom five examinees, this would result in upper and lower groups representing 31.25% (5/16 = .3125) each. It might have proven more convenient to have divided them into an upper group of four examinees (25%) and a lower group of four examinees (also 25%). Clearly, groups of examinees do not always come in nice round numbers that are evenly divisible by three so some flexibility is necessary.

Once the data are separated into the upper and lower groups, discrimination indices can be calculated. The item facility for the upper and lower groups should be calculated separately. The IF for the upper group will be calculated by dividing the number of examinees answering correctly in the upper group by the total number of examinees in that group. Similarly, the IF for the lower group will be calculated by dividing the number who answered correctly in the lower group by the total number of examinees in the lower group. Finally, the ID statistic is calculated by subtracting the IF for the lower group from the IF for the upper group as follows:

$$ID = IF_{upper} - IF_{lower}$$

Where:
ID = item discrimination
IF_{upper} = item facility for the upper group on the whole test
IF_{lower} = item facility for the lower group on the whole test

The calculations represented by the above formula are not difficult. However, because they must be done for each item, they may become tedious.

Consider the example shown in Table 4.5. The IF for the upper group on item 3 is 1.00 (that is, all examinees answered it correctly). The IF for the lower group on that item is .00 (everyone in the lower group got it wrong). If the IF for the lower group is subtracted from the IF for the upper group, the result is an item discrimination index that contrasts the performance of those examinees who scored the highest on the whole test with those who scored the lowest. On item 3, the item discrimination turns out to be 1.00 ($ID = IF_{upper} - IF_{lower} = 1.00 - .00 = 1.00$) as is reported in Table 4.6.

A discrimination index of 1.00 like that found on item 3 would be considered a very good discrimination index for an NRT. Such a finding means that the maximum possible contrast was obtained between the upper and lower groups. In other words, all of the upper group answered correctly and everyone in the lower group had wrong answers. Item discrimination statistics can be used effectively to revise and improve norm-referenced tests. The revisions involve selecting, or keeping, only those items which most effectively separate examinees into groups in the way that the whole test scores do. An

Table 4.6. *Item facility and discrimination statistics*

ITEM STATISTIC	ITEMS									
	1	2	3	4	5	6	7	8	9	10
IF_{total}	.53	.47	.67	1.00	.40	.53	.67	.33	.00	.93
IF_{upper}	.60	.60	1.00	1.00	.80	.00	.80	.20	.00	1.00
IF_{lower}	.60	.20	.00	1.00	.20	1.00	.40	.60	.00	.80
ID	.00	.40	1.00	.00	.60	−1.00	.40	−.40	.00	.20

item like item 3 in Tables 4.5 or 4.6 is therefore ideal for retention in a revised test because of its ID of 1.00. (Naturally, the adequacy of the item content would also be considered.)

ID indices can range from 1.00 (if all of the upper group answer correctly and all of the lower group answer incorrectly) to -1.00 (if all of the lower group answer correctly and all of the upper group answer incorrectly as on item 6 in the tables). Consider item 5, in which the examinees in the upper group have an IF of .80 and those in the lower group have an IF of .20, giving an ID of .60 $(.80 - .20 = .60)$. This ID indicates that the item is discriminating reasonably well between those examinees who are in the upper and lower groups on the basis of total test scores. In contrast, in item 8, the upper group has an IF of .20 and the lower group has .60 for an ID of $-.40$ $(.20 - .60 = -.40)$. Item 8 appears to be testing something quite different from the total scores (that is, a higher proportion of examinees in the lower group on the whole test managed to correctly answer this item than was the case in the upper group). Thus item 8 would probably be left out of a revised version of this test if it were being revised for norm-referenced purposes.

Another statistic that is often used in place of the ID index described above is the point-biserial correlation coefficient. This coefficient is often lower in magnitude when compared directly with the ID for a given item but is analogous in interpretation. (See Guilford & Fruchter, 1973 for more information on this statistic.) ID is shown here because it is easier to understand conceptually and to calculate.

In developing an NRT, the test revision process is accomplished by keeping the "best" items and discarding weak ones. The choices are generally made on the basis of some set of rules. Typically, items are selected if they have an item facility value of between 0.40 to 0.70 and a fairly high positive discrimination index (generally 0.40 and above). ID values below these may be marginally acceptable, but subject to improvement (Popham, 1981). As Cziko (1983) points out, these items are selected because they maximize variance (individual differences) and this, in turn, produces higher estimates of reliability and validity when traditional correlational statistics are used.

Criterion-referenced item analysis

While it is possible to employ the traditional item facility index in CRT item analysis, its interpretation will be somewhat different. CRTs are most often used to measure achievement, categorical status, or mastery level, and if we apply NRT interpretations of item facility to such uses we get caught in what Popham (1978) has called a "psychometric snare." That is, we would not be inclined to select those items which a high proportion of examinees are answering correctly. Thus, items measuring parts of the curriculum that have been given the most emphasis, items measuring anything for which we can expect high achievement, or items measuring mastery of tasks that the examinees have mastered will be systematically excluded from the test, regardless of their descriptive value. Items keyed to particular functional tasks that have been mastered would be excluded even though they are representative of the functional level under consideration. Further, there has been some argument in the CRT literature that item statistics should not be used at all in the construction of test forms (Popham, 1978; Millman, 1974) because the item pool developed from particular domains is considered to represent a random sample of the entire domain of behaviors. Williams and Slawski (1980), however, claim that this approach assumes an invariance in item statistics which is not justified.

Hambleton and de Gruijter (1983) point out that the distinction between NRT and CRT approaches to item statistics results from the inherent differences in the kinds of inferences made about item statistics in NRT and CRT. In classical item analysis, IF is usually reported on a scale from 0 to 1 and is defined for a population of examinees. However, for CRT, the item facility, while also reported on a scale from 0 to 1, is defined for a collection of test items. In the case of NRT classical item facility, inferences are made from IF for a well-defined population of examinees. In the case of the CRT domain score scale, inferences are made from a sample of test items in a well-defined content domain. That is, the domain score is defined as the expected score over all items from the domain. Thus, the first NRT inference is to a pool of examinees, while the second CRT inference is to a domain of content. On an NRT, if an item has an IF of 0.80, it means that 80% of the examinees answered the item correctly. It does not mean that the items distinguish between examinees who have mastered 80% of a domain content and those who have not, which is a concern of CRT. This distinction is important in the selection of items for inclusion on a test using item facility.

Traditional item discrimination indices can also be employed in CRT analyses, provided there is sufficient variance in examinee scores. The potential for reduced variance affects any statistic involving correlation, including NRT item discrimination indices. One way of dealing with this problem is to combine data from mastery and non-mastery groups (see Haladyna, 1974; Bernknopf & Bashaw, 1976). While such an approach renders the discrimination indices more reliable, the interpretation on CRTs will, again, differ from an NRT interpretation. Selecting only the best discriminators may weaken the test, from a CRT point of view, in that items associated with particular functional objectives might be systematically excluded.

There are, however, item discrimination indices that have been developed specifically for CRT. All of them involve discriminating between mastery and non-mastery examinees, usually in instructional settings.

Difference index

The simplest index to calculate is the *difference index*. The difference index (or DI, which is easily confused with ID) indicates the degree to which an item is reflecting gain in knowledge or skill. In contrast to item discrimination, which shows the degree to which an NRT item separates the upper and lower groups on an NRT, the difference index indicates the degree to which a CRT item is distinguishing between the students, called *masters*, who know the material (or have the skill being taught) and students, labeled *non-masters*, who do not. To calculate the difference index, the IF for the non-masters is subtracted from the IF for masters. The masters and non-masters groups can be established in one of two ways: an intervention study or a differential groups study.

The difference index is found by subtracting the proportion of the non-mastery group answering the item correctly from the proportion of the mastery group answering the item correctly. For example, if 20% of the non-mastery group answered the item correctly and 90% of the mastery group answered the item correctly, the difference index would be 0.70 (.90 − .20 = .70). This index is interpreted similarly to the traditional NRT indices, with the previously mentioned caution against selecting only those items with high discrimination. Certainly, negative difference indices indicate that the item and/or objective (or instructional treatment) should be revised or discarded. As with item facility, whether the index is high enough to consider an item to be acceptable or not will depend on the nature of the objective being tested, the characteristics of the examinees, and the hypothesized distance between masters and non-masters.

Intervention studies. In an intervention study, a group of students is tested in a pre-test on a specified set of material. This group is presumably made up of non-masters because they have not yet studied the material. After the intervention of teaching the material, the students are tested again in a post-test, where they are treated as masters because they presumably know the material. Because of human nature, these groupings will seldom create absolute and

Table 4.7. *Calculating the difference index (taken from the research reported in Brown, 1989a)*

ITEM NUMBER	POST-TEST IF	–	PRE-TEST IF	=	DIFFERENCE INDEX
41	.770	–	.574	=	.196
42	.623	–	.492	=	.131
43	.836	–	.689	=	.147
44	.787	–	.639	=	.148
45	.738	–	.656	=	.082
46	.328	–	.246	=	.082
47	.869	–	.574	=	.295
48	.689	–	.344	=	.345
49	.623	–	.311	=	.312
50	.557	–	.262	=	.295
51	.820	–	.639	=	.181
52	.262	–	.246	=	.016
53	.754	–	.623	=	.131
54	.639	–	.508	=	.131
55	.689	–	.541	=	.148
56	.508	–	.426	=	.082
57	.656	–	.492	=	.164
58	.426	–	.361	=	.065
59	.492	–	.311	=	.181
60	.639	–	.443	=	.196

distinct groups of masters and non-masters. None the less, they serve as a starting point.

Examples of calculations for the DI in an intervention study are shown in Table 4.7. The statistics in the table are derived from pre-test and post-test results in the ESL academic reading course at the University of Hawai'i (from a study reported in Brown, 1989a). Notice that only the results for items 41 to 60 are presented. From these examples, it should be clear that the calculation of the DI is relatively easy. Yet this simple statistic is also meaningful because, as you will see below, it can help select those test items for a CRT which are most highly related to the material being taught in a given course.

Consider item 48: the post-test IF was .689 and the pre-test IF was .344. These IFs indicate that only 34.4% of the students knew the concept (or had the skill) at the beginning of instruction while 68.9% knew it at the end of the course. The difference index for this item would be the relatively high DI of .345 (.689 – .344 = .345).

DIs can range from -1.00 (indicating that students knew but somehow unlearned the material in question) to $+1.00$ (showing that none of the students knew the material at the beginning of the course while all of the students knew it by the end of the course). The DI is interpreted similarly to the traditional NRT indices. Certainly, negative difference indices indicate that the item and/or objective (or instructional treatment) should be revised or discarded. As with IF, whether the index is high enough to consider an item to be acceptable or not will depend on the nature of the objective being tested, the characteristics of the examinees, the hypothesized distance between masters and non-masters, and the standards and practices of the institution.

For item selection, Berk (1980b) suggests that "good" items (those items to be kept) would be those which the mastery group tends to answer correctly (that is, with mastery group IF values ranging from 0.70 to 1.00), and the non-mastery group answers incorrectly (that is, with non-mastery group IF values of 0.00 to 0.50). He also suggests that judgments concerning IF be made relative to the content and importance of the objective being measured (pp. 66–67). Thus difference indices of .20 ($.70 - .50 = .20$) to 1.00 ($1.00 - .00 = 1.00$) would appear to be acceptable for selecting items to remain in revised versions of a CRT, depending on the testing/instructional context.

Differential groups studies. Another way to establish master and non-master groups is to find two groups of students who are masters and non-masters. In other words, to use this strategy, two groups of students must be identified: one group which has the knowledge or skills that the test is measuring and another group that lacks them. To calculate the difference index under these conditions, it is again necessary to compare the item facility index of the masters with the item facility for the non-masters.

Whether to choose an intervention or differential groups strategy will naturally depend on the particular teaching or research situation in which the items are to be analyzed. In some cases, it will be convenient to use a differential groups strategy and in other cases it will be logical to use an intervention study. In either case, the item statistic that you calculate to estimate the degree of contrast between the two administrations of the test is called the difference index.

Cut-score indices

One problem with using the difference index is that it requires *two* administrations of the CRT or administration of the test to two groups of students. To circumvent this problem, other indices have been developed. These indices assess the sensitivity of CRT items to differences in knowledge (of the content being tested) in terms of whether or not the students have passed the test (see Shannon & Cliver, 1987 for more on these statistics). In other words, when master–non-master results are not available, there are indices which indicate the discrimination at the cut-score, or standard, on a single administration of a test. Three such indices are mentioned by Shannon and Cliver (1987): the *B*-index, the agreement statistic, and the item phi (ϕ).

B-index. The most straightforward of the cut-score indices is called the *B*-index. The *B-index* used here (after Brennan, 1972) is an item statistic based on differences in the item facilities of those students who passed a test as opposed to those who failed it. This is somewhat like identifying the masters and non-masters on the test by whether or not they passed the test. Once the groups have been identified, the items are analyzed in terms of the contrasting performance of these two groups. Thus to calculate the *B*-index, it is first necessary to determine what the cut-point is for passing or failing the test.

Table 4.8 shows item-by-item performance on a CRT post-test at the end of a course. Notice that the cut-point has been identified as being 70% and that, at the bottom of the table, the IFs for those students who passed and those who failed are given separately for each item. To calculate the *B*-index for each item, you need only subtract the IF for those students who failed from that for those who passed. This can be expressed in the following simple formula:

Simple *B*-index $= IF_{pass} - IF_{fail}$

Where:

B-index = difference in IF between students who passed and failed a test
IF_{pass} = item facility for students who passed the test
IF_{fail} = item facility for students who failed the test

In Table 4.8, notice that 100% of the students who passed the test answered item 3 correctly and all of those who failed the test also failed item 3. Notice that the *B*-index, based on an item facility of 1.00 for the students who passed and 0.00 for those who failed, would be:

$$B\text{-index} = IF_{pass} - IF_{fail}$$
$$= 1.00 - 0.00$$
$$= 1.00$$

This item maximally separates the masters from the non-masters and its *B*-index is as high as this statistic can go.

The overall results for all ten items are shown in Table 4.9.

Table 4.8. *Item analysis data (first 10 items only)*

STUDENTS	ITEMS											TOTAL
	1	2	3	4	5	6	7	8	9	10	etc ...	%
Shira	1	1	1	1	1	0	1	1	0	1	......	96
Diana	0	1	1	1	1	0	1	0	0	1	......	95
Kathy	0	0	1	1	1	0	1	0	0	1	......	92
Kate	1	0	1	1	1	0	0	0	0	1	......	91
Carolyn	1	1	1	1	0	0	1	0	0	1	......	90
Marsha	1	0	1	1	0	1	1	1	0	1	......	90
Gabi	0	1	1	1	1	0	1	0	0	1	......	88
Sasha	1	0	1	1	0	0	1	0	0	1	......	80
Robert	0	1	1	1	0	1	1	0	0	1	......	79
Eric	0	1	1	1	0	1	0	0	0	1	......	72
Michael	1	0	0	1	1	1	1	1	0	1	......	67
Thom	1	0	0	1	0	1	0	1	0	1	......	66
Graham	1	1	0	1	0	1	0	0	0	1	......	64
James	0	0	0	1	0	1	0	1	0	1	......	64
Byron	0	0	0	1	0	1	1	0	0	0	......	61

Table 4.9. *Item facility and three cut-score item statistics*

ITEM STATISTIC	ITEMS									
	1	2	3	4	5	6	7	8	9	10
IF_{total}	.53	.47	.67	1.00	.40	.53	.67	.33	.00	.93
IF_{pass}	.50	.60	1.00	1.00	.50	.30	.80	.20	.00	1.00
IF_{fail}	.60	.20	.00	1.00	.20	1.00	.40	.60	.00	.80
B	$-.10$	.40	1.00	.00	.30	$-.70$	.40	$-.40$	.00	.20
A	.46	.66	.99	.99	.59	.20	.73	.27	.33	.73
ϕ	$-.11$	.36	1.00	.00	.28	$-.66$	.37	$-.41$	.00	.39

Interpretation of the simple *B*-index is similar to that for the difference index (DI). However, this version of the *B*-index indicates the degree to which an item distinguishes between the students who passed the test and those who failed rather than contrasting the performances of students before and after instruction as is the case with the difference index. Nevertheless, the *B*-index does have the advantage of requiring only one administration of a CRT, and therefore may prove useful.

Agreement statistic. Harris and Subkoviak (1986) presented the agreement statistic (*A*): the probability of agreement between outcomes on a given item and outcomes on the test as a whole. Agreement occurs when an examinee either answers the item correctly and passes the test or fails the item and fails the test. It may be expressed as follows:

$$A = 2P_{iT} + Q_i - P_T$$

Where:
P_{iT} = proportion of total examinees who answered the item correctly and passed test
Q_i = proportion of examinees who answered the item incorrectly
P_T = proportion of examinees who passed test

For example, for item 2 in Table 4.8, the proportion of total examinees (P_{iT}) who answered the item correctly and passed the test would be .40; the portion of examinees (Q_i) who answered the item incorrectly overall would be .53 ($1 - IF = 1 - .47 = .53$); the proportion of examinees (P_T) who passed the test overall was .67. Substituting these values into the formula yields the following result:

$$
\begin{aligned}
A &= 2P_{iT} + Q_i - P_T \\
  &= 2(.40) + .53 - .67 \\
  &= .80 + .53 - .67 \\
  &= .66
\end{aligned}
$$

In the above discussion, Q_i may be the passing score on an item when the item is not dichotomously scored or is scored using a rating scale. As such, the estimate is not restricted to items which are scored correct or incorrect, but rather can apply to items that are rated along a scale of measurement. (See Chapter 6 for issues in setting a passing score.) The agreement statistic ranges from a minimum value of 0.00 to a maximum value of 1.00. Notice that values obtained for the agreement statistic are sometimes quite different from those obtained using the *B*-index. This difference arises because the *B*-index indicates the degree to which an item distinguishes between the students who passed the test and those who failed, in contrast to the *A*-statistic which indicates the degree to which those answering the item correctly (passing the item) are the same as those who passed the test (without particular reference to those who failed the test). The difference can be seen by contrasting the response patterns and results for items 3 and 4 in Tables 4.8 and 4.9. Whereas the agreement statistic is .99 for both items 3 and 4, the *B*-index is 1.00 and 0.00, respectively. Thus the *B*-index is sensitive to the fact that all of those who failed the test answered item 3 incorrectly and item 4 correctly, while the agreement statistic is not. It is productive, then, to examine both statistics in item analysis.

Item phi. The item phi (Glass & Stanley, 1970) is essentially a Pearson correlation (see next chapter for an explanation of the Pearson correlation) between examinee item and test performance outcome, their mastery of the item to their mastery of the test. Item phi (ϕ) can be expressed using Shannon and Cliver's conventions as follows:

$$\phi = (P_{iT} - P_i P_T / \sqrt{P_i Q_i P_T Q_T}$$

Where:

P_i = the proportion of examinees who answered the item correctly

Q_i = the proportion of examinees who answered the item incorrectly, or $(1 - P_i)$

P_T = the proportion of examinees who passed the test

Q_T = the proportion of examinees who failed the test, or $(1 - P_T)$

P_{iT} = the proportion of examinees who answered the item correctly and passed the test

Once again using item 2 from Table 4.8 as an example, calculating item phi is a bit more complicated but, if done systematically, is fairly straightforward. The portion of examinees (P_i) who answered the item correctly overall would be the same as the overall IF, which was shown to be .47 (in Table 4.6 or 4.9); the portion of examinees (Q_i) who answered the item incorrectly overall would be .53 ($1 - IF = 1 - .47 = .53$); the proportion of examinees (P_T) who passed the test was .67; the proportion of examinees (Q_T) who failed the test overall was .33 (that is, $1 - .67$); and the proportion of total examinees (P_{iT}) who answered the item correctly and passed the test was .40. Substituting these values into the formula results in the following:

$$\phi = (P_{iT} - P_i P_T / \sqrt{P_i Q_i P_T Q_T}$$

$$= (.40 - .47 \times .67) / \sqrt{.47 \times .53 \times .67 \times .33}$$

$$= (.40 - .3149) / \sqrt{.0551}$$

$$= .0851 / .2347$$

$$= .3626$$

$$\approx .36$$

Shannon and Cliver (1987) indicate that the range of possible values of ϕ is restricted by the proportion of examinees who pass an item as well as by the proportion of examinees who pass the test. Notice in Table 4.9 that the values obtained for the item phi are in most cases very similar to those obtained for the B-index.

Interpreting cut-score item statistics. As with NRT item statistics, all three of these CRT cut-score item statistics are sensitive to the ability levels of the groups and the difficulty of the items drawn from a domain. Since all of these statistics are dependent upon the cut score, items should not be rejected solely on the basis of these values. Low values may be an indication that the domain has been mis-specified rather than that the item itself is bad. If no other confirmatory information is available to indicate that the item is bad then, rather than rejecting the item outright, the domain should be carefully examined and the item should be refined.

Criterion-referenced item selection

Having analyzed the items on a CRT using one or more forms of the difference index or cut-point indices, the ultimate goal will be to revise the test by selecting those items that are functioning well for criterion-referenced purposes. The item quality analysis discussed in the previous chapter should be used in this selection process because it provides information about how items fit the objectives or content being measured. However, calculating a difference index can provide additional information of interest in this process. Still further information will be provided if the B-index, agreement statistic, or item phi are also calculated. Difference indices give information about how sensitive each item is to instruction or to master and non-master differences, but cut-point indices indicate how each item is related to the distinction between students who passed and failed the course.

In other words, the entire picture (including the actual quality of the items) must be considered rather than becoming overly fascinated with any one statistic. The statistics are just numerical tools that can aid in selecting the best items for a revised version of a test.

Consider Table 4.7 once again. Which of the items would you be tempted to select if you were to need only the five best ones? Numbers 47 through 50 would be attractive and obvious choices. But what about the fifth item? Would you choose number 41 or 60 (both of which have DIs of .196) or would you choose 51 or 59 (which are not far behind with DIs of .181)? This last choice is much more difficult and will no doubt involve looking at the items in terms of their other qualities, particularly item quality and item format analyses. Also consider what you would do if you had the *B*-indexes on the post-test and the one for number 47 turned out to be only .02.

In short, the IF, DI, agreement statistic, ϕ-index, and *B*-index can all help in the selection of a subset of sound CRT items that are also related to the gains being made by the students who are studying the content and/or related to the distinction between students who passed or failed the course. In the process of developing CRTs for that content, you may find that there are some startling differences between what you think you are teaching and what the students seem to be learning. Thus with sound CRTs in place, teachers may be able to not only judge the performance of the students but also examine the fit between what they believe they are teaching and what the students are actually absorbing. It seems strange that some teachers may be examining this issue for the first time in their careers.

Item response theory and CRT

Three practical issues are periodically encountered in test development and administration that create problems difficult to address with traditional CRT or NRT approaches. First, in cases where examinees do not pass a test or are in programs requiring multiple exposures to an examination measuring a particular domain over time, problems exist with how to continually develop alternative test forms that are equivalent in terms of difficulty and discriminating power around the selected cut-score. Frequently examinees remember items from the previous test, and that memory has a contaminating effect on any subsequent encounter with those items. Thus, in such settings there is a need to develop a large item bank from which items can be selected that meet pre-established statistical criteria for purposes of comparison.

Second, items and test forms constructed for one group of learners may not yield score results that are comparable or interpretable for a more able or less able group of learners because the distribution of scores will be very different between the two groups. This situation results from the fact that test and item scores in traditional analyses are dependent upon the particular set of items on the test and on the particular sample of examinees who took the test. For example, a thirty item reading test given to a group of students at the beginning of a term might have a mean of 15 and a standard deviation of 5. That same test might be given to a different group of students and produce a mean of 19 and a standard deviation of 3. Consequently, the interpretation of each examinee's score is dependent upon the particular test form taken and upon the particular group of examinees who took the test at the same administration. A person's score will be low on a "hard" test and higher on an "easy" test. Similarly, the test mean will be low for a group of very "poor" examinees and will be high for a group of very "able" examinees. Suppose Examinee A is in fact quite a bit weaker than Examinee B as a language user. If we give both of them an easy test, they may both get the same perfect score. If we give both of them a very hard test, they may both get the same very low score. However, we are not able to discover the actual ability of each learner. Likewise, item facilities for the items would change with different testing groups of high and low ability levels. As the test is continually administered, these statistics would continue to change depending upon the particular ability level of the examinees in each administration.

Third, item statistics are reported on a scale that indicates the percentage of people who answered the item correctly while an examinee's score is reported in relation to the number or average number of items answered correctly across the test form. There is no way in these traditional approaches to interpret the examinees' ability on a scale that is comparable to the actual difficulty of the particular items. It would be desirable to have items with item statistics that are not group dependent, scores that describe an examinee's ability independently of the particular test form difficulty, and tests that allow the matching of a test item's difficulty and an examinee's ability on the same scale. There is, then, a need to find some way to standardize across tests with reference to examinees' abilities, not just their relative standing to one another, and to standardize item difficulties independent of the particular group of examinees who took that form of the test.

One approach that has strong potential for assisting in addressing the concerns just mentioned is called *item response theory* (IRT). This theory is comprised of a family of statistical approaches that provide probabilistic models linking item difficulty with an examinee's ability. In IRT, a person's trait level is estimated from a pattern of responses to test items. This is congruent with notions that psychological constructs, such as language ability, can be conceptualized as latent variables underlying behavior (Embretson & Reise, 2000). Any person's responses on a test are seen as some indication of the person's ability on the latent variable. As discussed in Chapter 1, the nature of that latent variable in the assessment of communicative language ability may be hotly debated. However, in the end, the results of measurement are generalized to ability on some latent variable regardless of how global or local that variable may be conceived. In short, a test is given and some generalization to a type of ability represented by the items on the given test is made. In IRT terms, that estimated ability is the latent variable.

The discussion of IRT in this book will necessarily be an overview, without extensive recourse to the mathematical bases of the various IRT models, the details of the computer programs usually employed in conducting IRT analysis, or the frequent rather contentious arguments about which particular IRT model is most elegant and/or, "right". That is not to negate the value of thoroughly understanding the underlying derivations of the different models, or the passion (yes, passion) that advocates of particular IRT models feel about their adopted approach. Rather, it simply recognizes that this text is focused on CRT and space here is too limited for a complete discussion of IRT. Other authors have presented these discussions eloquently and in detail elsewhere. Readers are referred to such sources as Hulin, Drasgow, and Parsons (1983), Hambleton and Swaminathan (1985), Suen (1990), McNamara (1996), Wright (1999), and Embretson and Reise (2000). In practice, IRT analysis is generally conducted with the aid of fairly advanced statistical computer programs, such as BILOG, FACETS, Logist, Quest, Xcaliber, etc. The discussion which follows will only provide an overview of how IRT can assist specifically in CRT development. Hence, it is beyond the scope of the present text to provide a primer in the details of how the different programs operate. Reference to other sources, such as McNamara (1996), Linacre (1988), Assessment Systems Corp. (1996–1997), and Mislevy and Bock (1990) will help in answering questions related to specific computer programs.

An introduction to three common IRT models

There are three different IRT models in common use, each addressing different concerns. The three different models discussed here vary in the number of parameters that are used to describe an item's characteristics. The three different parameters relate to item *difficulty* identified as b, expressed on a logistic scale in units called logits, item *discrimination* (slope, designated as a) and the extent to which *guessing* might be a factor in the item characteristics of dichotomously scored items, designated as c. The three models are called the *one-*, *two-*, or *three*-parameter models, respectively, depending on how many of the three parameters just mentioned are incorporated into calculations of the model. Each of the models incorporates different assumptions about item properties, and requires different numbers of examinees in the calibration group. Additionally, proponents of the different models disagree about the extent to which various of the parameters can in fact be adequately measured or, in other cases, legitimately omitted from inclusion in the item estimates. Thus, there are practical and theoretical issues involved in which of the models is chosen for building a test item pool. As a first principle, these models attempt to define item difficulty in a manner that is independent of the particular sample of examinees and to estimate the ability of individuals independent from the particular items the examinee has taken, assuming that both the examinee and set of items are generally representative of the population and item pool upon which the calibration was made. In the following discussion, the relevant formulas are provided for those who are interested in examining the specific types of differences that are associated with the different models.

The one-parameter model

The one-parameter model, often termed the Rasch model after the Danish mathematician Georg Rasch, is perhaps the most popular of the IRT *latent trait* models. It differs from the other two models to be discussed in that all items are assumed to have equal discriminating power and vary only in terms of item difficulty. The one-parameter model takes the form:

$$P_i(\Theta) = \frac{e^{(\Theta_s - b_i)}}{1 + e^{\Theta_s - b_i}}$$

Where:
$P_i(\Theta)$ = the probability that an examinee with an ability Θ answers item i correctly
e = a constant equal to 2.71828 (i.e., a natural or Naperian log)
b_i = the item difficulty in logit value
Θ_s = the person's trait score (ability) in logit value

The item difficulty parameter (b_i) and the ability parameter (Θ_s) are defined on the same scale. In the scale used here, the probabilities of obtaining the person ability or item difficulty are transformed into units called logits. The formula above for the one-parameter model indicates that in the numerator a constant represented as the natural (or Naperian) log is taken to an exponential power of the difference between a person's ability and the item's difficulty. This produces a scale representing the logarithmic odds of the probability of a response with units in logit measures (McNamara, 1996). This scale may undoubtedly be a new concept to many readers. However, it can be seen as analogous to other scales based on transformed data, such as z-scores or T-scores. Over time, with increased exposure, the scale will become familiar to IRT consumers. While the value of b or Θ can theoretically extend from minus infinity to positive infinity, in practice, the values typically extend from about -3 or -4 to $+3$ or $+4$. When the items have a negative value, they are on the easy end of the continuum and when they are positive, the items are more difficult. Because it has fewer parameters than the other two models, calibrations based on the one-parameter model can be made with fewer examinees and shorter tests. Sometimes as few as a hundred examinees and 25 item tests are needed (McNamara, 1996).

The two-parameter model

The two-parameter model (Birnbaum, 1968) produces item characteristic curves (ICCs) that incorporate the item discrimination (slope) in the equation. ICCs are discussed in more detail in the next section. The model takes the following form:

$$P_i(\Theta) = \frac{e^{a_i(\Theta_s - b_i)}}{1 + e^{a_i(\Theta_s - b_i)}}$$

Where:

$P_i(\Theta)$ = the probability that an examinee with an ability Θ answers item i correctly
e = a constant equal to 2.71828 (i.e., a natural or Naperian log)
b_i = the item difficulty in logit value
Θ_s = the person's trait score (ability) in logit value
a_i = the item discrimination of item i

The item discrimination parameter (a_i) can theoretically range from minus infinity to plus infinity. Any items that are negatively discriminating would be removed from an operational test. Further, values of above $+2$ are in practice rarely obtained. High values of a_i produce ICCs with very steep curves and low values produce curves that increase more gradually. In the formula, item discrimination is a multiplier of the difference between ability and difficulty levels. This item discrimination is related to traditional biserial correlations between the examinees' responses and total scores, although these correlations are not on a -1 to $+1$ scale (Embretson & Reise, 2000). As item discrimination increases, the magnitude of the effect of the differences between ability and difficulty increases. For lower item discriminations, the relative difference between trait level and difficulty level decreases. Thus, in the two-parameter model, items with low discrimination contribute less to trait level estimation than do items with high discriminations. In essence, then, items that have a very high a_i value discriminate across a narrow range of ability while items that have a very low a_i value discriminate across a wide band of abilities, but not as strongly. There is, then, a tradeoff between the level of discrimination and the range of abilities over which the item is of strong utility.

The three-parameter model

The three-parameter model is constructed from the two-parameter model, but adds a guessing parameter (c_i). It takes the following form:

$$P_i(\Theta) = c_i + (1 - c_i) \frac{e^{a_i(\Theta_s - b_i)}}{1 + e^{a_i(\Theta_s - b_i)}}$$

Where:
$P_i(\Theta) =$ the probability that an examinee with an ability Θ answers item i correctly
$e \ \ =$ a constant equal to 2.71828 (i.e., a natural or Naperian log)
$b_i =$ the item difficulty in logit value
$\Theta_s =$ the person's trait score (ability) in logit value
$a_i \ =$ the item discrimination of item i
$c_i \ \ =$ the probability of a low ability examinee correctly guessing the item i

This model was developed to account for any guessing that might occur at lower ability levels for selected response items such as multiple-choice. In practice, c_i is sometimes set at values lower than would occur if a person guessed randomly. That is, with effective distractors, responses will not occur in a random fashion. While with the one- and two-parameter models the probability that a person will get the answer correct can range from zero to 1, with the three-parameter model the lower value is generally greater than 0.

Three different models: advantages and disadvantages

Which particular model to choose is not a clear issue, and the selection frequently depends upon practical issues of sample size and number of items on a test form as much as on theoretical assumptions held by the testing practitioner. Hulin, Lissik, and Drasgow (1982) indicate that for the two-parameter model, 30 items with any sample size down to 200 would be sufficient for accurate estimation of Θ. Lord (1968) indicates that as many as 50 items and 1,000 examinees would be required for estimation of the three-parameter model. Hulin, Drasgow, and Parsons (1983) contend that this criterion might be too stringent. In their studies, they found relatively stable results with tests of 60 items and samples of 500. So, the decision regarding which model to select is both aesthetic and practical. If one assumes that guessing is a serious problem, then the three-parameter model might be selected. However, some, such as Mislevy and Bock (1982), have doubts that guessing is a constant across all people to the extent that some people guess freely while others are reticent and rarely guess. Thus, positing that the guessing probability is constant for all people will not provide an accurate picture. On the other hand, the one-parameter model is open to criticism for its assumptions that no guessing takes place and that all items should have the same item discrimination. Because only items with close item discriminations are allowed on a test, this narrows the potential significance of the test. The two-parameter model is criticized for the lack of stability in item discrimination estimation when small numbers of examinees are used. None of the three models is perfect and none is totally disreputable. While criticisms have been made of each model, these criticisms are not always empirically based. The choice of which model to select should be based on acknowledgment of the limitations and the goals of the analysis.

Practical applications of IRT to CRT issues

IRT offers methods for addressing the problems mentioned at the beginning of this section that may affect CRT contexts – problems such as the need for item independent person measurement and person free item estimation. There is a need to reference both items and persons to an external scale. In IRT, that scale is the probability scale discussed in relation to the three IRT models above. The IRT models begin with a mathematical statement as to how each expected response depends minimally on the level of examinee ability or skill, expressed as Θ (theta), and the difficulty, expressed as b, of any encountered test item. This relationship is shown by the item response function, or item characteristic curve (ICC). The shape of the ICC will differ depending upon the particular IRT model that is chosen. For simplicity of presentation, the following discussion will generally be based on the one-parameter model. However, this is not to deny the potential utility of the other models in practice. An example of an ICC is shown in Figure 4.6.

This curve is a mathematical expression of the probability of success on an item as a function of the person's ability and the

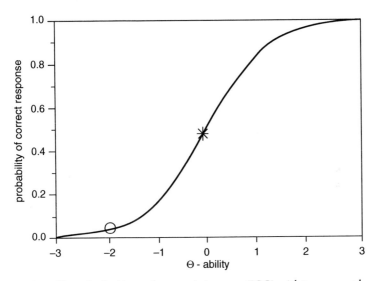

Figure 4.6. Hypothetical item characteristic curve (ICC) with two example ability levels

difficulty of the item. It describes how changes across trait ability level correspond to changes in the probability of a particular response, in this case, the probability of a correct answer. The ICC is a monotonic (S-shaped) curve. Note in Figure 4.6 that the inflection of the curve for this test item is located at the middle of the x-axis (that is, at the asterisk). A vertical line from the point labeled 0 would intersect the ICC at a point that separates the upper half of the curve from the lower, symmetrical, half of the curve. The item is, thus, said to have a difficulty (b) of 0. As mentioned, both difficulty (b) and ability (Θ) can in theory range from $-\infty$ to $+\infty$, though in practice values tend to cover the span between -3 or -4 and +3 or +4. The probability of a correct response on an item increases steadily as abilities increase. As the curve in Figure 4.6 indicates, relatively small changes in ability near the middle reflect large changes in probabilities, but not at extreme ability levels. Note that the units along the x-axis are in logit values discussed above. A logit value of 0, represents the middle of the difficulty or ability continuum. Higher values indicate increased difficulty and ability, while lower values are interpreted as being lower in difficulty or ability. One advantage of using logit scores with ICCs is that their use removes the effect of raw score dependencies upon number of items and relative ability of one examinee in relation to other examinees.

In the example ICC presented in Figure 4.6, a person whose ability is designated as 0 (shown as the asterisk on the curve) has a 50% chance of getting this item correct. However, a person with a trait of -2.0 (the "O" on the curve) has only about a 5–10% chance of getting the item correct. The probability that any particular examinee will answer the item correctly is independent of the distribution of abilities in the population of other examinees being tested on the same test (Hambleton, Swaminathan, & Rogers, 1991). Because of this independence, the probability of a correct response will not depend upon the number of other examinees at the same or other points along the score continuum. Additionally, the characteristics of the ICC for each item will maintain their features regardless of which other items are on the test form that an examinee confronts. This independence feature of IRT addresses the shortcomings of traditional NRT and CRT mentioned above regarding examinee scores being related to the particular group of examinees and the particular items on the test.

Further, knowing the ICCs associated with a large pool of items potentially allows the construction of multiple equivalent measures for candidates needing multiple assessments. Suppose we had a listening comprehension test with three open-ended questions that are scored as correct or incorrect. Figure 4.7 shows the ICCs for each of these test items.

Several characteristics of the test items can be seen. All three ICCs have the same S-shape, but they are situated at different locations along the ability trait scale on the x-axis. This difference in location indicates that the items are of different difficulty levels. Item 1 is the easiest and Item 3 is the most difficult. Note how none of this is based on NRT needs for relative ranking or ordering of test takers. Hence, this approach relates the assessment to Glaser's (1963) notions of CRT representing a continuum of ability, as mentioned in Chapter 1. If one were constructing a test for a number of very able examinees, several items like Item 2 and Item 3 could be selected. Similarly, if it were important to provide assessment for less able examinees, items similar to Item 1 and Item 2 could be selected.

Figure 4.8 presents the ICCs associated with eight different hypothetical items. Notice that Items 4–6 are all of similar item difficulty. Likewise, Items 2 and 3 have very similar difficulty values. In the construction of a test for examinees of medium ability levels, the test constructor could select Item 2, Item 5, and Item 7. This selection would adequately bracket the examinee ability levels. It would not be necessary to administer each item in the group represented by Items 4–6 since there is a great deal of overlap in the

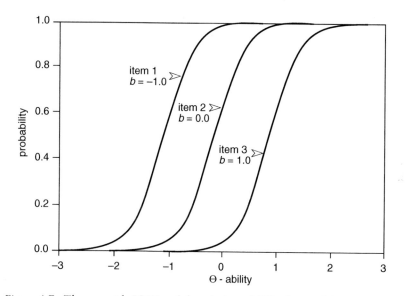

Figure 4.7. *Three sample ICCS and the relation of difficulty to ability*

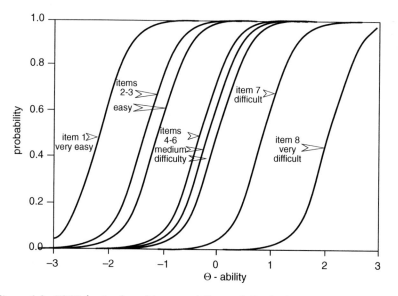

Figure 4.8. *ICCS for 8 selected items at different difficulty levels*

Table 4.10. *Example of item selection for alternate tests*

Item #	Item Facility	Logit Value
1	.27	1.158
2	.79	−1.535
3	.68	−0.843
4	.54	−0.211
5	.05	0.002
6	.39	0.528
7	.56	−0.275
8	.20	1.617
9	.44	0.275
10	.65	−0.779

ability level that they measure. Thus, the information from the ICCs can help to develop shorter tests that are directed at a particular level of ability. Not only does this save time for the examinee, it also conserves some of the items such that they need not be exposed until they are used in a subsequent form of the test.

Thus, one of the basic functions of IRT in test construction is to allow items with specific characteristics to be selected for different versions of a test and to allow the tests to be customized to the ability level of the particular group of examinees. For example, suppose a test has been administered to a large group of examinees across several grades or levels in a school and analyzed using the one-parameter model. From the analysis, the ten item difficulties presented in Table 4.10 were obtained. Note that as the IF increases, indicating that the items are easier, the logit value decreases. The lower the logit value, the easier the item.

The logit values obtained provide information for at least three uses. First, the information allows tailoring tests to different groups of examinees. Suppose, for example, that a pre-test must be constructed for potential students in the lower ability levels of the language program. It is assumed that these examinees are at a level generally lower than the entire cohort of examinees represented in Table 4.10. Items with difficulty characteristics such as Item 2, Item 3 and Item 10 could be selected in order to fit the difficulty level of the test to this particular group of students. Using logit values in this way allows the construction of more parsimonious tests.

Second, knowledge of the IRT parameters can allow the production of larger item banks based on a common frame of reference.

For example, suppose the items presented in Table 4.10 represent a set of items that are central to the curricular framework of the hypothetical language program under discussion here. All teachers and administrators involved in the program have internalized what the scores on these items mean in terms of student ability. However, there may be a need to expand the item pool in order to accommodate expanded course offerings or new course levels. The existing items can be used as anchor items for novel piloted items – items necessarily piloted on different examinee groups from the initial norming group. The new items can be calibrated in such a way that the scale that is in place within the institution incorporates the new items. This would not be completely possible with item raw scores alone because of the dependence of item statistics on the particular sample of test takers.

Third, IRT parameter estimation allows referencing person abilities with items tied to particular functional descriptors. For example, suppose a reading test had been given to a large sample of examinees but a program was interested in how four of the examinees fared. The distribution and standings of the four examinees are presented in Figure 4.9.

Clearly George has the lowest score of the four examinees and Pat obtained the highest. However, this alone does not provide the kind of descriptive information that might be desired. Figure 4.10 shows how the examinee logit ability scores can be related directly to specific language items.

In this instance, the qualitative differences in reading performance between the four examinees are reflected in the items associated with the different ability levels. Although it may be difficult in practice to find items that are so clearly ordered, when available, this kind of information can be used to help establish criterion levels for promotion from one curricular level to another. There will be more on this topic of criterion levels in the validity discussion in Chapter 6.

A number of considerations are involved in detecting which items are to be considered unacceptable and which items should be available for inclusion on forms of a test. Some of these identification approaches have parallels in traditional CRT and NRT techniques and some are specific to IRT methodologies. For example, IRT decisions may opt to view as unacceptable those items with low or negative discrimination indices, that is, those with a_i below .30. Such items may simply be seen as not demonstrating sufficient discrimination to justify maintenance in the test pool. Similarly, difficulty estimates – b_i values – should not be too low or too high for the intended group of examinees. The items may represent difficulty/

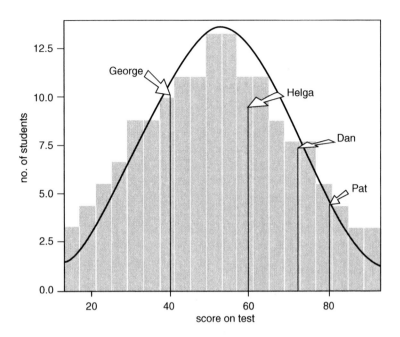

Figure 4.9. Raw score distribution

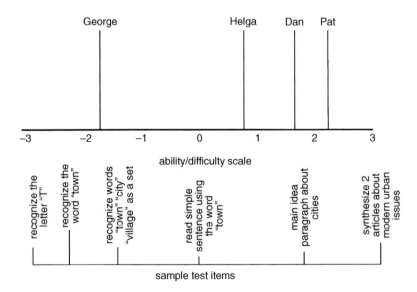

Figure 4.10. Persons and items related on the ability/difficulty scale

ability levels that are of no practical interest. However, IRT employs greater sensitivity to the match of ability and item difficulty than do traditional NRT and CRT techniques.

Other methods of item selection and evaluation are unique to IRT. These methods essentially examine the extent to which the obtained item response patterns fit the response patterns that are predicted, based on the responses of examinees at all ability levels across all items (cf. the discussion of *unidimensionality* and fit in Chapter 5 for a more extensive discussion). These models identify which items do not behave in a predictable manner. They may behave in these unpredictable ways for many of the same reasons that affect item dependability in CRT and NRT approaches, (e.g., item bias, prior knowledge, incidental vocabulary load, etc.).

Additionally, CRT development may involve ICCs in the determination of *item information functions* (IIF). Without initially employing a technical notion of *information*, we can take refuge in a very common and ordinary day-to-day notion of *information*. We can all agree that it is important that our tests provide the most information possible. The reason for this is that the more information we have, the less uncertainty we have to deal with, and the less uncertainty we have to deal with then the better able we are to make justifiable decisions. Key to having information that reduces uncertainty and allows the making of justifiable decisions is being able to pinpoint just where we have the most information and where we do not have much information. For instance, if we have a lot of information about the performance of non-native speakers of English attending an English medium university and how they perform on a particular examination, we would feel reasonably comfortable making certain decisions about these candidates. However, we would not have much information about students in secondary schools studying English in Japan, for example. We would need to get more information on that level of student in order to reduce the uncertainty we have in making any decisions regarding them.

IRT has taken this concept of information and incorporated it into a technical definition that allows the quantitative estimation of the *item information function* (IIF) mentioned above. The IIF reflects the amount of information a particular item provides, and is a function of the discrimination of the ICC and the amount of variability (or error) at each difficulty level. Lord (1980) indicated that item information functions (IIFs) can be interpreted as measures of the amount of information provided by an item at a specified ability level. Hambleton and de Gruijter (1983) consider IIFs to be superior

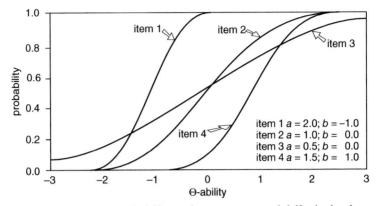

Figure 4.11. Four items with differing discrimination and difficulty levels

to conventional indices as measures of item discrimination power at passing scores (Shannon & Cliver, 1987).

The IIF informs the researcher how much discrimination an item provides at each level on the difficulty/ability axis. Further, the amount of information any item provides at that level is a function of the discrimination power of the item as well as its difficulty parameter. Because of the inclusion of the *a* discrimination parameter, it will now be informative to consider the contribution of the two-parameter model. As concrete examples, look at the ICCs for the four items in Figure 4.11.

Item 1 is a relatively easy item with a steep item slope of 2.0, indicating a high item discrimination. It would have most of its explanatory value near the *b* difficulty index of -1.0. Item 2 has a moderate slope of 1.0 and a difficulty in the center of the scale at 0.0. Item 3, while also having a difficulty of 0.0 at the center of the scale, has a relatively low slope at 0.5. Hence, it discriminates over a larger band of abilities, but is not as discriminating at any one point as the other items. Item 4 has a steep slope of 1.5 and a higher difficulty estimate than the other items at 1.0.

In selecting the items for a test, we can take the item parameters and information associated with the items just discussed into account. Figure 4.12 presents the IIFs associated with the four items shown in Figure 4.11.

Note that each of the IIFs has its peak at the item difficulty level and the amount of information (the height of the curve) is a function of the item discrimination. The greater the item discrimination, the greater the amount of information provided at the *b* value. Notice, however, that the items do provide some information at areas other

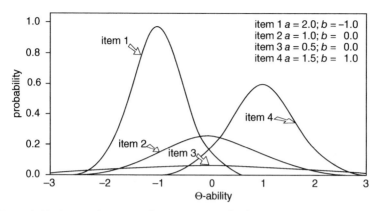

Figure 4.12. Item information functions (IIFs) for four items with differing discrimination and difficulty levels

than their particular difficulty level. The IIFs provide important information in test construction and interpretation. First, the information provided by each item is additive across the items on a test form. This allows the test users to determine which items will be valuable for any ability level of interest. For example, if a test developer were interested in making decisions around the $\Theta = 1.0$ level, information from Item 2, Item 3, and Item 4 would all contribute, providing test information of about $.20 + .50 + .05 = .75$. A researcher can determine the amount of information provided by a set of items at a particular level by adding the corresponding values from each IIF. If it is determined that .75 is too low in this case, and that more reduction of uncertainty is needed, more items can be added to provide more information.

The IIF scale will also likely be in units that are not readily identifiable to many readers. Suen (1990) notes that although the IIF can be derived from other mathematical perspectives, at a particular Θ value the IIF is "conceptually a ratio of the slope of the ICC and the expected measurement error at that Θ" (p. 96). So, although the actual scale units may represent an unfamiliar metric, as with the logit scale, it can be conceptualized as representing a decrease in the amount of uncertainty about how stable the ability estimate is at any given level. As the discrimination increases, it compensates for any degree of measurement error in the test item associated with that difficulty level. Increasing the number of items with information about that selected level of ability will increase the amount of total information available for making decisions at that point.

The IIF is in part a function of the item's difficulty level and level of discrimination. Items are selected on the basis of the amount of information they supply to the test for a designated sample of examinees at the selected cut-score. Lord (1977) outlines the steps of this procedure for test construction as follows:

1. Determine the shape of the desired test information curve.
2. Select items with information curves that will fit the "hard-to-fill" areas under the item information curve.
3. After each item is added to the test, calculate the test information curve for the selected items.
4. Continue selecting items until the test information curve approximates the target information curve to a satisfactory degree.

Thus, the test may be tailored to maximize information at particular abilities of interest. Shannon and Cliver (1987) found that conventional CRT indices such as ϕ and B may be comparable to IIFs as measures of discrimination power at passing scores. Thus, in the absence of mastery/non-mastery groups, it may be possible to utilize IIFs to inform CRT data analysis.

It should be noted that, as with NRTs, items may be rejected on statistical grounds alone, even if they continue to appear to subject experts to measuring skills or concepts highly relevant to the domain of concern. Tall (1981) refers to the Rasch model, though the criticism may apply equally to the three- and two-parameter models, as "self-justifying" in that the process used to create the item bank serves to reject items which are sensitive to instruction or which are rapidly changing. However, this iterative process of test refinement through cyclical selection and revision of items is certainly just as much a part of general NRT procedures in test pool construction. Henning (personal communication) notes that while Tall's criticism may be true in determining linking items, it would not be the case with a well-designed item bank.

In short, several applications for IRT in CRT construction have been identified. For example, apropos the previous discussion of the role of linking items, it would seem appropriate for language tests to employ linking items that are not sensitive to instruction. With linking items that are keyed to a more global proficiency, it may be possible to identify the band within which those items that are sensitive to instruction operate. In that way, a taxonomy of skills and relative order of acquisition of skills might be developed. When used with an approach which incorporates content domains as CRT does, IRT may very well aid in the development of more precise and interpretable tests.

Further, very practical applications within language programs are available. Hambleton (1979) argues that with a pool of items that fit a particular model of ability, a test that "discriminates" well at any particular region of the ability continuum can be constructed. This would provide an efficient method for criterion-referenced testing, where it is common to observe low test performance on a pre-test. The pre-test could be constructed with easier items and the post-test with more difficult items. Since the tests fit the ability level of the examinees more closely, the precision of measurement will be higher than with less well fitting tests. Furthermore, since the ability estimates are not dependent upon the particular test items, gain can be estimated by subtracting the pre-test ability estimate from the post-test ability estimate (Hambleton, 1979). This could be used in constructing mastery tests. The level of difficulty could be set to the desired level of ability for mastery vs. non-mastery decisions. Additionally, Williams and Slawski (1980) propose IRT as an aid in the construction of equivalent test forms in CRT testing. In this way, the invariance of item statistics across samples from the same population may be capitalized upon in developing alternate forms for domains. That is, the sample invariance property of IRT may aid in an examination of the equivalence properties which should appear in CRT alternate forms.

Multi-faceted Rasch IRT

Much current language testing and research involves items that are judged by raters on a scale of some sort. While the two- and three-parameter IRT models are basically limited to dichotomously scored items, the one-parameter Rasch model has been extended to work with analysis of rating scales and items which may yield partial credit (Wright & Masters, 1982). This model is helpful in the development of performance assessment test instruments and when working with questionnaires and scales in general.

As with dichotomously scored one-parameter items, the multi-faceted Rasch approach locates an examinee's ability and an item's difficulty estimates on a common scale. For example, in research by Brown, Hudson, Norris, and Bonk (2001) results from a performance test are reported. Items on this test asked the examinee to perform such tasks as: listening to a message on voice mail and then responding appropriately in writing; listening to a group of friends' preferences for pizza and then ordering the correct pizza types; or listening to someone's instructions about information needed on a university form and then filling out the form correctly. The results from each item were rated on a scale from 1 to 5 by three different raters. We need to know two pieces of information in determining the quality of the test: the difficulty of each of the performance tasks, and the probability that people of different abilities would get one of the ratings from 1 to 5. This, among other things, is precisely what the multi-faceted Rasch model allows us to do.

In Figure 4.13, the output of an analysis using the FACETS computer program (Linacre, 1989–1996) is presented. The first column (Measr) represents the logit values obtainable in the data set. Here, the obtainable scale values go from a high of 3 to a low of −2. The second column (Examinee) contains a histogram of the ability range of the examinees who were rated on the scale of 1 to 5. The third column (Tasks) indicates the difficulty of each of the items (tasks) on the performance test. Here the task labeled F09 (evaluating credit card offers based on banking 'tips' sheet) was the most difficult task for the examinees and the task labeled E20 (answering questions from the international student office) was the least difficult task for these examinees. The fourth column (Rater) indicates that the three raters were similar in the severity of their ratings. (More on this issue of rater severity is in Chapter 5). Finally, the column to the far right (Rating) indicates the spread of the ratings on these tasks. That is, it indicates which levels are associated with successful performance on particular tasks.

An analysis such as that in Figure 4.13 is helpful in test construction. For example, it is clear that most of the tasks target the ability estimates between a +1 ability level and a −1 ability level. Likewise, these tasks tend to get ratings of 4, 3 and 2. In further test construction, the data indicate that items A09, E21 and F07 are largely redundant since all three of them have a difficulty estimate of about .30. The data further indicate that there is a need to include more items at the upper and lower end of the scale since all tasks tend to fall in the difficulty band of −1.1 and .30. Thus, IRT is useful in tests that use ratings of behavior across some scale.

Although IRT approaches have been advocated for use in CRT test development and have been claimed to be superior to conventional discrimination indices at established cut-scores (Hambleton & de Gruijter, 1983), IRT statistics have limited application in settings with few examinees or when IRT computer programs are unavailable (Shannon & Cliver, 1987). Thus, CRT development in language program settings is often unable to utilize the scaled item difficulty and item discrimination information provided by IRT analysis. Nevertheless, with ongoing language programs that have a reasonably stable population of students as well as a stable curriculum, IRT

```
----------------------------------------------------------------------
| Measr |  +Examinee  | -Tasks              | -Rater #   | Rating
----------------------------------------------------------------------
+   3   +             +                     +            + (5)      +
        |   *
        |
        |
        |
        |
        |   *
+   2   +             +                     +            +          +
        |   *
        |   *
        |   * *
        |   *
        |                 F09
        |                                                  -----
        |   * * *         C14
+   1   + * *           +                   +            +          +
        |   * *
        |   *
        |
        |   * * *                                          (4)
        |   * *
        |   * *
        |   *             A09    E21    F07
        |   * *           E22                              -----
        |   * * * * *
*   0   * * * * * * *   * F05                 * 1  2  3   *          *
        |   * * *         A18                              (3)
        |   * * *
        |   * * * *       B20                              -----
        |   * *
        |   * * *         A21    C15
        |   * * * *                                        (2)
        |   * * * * * * * * * *
        |   * * * * *
        |   * * *
+  -1   + * * * * *     + A20                 +            +         +
        |   * *           E20                              -----
        |   * * *
        |   * * * *
        |   * *
        |   * * * *
        |
        |   *
        |
+  -2   +             +                      +            + (1)      +
----------------------------------------------------------------------
| Measr |  * -1       | -Tasks              | -Rater     | Rating
----------------------------------------------------------------------
```

Figure 4.13. Multi-faceted output

can be an important tool, even though it may initially appear complex and rather arcane. Systematic and judicious use of IRT approaches in CRT test development can help testing programs to develop consistent and stable assessment instruments.

See uk.cambridge.org/elt/crlt/ for chapter summary and exercises.

5 Reliability, dependability, and unidimensionality

Introduction

In this chapter, we will begin by addressing three central issues involved in test consistency: reliability, dependability, and fit. As we will explain, these issues arise because tests are never perfect, that is, any set of test scores contains error. Estimating just how much that error contributes to the scores of examinees centers on notions of *reliability* in norm-referenced testing (NRT), *dependability* in criterion-referenced testing (CRT), and what is termed *fit* in item response theory (IRT).

NRT reliability estimation relies heavily on correlational approaches. So, we will necessarily have to provide a brief explanation/review of how the Pearson product-moment correlation coefficient works and how it should be interpreted. Three basic correlational approaches will then be explained: (a) test–retest reliability, (b) equivalent forms reliability, and (c) internal consistency reliabilities (including split-half adjusted by the Spearman-Brown prophecy formula, alpha, K-R20, and K-R21).

CRT dependability will be discussed in terms of two general approaches to consistency estimation: threshold-loss methods and generalizability theory approaches. The threshold-loss methods will include the original agreement and kappa coefficients based on two administrations of a CRT, and Subkoviak's (1980) short-cut methods that allow for estimating the agreement and kappa coefficients from a single test administration. The generalizability theory approaches will include discussion of single and multiple sources of error as well as in terms of the domain score approach, phi (Φ), and squared-error loss approaches including Livingston's statistic and the more effective phi(lambda). Other uses of generalizability will also be shown.

IRT will be explored in terms of a key concept known as *unidimensionality*, which is the idea that each test (or subtest) should measure a single trait. Unidimensionality turns out to be a useful concept for criterion-referenced testing because CRTs are typically designed to measure well-defined domains of relatively homogeneous content. Several approaches will be discussed for establishing uni-dimensionality in tests. These will center around the degree to which items may misfit the measurement model, that is, the item response patterns of examinees may suggest that some items are measuring a different trait from the rest.

Preliminary definitions: consistency, reliability, and dependability

Regardless of the approach to measurement that is adopted, *consistency* is a critical issue. It is clear that there will always be individual variability in performance. Just recall playing darts, golf, or jogging. Recall Olympics gymnastics or skating performances. Recall any of the Educational Testing Service examinations that you may have taken, like the *Graduate Record Examination* (Educational Testing Service, 2000a) or the *Test of English as a Foreign Language* (Educational Testing Service, 2000b), or any of the examinations available through the University of Cambridge Local Examinations Syndicate, like the *Certificate of Proficiency in English* (UCLES, 1998), the *First Certificate in English* (UCLES, 1997), or the *International English Language Testing System* (UCLES, 1999, 2000) examinations. Or simply think about some in-class test that you took. Sometimes, you may have excelled at these activities and at other times you may have performed very poorly. Such variations in performance may be due to external factors, such as temperature, wind, noise, or poor instructions, or they may be due to internal factors such as fatigue, mood, or motivation. Regardless of where it comes from, variance need not always be a negative factor in testing. Sometimes an examinee performs well beyond expectations due to concentration, determination, lots of sleep, extra stamina, or looking at someone else's test paper. Some of the variance may be due to actual changes in ability, but some of it may be caused by error. In either case, it is necessary, at least in language assessment, to account for this variance and to understand how much consistency there is in any set of test scores.

For the sake of clarity, in this text the term *reliability* will be used with reference to consistency in NRT test uses while the term *dependability* will be associated with consistency in CRT test settings. For NRTs this consistency may be in terms of multiple test administrations over time (stability), between two or more forms of the same test (equivalence), or within one test (internal consistency).

For CRTs, the consistency is generally discussed in terms of the dependability of the classifications made on the basis of the test, classifications such as master vs. non-master or pass vs. fail. However, while this book is primarily about CRT use in language assessment, it is important to discuss NRT approaches to reliability because, for computational reasons, the NRT reliability coefficients are sometimes used in CRT equations. Further, as a practical matter, even most CRTs will in fact have variance, and their interpretation may benefit from NRT statistics.

NRT reliability

NRT approaches to reliability are derived from classical test theory, which has as one of its basic assumptions the concept of a normal and heterogeneous distribution of scores. This means that test scores are assumed to vary around the test mean in such a way that the relative status of each examinee can be determined in relation to this variance. The basic assumption is that when people take a test, their observed score represents their abilities on those particular items at a particular point in time (Suen, 1990). The general definition for *NRT reliability* is the proportion of observed score variance that is true score variance – true score variance being the proportion of observed score variance that is without error. A consequence of the restrictive assumptions of classical test theory is that, when estimating the *variance components* (or factors contributing to the score differences on a test) that determine reliability, the variance associated with items as a main effect is ignored, that is, it is assumed to be zero. In other words, it is assumed that no interaction exists between items and people such that people are affected only by the difficulty of the items and not by any other characteristic. Thus, NRT reliability focuses on specifying the variance component for persons (and error) in order to rank individuals for *relative* judgments and decisions. In this view, the relationship between an examinee's observed score and that person's true score is represented by the following equation:

$$X = T + E$$

where X is the observed score, T is the true score and E is random error (Pedhazur & Schmelkin, 1991; Li & Wainer, 1997). Here, true score is the result that would have been obtained under absolutely perfect conditions of measurement. However, since absolutely perfect conditions never occur in reality, some amount of error is always present (Pedhazur & Schmelkin, 1991).

A classical theory NRT reliability estimate can be expressed as the ratio of true score variance to observed score variance, or the ratio of true score variance to true score variance plus error variance, as follows:

$$reliability = \frac{T}{X} = \frac{T}{T+E}$$

The goal of the assessor is to reduce the amount of error variance as much as possible.

A note on correlation

Before examining the primary types of NRT reliability estimates, we must briefly discuss the concept of correlation because correlation is generally at the heart of NRT reliability estimation. Fundamentally, language assessment is trying to explain variations in performances among language learners. Such variance can occur on variables such as attitude, aptitude, a test, an item, and so forth, and understanding how such variables relate to each other is a fundamental component of language research, that is, we are often interested in seeing how one variable changes as another variable changes.

One basic method for examining these relationships is through *correlation*. The underlying concept of correlation was introduced in the discussion of item analysis in previous chapters. In those discussions, we were interested in such relationships as how one item relates to total test scores or whether an examinee who gets a particular item correct also is classified as a master, while an examinee who gets the item incorrect is classified as a non-master. Here, we are basically interested in looking at the *strength of relation* between variables. The Pearson product-moment correlation is essential to many concerns in NRT.

Numerous strategies help in exploring how variables relate to one another. One of the most basic strategies is to examine data graphically using scatterplots. *Scatterplots* indicate the location of individual scores on two variables. For example, if we wanted to see how the reading, listening, and grammar scores of people related to one another, we could take the set of data shown in Table 5.1a and plot them. Table 5.1a presents the results for 45 examinees, who took a test with 30 items on it. The first ten items (l01–l10) were listening items, the second ten items (r01–r10) were reading ability items, and the last ten items (g01–g10) measured the knowledge of grammatical structures.

If we first score each of the three subtests separately and put the subscores in a table like that shown in Table 5.1b, we can then plot

Table 5.1a. *Data for 45 examinees on 30 test items*

	Listening										Reading										Grammar									
ID	1	2	3	4	5	6	7	8	9	10	1	2	3	4	5	6	7	8	9	10	1	2	3	4	5	6	7	8	9	10
1	1	1	1	1	0	0	0	0	0	1	0	0	1	1	1	0	0	0	0	0	1	1	0	1	0	1	0	0	0	0
2	1	0	1	1	1	1	1	1	1	1	1	0	0	1	1	0	1	1	1	1	0	1	1	1	1	1	1	0	1	1
3	0	1	1	0	0	0	0	0	0	0	1	1	1	1	0	0	0	0	1	0	1	0	1	0	1	0	0	0	0	0
4	1	1	1	0	0	0	1	1	1	0	1	1	0	1	1	0	0	1	1	0	1	1	0	1	1	0	0	1	1	1
5	1	0	0	0	1	0	0	0	0	0	0	1	1	0	0	0	1	0	0	0	1	1	0	1	1	0	0	1	0	0
6	1	1	1	1	1	0	1	1	0	1	1	1	1	1	1	1	1	1	0	0	1	1	1	1	1	1	1	0	0	1
7	1	0	0	0	0	0	0	0	0	0	1	1	0	0	0	0	0	0	0	0	1	0	1	1	0	0	0	0	0	0
8	1	1	1	1	1	0	0	0	0	1	1	1	0	1	1	1	0	0	0	0	1	1	1	1	1	1	0	0	0	0
9	0	1	0	0	0	0	0	1	0	0	1	1	0	0	0	0	0	1	0	0	1	0	1	1	0	0	1	0	0	0
10	1	1	1	1	1	1	1	1	0	0	1	1	1	1	1	1	1	1	0	0	1	1	1	1	1	1	1	1	0	0
11	1	1	0	0	1	0	0	0	0	0	1	1	1	0	0	0	0	0	0	0	1	1	0	1	0	0	0	0	0	0
12	0	1	1	1	1	1	0	0	1	1	1	0	1	0	1	1	1	0	0	0	1	1	1	1	1	1	1	0	0	0
13	1	1	1	1	1	1	1	0	1	1	1	1	1	1	0	1	1	1	1	1	1	0	1	1	1	1	1	1	1	1
14	1	0	1	1	1	1	0	0	0	1	1	1	1	1	1	0	0	0	0	1	1	1	1	1	1	1	1	0	0	0
15	1	1	1	1	1	1	1	1	1	0	1	1	1	1	1	1	1	1	1	0	1	1	1	1	1	1	1	1	1	1
16	1	1	1	1	1	0	0	0	0	1	1	1	0	1	1	1	0	0	0	0	1	1	1	1	1	1	0	0	0	0
17	1	1	1	1	1	1	1	0	0	0	1	1	1	1	1	1	1	0	0	0	1	1	1	1	1	0	1	0	0	0
18	0	1	1	1	0	0	0	0	0	0	1	0	1	1	1	0	0	0	0	1	1	1	0	0	0	0	0	0	0	0
19	0	1	1	1	0	1	1	0	1	0	1	1	1	1	0	1	1	0	0	0	1	1	1	1	1	0	1	0	0	0
20	1	1	1	0	0	1	0	0	0	0	1	1	1	1	0	0	1	0	0	0	1	1	1	1	1	0	0	0	0	0
21	1	1	1	1	1	1	1	1	0	0	1	1	1	1	1	1	1	1	1	0	1	1	1	1	1	1	1	1	0	1
22	0	1	0	0	0	0	0	0	0	0	0	1	1	0	0	0	0	0	0	1	1	1	1	0	1	0	0	0	0	1
23	1	1	1	1	1	1	0	0	1	1	1	1	1	1	1	1	1	0	0	0	1	1	1	1	1	1	0	1	0	0
24	1	0	0	1	0	0	1	0	0	0	0	1	1	0	0	0	0	1	0	0	1	1	0	1	0	0	1	1	1	0
25	0	1	1	1	1	1	0	0	1	1	0	1	1	1	1	1	1	0	1	1	1	1	1	1	1	1	1	0	1	0
26	1	1	0	0	0	0	0	0	0	0	1	0	0	0	0	0	0	0	1	0	1	1	1	0	0	0	0	1	0	0
27	1	0	1	1	1	0	0	0	0	0	1	1	1	1	1	1	0	0	0	1	0	0	1	0	0	0	0	0	0	0
28	0	0	0	0	1	0	0	0	1	0	1	0	1	0	0	0	0	0	0	0	1	1	0	1	0	0	0	0	0	1
29	1	0	1	1	1	0	0	0	1	0	0	1	0	1	1	1	0	0	0	0	1	1	1	1	1	1	0	0	0	0
30	1	1	1	1	1	0	0	0	0	1	1	1	0	1	1	1	0	0	0	0	1	1	1	1	1	1	0	0	0	0
31	1	0	1	0	0	0	0	0	0	0	1	1	0	1	0	0	0	0	0	0	0	1	1	1	1	0	0	0	0	0
32	1	1	1	1	1	0	0	0	0	1	1	1	0	1	1	1	0	0	0	0	1	1	1	1	1	1	0	0	0	0
33	0	1	0	0	0	0	0	0	0	0	1	0	1	0	0	0	1	0	0	0	0	0	1	1	1	0	1	0	0	0
34	1	1	1	1	1	1	0	1	0	1	1	1	1	1	1	1	0	1	0	1	1	1	1	0	1	1	1	0	0	1
35	1	1	0	1	0	0	0	1	1	0	0	1	0	0	0	1	1	1	1	0	0	0	0	1	1	0	1	0	1	1
36	1	1	1	1	1	1	1	0	0	0	0	1	1	1	1	1	1	0	0	0	0	1	1	0	1	1	1	0	0	1
37	1	1	0	0	0	0	0	1	0	0	0	0	0	0	0	0	1	0	0	1	1	0	0	1	0	0	0	0	0	0
38	1	0	1	1	1	1	1	1	0	1	0	0	1	1	1	1	1	1	0	1	0	1	1	1	1	1	1	1	0	0
39	0	0	0	0	1	0	0	0	0	0	1	0	1	0	0	0	0	0	1	0	0	0	0	1	0	0	0	0	1	0
40	1	1	1	1	1	1	0	0	1	1	0	1	1	1	1	1	1	0	1	0	0	1	1	1	0	1	1	0	1	1
41	0	0	0	1	1	1	1	1	1	1	0	1	1	1	1	1	1	1	1	0	1	0	1	0	1	1	1	1	1	1
42	1	1	1	1	1	1	0	0	0	1	1	1	0	1	1	1	0	1	1	1	1	1	1	0	0	1	1	0	1	0
43	0	0	0	0	1	1	1	1	1	0	1	0	1	1	1	1	1	1	1	0	0	0	1	1	1	1	1	1	1	1
44	0	1	0	1	1	0	0	0	1	0	1	1	0	1	1	1	0	0	0	1	1	1	0	0	1	1	0	0	1	1
45	0	0	0	0	0	0	0	1	1	1	0	0	0	0	0	1	1	1	1	0	0	0	0	0	1	1	1	1	0	1

Table 5.1b. *Subscores for the listening, reading, and grammar subtests*

ID	Listening	Reading	Grammar	Total
1	5	3	4	12
2	9	7	8	24
3	2	5	3	10
4	6	6	7	19
5	2	3	5	10
6	8	8	8	24
7	1	2	3	6
8	6	5	6	17
9	2	3	4	9
10	8	8	8	24
11	3	3	3	9
12	7	5	7	19
13	9	9	9	27
14	6	6	7	19
15	9	9	10	28
16	6	5	6	17
17	7	7	7	21
18	3	5	4	12
19	6	6	6	18
20	4	5	5	14
21	8	9	9	26
22	1	3	5	9
23	8	7	8	23
24	3	3	6	12
25	7	8	8	23
26	2	2	4	8
27	4	7	1	12
28	2	2	4	8
29	5	4	6	15
30	6	5	6	17
31	2	3	4	9
32	6	5	6	17
33	1	3	4	8
34	8	8	7	23
35	5	5	5	15
36	7	6	6	19
37	3	2	2	7
38	8	7	7	22
39	1	3	2	6
40	8	7	7	22
41	7	8	8	23
42	7	8	6	21
43	5	8	8	21
44	4	6	6	16
45	3	4	5	12
Mean	5.11	5.40	5.78	16.29
SD	2.51	2.14	2.02	6.27
n	45	45	45	45
k	10	10	10	30

the score relationships on the different subtests and get the scatter-plots shown in Figures 5.1, 5.2, and 5.3.

These plots indicate graphically that as a person's score on one of the subtests increases, the scores on the other subtests also increase. However, we can see that there are *outliers* in the data sample. For example, in Figure 5.2, one person had a score of 1 on the listening subtest but a score of 7 on the grammar subtest. Likewise, in Figure 5.3, one person got a score of 1 on the grammar subtest but a score of 4 on the reading subtest. Although all of the subtests appear to correlate, we need to see how much these outliers affect that correlation and determine just how strong the general relationship is between the different pairs of tests.

In order to quantify the degree of relationship in the plots of the variables above, we can calculate a correlation coefficient, generally designated as r_{xy}. A correlation coefficient can range from -1.00 to $+1.00$. Any *negative values* indicate that the two variables are inversely related, that is, as the value of one increases the other decreases. *Positive values*, on the other hand, indicate that as one variable increases so does the other. The Pearson product-moment correlation coefficient can be calculated as follows:

$$r_{xy} = \frac{\sum (X - M_x)(Y - M_y)}{N S_x S_y}$$

where: r_{xy} = Pearson product-moment correlation coefficient
X = each score on variable X
M_x = mean score for variable X
Y = each score on variable Y
M_y = mean score for variable Y
S_x = standard deviation for variable X
S_y = standard deviation for variable Y
N = number of examinees who took both tests

Steps for calculation of the correlation between the listening and reading subtests are shown in Table 5.2 (see pp. 158–9). There are eight columns in the table. The first column contains the examinee identification number. Column 2 contains the examinee's score on the listening subtest while column 5 shows the examinee's score on the reading subtest. Columns 3 and 6 provide the mean score of the listening and reading tests, respectively. Columns 4 and 7 indicate the extent to which the examinee differed from the mean score on each test ($X - M_x$ and $Y - M_y$). Finally, column 8 shows the product of the deviation scores presented in columns 4 and 7 $[(X - M_x)(Y - M_y)]$. These column 8 cross-products sum $[\sum (X - M_x)$

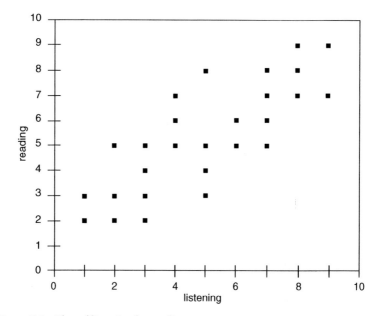

Figure 5.1. Plot of listening by reading

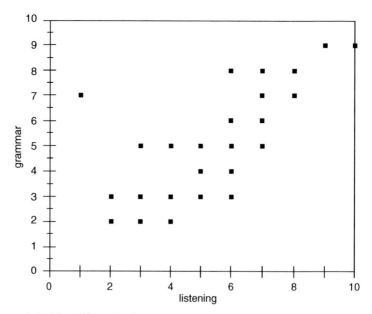

Figure 5.2. Plot of listening by grammar

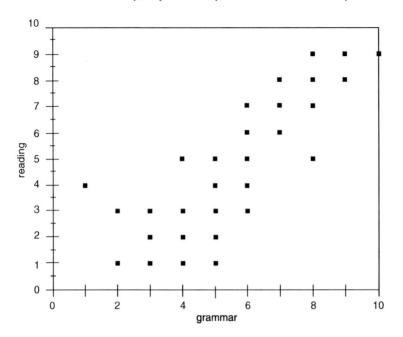

Figure 5.3. Plot of reading by grammar

$(Y - M_y)]$ to 207. At the bottom of the table, the calculation of NS_xS_y leads to 241.71.

To find the correlation between the listening and reading subtest scores, we simply divided the sum of the cross-products shown in column 8 $[\sum(X - M_x)(Y - M_y)]$ by the result of NS_xS_y or $\sum(X - M_x)(Y - M_y)/NS_xS_y = 207.00/241.71 = .8564 \approx .86$ (as shown at the bottom of Table 5.2). For the correlation between the listening and reading subtests, we find a coefficient of .86. This is a reasonably strong correlation for tests with 45 examinees and only 10 items on each subtest.

The full correlation matrix for the three subtests is given in Table 5.3. These correlations appear to be reasonably strong, although the relationship between the reading and the grammar subtests is weaker than the others. These relatively strong correlations indicate that the different subtests order the examinees in similar ways. Such ordering is a key concept in NRT reliability, as will be discussed in more detail.

There are two concerns in interpreting correlation coefficients. The first concern is whether this correlation is a result of error, that is, does it occur simply by chance on this administration. The second concern is related to whether the obtained correlation coefficient is

Table 5.2. *Calculation of correlation between listening and reading columns*

1	2	3	4	5	6	7	8
ID	X Listening	M_x	$X - M_x$	Y Reading	M_y	$Y - M_y$	$(X - M_x)(Y - M_y)$
1	5	5.11	−0.11	3	5.4	−2.4	0.26
2	9	5.11	3.89	7	5.4	1.6	6.22
3	2	5.11	−3.11	5	5.4	−0.4	1.24
4	6	5.11	0.89	6	5.4	0.6	0.53
5	2	5.11	−3.11	3	5.4	−2.4	7.46
6	8	5.11	2.89	8	5.4	2.6	7.51
7	1	5.11	−4.11	2	5.4	−3.4	13.97
8	6	5.11	0.89	5	5.4	−0.4	−0.36
9	2	5.11	−3.11	3	5.4	−2.4	7.46
10	8	5.11	2.89	8	5.4	2.6	7.51
11	3	5.11	−2.11	3	5.4	−2.4	5.06
12	7	5.11	1.89	5	5.4	−0.4	−0.76
13	9	5.11	3.89	9	5.4	3.6	14.00
14	6	5.11	0.89	6	5.4	0.6	0.53
15	9	5.11	3.89	9	5.4	3.6	14.00
16	6	5.11	0.89	5	5.4	−0.4	−0.36
17	7	5.11	1.89	7	5.4	1.6	3.02
18	3	5.11	−2.11	5	5.4	−0.4	0.84
19	6	5.11	0.89	6	5.4	0.6	0.53
20	4	5.11	−1.11	5	5.4	−0.4	0.44
21	8	5.11	2.89	9	5.4	3.6	10.40
22	1	5.11	−4.11	3	5.4	−2.4	9.86
23	8	5.11	2.89	7	5.4	1.6	4.62
24	3	5.11	−2.11	3	5.4	−2.4	5.06
25	7	5.11	1.89	8	5.4	2.6	4.91
26	2	5.11	−3.11	2	5.4	−3.4	10.57
27	4	5.11	−1.11	7	5.4	1.6	−1.78
28	2	5.11	−3.11	2	5.4	−3.4	10.57
29	5	5.11	−0.11	4	5.4	−1.4	0.15
30	6	5.11	0.89	5	5.4	−0.4	−0.36
31	2	5.11	−3.11	3	5.4	−2.4	7.46
32	6	5.11	0.89	5	5.4	−0.4	−0.36
33	1	5.11	−4.11	3	5.4	−2.4	9.86
34	8	5.11	2.89	8	5.4	2.6	7.51
35	5	5.11	−0.11	5	5.4	−0.4	0.04
36	7	5.11	1.89	6	5.4	0.6	1.13
37	3	5.11	−2.11	2	5.4	−3.4	7.17
38	8	5.11	2.89	7	5.4	1.6	4.62
39	1	5.11	−4.11	3	5.4	−2.4	9.86
40	8	5.11	2.89	7	5.4	1.6	4.62
41	7	5.11	1.89	8	5.4	2.6	4.91
42	7	5.11	1.89	8	5.4	2.6	4.91

43	5		5.11	−0.11	8		5.4	2.6	−0.29
44	4		5.11	−1.11	6		5.4	0.6	−0.67
45	3		5.11	−2.11	4		5.4	−1.4	2.95

$$\sum (X - M_x)(Y - M_y) = 207.00$$

$$NS_xS_y = 45(2.51)(2.14) = 241.713 \approx 241.71$$

$$r_{xy} = \frac{\sum (X - M_x)(Y - M_y)}{NS_xS_y} = \frac{207.00}{241.71} = .8564 \approx .86$$

Table 5.3. *Correlation matrix for the three subtests*

	Listening	Reading	Grammar
Listening	1.00	.86	.83
Reading	–	1.00	.78
Grammar	–	–	1.00

meaningful for our uses, that is, it may turn out that the correlation is not due to chance, but the magnitude of the correlation is not very high. These two concerns are addressed in different ways.

In order to determine whether the coefficient is statistically significant, that is, that it did not occur by chance alone, its value can be compared to the values in Table 5.4. Two decisions need to be made in using this table. First, a decision must be made regarding whether we are making a one-tailed (directional) decision or a two-tailed (non-directional) decision. A directional decision is used if either a positive or negative relationship is predicted on the basis of theory or previous empirical research. For example, if we were to hypothesize that there is a strong relationship between vocabulary and reading ability, then a directional decision would make sense, and those columns in the table should be used. However, if there is no known or theoretical relationship between the variables, for instance between hat size and attitude toward language learning, then we would have a non-directional decision and would use those columns in the table. In the listening, reading, and grammar data presented here, we can safely assume that since all of the variables are related to some concept of language and they are all measured on paper-and-pencil tests, they should be related to some degree in a positive direction. Thus, we look in the directional columns.

Note that the column on the far left begins with $N-2$, that is, the number of examinees is reduced by two in finding the appropriate

Table 5.4. *Critical values of the Pearson product-moment correlation coefficient*

(N−2)	Directional Decision: Sound reasons to expect either a positive or a negative correlation		Non-directional Decision: Do not know which direction correlation might be	
	95% Certainty p<.05	99% Certainty p<.01	95% Certainty p<.05	99% Certainty p<.01
1	.9877	.9995	.9969	1.0000
2	.9000	.9800	.9500	.9900
3	.8054	.9343	.8783	.9587
4	.7293	.8822	.8114	.9172
5	.6694	.8329	.7545	.8745
6	.6215	.7887	.7067	.8343
7	.5822	.7498	.6664	.7977
8	.5494	.7155	.6319	.7646
9	.5214	.6851	.6021	.7348
10	.4973	.6581	.5760	.7079
11	.4762	.6339	.5529	.6835
12	.4575	.6120	.5324	.6614
13	.4409	.5923	.5139	.6411
14	.4259	.5742	.4973	.6226
15	.4124	.5577	.4821	.6055
20	.3598	.4921	.4227	.5368
25	.3233	.4451	.3809	.4869
30	.2960	.4093	.3494	.4487
35	.2746	.3810	.3246	.4182
40	.2573	.3578	.3044	.3932
45	.2428	.3384	.2875	.3721
50	.2306	.3218	.2732	.3541
60	.2108	.2948	.2500	.3248
70	.1954	.2737	.2319	.3017
80	.1829	.2565	.2172	.2830
90	.1726	.2422	.2050	.2673
100	.1638	.2301	.1946	.2540

(adapted from Fisher & Yates, 1963)

level of significance. This reduction is related to the statistical issue of *degrees of freedom* (for explanations, see Brown, 1988a, or Hatch & Lazaraton, 1990). The question that is being asked in testing the significance of a correlation coefficient is whether the cluster of observations could have occurred by chance. We are examining a linear relationship between the two sets of data. Thus, in constructing the line, we identify two points at the extremes of the cluster, and draw a line (Henning, 1987). All of the other points are free to vary around that line, but the two initial points cannot vary at all. In essence, the correlation coefficient loses those two degrees of freedom, and that is why we subtract $N - 2$.

In using Table 5.4, one of two confidence levels is typically used: a 95% level of certainty or a 99% level of certainty. This choice centers around how serious an incorrect decision might be. In most educational contexts, the 95% confidence level is selected since any error in interpretation can be remedied without serious ramifications. However, if there is a context where an error would have serious implications, such as effectiveness of a medicine or airplane fuel use, then a 99% confidence level might be warranted. When we look at Table 5.4, because we have 45 people, we look at the value in the left-hand column that most closely corresponds below 43, in this case 40, then look over to the directional decision columns, and find a value of .2573 for the 95% level and .3578 for the 99% confidence level. The three correlation coefficients shown in Table 5.3 exceed both of these values, so those coefficients can be considered statistically significant at the 99% confidence level, or put another way, $p < .01$. If the coefficients had been less than the tabled values, they would not have been statistically significant.

The second concern when interpreting a correlation coefficient is whether the correlation is meaningful. In looking at Table 5.4, as the number of examinees increases, the value that is needed to reach significance clearly decreases. If there are 12 examinees, a value of .4575 is needed for a directional decision at the 95% level, while, in the case of 100 examinees, only a value of .1638 is needed. Thus, reaching significance is in part a function of the number of people in the study.

The correlation coefficient simply states whether the trends in the data are likely to have happened by chance alone, not whether the correlation is meaningful in any way. We are frequently left with the question of how high does a correlation have to be in order to be considered high, and how low does a correlation have to be to be considered low. As with many of the issues dealt with in language testing, the answer is usually "it depends". The correlation coefficient squared (r_{xx}^2) is known as the coefficient of determination (Brown, 1996). That value indicates how much of the variance in the two variables is shared variance. In short, it represents the amount of overlap between the two variables. In the examples above that equals $.84^2$, or .71, for the correlation between Reading and Listening, $.83^2$, or .69, for the correlation between Grammar and Listening, and .78[2], or .61, for the correlation between Grammar and Reading. Are these meaningful? In part, the meaningfulness depends upon what decisions and interpretations are going to be made on the basis of the information. If a program is going to commit considerable resources to changing the curriculum based on whether the correlations are significant or not, then these might not be considered meaningful. However, if a teacher is going to alter a lesson plan, it might be considered useful and meaningful information to be able to see any relationship at all between the variables.

Correlation is important in NRT reliability estimation. Generally, NRT reliability is estimated by determining the extent to which variables *covary*, that is, whether two forms of a test order examinees in the same way, whether the same test orders the examinees in the same way over two different administrations, or whether examinees are ordered in the same way across all of the different test items. The correlation coefficient is frequently used as an indicator of the extent to which such relationships exist. However, unlike correlation coefficients, reliability estimates are reported on a scale from 0 to 1.00, because, logically, a test cannot be any less reliable than 0. The details of the three main NRT reliability approaches will be discussed in the next three sections.

Test–retest reliability

An assumption underlying classical test theory is the notion of parallel tests. This assumption is that, under appropriate conditions of administrative control, observed scores on two administrations will be parallel. The classical definition of parallel for two administrations is that they will have equal means, equal variances, and equal correlations with an external criterion (Allen & Yen, 1979). Testing this assumption is one approach to establishing NRT reliability. This type of reliability, called *test–retest reliability*, examines the consistency of a test over time. The correlation of the scores between the two administrations is an indication of the test reliability. The assumption is that those factors that contribute to a low correlation represent error.

Several potential problems crop up when using the test–retest method. First, carry-over effects from the first administration can affect the second administration, particularly if the test contains non-trivial material. Second, the length of time between the two administrations must be long enough so examinees do not remember the material, but short enough so the examinees have not gone through any real changes, such as learning or mood fluctuation. Furthermore, simply obtaining a high correlation between the two scores only indicates that the examinees have been ordered in a similar manner on the two administrations, it does not mean that the examinees obtained similar raw scores. Because of these potential problems, test–retest reliability is seldom used in language testing.

Equivalent forms reliability

In order to avoid the problems with content contamination in the test–retest approach to reliability estimation, *equivalent forms reliability* is sometimes used. In this approach, different forms of a test are constructed. Both forms are designed to measure the same construct, sometimes consisting of items from a larger item pool. In constructing the equivalent forms, the statistical characteristics of the items must be well known. To calculate equivalent forms reliability, the two forms are administered to the same examinees, and the correlation coefficient between the scores is interpreted as the reliability estimate. Equivalent forms reliability is particularly of interest in settings which have clear objectives and item specifications that are used to generate test items. It provides some indication about the stability of the attributes that are being tested.

As with test–retest, practical problems occur when conducting equivalent forms reliability studies. First, it involves administering two forms of the test, which is a time-consuming process. Second, in many settings, generating truly parallel forms of a test is difficult. It involves piloting the items well ahead of time and building an item pool that can be used for selecting parallel items (see the previous chapter discussion of item response theory). Finally, in most practical instructional settings, a primary goal is to get students to improve their language as quickly as possible. Thus, there is a limit to the time span that can be allowed between administrations of the two forms. This can lead students to feel that they are constantly being tested.

Internal consistency

Both the test–retest and the equivalent forms approaches to reliability are subject to problems additional to those mentioned above. First, it is frequently difficult to get cooperation from the subjects. In a study in which one of the authors was involved, examinees took a test and then were to re-take the test during their regular class period after a two-week time span. During that time span, the examinees recognized that their grades did not depend upon their performance. They merely had to take the exam to get credit. So, in the interval between the administrations they colluded with one another and decided to answer all of the items on this multiple-choice test with option A. This lack of variance in the second test certainly interfered with determining the reliability through test–retest. A second drawback to test–retest or equivalent forms reliability is that some attrition inevitably occurs in such methods. Examinees fail to return for the second administration, either due to illness or by simply opting out of the process. Clearly, several potential advantages would accrue to being able to establish reliability from a single administration of a single test.

Such is the case with *internal consistency reliability* approaches, which examine how different parts of a single test relate to each other. Internal consistency approaches examine how two halves of a test correlate, or in some way estimate the average correlations among all individual items on the test across all of the examinees. Such approaches examine whether parts of a test behave in the same way in terms of ranking the examinees. Naturally, there are two assumptions underlying these reliability approaches. First, there must be more than one test part. If the test is a single item, such as a single essay composition, it is not possible to perform internal consistency estimates. Second, the test parts must be homogeneous in their content domain. If the test instrument is attempting to measure several different traits, internal consistency is not an appropriate approach. For example, batteries of subtests that measure attitude, aptitude, brain hemisphere dominance, listening ability, anxiety level, and hygiene would not necessarily be expected to demonstrate high internal consistency across the subtests unless the scores of each of these is the result of some external variable, such as socio-economic status. However, such heterogeneous tests are generally designed to measure different traits, so, while it might make sense to examine the internal consistency of each subtest separately, internal consistency reliability would not make sense across the subtests.

Generally, internal consistency estimates are made by using the split-half approach, or by using internal consistency formulas such as alpha, K-R20, K-R21, and the associated standard error of measurement.

Split-half reliability. The *split-half reliability* involves dividing the test into two halves, usually scoring the even numbered items and odd numbered items separately, and then examining the correlation between the two halves of the test. This is similar to the parallel forms approach to reliability, only the two forms are being administered on a single occasion. A major drawback of the split-half approach is that each half of the test is shorter than the whole test. Thus, the correlation between the two halves reflects the reliability of scores from half of the test. However, typically, the more items there are on a test, the higher the correlation will be. So, the reliability of a test is in part contingent upon its length. The Pearson correlation between the two tests will thus underestimate the reliability because the test has basically been reduced to half its actual length. In order to compensate for this, the resulting correlation is adjusted using the Spearman-Brown Prophecy formula, so named after the two people who independently developed the formula (Pedhazur & Schmelkin, 1991). The formula is as follows:

$$r_{xx} = \frac{2r_{x^1x^2}}{1 + r_{x^1x^2}}$$

where: r_{xx} = the reliability of the measure

$r_{x^1x^2}$ = the correlation coefficient between the two halves of the test

So, for the data set in Table 5.1a the correlation between the odd numbered items and the even numbered items is .86. The full-test reliability would be determined as follows:

$$r_{xx} = \frac{2(.86)}{1 + .86} = \frac{1.72}{1.86} = .92$$

It should be noted that the above formula is the split-half case of the more general Spearman-Brown formula which follows (Pedhazur & Schmelkin, 1991):

$$r_{kk} = \frac{kr_{x^1x^2}}{1 + (k - 1)r_{x^1x^2}}$$

where: k = the factor by which the test is to be increased or decreased

r_{kk} = the estimated reliability of a test k times longer or shorter

$r_{x^1x^2}$ = the half test reliability (correlation coefficient between the two halves of the test)

This more general formula can be used to estimate what level of reliability might be obtained if a test is increased in length by a number of multiples, or reduced in length by a number of multiples. In other words, if a language program is interested in making its existing examinations shorter in order to save time or in order to introduce an additional type of test, it can estimate the potential effect of making the test shorter. However, the basic assumption is that any additional items or the items that are reduced are parallel to the existing test. For example, when applied to the data set in Table 5.1a, where the half test correlation was .86, if we wanted to know what the reliability would be if we increased the length of the test by five times its length (instead of two times), the reliability estimate would be:

$$r_{kk} = \frac{5(.86)}{1 + (5 - 1).86} = \frac{4.30}{1 + 3.44} = \frac{4.30}{4.44} = .968$$

Alpha, K-R20, and K-R21. The split-half method of estimating reliability can sometimes be problematic in that the two halves of the test should be homogeneous. Using the odd and even numbered items is an attempt to make the two halves homogeneous. That strategy minimizes the problem that occurs if, for instance, the first half of the test is selected as one half and the second part of the test is selected as the second half. Not only might there be differences in content in the two halves, but the second half would likely be more affected by fatigue. Likewise, in a test with items ordered in terms of their difficulty, even taking odd and even numbers as the basis for the halves might lead to the even numbered half being more difficult than the odd numbered half. One way around these problems is to have the parts that are compared essentially be every item on the test. In this way, there are as many comparisons as there are items. Cronbach's α (*alpha*) is an approach to establishing reliability in this way. It sometimes takes the following form:

$$\alpha = \frac{k}{k - 1} \left(1 - \frac{\sum pq}{S_x^2} \right)$$

where: k = number of items on the test
S_x^2 = the variance of the total score
p = the proportion of examinees who got the item correct
q = the proportion of examinees who got the item incorrect

The equation above is for dichotomously scored items and is generally known as K-R20, the Kuder-Richardson 20 formula. It is a stronger reliability estimate than the split-half approach in that it takes into account the inter-relationships among all items. When applied to the data set in Tables 5.1a and b, the reliability is calculated as follows:

$$\alpha = \frac{30}{29} \left(1 - \frac{6.57}{6.27^2} \right) = 1.0345 \left(1 - \frac{6.57}{39.31} \right) = 1.0345(1 - .1671)$$
$$= 1.0345(.8329) = .862$$

A final NRT estimate of reliability is the Kuder-Richardson coefficient 21, known as K-R21. This is an estimate that can be made by merely having access to the score mean, standard deviation, and number of items. Computationally it is much simpler than the approaches just discussed:

$$K - R21 = \frac{k}{k - 1} \left(1 - \frac{M(k - M)}{kS^2} \right)$$

where: k = number of items on the test
        M = the mean
        S^2 = the variance of the total score

For the data above, this would yield:

$$K - R21 = \frac{30}{29} \left(1 - \frac{16.29(30 - 16.29)}{30(39.31)} \right) = 1.034 \left(1 - \frac{223.34}{1179.30} \right)$$
$$= 1.0345(1 - .1894) = .839$$

The K-R21 procedure is generally an underestimate to the reliability of a test. Basically, it assumes that all items have the same item difficulty. To the extent that items vary in their difficulty, the K-R21 value will decrease. However, it is useful if item data are not available, and is helpful in interpreting research reports that present descriptive statistics but fail to report the reliability of the instruments used.

The standard error of measurement. Closely associated with concerns of reliability are concerns about how the strength of consistency, or lack thereof, affects how representative an observed score is of the examinee's *true score*, or true ability. This is an issue of the precision of measurement (Kane, 1996). If an examinee obtains an observed score of 25 on the test we have been examining, but the reliability of the test administration is .862, how sure are we that a score of 25 is reflective of the examinee's true ability. The *standard error of measurement (SEM)* represents a confidence interval around the examinee's score within which we feel confident the examinee's score would fall if we administered the test to the examinee many times. We assume that errors are normally distributed around the examinee's scores and that the variability is constant for all scores. The formula for the *SEM* is as follows:

$$SEM = S_x \sqrt{1 - r_{xx}}$$

where: SEM = standard error of measurement
  S_x = standard deviation of the test
  r_{xx} = the reliability of the test

Using the K-R20 estimate obtained above, the SEM for the data in Table 5.1a would be:

$$SEM = 6.27\sqrt{1 - .862} = 6.27\sqrt{.138} = 6.27(.3715) = 2.329$$

This value can be interpreted as a standard deviation of the examinee's scores across multiple administrations. So, for the examinee with an observed score of 25, we can assume with a 68% confidence that the true score is ± 2.329 on either side of the observed score of 25. In this case, we can be 68% certain that the examinee's true score is between 22.671 and 27.329. Thus, while the reliability coefficient is helpful as an indicator of test consistency, the confidence interval represented by the SEM provides information about the precision of interpreting any particular score. The SEM provides an awareness that observed scores contain some amount of error and that we should take due care in interpreting the differences between scores.

CRT dependability

As noted earlier, one of the major concerns for CRT has been the development of an appropriate method for estimating the consistency of decisions. As early as 1969, Popham and Husek pointed out the potential inappropriateness of classical test theory reliability for CRT. CRT tests tend to be used in settings designed to produce the largest number of "low scores" (i.e., pre-test scores) or "high scores" (i.e., mastery of a well-defined domain). The resulting potential restriction of range causes a reduction in observed variance which, in turn, lowers reliability as estimated by correlation of scores between parallel tests, between scores derived from repeated administrations of the same test, or internal consistency estimates (Allen & Yen, 1979). In addition, CRT tests which measure specified domains tend to be shorter than traditional NRT tests, and this poses further problems for accurately estimating reliability using traditional statistics given that the longer a test is, the higher its reliability will likely to be.

Whereas NRT results are concerned with *relative decisions* (i.e., decisions based on their standing among examinees relative to each other, such as admissions or placement decisions), a CRT approach is primarily concerned with the consistency of *absolute decisions* (i.e., decisions based on the amount of material they know regardless of their relative standing) (Hambleton, 1994). Many researchers in CRT thus avoid the term *reliability* in favor of the terms *dependability* or *agreement*. We will use the term *dependability*, with the associated notions of *agreement*, rather than the term *reliability* in this book. We choose this path because many of the indices used in the CRT approach fall outside of classical test theory assumptions. For example, they do not necessarily assume parallel forms and/or they are not defined in terms of the traditional ratio of true score variance to observed score variance. These CRT indices can be classified (after Berk, 1980c and Hambleton et al, 1978) into two main categories: threshold-loss agreement methods and generalizability theory approaches.

Threshold-loss agreement methods

Subkoviak (1980) reviews the *threshold-loss agreement methods*. These all involve calculation of the agreement coefficient (p_o) and the kappa coefficient (κ), where p_o is the proportion of examinees consistently classified as masters or non-masters (or some other non-overlapping intervals of mastery), and κ is the proportion of consistent classifications beyond that expected by chance. Thus, p_o represents the proportion of decision consistency that occurs for whatever reason on two tests, while κ represents the proportion of decision consistency attributable solely to the test. For example, a cut-score could be set at either 100% or 0% for a set of test results. The outcome of classifying examinees as either masters or non-masters would likely to be perfect consistency. There would either be all masters or all non-masters. This represents the value of p_o. However, the amount of consistency is not due to the test itself. The value of κ would represent this, and would consequently be a low value. It is important to examine both coefficients in evaluating a test. This correction for chance in coefficient κ has been criticized because it assumes that the attained percentage of masters is the chance percentage for the test (see Berk, 1980c). That is, if 90% of the examinees were classified as masters on the initial test, then 90% would be used as the chance estimate for the second test. While always lower than p_o, κ tends to be higher if the cut score used to assign mastery/non-mastery is near the test mean, whereas p_o tends to be lower at this point. It should be pointed out that the threshold-loss agreement approaches do assume parallel forms (like NRT reliability approaches). Furthermore, these indices assume that the consequences associated with classification errors are equally serious at all distances from the cut score. Brown (1996) presents a convenient way to calculate p_o and κ based on methods developed by Subkoviak (1980) and by Huynh (1976, 1978). Assume that there have been two administrations of a test in a test–retest situation. The tests are close enough in time that no learning has taken place, yet far enough apart that the examinees do not remember the content of the test (not an easy task). The examinees are classified as masters or non-masters on the two tests. There are four possible outcomes for the classification of each examinee as indicated in Figure 5.4.

Thus, an examinee could be classified as a:

1. master on both administrations of the test (A);
2. master on the first administration but a non-master on the second administration (B);
3. non-master on the first administration and master on the second administration (C); or
4. non-master on both administrations (D).

Categories A and D represent consistency, while categories B and C represent inconsistencies. The formula for calculating p_o is:

$$p_o = \frac{A + D}{N}$$

where: p_o = agreement coefficient
A = number of examinees in cell A
D = number of examinees in cell D
N = total number of examinees

In examining the consistency due to the test itself, κ can be estimated as follows:

$$\kappa = \frac{p_o - p_{chance}}{1 - p_{chance}}$$

where: κ = coefficient kappa
p_o = agreement coefficient
p_{chance} = proportion of consistent classifications that could be due to chance

Thus, it is necessary to estimate the chance factor in order to arrive at κ. This value is obtained as follows:

$$p_{chance} = \frac{(A + B)^*(A + C) + (C + D)^*(B + D)}{N^2}$$

| | | Time 2 | | |
		Masters	Non-masters	
	Masters	A	B	A + B
Time 1	Non-masters	C	D	C + D
		A + C	B + D	A + B + C + D

Figure 5.4. Possible outcomes for mastery/non-mastery on two administrations

Suppose the examinees represented by the current data set took the examination a second time. Their results are indicated in Table 5.5.

Of the 45 examinees, 13 are classified in category A, 2 in category B, 5 in category C, and 25 in category D. The agreement coefficient would be:

$$p_o = \frac{A + D}{N} = \frac{13 + 25}{45} = \frac{38}{45} = .84$$

There is, then, 84% consistent classification of examinees across the two administrations. That represents a fairly strong consistency in the way examinees are classified. However, it is also important to determine the proportion of those consistent classifications that are beyond chance. That value is calculated as follows:

$$p_{chance} = \frac{(A + B)^*(A + C) + (C + D)^*(B + D)}{N^2}$$

$$r = \frac{(13 + 2)^*(13 + 5) + (5 + 25)^*(2 + 25)}{45^2} = \frac{(15^*18) + (30^*27)}{2025}$$

$$r = \frac{(270) + (810)}{2025} = \frac{1080}{2025} = .53$$

This indicates that 53% of the consistent classification could occur by chance alone. When that value is inserted into the formula for kappa, the following agreement coefficient is obtained:

$$\kappa = \frac{p_o - p_{chance}}{1 - p_{chance}} = \frac{.84 - .53}{1 - .53} = \frac{.31}{.47} = .66$$

Table 5.5. *Hypothetical results on two administrations of the same CRT*

ID	Time 1	Time 2	Classification
1	12	17	D
2	24	22	A
3	10	14	D
4	19	20	D
5	10	9	D
6	24	25	A
7	6	8	D
8	17	22	C
9	9	11	D
10	24	23	A
11	9	10	D
12	19	22	C
13	27	28	A
14	19	20	D
15	28	29	A
16	17	22	C
17	21	22	A
18	12	15	D
19	18	15	D
20	14	14	D
21	26	28	A
22	9	11	D
23	23	24	A
24	12	13	D
25	23	22	A
26	8	9	D
27	12	11	D
28	8	8	D
29	15	14	D
30	17	18	D
31	9	9	D
32	17	21	C
33	8	9	D
34	23	22	A
35	15	18	D
36	19	21	C
37	7	8	D
38	22	22	A
39	6	6	D
40	22	23	A
41	23	21	A
42	21	19	B
43	21	20	B
44	16	14	D
45	12	16	D

Thus, while 53% of the consistency could have occurred by chance, in fact 66% of the consistent classification is not due to chance. It is due to the effects of the measurement.

As with the NRT test–retest reliability procedure, this method of establishing consistency requires two administrations of the same test. As noted, any multiple administration approach is prone to carryover effects, particularly with more complex language assessment. It is also a rather cumbersome and time-consuming exercise. Brown (1996) presents a method by Subkoviak (1980), again based on Huynh (1978), for determining p_o and κ from the results of a single test administration. This approach utilizes tabled values, which require only a reliability estimate and basic descriptive statistics from the test. The formula for approximating the two coefficients begins with an estimation of the z score for the cut-score that is used to make classifications. That formula is as follows:

$$z = \frac{c - .5 - M}{S}$$

where: z = standardized cut-score
         c = raw cut-score
       M = test mean
        S = test standard deviation
       $.5$ = a constant adjustment factor

After obtaining the z score that corresponds to the cut-score, it is necessary to calculate one of the NRT reliability estimates. With these two values, it is possible to enter the Tables 5.6 and 5.7 and estimate both p_o and κ. Notice in Tables 5.6 and 5.7, for a test that has a standardized cut-score of 1.00 and a K-R20 of .90, the p_o value would be .91 and κ would be .68. Notice that as the values for z increase, the estimates for p_o increase while the estimates for κ decrease. This reflects the information that each coefficient provides. The p_o coefficient indicates how many consistent classifications there are, in part a function of the distance of the cut-score from the mean, while κ provides information about how much of the consistent classification is due to the test, in part a function of the test consistency.

For the data set we are examining here, with a cut-score of 21 (70%), we have the following:

$$z = \frac{c - .5 - M}{S} = \frac{21 - .5 - 16.29}{6.27} = \frac{4.21}{6.27} = .67$$

Table 5.6. *Approximate values of the agreement coefficient*

z	Reliability (r_{xx})								
	.10	.20	.30	.40	.50	.60	.70	.80	.90
.00	.53	.56	.60	.63	.67	.70	.75	.80	.86
.10	.53	.57	.60	.63	.67	.71	.75	.80	.86
.20	.54	.57	.61	.64	.67	.71	.75	.80	.86
.30	.56	.59	.62	.65	.68	.72	.76	.80	.86
.40	.58	.60	.63	.66	.69	.73	.77	.81	.87
.50	.60	.62	.65	.68	.71	.74	.78	.82	.87
.60	.62	.65	.67	.70	.73	.76	.79	.83	.88
.70	.65	.67	.70	.72	.75	.77	.80	.84	.89
.80	.68	.70	.72	.74	.77	.79	.82	.85	.90
.90	.71	.73	.75	.77	.79	.81	.84	.87	.90
1.00	.75	.76	.77	.77	.81	.83	.85	.88	.91
1.10	.78	.79	.80	.81	.83	.85	.87	.89	.92
1.20	.80	.81	.82	.84	.85	.86	.88	.90	.93
1.30	.83	.84	.85	.86	.87	.88	.90	.91	.94
1.40	.86	.86	.87	.88	.89	.90	.91	.93	.95
1.50	.88	.88	.89	.90	.90	.91	.92	.94	.95
1.60	.90	.90	.91	.91	.92	.93	.93	.95	.96
1.70	.92	.92	.92	.93	.93	.94	.95	.95	.97
1.80	.93	.93	.94	.94	.94	.95	.95	.96	.97
1.90	.95	.95	.95	.95	.95	.96	.96	.97	.98
2.00	.96	.96	.96	.96	.96	.97	.97	.97	.98

(adapted from Subkoviak, 1988)

Entering Tables 5.6 and 5.7 respectively with a K-R20 of .862 and a z of .67, we arrive at an agreement coefficient of approximately .85 and a κ of approximately .63. These values are reasonably close to the values obtained from the two-test administration calculated above.

At first perusal of the literature, using Subkoviak's tables would appear to be relatively safe; as Berk put it, Subkoviak's approach "provides relatively precise though conservatively biased estimates of p_o and κ" (p. 245). However, in interpreting the results of Subkoviak's method, it is also important to take into account Berk's (1984) two warnings: (a) ". . . since the estimates are based on only one test administration, they do not reflect all sources of instability across repeated testings," and (b) "the method may overestimate decision consistency even though the estimates of the parameters are conservatively biased" (both quotes on p. 245).

Table 5.7. *Approximate values of the kappa coefficient*

z	Reliability (r_{xx})								
	.10	.20	.30	.40	.50	.60	.70	.80	.90
.00	.06	.13	.19	.26	.33	.41	.49	.59	.71
.10	.06	.13	.19	.26	.33	.41	.49	.59	.71
.20	.06	.13	.19	.26	.33	.41	.49	.59	.71
.30	.06	.12	.19	.26	.33	.40	.49	.59	.71
.40	.06	.12	.19	.25	.32	.40	.48	.58	.71
.50	.06	.12	.18	.25	.32	.40	.48	.58	.70
.60	.06	.12	.18	.24	.31	.39	.47	.57	.70
.70	.05	.11	.17	.24	.31	.38	.47	.57	.70
.80	.05	.11	.17	.23	.30	.37	.46	.56	.69
.90	.05	.10	.16	.22	.29	.36	.45	.55	.68
1.00	.05	.10	.15	.21	.28	.35	.44	.54	.68
1.10	.04	.09	.14	.20	.27	.34	.43	.53	.67
1.20	.04	.08	.14	.19	.26	.33	.42	.52	.66
1.30	.04	.08	.13	.18	.25	.32	.41	.51	.65
1.40	.03	.07	.12	.17	.23	.31	.39	.50	.64
1.50	.03	.07	.11	.16	.22	.29	.38	.49	.63
1.60	.03	.06	.06	.15	.21	.28	.37	.47	.62
1.70	.02	.05	.09	.14	.20	.27	.35	.46	.61
1.80	.02	.05	.08	.13	.18	.25	.34	.45	.60
1.90	.02	.04	.08	.12	.17	.24	.32	.43	.59
2.00	.02	.04	.07	.11	.16	.22	.31	.42	.58

(adapted from Subkoviak, 1988)

Generalizability theory and domain score dependability

Generalizability theory (G theory) was originally introduced in educational measurement circles by Cronbach, Rajaratnam, and Gleser (1963). Bolus, Hinofotis, and Bailey (1982) should be credited with first suggesting the use of G theory to help in improving the reliability of language tests. Brown (1984c) actually used G theory to investigate the effects of numbers of items and numbers of passages on the dependability of an engineering English reading comprehension test. Brown and Bailey (1984) reported on a study of the effect of numbers of raters and numbers of scoring categories on the dependability of writing scores. Later, Stansfield and Kenyon (1992) used G theory to study the effects of numbers of tests and numbers of raters on the dependability of oral proficiency interview scores. Brown (1990a, 1993) used G theory to estimate score dependability in criterion-referenced language tests. Kunnan (1992) also applied G theory to a criterion-referenced test at UCLA. Bachman, Lynch, and Mason (1995) used G-theory to study the variability in test tasks and rater judgments on a speaking test. Brown and Ross (1996) studied the contributions of item types, sections, and tests to the dependability of norm-referenced TOEFL scores. And most recently, Brown (1999) investigated the relative contributions of various numbers of persons, items, subtests, languages, and their various interactions to TOEFL score reliability.

In *generalizability theory*, reliability or dependability is a question of generalizing from one observation to a universe of observations (Cronbach, Gleser, Nanda, & Rajaratnam, 1972, p. 15). G-theory takes the view that an observed score is the *universe score* and allows for generalizing from a specific sample to the universe of interest by means of a set of clearly defined estimation procedures (Shavelson & Webb, 1981, pp. 133–137).

Single source of variance. In its most basic form, generalizability theory provides a conceptual framework for assessing a single *facet*, or source of measurement error, within a given testing situation. The first step is a *generalizability study* (G study), in which analysis of variance (ANOVA) procedures are used to estimate the variance components for persons and items.

Consider, for example, a set of results from the achievement test (form A) administered at the end of the intermediate level ELI reading course (ELI 72) at UHM. The items were developed by the course teachers to test the particular objectives of ELI 72. The teachers administered the test to 42 students during their regular final examination period in its original 46-item format. A subset of 30 items was then selected on the basis of difference indexes to create a better, revised version of the test. The results shown in Table 5.8 are for the 30-item revised version of the test (for more on this test, see Brown 1990a, 1993).

In the overall G study of these data, we began by conducting an analysis of variance (ANOVA) procedure. In reanalyzing these data for this book, we used the SPSS for Windows (version 10) statistical program to perform a repeated-measures ANOVA in the general linear model (GLM) module with items as levels of the repeated variable and persons' ID numbers (1–42) as the between subjects factor. We took the sums of squares, degrees of freedom, and mean squares shown in Table 5.9 for items and the persons-by-items interaction directly from the within-subjects effects table in the printout and took the same statistics for persons from the table for within-subjects effects (to see how this works, try entering our data

Table 5.8. *Example data set for G study (ELI 72 reading course final achievement test)*

ID	I01	I02	I03	I04	I05	I06	I07	I08	I09	I10	I11	I12	I13	I14	I15	I16	I17	I18	I19	I20	I21	I22	I23	I24	I25	I26	I27	I28	I29	I30	Total
33	1	1	1	1	1	1	1	1	1	1	1	1	1	1	1	1	0	1	1	1	1	1	1	1	1	1	1	1	1	1	29
3	1	1	0	1	1	1	1	1	1	1	1	1	1	1	1	1	0	1	1	1	1	1	1	1	1	1	1	1	1	1	28
39	1	1	1	1	1	1	1	1	1	1	1	1	1	1	1	1	1	1	1	1	1	0	1	1	0	0	1	1	1	1	27
15	1	1	1	0	1	1	1	1	1	1	1	1	0	1	1	1	1	1	1	1	1	0	1	0	1	1	1	1	1	1	26
5	1	0	1	1	1	1	1	1	1	0	1	1	1	1	1	1	1	1	1	1	0	1	1	0	1	1	1	1	1	1	26
9	1	1	1	1	1	0	1	1	1	0	1	1	1	1	1	1	1	0	1	1	1	1	1	1	1	1	1	1	0	1	26
2	1	0	0	1	1	1	1	1	1	0	1	1	1	1	1	1	1	1	1	1	1	0	1	1	1	1	1	1	1	1	26
40	1	1	1	1	1	1	1	0	1	0	1	1	0	1	1	1	1	1	1	1	1	1	1	0	1	1	0	1	1	1	25
31	1	1	0	1	1	1	1	1	1	1	1	1	0	1	1	1	0	1	1	1	1	0	1	1	1	1	0	1	1	1	25
16	1	1	1	1	1	1	1	1	1	0	1	1	1	0	0	1	0	1	1	1	1	1	1	0	1	1	1	1	1	1	25
12	1	1	0	1	1	1	1	1	1	0	0	1	0	1	1	1	0	1	1	1	0	1	1	1	1	1	1	1	1	1	24
25	1	1	0	1	1	1	1	0	1	1	1	0	1	1	1	1	0	1	1	1	0	0	1	0	1	1	1	1	1	1	23
42	1	1	0	1	1	1	1	1	1	0	1	1	0	1	1	1	0	1	1	1	1	0	1	0	1	1	0	1	1	1	23
38	1	1	1	1	1	0	1	1	1	1	1	0	0	0	1	1	1	1	1	1	1	0	1	0	1	1	0	1	1	1	23
22	1	0	0	1	1	1	1	1	1	0	1	1	1	1	0	1	0	1	1	1	1	0	1	1	1	0	1	1	1	1	23
10	1	1	0	1	1	1	1	0	1	0	1	0	1	1	1	1	0	1	1	1	1	0	1	0	1	1	1	1	1	1	23
18	1	1	0	1	1	1	1	0	1	1	1	1	1	1	1	1	0	1	1	1	1	0	1	0	1	0	0	1	1	1	23
32	1	1	0	1	1	0	1	0	1	1	1	1	1	1	1	1	1	0	1	1	1	0	1	0	1	1	0	1	1	1	23
13	1	1	0	1	1	1	1	0	1	1	1	1	0	1	1	1	1	1	1	1	1	0	1	0	1	0	0	1	1	1	23
41	1	1	1	1	0	1	1	0	1	0	1	1	1	1	1	1	1	1	1	1	1	0	1	0	1	0	0	1	1	1	23
8	1	1	1	1	1	1	0	1	1	1	0	1	1	1	1	1	1	0	1	1	0	0	1	0	1	1	0	1	1	1	23
1	0	1	1	1	1	1	1	0	1	0	1	0	1	1	1	1	0	1	0	1	1	0	0	1	1	1	1	1	1	1	22
11	0	1	0	1	1	1	1	0	1	1	0	1	1	1	1	1	0	1	1	1	0	1	0	1	0	1	0	1	1	1	21
26	1	1	0	1	1	0	1	0	1	0	1	0	1	1	1	1	0	1	1	1	1	1	1	0	1	0	0	1	1	1	21
30	1	1	0	1	0	0	1	1	1	0	1	0	1	1	1	1	0	1	1	1	1	0	1	1	0	1	0	1	1	1	21
14	1	1	0	0	0	1	1	1	1	0	0	0	1	1	1	1	0	1	1	1	1	1	1	0	1	1	0	1	1	1	21

177

Table 5.8. (contd)

ID	101	102	103	104	105	106	107	108	109	110	111	112	113	114	115	116	117	118	119	120	121	122	123	124	125	126	127	128	129	130	Total
34	1	1	1	1	1	1	1	1	0	1	1	1	0	1	1	1	0	1	1	1	1	0	0	1	1	1	0	1	0	0	21
35	1	1	1	1	1	1	1	1	0	0	0	1	0	1	1	1	1	1	1	1	1	1	0	1	1	0	0	1	0	0	21
27	0	1	0	0	1	0	1	1	0	0	0	1	1	1	0	1	1	1	1	1	0	1	1	1	1	1	1	1	0	0	21
24	0	1	0	0	0	1	1	0	1	1	1	0	1	0	1	1	1	1	1	1	0	0	1	1	0	1	0	1	0	0	21
7	0	0	0	0	1	0	1	1	0	1	1	1	0	1	1	0	1	1	1	1	0	0	0	1	1	1	0	1	1	1	20
6	1	1	1	0	1	1	1	1	0	0	0	1	1	1	1	1	1	1	1	1	1	0	0	1	1	1	0	1	1	1	19
29	0	0	0	1	1	1	1	1	0	0	0	1	1	1	1	1	1	1	0	1	0	1	0	1	0	0	0	1	1	0	19
17	0	1	1	0	0	1	1	0	0	0	0	1	1	1	0	1	0	1	1	0	1	1	0	0	1	1	0	0	1	0	19
20	0	0	0	1	1	1	0	1	0	1	1	0	0	0	0	0	1	1	1	1	0	1	0	1	0	1	0	1	0	1	18
23	1	1	1	1	0	1	1	1	1	0	1	0	0	1	1	1	1	1	1	1	1	0	0	0	0	0	0	1	1	0	17
36	0	0	0	0	1	0	1	1	0	1	0	0	1	1	0	1	0	1	1	1	1	0	0	0	0	1	0	1	1	1	16
37	0	0	0	0	1	1	1	1	0	0	0	0	1	1	1	1	1	1	1	1	1	0	0	0	0	1	0	1	1	1	16
4	0	1	0	0	1	1	1	0	0	0	1	1	1	1	1	1	1	1	1	1	0	0	0	0	0	1	1	1	1	1	15
19	1	1	0	0	0	0	0	1	0	0	0	0	1	1	0	1	1	1	0	0	0	0	0	0	0	0	1	1	1	1	14
21	0	1	0	1	0	0	0	0	0	1	0	0	1	0	0	0	1	0	0	0	0	0	1	0	0	0	0	0	0	1	7
28	1	0	0	0	0	0	1	0	0	0	0	0	0	0	1	0	0	1	0	0	0	1	0	0	0	0	0	0	1	0	7

$$M = 21.2857$$
$$S = 4.6511$$
$$\text{K-R20} = .776296$$

Table 5.9. *ANOVA for persons by items (p × i) G study*

Source	SS	df	MS
persons	30.2857	41	.7386756
items	32.9238	29	1.1353034
p × i	196.4762	1189	.1652449
total	259.6857	1259	

Table 5.10. *Calculating estimated variance components for persons by items (p × i) G study*

Variance component	Estimated mean squares		Variance component calculations	Estimate
$\hat{\sigma}_p^2$	=	$[MS(p) - MS(pi)]/n_i$	= $[.7386756 - .1652449]/30$	= .0191143
$\hat{\sigma}_i^2$	=	$[MS(i) - MS(pi)]/n_p$	= $[1.1353034 - .1652449]/42$	= .0230966
$\hat{\sigma}_{pi}^2$	=	$MS(pi)$	= .1652449	= .1652449

and running the analysis in SPSS or some similar statistical analysis program).

Note that Table 5.9 does not show the *F* and *p* values that some readers may have expected to find on the right side of such a table. *F* and *p* values are not necessary or appropriate in reporting G-study results. As Brennan (1983) put it:

In generalizability theory the magnitudes of estimated variance components are of central importance, rather than their estimated statistical significance at some preassigned level. Even if an estimated variance component does not possess statistical significance, the usual procedure for estimating it yields an unbiased estimate. As such, it is better to use the estimate than to replace it by zero (Cronbach et al, 1972, p. 192). In particular, generalizability theory emphatically does *not* involve performing *F* tests on the ratios of mean squares. In generalizability theory, mean squares are used simply to estimate variance components. (p. 14)

We then used the mean squares in the ANOVA and the estimated mean squares equations from Brennan (1983) to estimate the G-study variance components (as shown in Table 5.10):

1. Starting at the bottom of Table 5.10, the variance component for the persons-by-items interaction was exactly the same as the mean squares for that interaction, .1652449.

2. Moving up the table, we calculated the items variance component by subtracting the mean square for items minus that for the interaction of persons and items $(1.1353034 - .1652449)$ and dividing the result by the number of persons (42), which equals .0230966.

3. Moving still further up the table, we calculated the persons variance component by subtracting the mean square for persons minus that for the interaction of persons and items $(.7386756 - .1652449)$ and dividing the result by the number of items (30), which equals .0191143.

Next, using the variance components in Table 5.10, we were able to calculate the appropriate generalizability coefficient in what is called a *decision study* (D study) – a study to determine the effects of various possible test designs on the generalizability coefficients associated with them. In the same sense that classical theory reliability was described above as the ratio of true score variance to observed score variance (with observed score variance being made up of true score variance plus error variance), a *generalizability coefficient* (G coefficient) is the ratio of universe score variance to observed score variance, where universe score variance is that variance attributable to persons and observed score variance is that variance attributable to both persons and error. Thus the G coefficient, represented by the none-too-transparent symbol $E\rho^2$, is the ratio of observed score variance to observed score variance plus error, or the variance components for persons to persons plus error as follows:

$$E\rho^2 = \frac{\hat{\sigma}_p^2}{\hat{\sigma}_p^2 + \hat{\sigma}_e^2}$$

Where: $E\rho^2$ = G coefficient

$\hat{\sigma}_p^2$ = variance component for persons

$\hat{\sigma}_e^2$ = error variance

In generalizability theory, the observed score variance is defined as the variance component due to persons regardless of the type of test. However, error variance is defined differently for norm-referenced tests and criterion-referenced tests, and for different sorts of G-study designs.

For **norm-referenced tests** error is typically labeled $\hat{\sigma}_\delta^2$. Thus the formula for the G coefficient for a norm-referenced test can be expressed as follows:

$$E\rho^2(\delta) = \frac{\hat{\sigma}_p^2}{\hat{\sigma}_p^2 + \hat{\sigma}_\delta^2}$$

Where: $E\rho^2(\delta)$ = G coefficient for relative decisions, i.e., for norm-referenced tests

$\hat{\sigma}_p^2$ = variance component for persons

$\hat{\sigma}_\delta^2$ = error variance for relative decisions, i.e., norm-referenced error

In the simplest possible one facet G study, a persons-by-items G study, norm-referenced error, $\hat{\sigma}_\delta^2$, is a single facet defined as the variance component for the interaction of persons-by-items divided by the number of items ($\hat{\sigma}_\delta^2 = \hat{\sigma}_{pi}^2/n_i$). Given that $\hat{\sigma}_\delta^2 = \frac{\hat{\sigma}_{pi}^2}{n_i}$, the norm-referenced G-coefficient can be further specified as:

$$E\rho^2(\delta) = \frac{\hat{\sigma}_p^2}{\hat{\sigma}_p^2 + \dfrac{\hat{\sigma}_{pi}^2}{n_i}}$$

Where: $\hat{\sigma}_{pi}^2$ = variance component for the persons-by-items interaction
n_i = number of items

Thus for the example data in Table 5.8, using the variance component estimates from Table 5.10 and what we know about the number of items on the test, we can calculate the norm-referenced G coefficient as follows:

$$E\rho^2(\delta) = \frac{\hat{\sigma}_p^2}{\hat{\sigma}_p^2 + \dfrac{\hat{\sigma}_{pi}^2}{n_i}} = \frac{.0191143}{.0191143 + \dfrac{.1652449}{30}} = \frac{0.191143}{.0191143 + .0055081}$$

$$= \frac{.0191143}{.0246224} = .7762971 \approx .78$$

For criterion-referenced tests in this one facet persons-by-items G-study, error is typically labeled $\hat{\sigma}_\Delta^2$. Thus the formula for the G-coefficient reliability estimate for a criterion-referenced test can be expressed as follows:

$$E\rho^2(\Delta) = \frac{\hat{\sigma}_p^2}{\hat{\sigma}_p^2 + \hat{\sigma}_\Delta^2}$$

Where: $E\rho^2(\Delta)$ = G-coefficient for absolute decisions, i.e., for criterion-referenced tests

$$\hat{\sigma}_p^2 = \text{variance component for persons}$$

$$\hat{\sigma}_\Delta^2 = \text{error variance for absolute decisions, i.e., criterion-referenced error}$$

Because CRTs are concerned with absolute decisions (in the form of absolute error, $\hat{\sigma}_\Delta^2$) and because generalizability theory is not restricted by all of the assumptions of classical test theory, the error term for the G-coefficient includes the variance component for items as well as the persons-by-items interaction. Thus in a persons-by-items G-study, criterion-referenced error, $\hat{\sigma}_\Delta^2$, is defined as the variance component for items divided by the number of items plus the variance component for the interaction of persons-by-items divided by the number of items($\hat{\sigma}_\Delta^2 = \hat{\sigma}_i^2/n_i + \hat{\sigma}_{pi}^2/n_i$). Given that $\hat{\sigma}_\Delta^2 = \frac{\hat{\sigma}_i^2}{n_i} + \frac{\hat{\sigma}_{pi}^2}{n_i}$, the criterion-referenced G-coefficient can also be expressed as:

$$E\rho^2(\Delta) = \frac{\hat{\sigma}_p^2}{\hat{\sigma}_p^2 + \dfrac{\hat{\sigma}_i^2}{n_i} + \dfrac{\hat{\sigma}_{pi}^2}{n_i}}$$

Where: $\hat{\sigma}_p^2$ = variance component for persons

$\hat{\sigma}_i^2$ = variance component for items

$\hat{\sigma}_{pi}^2$ = variance component for the persons-by-items interaction

n_i = number of items

Thus for the example data in Table 5.8, using the variance component estimates from Table 5.10 and what we know about the number of items on the test, we can calculate the criterion-referenced G-coefficient as follows:

$$E\rho^2(\Delta) = \frac{\hat{\sigma}_p^2}{\hat{\sigma}_p^2 + \dfrac{\hat{\sigma}_i^2}{n_i} + \dfrac{\hat{\sigma}_{pi}^2}{n_i}} = \frac{.0191143}{.0191143 + \dfrac{.0230966}{30} + \dfrac{.1652449}{30}}$$

$$= \frac{.0191143}{.0191143 + .0007698 + .0055081} = \frac{.0191143}{.0191143 + .0062779}$$

$$= \frac{.0191143}{.0253922} = .7527626 \approx .75$$

A short-cut estimate for the G-coefficient. Brennan (1980) uses the formula for the generalizability coefficient for absolute decisions as a "general purpose" estimate of the *domain-score dependability* for scores on CRT tests, without reference to a cut score. This formula, which he calls phi (Φ), is the ratio of universe score variance to observed score variance as follows:

$$\Phi = \frac{\hat{\sigma}_p^2}{\hat{\sigma}_p^2 + \hat{\sigma}_\Delta^2}$$

Where: $\hat{\sigma}_p^2$ = persons variance

$\hat{\sigma}_p^2$ = error variance for absolute decisions

Notice that the equation for Brennan's Phi (Φ) coefficient is exactly the same as that given for the generalizability coefficient. Thus Φ and $E\rho^2(\Delta)$ are interchangeable labels for the same thing. Thus the error term for Brennan's Φ coefficient includes the variance component for items as well as the persons-by-items interaction (as does the Generalizability coefficient, $E\rho^2(\Delta)$ for criterion-referenced absolute decisions) as follows:

$$\Phi = \frac{\hat{\sigma}_p^2}{\hat{\sigma}_p^2 + \hat{\sigma}_\Delta^2} = \frac{\hat{\sigma}_p^2}{\hat{\sigma}_p^2 + \dfrac{\hat{\sigma}_i^2}{n_i} + \dfrac{\hat{\sigma}_{pi}^2}{n_i}}$$

Brown (1990a, 1996) derived a relatively easy-to-calculate formula for estimating Φ for tests that are dichotomously scored (i.e., scored right or wrong). That formula is as follows:

$$\Phi = \frac{\dfrac{nS_p^2}{n-1}[K - R20]}{\dfrac{nS_p^2}{n-1}[K - R20] + \dfrac{M_p(1 - M_p) - S_p^2}{k-1}}$$

Where: n = number of persons taking the test
k = number of test items
M_p = mean of the proportion scores (or the mean divided by k)
S_p = standard deviation of the proportion scores (or the standard deviation divided by k)
K-R20 = Kuder-Richardson 20 reliability

For the data in the single facet persons-by-items example (where $k = 30$; $n = 42$; $M_p = 21.2857/30 = .7095233$; $S_p = 4.6511/30 = .1550366$; $S_p^2 = .1550366^2 = .0240363$; and   K-R20 $= .776296$, based on the mean, standard deviation, and K-R20 shown at bottom right of Table 5.8) the calculations are as follows:

$$\Phi = \frac{\dfrac{nS_p^2}{n-1}[K - R20]}{\dfrac{nS_p^2}{n-1}K - R20] + \dfrac{M_p(1 - M_p) - S_p^2}{k-1}}$$

$$\Phi = \frac{\dfrac{42^*.0240363}{41}[.776296]}{\dfrac{42^*.0240363}{41}[.776296] + \dfrac{.7095233(1 - .7095233) - .0240363}{29}}$$

$$= \frac{.0246225(.776296)}{(.0246225(.776296)) + .0062779} = \frac{.0191143}{.0191143 + .0062779}$$

$$= \frac{.0191143}{.0253922} = .7527626 \approx .75$$

This result, though conceptually less clear, is exactly equivalent to the result obtained from the full generalizability and decision studies for the example data in Table 5.8.[1] However, to obtain this result we only needed to know the number of items, the number of examinees, the mean proportion scores, the standard deviation of the proportion scores, and the K-R20 reliability estimate. Although it may seem odd to use an NRT reliability estimate to obtain a CRT dependability estimate, its use provides an effective short-cut in dependability estimation.

The confidence interval. Closely associated with the phi dependability index is the *confidence interval (CI)*. The CI represents a confidence interval around the examinee's score within which the examinee's score would probably fall 68% of the time if we were to administer the test many times. Thus the CI is similar to the SEM in NRT reliability. We assume that errors are normally distributed around the examinee's scores and that the variability is constant for

---

[1] Note that Brown (1996) provided four cautions that should be observed in calculating both the phi and phi(lambda) short-cut statistics provided in this chapter: (a) these formulas should only be applied to tests with items that are scored dichotomously (that is, right or wrong); (b) the *n* formulas (rather than the *n*−1 formulas) should be used in computing the means and standard deviations of the proportion scores for use in these formulas; (c) during all steps of the calculations, as many places as possible should be carried to the right of the decimal point (thus the decimal point and rounding should only be done once the final coefficient has been found); and (d) the full-blown versions of phi and phi(lambda) coefficients are based on the variance components for the test scores involved, so, if it is at all possible to do a full-fledged generalizability study, that is the best course of action.

all scores. Recall from earlier discussions that the phi coefficient was defined as follows:

$$\Phi = \frac{\hat{\sigma}_p^2}{\hat{\sigma}_p^2 + \hat{\sigma}_\Delta^2}$$

Thus phi is the ratio of the persons variance $(\hat{\sigma}_p^2)$ to the persons variance plus absolute error variance $(\hat{\sigma}_p^2 + \hat{\sigma}_\Delta^2)$. The confidence interval is simply the square root of that criterion-referenced absolute error as follows:

$$CI = \sqrt{\hat{\sigma}_\Delta^2}$$

Based on the variance components reported for the G-study above, we could calculate the *CI* for the example data as follows:

$$CI = \sqrt{\hat{\sigma}_\Delta^2} = \sqrt{\frac{\hat{\sigma}_i^2}{n_i} + \frac{\hat{\sigma}_{pi}^2}{n_i}} = \sqrt{\frac{.0230966}{30} + \frac{.1652449}{30}}$$

$$= \sqrt{.0007698 + .0055081} = \sqrt{.0062779} = .0792332 \approx .0792$$

Recall also that, for the special case of a test that is scored dichotomously, phi was also defined as follows:

$$\Phi = \frac{\dfrac{nS_p^2}{n-1}[K - R20]}{\dfrac{nS_p^2}{n-1}[K - R20] + \dfrac{M_p(1 - M_p) - S_p^2}{k-1}}$$

Combining the conceptual and computational equations, we find that:

$$\Phi = \frac{\hat{\sigma}_p^2}{\hat{\sigma}_p^2 + \hat{\sigma}_\Delta^2} = \frac{\dfrac{nS_p^2}{n-1}[K - R20]}{\dfrac{nS_p^2}{n-1}[K - R20] + \dfrac{M_p(1 - M_p) - S_p^2}{k-1}}$$

From the preceding, it should be easy to see that the portions of the equation that are common to the denominator and numerator are the persons variance and that the portion in the denominator to the right that is not common to both is the error variance as follows:

$$error = \frac{M_p(1 - M_p) - S_p^2}{k-1}$$

Since the square root of the error variance is the confidence interval, it follows that:

$$CI = \sqrt{\hat{\sigma}_\Delta^2} = \sqrt{\frac{M_p(1 - M_p) - S_p^2}{k - 1}}$$

Thus for a test that is dichotomously scored, the confidence interval can be defined as follows:

$$CI = \sqrt{\frac{M_p(1 - M_p) - S_p^2}{k - 1}}$$

In the example calculations for Φ in the previous section, the last two steps were as follows:

$$\hat{\sigma}_\Delta^2 = \frac{M_p(1 - M_p) - S_p^2}{k - 1} = \frac{.7095233(1 - .7095233) - .240363}{29}$$
$$= .0062799$$

So the confidence interval would be:

$$CI = \sqrt{.0062779} = .0792332 \approx .0792$$

Regardless of how it is calculated, the confidence interval in this particular case would be .0792. Recall that this statistic represents a confidence interval around the examinee's score within which we can feel confident the examinee's score would fall 68% of the time if we administered the test many times. More specifically, the .0792 confidence interval found in this example means that, by chance alone, an examinee's score might reasonably be expected to vary within plus or minus .0792 proportion score points 68% of the time. To put it another way, interpreted as a percent, this confidence interval indicates that an examinee's score might reasonably be expected to fall within plus or minus 7.92 percentage score points of where it did 68% of the time. Thus the confidence interval is the domain score analog to the standard error of measurement covered above in the discussion of NRT reliability.

The confidence interval is most useful in making decisions around specific cut-points. For example, given the CI of 7.92% and a decision being made at a 70% cut-point, making responsible decisions would involve gathering further information about any student within ±7.92% of the cut-point. The confidence interval indicates that students below the cut-point by as much as 7.92% points, that is, as low as 62.08% points (70% − 7.92% = 62.08%) might score above the cut-point by chance alone if they were to take the test again. Thus additional information in the form of other test scores or other types of observations should be used for students in this range to make sure they should *not* pass. Similarly, the *CI* shows that students above the cut-point by as much as 7.92% points, that is, as high as 77.92% points (70% + 7.92% = 77.92%) might score below the cut-point by chance alone if they were to take the test again. Thus additional information in the form of other test scores or other types of observations should be used for students in this range to help in deciding whether or not they should pass.

Signal-to-noise ratios. These ratios provide another way to interpret G-study variance components. A *signal-to-noise ratio* simply involves examining the relative magnitudes of the appropriate variance components. For instance, in the single facet persons-by-items example G-study, the universe score and error variance were identified as the persons variance and the criterion-referenced error variance for absolute decisions: $\hat{\sigma}_p^2$ = .0191143 and $\hat{\sigma}_\Delta^2$ = .0062779, respectively. One interpretation of magnitude of the variance components is quite clear and straightforward: the magnitude of the variance component for persons, $\hat{\sigma}_p^2$ = .0191143, is quite large relative to the magnitude of the estimated absolute error component, $\hat{\sigma}_\Delta^2$ = .0062779. This is clearly reflected in the ϕ coefficient of .75, which is the ratio of the estimated variance component for persons to that variance component, plus the estimated variance component for absolute error. In addition, it is sometimes illuminating to express the relationship between these variance components in a signal-to-noise ratio (see Cronbach and Gleser 1964).

Signal-to-noise ratios have been discussed and demonstrated by Brennan and Kane (1977) for both Φ and $\Phi(\lambda)$. In the case of Φ, a signal-to-noise ratio would be expressed as $\hat{\sigma}_p^2/\hat{\sigma}_\Delta^2$. Using the estimated variance components from the example data $\hat{\sigma}_p^2/\hat{\sigma}_\Delta^2$ = .0191143/.0062779 = 3.0446964 ≈ 3.0446. In other words, there is a more than three to one ratio in the magnitudes of the estimated variance components for persons and criterion-referenced absolute error. This is not such a startling revelation in itself. After all, it is evident that the coefficient of .75 is three times as large as the error term of .25 (i.e., 1 − .75 = .25). None the less, the signal-to-noise ratio is a way of looking at the dependability of a test that may prove useful when coupled with the idea that such ratios are between estimated variance components for a given test.

Multiple sources of variance. Clearly then, G-theory can be used to examine a single facet, or source of measurement error, in relation to the universe score, but the real strength of G-theory is its potential for examining *multiple sources of measurement error*, within a given testing situation (Suen, 1990, pp. 41–42). The G-study not only investigates sources of error in a way that is multifaceted but, more importantly, in a way that provides a comprehensive and differentiated explanation of variance that was never possible in classical theory (Shavelson & Webb, 1981, p. 133).

Many different designs can be analyzed using the full generalizability theory procedures to study the effects of any source of testing error that may be of interest. Examples of sources of error that might prove of interest in criterion-referenced testing are: items, subtests, passages, testing occasions, raters, prompt topics, prompt types, students' language backgrounds, etc. Such sources of error can be studied singly or in combination. Each such source of error included in these more complex generalizability studies are called *facets* (just as in a single facet G-study). To date, practical considerations have typically limited designs to three such facets, but there is no theoretical reason why more facets could not be studied simultaneously. For an overview of the wide variety of designs that could be studied using G-theory, see Cronbach, Gleser, Nanda, and Rajaratnam (1972), Shavelson and Webb (1981), or Brennan (1983).

Regardless of the design that is chosen, analysis of variance (ANOVA) procedures are used to estimate the variance components for each of the several facets of measurement in a generalizability study. As in a single facet design, the variance components can be further analyzed in a D study to determine the effects of various possible test designs on the generalizability coefficients associated with them. Test design decisions can then be informed by estimates of the effects of error on various options. Shavelson and Webb (1991) give a theoretical overview of these G-study techniques, and Brennan (1983) provides more practical, how-to-do-it explanations.

An example is provided here for a criterion-referenced approach to decision making for a writing test for native speakers of English at the University of Hawai'i at Manoa.

The Manoa Writing Placement Test (MWPE) is typically used for norm-referenced placement of undergraduate students into four different courses in English composition: English 22 (a remedial composition course), English 100L (regular English composition with a one unit tutorial added on), English 100 (regular English composition), and English 100A (accelerated English composition). However, the analysis reported here provides an exploration of the appropriateness and dependability of the MWPE for criterion-referenced achievement testing at the end of each of the courses.

Table 5.11. *ANOVA for G study (p × r:t) with estimated variance component formulas*

Source	SS	df	MS
persons	10495.8097	6874	1.5268842
topics	.8624	1	0.8624000
ratings: topics	2.5543	2	1.2771500
p × t	4612.6376	6874	0.6710267
p × r:t	4769.4457	13748	0.3469192
total	19811.3097	27499	

Each of 6,875 students wrote two essays on topics which were purposely made to be different: one we called a read-to-write topic because students were asked to read a two-page article and respond to it in some way, and the other we called a personal-experience topic because it required a narrative essay based on the students' personal experiences. One issue of interest to the members of the Manoa Writing Committee was whether we needed to use two topic types. Would the test scores have been equally consistent with only one topic? Would three topic types have been more effective? In short, we were interested in the degree to which the number of different topic types affected the consistency of the test scores. To answer such questions, the number of topic types was designated as one facet in a G study.

Since the number of ratings has often been reported in the literature to be a major source of variance in writing test scores, a ratings facet was also included in this G study. The question was whether the present system of doing four ratings for each student's essays (two for each of the two topic types) was necessary. Would a total of two ratings be enough? Would six ratings be more effective? To answer such questions, the second facet of interest in this G study was the degree to which the number of different ratings affected the dependability of the scores. Both the types and ratings facets were treated as what are called random effects in this study because the topic types and raters were assumed to be random samples from all possible topic types and raters, an assumption that was justified based on the concept of "exchangeability" discussed in Shavelson and Webb (1981, p. 143).

Table 5.11 shows how analysis of variance (ANOVA) procedures were used to isolate the variance components for each facet in the design, as well as for interactions of those facets. In this case,

ANOVA was used to investigate the degree to which the number of different topics and ratings and their interactions were affecting the consistency of the variance in the MWPE scores. Table 5.11 shows the sources of variance, sums of squares (SS), degrees of freedom (df), and mean squares (MS) that are typical of an ANOVA table. As explained in association with Table 5.9, Table 5.11 does not show the F and p values that some readers may have expected to find on the right side of such a table, because F and p values are not necessary or appropriate in reporting G-study results (Brennan, 1983).

Next, Table 5.12 shows how the variance components were calculated from the variance component formulas (taken from Brennan, 1983, p. 130) using the various mean squares (MS) shown in Table 5.11. For instance, to calculate the variance component for persons ($\hat{\sigma}_p^2$), the result of the mean squares for persons minus the mean squares for the persons-by-topics interaction was divided by the product of the number of raters times the number of topics, yielding an estimate of .2139643. Expressed as a formula, that would be:

$$[MS(p) - MS(pt)]/n_r n_t = [1.5268842 - .6710267]/[(2)(2)] = .2139643$$

Where: $MS(p)$ = mean squares for persons
$MS(pt)$ = mean squares for the persons-by-topics interaction
n_r = number of raters per topic
n_t = number of topics

Similarly, the other formulas in Table 5.12 were used to calculate the estimated variance components for topics ($\hat{\sigma}_t^2$), raters nested within topics ($\hat{\sigma}_{r:t}^2$), the persons-by-topics interaction ($\hat{\sigma}_{pt}^2$), and the persons-by-raters nested within topics interaction ($\hat{\sigma}_{pr:t}^2$).

With the variance components in hand, the generalizability coefficients were calculated for various combinations of numbers of topic types and numbers of ratings using the general conceptual formula given earlier in the chapter.

$$E\hat{\rho} = \frac{\hat{\sigma}_p^2}{\hat{\sigma}_p^2 + \hat{\sigma}_\Delta^2}$$

Where: $\hat{\sigma}_p^2$ = persons variance
$\hat{\sigma}_\Delta^2$ = error variance for absolute decisions

Since the estimated error variance for absolute decisions, $\hat{\sigma}_\Delta^2$, in this G-study includes the variance components for topics ($\hat{\sigma}_t^2$), raters nested within topics ($\hat{\sigma}_{r:t}^2$), the persons-by-topics interaction ($\hat{\sigma}_{pt}^2$), and the persons-by-raters nested within topics interaction ($\hat{\sigma}_{pr:t}^2$), a general

Table 5.12. *Calculating estimated variance components for G-study* $(p \times r : t)$

Variance Component		Variance component formulas	Variance component calculations		Estimate
$\hat{\sigma}_p^2$	=	$[MS(p) - MS(pt)]/n_r n_t$	=	$[1.5268842 - .6710267]/[(2)(2)]$	= .0191143
$\hat{\sigma}_t^2$	=	$[MS(t) - MS(r{:}t) - MS(pt) + MS(pr{:}t)]/n_p n_r$	=	$[.8624 - 1.27725 - .6710267 + .3469192]/[(6875)(2)]$	= .0000000
$\hat{\sigma}_{r{:}t}^2$	=	$[MS(r{:}t) - MS(pr{:}t)]/n_p$	=	$[1.27725 - .3469192]/6875$	= .0001353
$\hat{\sigma}_{pt}^2$	=	$[MS(pt) - MS(pr{:}t)]n_r$	=	$[.6710267 - .3469192]/2$	= .1620537
$\hat{\sigma}_{pr{:}t}^2$	=	$MS(pr{:}t)$	=	$.3469192$	= .3469192

formula for calculating various G-coefficients for different numbers of raters (n_r) and topics (n_t) in this design would include those facets as follows:

$$E\hat{\rho}^2 = \frac{\hat{\sigma}_p^2}{\hat{\sigma}_p^2 + \dfrac{\hat{\sigma}_t^2}{n_t} + \dfrac{\hat{\sigma}_{r:t}^2}{n_r} + \dfrac{\hat{\sigma}_{pt}^2}{n_t} + \dfrac{\hat{\sigma}_{pr:t}^2}{n_t n_r}}$$

By inserting the variance components from the facets in the specific study in question here and varying the *n*-sizes for raters and topics, the G-coefficient for any combination of numbers of raters and topics can be calculated. Consider for instance, what would happen if we tried to calculate the G-coefficient for two topics and four raters:

$$E\hat{\rho}^2 = \frac{\hat{\sigma}_p^2}{\hat{\sigma}_p^2 + \dfrac{\hat{\sigma}_t^2}{n_t} + \dfrac{\hat{\sigma}_{r:t}^2}{n_r} + \dfrac{\hat{\sigma}_{pt}^2}{n_t} + \dfrac{\hat{\sigma}_{pr:t}^2}{n_t n_r}}$$

$$= \frac{.2139643}{.2139643 + \dfrac{.0000000}{2} + \dfrac{.0001353}{4} + \dfrac{.1620537}{2} + \dfrac{.3469192}{8}}$$

$$= \frac{.2139643}{.2139643 + .0000000 + .0000338 + .0810268 + .0433649}$$

$$= \frac{.2139643}{.2139643 + .1244255} = .6323012 \approx .63$$

The G-coefficient of .63 shown in Table 5.13 for two topics with four ratings each (see column two, row four of the numbers within Table 5.13) was calculated in just this manner. This statistic indicates that the scores are approximately 63 percent dependable and 36 percent undependable. G-coefficients are also presented for other possible numbers of topics and ratings. For instance, cutting back to one topic with four ratings would clearly make the procedure much less dependable (G-coefficient = .46). If three topics and three ratings were used, it would have the opposite effect of increasing the G-coefficient (G-coefficient = .70). This is important information in that it makes clear the relative value of increasing or decreasing the numbers in each facet (numbers of topics, or numbers of ratings) separately and together.

Table 5.13. *Generalizability coefficients for different numbers of topics and ratings*

	Topics														
Raters	1	2	3	4	5	6	7	8	9	10	20	30	40	50	60
1	0.30	0.46	0.56	0.63	0.68	0.72	0.75	0.77	0.79	0.81	0.89	0.93	0.94	0.95	0.96
2	0.39	0.56	0.66	0.72	0.76	0.79	0.82	0.84	0.85	0.86	0.93	0.95	0.96	0.97	0.97
3	0.44	0.61	0.70	0.75	0.79	0.82	0.84	0.86	0.87	0.88	0.94	0.96	0.97	0.97	0.98
4	0.46	0.63	0.72	0.77	0.81	0.84	0.86	0.87	0.89	0.90	0.94	0.96	0.97	0.98	0.98
5	0.48	0.65	0.73	0.79	0.82	0.85	0.87	0.88	0.89	0.90	0.95	0.97	0.97	0.98	0.98
6	0.49	0.66	0.74	0.80	0.83	0.85	0.87	0.89	0.90	0.91	0.95	0.97	0.97	0.98	0.98
7	0.50	0.67	0.75	0.80	0.83	0.86	0.88	0.89	0.90	0.91	0.95	0.97	0.98	0.98	0.98
8	0.51	0.68	0.76	0.81	0.84	0.86	0.88	0.89	0.90	0.91	0.95	0.97	0.98	0.98	0.98
9	0.52	0.68	0.76	0.81	0.84	0.86	0.88	0.90	0.91	0.91	0.96	0.97	0.98	0.98	0.98
10	0.52	0.69	0.77	0.81	0.84	0.87	0.88	0.90	0.91	0.92	0.96	0.97	0.98	0.98	0.98
20	0.54	0.70	0.78	0.83	0.86	0.88	0.89	0.91	0.91	0.92	0.96	0.97	0.98	0.98	0.99
30	0.55	0.71	0.79	0.83	0.86	0.88	0.90	0.91	0.92	0.92	0.96	0.97	0.98	0.98	0.99
40	0.56	0.71	0.79	0.83	0.86	0.88	0.90	0.91	0.92	0.93	0.96	0.97	0.98	0.98	0.99
50	0.56	0.72	0.79	0.84	0.86	0.88	0.90	0.91	0.92	0.93	0.96	0.97	0.98	0.98	0.99
60	0.56	0.72	0.79	0.84	0.86	0.88	0.90	0.91	0.92	0.93	0.96	0.97	0.98	0.98	0.99

Generalizability theory and squared-error loss dependability

A second category of CRT agreement indices (in the generalizability theory framework) is squared-error loss dependability. Unlike the threshold-loss agreement indices discussed much earlier in this chapter, squared-error loss dependability approaches are sensitive to the degree of mastery or non-mastery and assume that the consequences of misclassifying individuals who are at the extreme distances from the cut-score are more serious than those for individuals close to the cut-score.

One of the first indices developed as an estimate for CRT tests comes under this category. Livingston (1972) derived what is cleverly called the *Livingston statistic* from NRT/classical test theory by substituting the cut-score for the group mean. His equation (using the same symbols as those for other formulas in our book) is as follows:

$$k^2(XT) = \frac{K-R20(S^2) + (M - \lambda)^2}{(S^2) + (M - \lambda)^2}$$

where: k^2 *(XT)* = Livingston's criterion-referenced dependability estimate

S^2 = variance of the test scores (that is, the standard deviation squared)

M = mean of the test scores

λ = the cut-point for the test

$K-R20$ = the Kuder-Richardson formula 20 reliability

For example, based on the data in Table 5.1a, we know that the $K-R20$ reliability is .862 and, from the bottom of Table 5.1b, we know that the mean is 16.29, the standard deviation is 6.27, and the total number of items is 30. If we set the cut-point at 50% or 15 raw score points, Livingston's coefficient would turn out to be about .87, as shown in the following:

$$k^2(XT) = \frac{K-R20(S^2) + (M - \lambda)^2}{(S^2) + (M - \lambda)^2} = \frac{.862(6.27^2) + (16.29 - 15)^2}{(6.27^2) + (16.29 - 15)^2}$$

$$= \frac{33.89 + 1.66}{39.31 + 1.66} = \frac{35.55}{40.97} = .8677 \approx .87$$

Three rather convincing arguments have been advanced against the use of Livingston's statistic for criterion-referenced testing:

1. As Livingston (1972, p. 20) himself points out, his statistic is "valid for any set of data only to the extent that it meets the assumptions of classical test theory." In most cases, those assumptions are neither tenable nor desirable on a criterion-referenced test.
2. Harris (1972) showed how Livingston's statistic would best be interpreted as "primarily a careful spelling out of what occurs when one pools two populations with different means, but similar variances and (conventional) reliability coefficients. If this view is correct, we must conclude that his [Livingston's] work fails to advance reliability theory for the special case of criterion-referenced testing" (p. 29).
3. Based on the derivations of Livingston's coefficient and phi (lambda) [$\Phi(\lambda)$], Brennan (1984) argues that ". . . it can be shown that equation 21 [$\Phi(\lambda)$] is identical to Livingston's coefficient when $s^2(\Delta)$ equals $s^2(\delta)$ – that is, when $s^2(I)$ is zero. This is consistent with the fact that Livingston's coefficient is based on the assumption of classically parallel tests, which precludes distinguishing between $s^2(\Delta)$ and $s^2(\delta)$. By contrast, the development of $\Phi(\lambda)$ is based on the assumption of randomly parallel tests" (p. 307).

Hence, we generally avoid using Livingston's formula in favor of using the phi(lambda) coefficient because $\Phi(\lambda)$ is much more firmly linked with criterion-referenced test theory (that is, randomly parallel tests and provision for the variance component due to absolute error, $\hat{\sigma}^2_\Delta$, which includes $\hat{\sigma}^2_i$), rather than to norm-referenced testing assumptions (that is, classically parallel tests and reliance on the variance component for relative error, $\hat{\sigma}^2_\delta$). In view of the fact that the formula for $\Phi(\lambda)$ given below is as easy to calculate as Livingston's statistic, there is no practical advantage to using Livingston's statistic, while there are numerous theoretical disadvantages.

Brennan's $\Phi(\lambda)$ is an "index of dependability" for criterion-referenced tests (Brennan, 1980, p. 211). This approach is outside the classical theory assumptions of parallel tests and zero variance across items. That is, it assumes that test items have been randomly sampled from the "universe" of interest (i.e., the domain being tested), and that the proper error term for absolute decisions includes a variance component for items (that is, the effect for items is *not* assumed to be zero). To calculate $\Phi(\lambda)$, a random effects, persons-by-items ANOVA is computed and a one-facet G study is carried out with items as the facet. The estimated variance components from this analysis and the distance of the observed mean for items from the cut score are then used to calculate the index. The conceptual formula for this index is as follows:

$$\Phi(\lambda) = \frac{\hat{\sigma}^2_p + (X_{PI} - \lambda)] \left[\frac{\hat{\sigma}^2_p}{n_p} + \frac{\hat{\sigma}^2_i}{n_i} + \frac{\hat{\sigma}^2_{pi}}{n_p n_i} \right]}{\hat{\sigma}^2_p + (X_{PI} - \lambda) - \left[\frac{\hat{\sigma}^2_p}{n_p} + \frac{\hat{\sigma}^2_i}{n_i} + \frac{\hat{\sigma}^2_{pi}}{n_p n_i} \right] + \hat{\sigma}^2(\Delta)}$$

where: $\Phi(\lambda)$ = phi(lambda) estimate

λ = the cut score as a proportion

$\hat{\sigma}^2_p$ = estimated variance component for persons

$\hat{\sigma}^2_i$ = estimated variance component for items

$\hat{\sigma}^2_{pi}$ = estimated variance component for item x person interaction

X_{PI} = mean across all items

n_p = number of persons

n_i = number of items

$\hat{\sigma}^2(\Delta)$ = error term for absolute decisions

What is important to note here is that variance due to the interaction of persons and items is included. Additionally, the inclusion of the error term in the denominator shows how as the error increases, the value of $\Phi(\lambda)$ will decrease. Note that this absolute error term is the sum of variance due to items and the variance due to any person-by-item interactions. Brennan (1980, 1984) also provides a computational formula that can be used in calculating the $\Phi(\lambda)$ index directly from commonly available test statistics for dichotomously (right/wrong) scored tests without having to use ANOVA. That formula (using the symbols of this book) is as follows:

$$\Phi(\lambda) = 1 - \frac{1}{k-1}\left[\frac{M_p(1-M_p) - S_p^2}{(M_p - \lambda)^2 + S_p^2}\right]$$

where: λ = cut-point as a proportion
k = number of test items
M_p = mean of the proportion scores
S_p = standard deviation of the proportion scores

Using the single facet persons-by-items G-study example data in Table 5.8 (where $k = 30$; $n = 42$; $M_p = 21.2857/30 = .7095233$; $S_p = 4.6511/30 = .1550366$; and $S_p^2 = .1550366^2 = .0240363$) with a cut-point of 60%, or $\lambda = .60$, the calculations for $\Phi(\lambda)$ would be as follows:

$$\Phi(.60) = 1 - \frac{1}{k-1}\left[\frac{M_p(1-M_p) - S_p^2}{(M_p - \lambda)^2 + S_p^2}\right]$$

$$= 1 - \frac{1}{30-1}\left[\frac{.7095233(1 - .7095233) - .0240363}{(.7095233 - .60)^2 + .0240363}\right]$$

$$= 1 - .344827\left[\frac{.2060999 - .0240363}{.0119953 + .0240363}\right] =$$

$$1 - .0344827\left[\frac{.1820636}{.0360316}\right]$$

$$= 1 - .0344827(5.0528869) = 1 - .1742371 =$$

$$.8257629 \approx .83$$

The dependability estimate is then about .83. This is a moderately high value, indicating a fair amount of consistency in classifications. This result may, in part, be due to the distance from the mean proportion score of .7095 from the cut-score proportion of .60.[2]

---

[2] Recall that Brown (1996) suggested four cautions when calculating phi or phi(lambda)

The squared-error loss approach has been criticized (see Shavelson et al, 1972) because of its sensitivity to the cut-score. Berk (1980c) and others see this sensitivity as a desirable characteristic from the CRT concern for decision consistency. The position taken by Shavelson et al is that a CRT coefficient of reliability should not be affected by the choice of a particular standard or cut-score. Berk, on the other hand, would argue that the primary concern in CRT testing is the dependability of the absolute decisions being made. This concern makes the inclusion of the cut-score in the reliability formula essential for the coefficient to reflect the dependability of the decisions being made. As such, the decision reliability is free to vary with the particular cut-score selected. One limitation, however, is that the value of $\Phi(\lambda)$ will increase as a function of the distance the proportion score mean is from the cut-score regardless of the direction. That is, if the proportion score mean is 0.70, a higher value of $\Phi(\lambda)$ will be obtained at an unrealistic cut-score of 0.10 than a more realistic cut-score of 0.80.

Because the consistency of decisions based on test scores may vary depending on where the cut-points are placed in the continuum of possible scores, it is also often useful to examine the dependability of scores at various cut-points used for making decisions. The $\Phi(\lambda)$ dependability index is one statistic that can be used to study this issue. In fact, the single biggest advantage of $\Phi(\lambda)$ is that it can be used to estimate dependability for different decision points.

Table 5.14 presents $\Phi(\lambda)$ estimates for the writing test data shown in Tables 5.11–5.13. The $\Phi(\lambda)$ estimates are given for a variety of different possible cut-scores (when four ratings are used to judge two essays as they typically are on the MWPE). If the cut-score for an achievement decision were on the mean of 11.23, the table indicates that the dependability would be .63, or the lowest $\Phi(\lambda)$ reported in the table. It turns out that the dependability of such decisions is always lowest at the point that corresponds to the mean on the test (Brennan, 1980, 1984). Fortunately, none of the actual cut-points currently used on the MWPE is near the mean. A glance at the table will indicate that the decision dependability for ENG22 is a satisfactory .94, while the corresponding statistics for ENG101 and ENG100 are .81 and .85, respectively. However, only by using $\Phi(\lambda)$ were we able to determine the CRT dependability of our decision points.

from the short-cut formulas provided in this chapter. They are listed in footnote 1 at the end of the explanation of the phi coefficient.

Table 5.14. *Various cut-points and associated phi(lambda) dependability indexes*

Cut-point	Decisions	$\Phi(\lambda)$
2.00		.98
4.00		.97
6.00	ENG22	.94
8.00		.87
9.00	ENG101	.81
10.00		.71
*11.23		.63
12.00		.67
14.00	ENG100	.85
16.00		.93
18.00		.96
20.00		.98

*overall mean = 11.23

Useful relationships among reliability and dependability indexes

A number of predictable relationships exist among the NRT reliability coefficients and the CRT dependability indexes. First, Berk (1984, p. 246) points out that, when the cut-score is set at the mean, two interesting relationships exist: (a) $k^2(XT)$ turns out to be the same as K-R20 and (b) $\Phi(\lambda = M)$ turns out to be the same as K-R21. Second, it is also true that the values of both $k^2(XT)$ and $\Phi(\lambda = M)$ are lowest when the cut-point is set at the mean (see for instance, the figure on p. 317 of Brennan, 1984). Third, Brennan (1984, pp. 315–316) demonstrates that, for any particular test, the result for K-R21 will always be less than or equal to Φ, which will in turn be less than or equal to K-R20. These relationships can be expressed as follows:

$$K-R21 \leq \Phi \leq K-R20$$

For example, for the data in Table 5.1a, K-R21 = .839, Φ = .845, and K-R20 = .862, and indeed:

$$.839 \leq .845 \leq .862$$

These facts combined have three important implications in practice:

1. If the $k^2(XT)$ estimate is lowest when the cut-point is at the mean

and if $k^2(XT)$ turns out to be the same as $K\text{-}R20$ when the cut-point is at the mean, then $K\text{-}R20$ can serve as a conservative quick-down-and-dirty underestimate of $k^2(XT)$.

2. If the $\Phi(\lambda)$ estimate is lowest when the cut-point is at the mean and if $\Phi(\lambda)$ turns out to be the same as $K\text{-}R21$ when the cut-point is at the mean, then $K\text{-}R21$ can serve as a conservative quick-down-and-dirty underestimate of $\Phi(\lambda)$ when the cut-point is at the mean.

3. If indeed $K\text{-}R21$ is always lower than or equal to Φ, then $K\text{-}R21$ can be used as a conservative quick-down-and-dirty underestimate of the domain-referenced dependability (Φ) of a criterion-referenced test (Brennan 1984, pp. 331–332).

Thus, in a pinch, when doing criterion-referenced testing, you could consider calculating $K\text{-}R20$ and $K\text{-}R21$ (or getting them off some norm-referenced computer printout) and interpreting the $K\text{-}R20$ as a conservative estimate of $k^2(XT)$ and the $K\text{-}R21$ as a conservative estimate of both Φ and $\Phi(\lambda = M)$. Thus you will know that the $k^2(XT)$ is at least as high as the value you get with $K\text{-}R20$ and that Φ and $\Phi(\lambda = M)$ are at least as high as the values you get with $K\text{-}R21$.

However, you must also recognize that, because these quick-down-and-dirty estimates are conservative, they may be lower, even much lower, than the actual state of affairs in your data. If these estimates turn out to be unacceptably low, you may want to go ahead and do the calculations using the short-cut formulas or generalizability theory approaches described in this chapter. If the results of these latter calculations are different, they are likely to be higher, and finding out that your test is more dependable may be worth the effort.

IRT consistency issues: unidimensionality, local independence, and model fit

IRT proponents criticize the NRT classical test model for a number of basic limitations in interpretation (Hambleton, 1982). As already noted, these difficulties stem from analyses that are limited by the item and person dependence inherent in traditional measurement paradigms. These restrictions on utility extend, from the IRT proponents' perspectives, into areas of test consistency that are usually associated with reliability and dependability. These limitations will be addressed below and then a discussion will be presented of the IRT issues most closely associated with consistency as it has been viewed thus far.

Of primary importance in discussions of reliability is the fact that the estimations of reliability based on parallel-forms, test–retest, or internal consistency approaches are all sample specific. That is, a slight change in the composition of the group of people who take the test or the particular set of items selected for the test will create a need to recalculate and evaluate the test reliability. Since IRT is based upon the probabilities of given response patterns, the particular set of examinees is less important than in NRT approaches and the test consistency will be additively based on the cumulative item character-istics across the set of items selected for the test form. Those characteristics will not be confounded with the characteristics of other items that happen to be chosen for the test. In short, the IRT approach to test development and delivery claims to obviate some of these test and sample dependencies.

A second issue raised in the IRT framework addresses the assump-tion in classical NRT theory that the standard error of the measure-ment (*SEM*) is a group estimate of standard deviation errors in individual test scores. Related to this assumption is the assumption that reliability is a constant across the test regardless of the ability or difficulty level being evaluated. However, such reliability estimates are in fact derived without due recognition that the size of errors in test scores is related to the "true scores" of the examinees taking the test (Hambleton, 1979; Bock, Thissen, & Zimowski, 1997). IRT, on the other hand, estimates the *SEM* at each ability level. Thus, conceptually, the standard deviation of scores obtained for the subset of examinees who are at a particular ability level is determined and that is seen as representative of the amount of error at that Θ level. This is known as $SE(\Theta)$, and is the IRT parallel to the *SEM*. This approach recognizes that error is not a constant group attribute, but can be estimated across a range of ability levels measured by the test item pool.

Related to this issue of error at a given ability level is the IRT concern for how much information a test form supplies. The basic concepts employed here should be familiar from the discussion in Chapter 4 of IIFs (item information functions). In discussing IRT, Lord (1980, p. 52) claims to have "little use for test reliability coefficients"; however, he defines reliability as equal to the correla-tion of the relationships of X (raw score) to Θ (estimated logit ability). In general, one counterpart of reliability and the *SEM* for IRT is the test information (TI) function. The test information function is considered useful as a measure of accuracy of estimation in that: (a) its shape depends only on the items in the particular test, and (b) it provides an estimate of the error of measurement at each ability level (Hambleton, 1979). Hambleton, Swaminathan, and Rogers (1991) indicate the test information value as the sum of information provided by each item at a corresponding ability level.

$$TI(\Theta) = \sum_{i=1}^{n} I_i(\Theta)$$

Thus, the information that is provided by a test is merely the sum of the item information functions at the particular ability level of concern. Further, the standard error of estimation, $SE(\Theta)$, of ability dealt with conceptually in the previous paragraph can be calculated as equal to one over the square root of the information value (Hambleton & Cook, 1977).

$$SE(\Theta) = \frac{1}{\sqrt{I(\Theta)}}$$

If information is low, then there is a wide confidence band around the estimate. If information is high, there is a narrow confidence band. Since the information varies with ability level, some theoreticians suggest that test information curves replace classical reliability estimates and standard errors of measurement (Hambleton & Cook, 1977). Thus, IRT can estimate the standard error of estimation, and hence a confidence band can be constructed around any particular ability level on the test (Hambleton, Swaminathan, & Rogers, 1991).

IRT, then, attempts to address the three limitations on analysis by NRT just discussed. However, the utility of the IRT model proposed advantages are obviously limited, as is any analytic model, to the degree to which the data are consistent with the underlying assumptions of IRT measurement. For example, in classical testing internal consistency, items are assumed to measure in a manner congruent with that of the overall test. If that is not the case, internal consistency reliability estimates are low, which in part indicates the degree of violation of the assumption.

In IRT, there are three basic assumptions that need to be addressed in some manner. These three assumptions relate to *unidimensionality*, *local independence*, and *model to data fit*. Each of these will be addressed in turn.

Unidimensionality

Closely linked to reliability/dependability for the IRT framework are concerns of *unidimensionality* (see Hattie, 1985). That is, one of the most critical assumptions of most commonly employed IRT models is that the items on a test or subtest measure only one dominant attribute or trait. It is assumed that a single latent trait dimension can explain the common variance associated with the item responses (Embretson & Reise, 2000). With CRT testing, unidimensionality is often partially ensured by the fact that the tests are designed to measure carefully defined domains of behavior. Unfortunately, few, if any, more precise definitions of *unidimensionality* exist. As Hambleton and Rovinelli (1986) point out, the definitions of *unidimensionality* are typically abstract and non-operational. They note that a typical example is, "A set of test items is unidimensional when a single trait can explain or account for examinee test performance" (p. 287).

Not all differences in dimensionality are the same. There are differences in *degree* and there are differences in *kind*. The fact that all items on a test may vary in terms of their difficulty does not make a test violate the assumption of unidimensionality. However, any items that require distinctly different cognitive processes to answer do violate the assumptions. An analogy from nature would be in the classification of the birds of North America. Types of differences from some hypothetical trait of "birdness" will vary. Penguins and hummingbirds are different in both degree and kind. Thrushes and finches on the other hand are different only in degree from the unidimensional hypothetical bird, which we picture when we think of "birdness." If we want to take a sample of birds from North America, we define the types and select them. We do not merely proceed with a net and wind up primarily with starlings and sparrows. The fact that we have robins and cardinals and thrushes as well as starlings and sparrows does not mean that there is a violation of unidimensionality, either with our birds or our CRTs. Likewise, with discretely defined CRTs, we have a defined collection of language skills. The notion of unidimensionality must be more than a statistical notion (Henning, 1992). There should also be a content and descriptive notion taken into account in decisions of whether a test demonstrates unidimensionality or not. The content and descriptive components in establishing unidimensionality are in part taken care of with CRTs through the development of test and item specifications.

While CRT approaches can assist in addressing conceptual concerns of dimensionality, the statistical approaches for testing IRT dimensionality assumptions are somewhat less clear. Hattie (1985) notes that a major problem in assessing indices of *unidimensionality* results from a confusion of the term with such other terms as *reliability, internal consistency, local independence,* and *homogeneity.* He states that "unidimensionality can be rigorously defined as the existence of one latent trait underlying the set of items" (p. 151). He presents thirty approaches to testing unidimensionality and notes that while "most proposers do not offer a rationale for their choice of index, even fewer assess the performance of the index relative to other indices, and hardly anyone has tested the indices using data of known dimensionality" (p. 140). After reviewing the 30 approaches, Hattie concludes that ". . . there are still no known satisfactory indices. None of the attempts to investigate unidimensionality has provided clear decision criteria for determining it" (p. 158).

While none of the approaches Hattie investigated provided clear decisions for the estimation of unidimensionality, subsequent approaches based on Stout (1987, 1990) and Nandakumar and Stout (1993, 1994) have produced promising practical approaches. Stout's approach recognizes that actual data are rarely strictly unidimensional. That is, items may be multiply determined because, in addition to a dominant dimension associated with a given trait, other attributes may prove to be unique to individual items or groups of items and may therefore contribute to variability in the outcomes. Variability may also be related to different examinee characteristics resulting from prior teaching methods or experiences. The approach that Stout has pursued is to establish what is termed *essential unidimensionality* (Stout, 1987, 1990). The procedures that determine whether a test is essentially unidimensional show the extent to which there is discrimination between one- and two-dimensional tests. In this framework, a test is determined to be essentially unidimensional when the covariances not associated with trait level are reduced to zero. The computer program DIMTEST (Stout, 1987) is utilized in this analysis. Of importance here is the recognition that there are approaches for helping determine the unidimensionality of tests and the consequent appropriateness of IRT methods.

With NRTs, Cronbach's alpha and *K-R20* have generally been the most widely utilized indices of unidimensionality. However, Hattie (1985) reviews several problems with interpreting high reliability coefficients as equivalent to unidimensionality. Alpha may be high even if there is no general factor (for example, Henning, 1988, found a *K-R20* of .98 for a two dimensional test). First, alpha is influenced by the number of items on the test. Second, it increases as the number of factors which pertain to each item increase. Third, judgments of unidimensionality should not be affected by test length. Cronbach

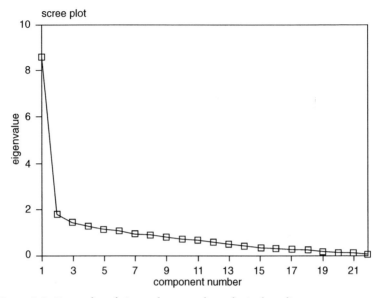

Figure 5.5. Scree plot of eigenvalues on a hypothetical reading test

(1951) was aware of the test length problem in interpreting alpha for unidimensionality and recommended using the Spearman-Brown formula to indicate the total test alpha. Clearly then, important drawbacks cloud the use of traditional reliability estimates as indicators of unidimensionality.

The literature contains numerous approaches for examining unidimensionality that may be particularly useful in CRT language assessment. One of these involves carrying out a factor analysis of the inter-item correlations (items using tetrachoric correlation coefficients for dichotomously scored items). To begin with, a plot of the *eigenvalues*[3] is examined to establish whether a dominant first factor is present or not. If a single factor solution appears to exist in the data, then the test is assumed to be unidimensional. However, Hambleton and Rovinelli (1986) found that nonlinear factor analysis was better than linear factor analysis, in that linear factor analysis tended to over-estimate the number of underlying dimensions.

Still, linear factor analysis has its uses in examining test dimensionality. One example of the use of factor analysis in investigating unidimensionality is shown in Figure 5.5. This is a scree plot of the

---

[3] In factor analysis, eigenvalues represent the relative importance of a factor in its contribution to the overall variation in scores.

Table 5.15. *Component matrix for the hypothetical reading test showing factor loadings on the six identified possible factors*

	Components					
	1	2	3	4	5	6
I31	.559	−.107	.080	.235	.187	.231
I32	.464	−.533	.378	−.236	−.138	.108
I33	.735	.225	.046	.077	.046	−.076
I34	.673	.225	−.411	−.082	−.067	.302
I35	.512	.172	.183	.667	−.014	.143
I36	.614	−.345	−.194	−.238	.280	−.016
I37	.542	.101	−.295	−.156	−.021	−.238
I38	.725	−.496	.116	−.155	.091	−.047
I39	.551	−.378	−.240	.370	−.189	−.268
I40	.660	.013	.133	−.281	.156	−.146
I41	.620	.264	.256	−.175	−.256	−.418
I42	.838	.010	.175	.173	.013	.105
I43	.505	−.333	−.040	.182	−.333	.447
I44	.883	.165	−.141	−.016	−.216	−.125
I45	.510	.284	.690	−.042	−.125	−.098
I46	.457	.350	.246	−.072	.187	.282
I47	.489	.491	−.107	−.363	.101	.383
I48	.455	.323	−.386	.146	.026	−.124
I49	.508	−.090	.091	.248	.457	−.056
I50	.859	.082	−.152	.075	−.317	−.139
I51	.704	−.280	−.134	−.299	−.156	.171
I52	.582	−.087	−.086	.055	.561	−.188

results from a hypothetical 22-item reading test. Although the scree plot indicates factors above the eigenvalue of 1.0, which is generally seen as indicating a factor that is contributing to the structure of the data, the first factor is clearly dominant. In fact, the largest eigenvalue is almost five times greater than the second largest and the rest of the factors are largely indistinguishable from each other in terms of magnitude. Further, Table 5.15 shows that almost all of the items load most heavily on the first factor. This pattern of the dominant first factor provides a strong argument for the unidimensionality of the particular test. If, however, no clear dominant factor had emerged, unidimensionality would still be in question. As we will show in the following chapter, these questions of unidimensionality, reliability, and dependability all have an impact on issues of validity in assessment.

Local independence

A second major assumption of IRT, also applicable to some degree in classical test theory, is the assumption that the success or failure of any item should not depend on the success or failure of any other item. This assumption of *local independence* means that when ability is held constant across examinees, the responses are statistically independent of one another. The assumption, then, is that the only factors affecting examinees' responses are their abilities on the latent trait. When there is a violation of local independence, no reliable method exists for establishing the item parameters, regardless of which IRT model is being used. Unfortunately, in such situations, test information and item discrimination will be overestimated (Yen, 1993).

Thus, test designers should avoid what Yen (1993) terms *local item dependence* (LID) from the very first stages of test development. Yen outlines several causes of LID, causes such as fatigue, passage dependence, item chaining, background knowledge, etc. Additionally, performance assessments are frequently prone to problems with LID because performance tasks may be linked and the scoring rubrics may not clearly separate the relative contributions of the different tasks.

Statistics have been developed to identify LID. Yen proposes what she terms the $Q3$ statistic (Yen, 1984). This statistic is the correlation between performances on two items after taking overall test performance into account. In calculating this statistic, the Θ value is estimated for each examinee using the examinee's responses on all of the items encountered. Then the examinee's expected performance on each item is estimated. The difference between the examinee's obtained and expected performance (or error) is determined. The measure of LID is the correlation across all examinees of this residual. With large samples, the value would be expected to be near zero, since there should be no systematic relationship between the error in each examinee's obtained score. The higher the value of $Q3$, the greater the violation of local independence.

Avoiding violations of local independence may be difficult, particularly as tests become more performance based. Naturally, the potential violations need to be addressed throughout the process of test development and administration. Additionally, when items are inherently related, test developers may need to incorporate the concept of "testlets" into test analysis (Embretson & Reise, 2000; Wainer & Kiely, 1987). *Testlets* are collections of items that are suspected of violating local independence by being related in some identifiable way. Such items might be multiple items associated with a single reading or listening passage or evaluations of abilities such as grammar, effectiveness of communication, appropriateness of expression, etc. based on a single language performance. Basically, any items or rating categories that might be correlated because they are part of a response set are candidates for inclusion on a testlet. The various testlets across the test setting are then seen to be independent of one another. The testlets become the unit of analysis and the problem with LID has been addressed.

Model to data fit

IRT can solve many practical measurement problems, but only if we ensure that there is a satisfactory fit between the model and the test data. Examining the *model to data fit* involves determining whether the appropriate IRT model has been selected. Making such a determination is a process of judging the fit of item and examinee behaviors to what the selected model would predict them to be.

Model selection. The first order of business is to determine whether the correct IRT model has been selected. Note, at the outset, that substantial differences may arise in the way this question is framed depending upon whether it is being addressed by proponents of the Rasch one-parameter model or by researchers who are just as likely to employ the two- or three-parameter models as they are to employ the one-parameter model. The basic issue is whether one begins by asking whether the data fit the model (the approach taken by Rasch proponents) or whether the model fits the data (the approach taken by those who accept the multi-parameter approaches). Researchers using the multi-parameter models attempt to select a model that will account for as much data as possible. Many Rasch proponents, on the other hand, take the perspective that any data not adhering to the assumptions of no guessing and constant item discrimination should not be included in the analysis. Such an approach often takes as its basis an assertion that guessing and item discrimination basically cannot be stably estimated. Although not entirely agnostic on this issue, we will simply point this issue out for the reader and proceed with the discussion of model fit.

Hambleton, Swaminathan, and Rogers (1991) discuss several possible methods for examining model appropriateness. First, in order to establish the assumption of equal item discriminations of the one-parameter model, the distribution of traditional biserial or point-biserial correlations can be reviewed. If the distribution of the correlations across the test is substantially homogeneous, the one-parameter model may be of interest. Individual items that are in violation can be identified by goodness-of-fit indices discussed in the next section. However, if there is wide variation in the discrimination indices, the one-parameter model may not be appropriate and it may be more reasonable to pursue the two-parameter model, which does not have this assumption. For the assumption of minimal guessing in the one- and two-parameter models, Hambleton et al (1991) propose examining the performance of the low ability students. They recommend that the performance of the low ability examinees be checked on the most difficult items. If their scores are close to zero, then guessing would not appear to be a problem. If, however, their scores are substantially above zero, guessing may be an issue and the three-parameter model would be most appropriate.

Hambleton et al (1991) also note the need to check the two IRT features that are independent of the decisions about which model should be selected: (a) invariance of ability and (b) invariance of item parameter estimates. To evaluate the *invariance of ability estimates*, the examinee abilities are estimated with different samples of test items. For example, ability would be estimated using predominately easy or predominately difficult items. Also, items from different content categories of the item pools could be used. To the extent that ability estimates do not vary more than the measurement errors, the invariance of ability assumption would hold. Likewise, the *invariance of item parameters* across examinees can be estimated from two or more sub-samples of the target population. Examinees from different geographical regions, ethnic groups, genders, etc. could be tested. A plot of the parameters across the different groups should yield a linear relationship. To the extent that the parameters differ, the groups may represent different populations or the items may be overly sensitive to examinee differences not projected to be part of the underlying trait.

Item and person fit. Attention has long been paid in IRT to assessing the fit of items and persons to the models. These concerns focus on whether the item obtains responses that are predicted given the ability level and difficulty levels of the item. Likewise, testers are concerned with determining whether a particular person provides a response pattern consistent with what would be predicted based upon that person's demonstrated ability. An item might not fit the data because it captures content that is not uniformly available to all examinees in the population. Thus, some very able examinees may not get a particular item correct while less able examinees do get the item correct. Examinees may also provide misfitting performances if they become ill part of the way through the test and consequently begin to answer items incorrectly that would have been predicted to be relatively easy for them. Part of the problem for IRT, then, is to devise methods for identifying those misfitting items or people.

Most approaches to fit estimation rely on a goodness-of-fit statistic such as a chi-square. The *chi-square* (χ^2) statistic examines the degree to which observed values deviate from predicted, or expected, values. If the observed values are very different from the predicted values, then it is assumed that the two distributions are different. In IRT, if the observed values and predicted values of an item are very different, then the item is seen as not fitting the rest of the data. This can be seen as analogous to a finding in traditional NRT of an item with very low point-biserial correlation. In both cases, the item does not behave in the same manner as the other items. In IRT, an item that is misfitting does not behave as it should, given the assumption of unidimensionality. In implementing the χ^2 test, examinees are rank-ordered according to their level and groups of examinees with similar ability levels are created. Then, within each of these groups, the proportion of examinees who answered correctly is calculated. This observed proportion of examinees in each group getting the item correct is compared to the proportion of examinees predicted by the item response function. Reise (1990) presents the χ^2 formula:

$$\chi^2 = \sum_{j-1}^{G} \frac{N_j(O_{ij} - E_{ij})^2}{E_{ij}(1 - E_{ij})}$$

Where: i = the item
j = the interval created by grouping the examinees based on their Θ estimates
G = the number of examinee groups
N_j = the number of examinees with Θ estimates in each interval j
O_{ij} = the observed proportion of correct responses on item i for interval j
E_{ij} = the expected proportion of correct responses on item i for interval j, based on the item response function at the median Θ estimate within the interval

High values of χ^2 indicate items that are performing differently from what would be predicted. Several χ^2 variants appear in the literature. One variation of these goodness-of-fit indices, used in one-parameter models, involves two fit statistics, *infit* and *outfit* (Wright & Linacre, 1984). Both are ways of assessing how large the residuals, the differences between observed and expected values, are in the data set.

Outfit is the standardized weighted mean square residual of unlikely items responses while *infit* is a weighted derivation of the outfit statistic, which is focused on the area where responses deliver the most information (Henning, 1988). The second of these statistics is not as sensitive to the unexpected effects in outliers distant from the items as is the outfit statistic. However, Hambleton and Rovinelli (1986) found drawbacks with residual analysis of this type, finding it generally unsatisfactory. In their study, residual analysis did not identify the presence of multidimensionality in the test data. Still, despite these shortcomings, these statistics are relatively well known and used in the one-parameter literature and do provide useful information.

Examination of person fit, regardless of which statistic is employed, is analogous to the process involved in determining item fit. The purpose is to identify examinees whose response patterns are not congruent with what is expected. Such aberrant response patterns may reflect examinee guessing, inattention, or specific educational deficits (Reise, 1990).

Reise (1990) has noted two basic problems with χ^2 fit indices. He points out that one initial problem exists with how the intervals, *j*, are established. For example, an interval could include examinees with ability estimates of 3 while another includes ability estimates of -2, and so on up to ability estimates of +3 or +4. On the other hand, an interval could contain examinees with ability estimates of both -3 and -2, another could contain ability estimates of -1 and 0, and so on up to the +3 and +4 range. The decision as to the width and makeup of these intervals can clearly affect the resulting χ^2 value. Second, χ^2 is sensitive to the number of examinees included in the analysis. With large samples, the χ^2 will tend toward a significant value, and hence indicate misfit. This can lead to finding a large number of misfitting items as an artifact of having a large sample size. However, although the fit statistics have limitations, they can be helpful in examining item and person fit.

Items or persons that are found to be misfitting can be interpreted in at least two different ways (McNamara, 1996). The designation of items as misfitting may signal poorly constructed items. For example, there may be more than one answer or the particular scale may not apply well. Second, the item may be perfectly fine in itself, but may not belong to the particular set of items to which it has been associated. For example, the item could be designed to measure reading ability, but contain an obscure lexical item unrelated to the topic or to general reading ability.

Similarly, the interpretation of misfitting persons is open to many possibilities. The first interpretation, and that frequently of concern early on in the development of fit analysis, might be that the examinee was cheating. If an examinee happens to glance frequently at a neighbor's test paper – a neighbor with a different Θ value – the resulting responses might indicate that a number of difficult items were unexpectedly answered correctly, given the examinee's answers on other items. This unpredicted response pattern would signal a misfit with the overall examinee ability. Second, the finding that a person is misfitting might indicate that the test is not appropriate as a measure of this particular candidate's ability. Thus, it is important to examine the test results to determine whether there might be an inordinate number of examinees who are found to have significantly high misfit estimates. A finding such as this could indicate a serious situation in which the test is not appropriate for some subgroup in the population. This would place severe restrictions on the interpretations that could be made on the basis of the test results.

In conclusion, while IRT is as concerned with consistency as the NRT and CRT frameworks, the way in which consistency is approached is different. The focus is on consistency of response patterns, and consistency of obtaining actual observed values that are close to the predicted values, given information about examinee ability and item difficulty. Further, a central feature of the concern with consistency in IRT is the extent to which the ability and difficulty estimates are invariant across specific items or test samples. Thus, if CRT tests are to be constructed utilizing the advantages that IRT has to offer, a careful analysis of the issues mentioned regarding reliability, dependability, and unidimensionality will need to be conducted.

See uk.cambridge.org/elt/crlt/ for chapter summary and exercises.

6 Validity of criterion-referenced tests

Introduction

Traditionally, *validity* has been defined as "the degree to which a test measures what it claims, or purports, to be measuring" (Brown, 1996, p. 231). For example, if a criterion-referenced test is designed to measure the objectives of a specific course, the validity of the test could be defended by showing that the test is indeed measuring those objectives. Naturally, making such arguments from a number of perspectives will be more convincing to you and other users of the tests. The perspectives that have traditionally been most useful for studying the validity of criterion-referenced tests are content validity and construct validity. Each of these validity strategies will be defined and discussed in turn in the sections that follow. In addition, ample examples will be provided to help illustrate how these concepts are applied in practice and how they can be combined.

Recently, expanded views of what validity ought to include have begun to surface in the educational measurement literature. Chief among the proponents of such expanded views are Messick and Cronbach. Messick (1988) discusses the evidential and consequential bases of test interpretation and use, and Cronbach (1988) covers the functional, political, economic, and explanatory perspectives on test validity. We feel that the considerations suggested by Messick and Cronbach may be especially important for criterion-referenced tests. This is particularly true to the extent that validity is viewed as being concerned with the *inferences* that are made on the basis of test scores, rather than being any intrinsic quality of the particular test form itself.

The chapter will end with a discussion of valid decision making based on criterion-referenced tests. This last section will include exploration of such topics as traditional cut-points and grading on a curve, the arbitrariness of cut-points, definitions of standards setting, alternative approaches to the setting of standards, as well as the relationships between standards setting and criterion-referenced decision making, between standards and dependability, and between validity and criterion-referenced decision making.

Content validity

Content validity approaches all require the systematic investigation of the degree to which the items on a test, and the resulting scores, are representative and relevant samples of whatever content or abilities the test has been designed to measure. Typically, content validity involves demonstrating that the content of a test is related to the content of a well-described course (that is, the objectives and/or item specifications) or domain (that is, a detailed description of the theoretical underpinnings and/or the item specifications related to those theoretical underpinnings). In criterion-referenced assessment, content validity may be supported through theoretical arguments or expert judgments or both. We will also contend that content validity approaches are much stronger and more convincing if linked to construct validity approaches.

Theoretical arguments approach to content validity

The *theoretical arguments approach* to content validity usually makes a case for the representativeness of the content of a test by (a) carefully planning a test on the basis of theoretical, research, or practical perspectives and (b) arguing for the content validity of the test on the basis of those perspectives. Thus the theoretical arguments for how a particular test ought to be designed will depend on the theory, research, and practical factors underlying the test. One ramification of this definition is that validity defined in this way is a moving target, that is, the content validity of a test defended on the basis of today's theoretical and practical notions may not be viewed as valid if those theories and practices change over the years. This is as it should be; it's called progress.

We will briefly discuss two examples here of the theoretical arguments approach to content validity; one is a task-based performance assessment project and the other is an engineering-English reading test for non-native speakers of English.

Task-based performance assessment example. In a task-based curriculum, the theory underlying the test might be task-based syllabus design. To defend the logic of such a test, it would be necessary to clearly delineate the theoretical underpinnings perhaps by doing a thorough literature review as we did in Norris, Brown,

Hudson, and Yoshioka (1998) for designing performance assessments. In fact, in writing up the design procedures, we provided a literature review that was organized into four chapters: (a) alternative assessments in general, (b) performance assessments, (c) task-based language teaching, and (d) task-based assessment. Only then were we ready to state clearly the theoretical validity arguments behind our choices in developing task-based performance assessments. That is not to say that we were simply reflecting a clearly developed consensus in the literature; quite to the contrary, we were instead choosing our own path on the basis of all available information on relevant topics. The degree to which our logic holds up for readers and future test users will clearly affect the degree to which those people will accept the validity of these performance assessment procedures.

Reviewing the literature in Norris et al (1998) led us to realize that a key element in performance assessment of any kind is clearly defining the task(s) that students must perform. That realization led us to the further recognition that the key to clearly defining task(s) is to understand what makes a task easy or difficult. In discussing our overall and specific test descriptors, we concluded (primarily on the basis of Skehan, 1996, and our own experiences with university-level L2 education) that we should devise a task difficulty matrix to help in exploring different ways to differentiate and sequence the difficulty of tasks. Our task difficulty matrix is shown in Table 6.1a, which shows three components that summarize our thinking at that time about the components of task difficulty (Norris et al, 1998, p. 77). For practical reasons, we reduced the matrix to the smaller version shown in Table 6.1b with the components and subcomponents of task difficulty defined as shown in Table 6.2.

For Norris et al (1998), the item generation and selection processes involved primarily two steps: task selection and task difficulty ratings. The task selection process focused on task themes like *deciding on a movie* or *planning the weekend* that "the authors of a variety of different language teaching textbooks found important enough to include in their language teaching materials" (p. 84). We then analyzed the difficulty level of the tasks they projected for each theme in terms of code complexity (including a + or − for both range and number of input sources), cognitive complexity (including a + or − for both input/output organization and input availability), and communicative demand (including a + or − for both mode and response level). A subset of our results for nine themes (out of the 114 identified) are shown in Table 6.3. Note that the first column in Table 6.3 contains labels for the task themes and that the six columns

Table 6.1a. *Revised assessment of language performance task difficulty matrix*

	easy→→→difficult		easy→→→difficult		easy→→→difficult	
	Range		**Number of input sources**		**Delivery of input**	
Code complexity	−	+	−	+	−	+
	Amount of info. to be processed		**Organization of input**		**Availability of input**	
Cognitive complexity	−	+	−	+	−	+
	Mode		**Channel**		**Response level**	
Communicative demand	−	+	−	+	−	+

Note: In the revised task difficulty matrix, a *minus* sign always indicates less difficulty with respect to the component and characteristic relative to the given task, whereas a *plus* sign always indicates greater relative difficulty.
(Norris et al, 1998, p. 77)

Table 6.1b. *Reduced assessment of language performance task difficulty matrix*

	easy>>>>>>>>>difficult		easy>>>>>>>>>difficult	
	Range		**Number of input sources**	
Code complexity	−	+	−	+
	Organization of input/output		**Availability of input**	
Cognitive complexity	−	+	−	+
	Mode		**Response level**	
Communicative demand	−	+	−	+

Note: In the reduced task difficulty matrix, a *minus* sign always indicates less difficulty with respect to the component and characteristic relative to the given task, whereas a *plus* sign always indicates greater relative difficulty.

Table 6.2. *Difficulty factors in planning task-based performance assessments*

I. **Code complexity.** The code complexity of a given task depends on the kind of language and information that is involved in successful task performance (i.e., the linguistic code). The primary variables for estimating code complexity are:

   A. **Range** addresses the extent to which the code that is inherent in the language of a given task represents a greater or lesser degree of *spread*.

   B. **Number of different input sources** addresses whether or not the examinee must *decode* multiple sources of information input, each source representing inherent code differences.

II. **Cognitive complexity.** The cognitive complexity of a given task essentially turns on the amount and kind of information processing that an examinee must engage in to successfully perform the task (mental gymnastics, in a sense). The primary variables for estimating cognitive complexity are:

   A. **Input/output organization** addresses the extent to which information must be significantly organized, re-organized, or just plain shifted about with respect to parameters of task success.

   B. **Input availability** addresses whether or not an examinee is required in some significant way to search for the information upon which a task performance is to be based.

III. **Communicative demand.** The communicative demand involved in a given task is determined by the type of communicative language activity that is required as well as by a number of moderator variables that can drastically influence the relative difficulty of a particular communicative act. The primary variables for estimating communicative demand are:

   A. **Mode** addresses whether or not a task is construed to have a productive element that is inherently connected to task performance success.

   B. **Response level** addresses the extent to which an examinee must interact with input in an *on-line* or *real time* sense.

(adapted from Norris et al, 1998, pp. 78–82)

on the right show their estimated + or − ratings for the various difficulty factors as they are applied to each task theme. Notice also that the second column from the left shows the overall estimated difficulty levels, based on the sum of the + signs.

The task themes shown in Table 6.3 were all part of what we called (A) Health and recreation/entertainment. The entire table in the original source included task themes organized into a total of seven areas: (A) Health and recreation/entertainment; (B) Travel; (C) Food and dining; (D) At work; (E) At the university; (F) Domesticity; (G) Environment/politics.

Table 6.3. *Task difficulty matrix for prototypical tasks: assessment of language performance*

Component:		Code >		Cognit. > Complx		Commu. > Demand	
Characteristic:		Range	#Input Sources	In/Out Organiz.	Input Avail.	Mode	Resp.
Task Themes	Diff. Index						
A.1 Deciding on a movie	5	+	+	−	+	+	+
A.2 Choosing the appropriate film	4	+	+	−	+	+	−
A.3 Planning the weekend	2	−	+	+	−	−	−
A.4 Getting directions to the party	2	−	−	+	−	−	+
A.5 Using the dating service	5	+	+	+	+	−	+
A.6 Giving medical advice	4	+	−	−	+	+	+
A.7 Be careful with medicine	1	−	+	−	−	−	−
A.8 Quit smoking cigars!	4	+	+	+	−	+	−
A.9 Getting advice from TEL-MED	6	+	+	+	+	+	+

(adapted from Norris et al, 1998, pp. 84–91)

Thus from the very beginning, we had already begun setting up our validity arguments for the test by prudently planning the types of items we would use on the basis of all available literature. Only then were we in a position to design and administer the test in various forms to find out how well we had measured what we thought we were assessing. We validated the adequacy of our assessment procedures through what you will see below is called a hierarchical-structure construct validity study.

Engineering-English reading test example. In order to discuss the validation of the engineering-English reading test in this example, we must provide some background. During the years from 1979 to 1982, Drs. Francis Butler and Russell Campbell, with the help of

J.D. Brown, guided six MA students[1] (in what was then called the TESL section of the English Department at UCLA) in developing and piloting three engineering reading tests and three engineering listening tests designed specifically for graduate engineering students whose native language was other than English. Three of the MA students focused on developing their own reading tests of 30 or more items on each of three different topics: (a) "Mechanics of Deformable Bodies," (b) "Refactories," and (c) "Thermodynamic Analysis of Heat Pumps." These are topics that language teachers may at first find somewhat impenetrable. Indeed, they read somewhat like the Jabberwocky to many of us. However, according to the three professors in the Engineering Department at UCLA that we used as informants, these are topics and passages (drawn from sophomore level engineering textbooks) that any native English speaking graduate level engineering student should be able to read and comprehend.

In designing the test, we carefully planned and justified the types of items we would use in the test based on interviews we did with three engineering professors and the reading we did in the English for specific purposes literature available at that time (for example, we examined Cowan, 1974; Inman, 1978; Lackstrom, Selinker, & Trimble, 1973; and Selinker, Todd-Trimble, & Trimble, 1976, 1978). As shown in Table 6.4, each of the three engineering reading tests were planned to include two major item types: what we called linguistic items and what we called engineering items.

Under linguistic items, we included what was then a hot topic (based on Halliday & Hasan, 1976): cohesion. Four of the five types of cohesion identified and discussed by Halliday and Hasan were included in the test as items: reference, substitution, lexical cohesion, and intersentential conjunction. Note that we did not include their fifth type of cohesion, ellipsis (defined as substitution by zero) because we could not figure out how to test it. We also included non-technical vocabulary (defined as vocabulary that any educated native-speaker could be expected to know) under the linguistic category.

Under engineering items, we included fact, inference, subtechnical vocabulary (defined here as vocabulary that any educated scientist could be expected to know), technical vocabulary (defined here as vocabulary that any educated engineer could be expected to know),

---

[1] To give them full credit for their hard work, the students were Melinda Erickson, Michael Linden-Martin, Barbara Miller, Josette Molloy, Anita Orlowski, and Philip Owen.

Table 6.4. *Item plan for an engineering-English reading test*

I. Linguistic factors
    A. Cohesion (after Halliday and Hasan, 1976)
        1. Reference items
        2. Substitution items
        3. Lexical cohesion items
        4. Conjunction items
    B. Non-technical vocabulary items
II. Engineering factors
    A. Fact items
    B. Inference items
    C. Lexis (after Cowan 1974; and Inman 1978)
        1. Subtechnical vocabulary items
        2. Technical vocabulary items
    D. Scientific rhetorical function items (after Lackstrom, Selinker, & Trimble
        1973; and Selinker, Todd-Trimble, & Trimble 1976, 1978)

(adapted from Brown, 1984c)

and scientific rhetorical functions (as defined and listed in Lackstrom, Selinker, & Trimble, 1973; and Selinker, Todd-Trimble, & Trimble, 1976, 1978).

To briefly summarize the reading test development, each of three MA students developed an engineering-English reading test of thirty or more items according to the plan shown in Table 6.4. The individual MA students wrote their own sets of items and later got feedback on their quality and their match to the item plan from all the others involved in the project. Then each of these three MA students piloted their tests using four kinds of graduate students: (a) native-speaker engineering students, (b) native-speaker humanities students, (c) non-native engineering students, and (d) non-native humanities students. Sample sizes ranged from 15 to 50 students in each category in each study. The MA students then analyzed their results, revised their tests on the basis of the results, and reported the descriptive statistics, reliability estimates, and validity conclusions as their MA theses.

Brown then used their pilot results to build a new test made up of the same three passages with the 20 best items for each passage combined into one test with a total of 60 items. All three of the MA students as well as Brown (1982) used content validity explanations based on the item plan shown in Table 6.4 to support the validity of their tests (see, for instance, Erickson and Molloy, 1982).

Thus again, as in the task-based performance assessment project, from the very beginning we were already setting up our arguments for the validity of the test by carefully planning our item types on the basis of the available literature and interviews with engineering professors. We did so by defining various theoretical categories of item types that we wanted to test. Only then did we take the next step, which was to administer the test and find out how well we had measured what we thought we were assessing (through a differential-groups construct validity study – explained below).

Expert judgments approach to content validity

The *expert judgments approach* to content validity first requires identifying experts. *Experts* are typically people who are trained in or knowledgeable about the content/processes being tested. The experts are then asked to judge the degree to which the test (or each individual test item) is testing the relevant content.

Clearly, the expert judgments approach will benefit greatly from first using the theoretical arguments approach, that is, the experts will better be able to judge the content validity of a criterion-referenced test if it has been carefully planned on the basis of theoretical, research, or practical perspectives. To some extent, then, the expert judgments approach depends on first applying the theoretical arguments approach. We will briefly discuss three examples of the expert judgments approach being applied to actual language tests: (a) a Tagalog listening proficiency testing project, (b) an English Language Institute testing project, and (c) a performance testing project.

Tagalog listening proficiency testing project. Our first example is drawn from Brown, Ramos, Cook, and Lockhart (1990), who report, among other things, using a scale for establishing the content validity of a Tagalog listening comprehension proficiency test. In the case of this example, for good or ill, the original purpose of the test was to measure Tagalog listening proficiency as defined in the ACTFL Proficiency Guidelines (American Council on the Teaching of Foreign Languages, 1986). After creating, piloting, and revising the test on the basis of item analysis techniques (as described in Brown, Ramos, Cook, & Lockhart, 1990; Brown, Cook, Lockhart, & Ramos, 1991; and briefly in Brown, 1996), they chose to explore the content validity of their revised test by convening a panel of Tagalog listening comprehension experts to judge how well the items on their revised test represented each of the ACTFL proficiency levels for Tagalog listening proficiency.

The experts were presented with a scale on which to judge the

Table 6.5. *Content validity judgment scale*

		No Match	Perfect Match
SEASSI PROFICIENCY EXAMINATION			
Rater's Name_____			
LISTENING COMPREHENSION SUBTEST			
MATCH TO ACTFL GUIDELINES			

INTERMEDIATE-LOW
13) MAGKANO MO IPINAGBIBILI ANG TELEBISYONG ITO?   1 2 3 4 5
   A. Opo, ang mahal.
   B. Isa po.
   C. P6,000.00 po.*
   D. Cash lang po.
14) NASAAN KA NITONG NAKARAANG SABADO AT LINGGO? 1 2 3 4 5
   A. Noong Linggo.
   B. Nasa Baguio po.*
   C. Dalawang araw po sa isang linggo.
   D. Tanghali na po akong gumising noong Linggo.
15) PAPASOK KA BA SA ESKUWELAHAN BUKAS?   1 2 3 4 5
   A. Opo, dahil kailangang pumasok.*
   B. Opo, pumasok po ako.
   C. Bukas po ang pasok sa eskuwela.
   D. May pasok po

(from Brown, Ramos, Cook, & Lockhart, 1990).

degree to which each item was "no match" to a "perfect match" with the ACTFL Proficiency Guidelines description for the appropriate level. A subset of items from the intermediate-low level items on that scale is shown in Table 6.5. Notice that the layout of the rating sheet focuses the experts on the individual test questions and that the stems are given in capital letters to alert the experts to the fact that these stems are only being heard by the students, while the four options are being read in the test booklet as shown. Notice further that the items are being rated on a five-point scale that asks for the expert to rate the degree to which the item matches the ACTFL Guidelines from "no match" (1) to a "perfect match" (5).

If the experts agree that the test items are representative of each level of the ACTFL Proficiency Guidelines (that is, the experts assign numerical "perfect match" values of 5 to each and every item), the testers would have built one fairly strong argument for the content validity of their test for purposes of testing Tagalog listening proficiency at least as defined by the ACTFL guidelines. If, in contrast, the experts disagreed as to whether the items represented Tagalog listening proficiency, the testers would have had to revise or redevelop at least some portions of the test. The degree to which further revisions were necessary depended on the ratings that the judges gave, and the degree to which the test developers were willing or obliged to attend to those ratings. Once revisions were made, it was necessary to get the judges to repeat their ratings, at least for those items that have been revised.

Note that expert judgments are only accurate to the extent that the views of the experts do not interfere with their judgments. Hence test developers may wish to take the following steps to make sure the experts' judgments are as useful as possible:

1. The test developers should insure that the experts share the kinds of professional viewpoints that the testers and their colleagues have. For instance, if the group developing the test is defining listening proficiency according to the *ACTFL Proficiency Guidelines*, they should probably consult experts who hold the same view of language teaching rather than experts who do not (for example, authors who have written articles criticizing the guidelines, like Savignon 1985, or Bachman & Savignon, 1986). Moreover, in reporting about their tests in articles or manuals, the test developers should be open about the fact that they have selected experts who share their view of the definition of the construct.

2. The test developers will have to acknowledge that such judgments of individual items will rarely be clear-cut. Such judgments will often be a matter of degrees rather than a simple yes or no. Hence, the test developers should provide the experts with some sort of rating scale, perhaps like the one shown in Table 6.5 with a scale from 1–5.

3. The test developers may feel that they need more information than that provided on a single scale, so they may wish to develop and use different 1–5 scales, say for instance, one for the form of the item, a second for the content of the item, and a third for the match to the overall goals of the test.

ELI testing project. For our second example, we use the ELI at the University of Hawai'i. During our tenures as directors of the ELI (over the course of eight years from 1986 to 1994), we organized the development of criterion-referenced tests for all of the ELI courses. We did so with the help of a series of excellent "lead teachers for testing" (individual teachers given release time to organize other teachers in test development and other curriculum development projects). We created these tests in two forms for each of eight courses. The items for these CRTs were written to closely fit with the course objectives. Since the objectives were the domain being assessed, every effort was made to write items with the content and skills being taught in the courses. Thus, content validity was an integral part of the item writing process. Since the course teachers wrote the actual items (with feedback from the ELI director and lead teachers), it was possible to not only design the items to fit the objectives, but also to match the objectives as they were actually taught in the courses.

Once criterion-referenced test developers were fairly sure the items they had written were content valid from their perspective, it proved useful to get feedback from outside "experts" in order to have independent judgments of how well the items fit the objectives.

Performance testing project. Recall that the performance assessment project described earlier in the chapter was reasonably well planned with carefully developed task difficulty levels based on task difficulty factors drawn from the literature (see Tables 6.1b and 6.2). A total of 114 potential language tasks (see examples shown in Table 6.3) were assigned to the different task difficulty levels. Expert judgments were used to verify the difficulty ratings of these tasks. Two trained ESL teachers examined the tasks and independently rated all six of the plus or minus categories shown in Table 6.1b to descriptions of the 114 tasks. In other words, in rating code complexity, the raters were assigning a + or − for both range and number of input sources; in rating cognitive complexity, they were assigning a + or − for both input/output organization and input availability; and in rating communicative demand, they were assigning + or − for both mode and response level.

Table 6.6 shows the correlations between scores given by the raters for each of the components and subcomponents. These correlations range from a low of .62 for input availability in cognitive complexity to .94 for response level in communicative demand. Generally, these correlations give moderate to strong support for the content validity of the difficulty ratings assigned to the 114 tasks in this performance testing project. Because there is a necessary connection between content and construct validity, this issue of the content validity of the performance test difficulty ratings will be revisited from a construct validity perspective in the next section.

The link between content and construct validities

Why do we say that content and construct validity are necessarily

Table 6.6. *Agreement of experts on content difficulty estimates*

Component	Subcomponent	Correlation
Code complexity	Range	.68
Code complexity	# of input sources	.77
Cognitive complexity	Input/output organization	.75
Cognitive complexity	Input availability	.62
Communicative demand	Mode	.88
Communicative demand	Response level	.94

connected? Messick (1989) argued the validity of the content of a test should be examined for both content representativeness and content relevance and, above, we showed that theoretical arguments or expert judgments can be used to accomplish both tasks. Messick also pointed out in that same chapter that content validity has its limitations as a sole basis for validity. His main point was that ". . . content validity is focused upon the test *forms* rather than test *scores*, upon *instruments* rather than *measurements*" (p. 41). A few lines later he restated this argument this way:

Strictly speaking, even from a content viewpoint, it would be more apropos to conceptualize content validity as residing not in the test, but in the judgment of experts about domain relevance and representativeness. The focus should not be on the test, but on the relationship between the test and the domain of reference. (p. 41)

Without laying out all of his reasoning, we will simply acknowledge that content validity should probably be conceptualized as residing in the judgments of experts, and that content validity is not sufficient unto itself. We further argue that, in criterion-referenced testing, content validity is a necessary, but not sufficient, precondition for the further demonstration of construct validity. As such, content and construct validity are probably inseparable. As Messick (1988, p. 38) put it: "Typically, content-related inferences are inseparable from construct-related inferences. . . . Test items and tasks are deemed relevant and representative because they are construct-valid measures of relevant and representative domain knowledge and skill." As we pointed out at the top of this chapter, arguments for the validity of test scores will be much more convincing to you and to others if they are accumulated from a number of perspectives. As such, considering several aspects of both the content and construct validity of any criterion-referenced test would seem prudent.

Another way to look at the content/construct validity connection is that content validity is just one aspect of construct validity. As Messick (1996, p. 248) puts it: "The content aspect of construct validity (Lennon, 1956; Messick, 1989) includes evidence of content relevance and representativeness as well as of technical quality. . .". However, even if we accept the view that content validity is one aspect of construct validity, that does not change the fact that careful consideration of the content validity of a criterion-referenced test from the theoretical arguments or expert judgments perspectives in terms of the representativeness and relevance of the items is a first crucial step to convincingly defending the validity of any criterion-referenced test.

Construct validity

In one way or another, *construct validity* approaches all rely on experimental studies of the degree to which a test is measuring the psychological construct or constructs that it claims to be measuring. Such experimental studies can take many shapes. For criterion-referenced tests, intervention or differential groups studies are usually the most appropriate and practical approaches to construct validity. However, hierarchical-structure studies of construct validity are sometimes also possible, as we will show below.

Intervention construct validity studies

Intervention studies usually entail three steps: (a) administering a pre-test, (b) teaching the students the construct, and (c) testing the students again at the end of instruction. If the criterion-referenced test is appropriately and accurately measuring the construct, the students' scores should increase significantly between the pre-test and post-test. This entire process is called an intervention study, and such a study can serve as the basis for one argument for the construct validity of the test involved.

In the criterion-referenced testing project discussed above and reported in Brown (1993), differences between pre-test and post-test means were shown for both forms of the criterion-referenced tests in each course. The results indicated that there were some gains in scores between the pre-test and post-test for each and every class involved. We therefore concluded that there was some relationship between the test scores and course instruction. These gains ranged from 5–8 percent. However, Brown concluded that the actual gains experienced by the students who took the courses may have been

Table 6.7. *Descriptive statistics for the original criterion-referenced forms A and B for ELI 72 intermediate ESL reading course (k = 46)*

		STATISTIC			
Test	N	Raw M	Raw SD	% M	% SD
PreA	35	31.11	5.18	67.63	11.26
PreB	29	30.90	5.47	67.17	11.89
PostA	26	34.73	4.86	75.50	10.57
PostB	35	33.57	3.81	72.98	8.28
Difference A		3.62		7.87	
Difference B		2.67		5.80	

considerably larger for a couple of reasons: (a) the pre-test/post-test differences were probably somewhat minimized because they included all students who took the pre-tests and post-tests – even those students who had high scores on the pre-test and were therefore exempted from the courses (thereby missing both the instruction and post-test); (b) the tests had not yet been extensively revised to select those items which are most sensitive to instruction (that is, they had not been item-analyzed to select those with high difference and B indexes).

Table 6.7 shows the pre-test/post-test results from the original two forms (A & B) of the ELI 72 (intermediate ESL reading) criterion-referenced tests analyzed in Brown (1993). Notice in the title for the table that each of the two forms contained 46 items (that is, $k = 46$). Notice also that inside the table the rows are labeled PreA and PreB for the pre-tests and PostA and PostB for the post-tests, and that the differences between pre-test and post-test for Forms A and B are given in the last two rows. Note also that the statistics included in the columns include the number of students taking each form, the raw score means and standard deviations, and the percent means and standard deviations. Finally, notice that average raw score differences between pre-tests and post-tests were 3.62, and 2.67 for Forms A and B, respectively, which is equivalent to 7.87% and 5.80%, respectively.

When we investigated the first of the two concerns reported in Brown (1993) (that is, the mismatch of students on the pre-tests and post-tests), we found as shown in Table 6.7 that indeed more people took the pre-tests (total $N = 35 + 29 = 64$) than took the post-tests (total $N = 26 + 35 = 61$) indicating that some of the students (presum-

Table 6.8. *Descriptive statistics-revised criterion-referenced forms A and B for ELI 72 intermediate ESL reading course (K = 30) with students matched on pre-test and post-test (N = 58)*

| | FORM A | | | | FORM B | | | |
	Raw M	Raw SD	% M	% SD	Raw M	Raw SD	% M	% SD
Pre-test	17.97	4.15	59.90	13.84	19.24	3.24	64.13	10.80
Post-test	22.28	4.05	74.27	13.52	22.76	2.61	75.86	8.69
Difference	4.31		14.37		3.52		11.73	

ably high scorers on the pre-tests) were not present for the post-tests. When we examined the data more closely, we found that only 58 of the 64 students had taken both tests. Some students had registered late and had therefore not taken the pre-test; others had been exempted from the courses on the basis of their pre-test scores; still others may have dropped the course for reasons of their own. Hence Brown (1993) was clearly justified to worry about mismatches in the students taking the pre-tests and post-tests.

In addition, item analysis of the 46 items for each test indicted that some of the items produced very low or even negative difference indexes and should therefore be revised, replaced, or eliminated. In each of the forms 16 items were found to have difference indexes that were .02 or lower (including negative values).

To investigate the effects of these two issues (the mismatch of students and the lack of item analysis), we reanalyzed the data for the ELI 72 course using only those students who had taken both tests and using only that reduced set of items that had adequate difference indexes. The results are shown in Table 6.8. Notice in the title of the table that the number of students is now the same 58 total for the pre-tests and post-tests (N = 58) and that the number of items is now 30 for each form (k = 30). Notice also that average raw score differences between pre-tests and post-tests in these revised results were 4.31, and 3.52 for Forms A and B, respectively, which is equivalent to 14.37% and 11.73%, respectively – approximately double the percent of gain found in the original, longer forms of the tests.

The question that usually springs to mind when examining the results of such an intervention study is how much of a difference between pre-test and post-test results is sufficient to make a good argument for the validity of a criterion-referenced test. The obvious answer is: the bigger the difference the stronger the argument.

Table 6.9. *Repeated-measures ANOVA results for ELI 72 reading test intervention validity study*

Source of Variation	SS	df	MS	F	p
BETWEEN-SUBJECTS					
Form difference	8.20	1	8.20	.44	.509
Within Cells	1039.66	56	18.57		
WITHIN-SUBJECTS					
Pre/post difference	440.13	1	440.13	57.36	.000
Form By Prepost	15.30	1	15.30	1.99	.163
Within Cells	429.67	56	7.67		

However, we are often asked the opposite question, which is how much of a difference is the smallest difference that could be used to support the validity of a criterion-referenced test. We would say that at least a statistically significant difference (based on *t*-test, ANOVA, or other statistical tests) between the pre-test and post-test would be the minimum difference that it would make sense to present as a positive argument for the validity of a test. Our reasoning is that any difference that is not statistically significant could have occurred by chance alone. Hence, non-significant (that is, chance) differences would not help at all in building arguments for the validity of any test. At the same time, just because a difference is significant does not imply that it is interesting or important. Judgment of the importance of a significant difference should be based on the magnitude of the difference, and must be considered within the context in which it was found, including factors like the length of instruction, the intensity of instruction, the level of proficiency of the students, the nature of the material being taught, and so forth.

Table 6.9 presents analysis of variance (ANOVA) results for the pre-test/post-test differences found for the revised ELI 72 intermediate ESL reading course criterion-referenced Forms A and B reported in Table 6.8. The ANOVA was conducted to answer three questions: (a) Is the observed difference in means between the pre-test and post-test scores significantly different? (b) Is the observed difference in means between Form A and Form B significantly different? (c) Is there any significant interaction effect between test times (pre and post) and forms (A & B)? (Full explanations of topics like *t*-tests, ANOVAs, effect size, interaction effects, etc. are well beyond the scope of this book; for amplification and clarification, see Brown, 1988a or Hatch & Lazaraton, 1990.)

There are three important things to notice in Table 6.9:

1. The mean difference for forms (A & B) is not significantly different ($p > .05$; indeed, $p = .509$ according to the table).
2. However, the difference for test times (pre & post) is significant ($p < .01$; indeed, $p = .000$ according the table).
3. In addition, no significant interaction effects were found between test times (pre- and post-) and forms (A & B) ($p > .05$; indeed, $p = .163$).

The first result indicates that we can only interpret the mean differences between forms as chance fluctuations. This result is good news because we would like our forms to be as parallel as possible, that is, we would not like them to be systematically different.

The second result indicates that the pre-test/post-test mean differences shown in Table 6.8 are significant, that is, they are probably not due to chance alone. This result is also good news because it means that the gains in scores between the pre-test and post-test are probably due to the intervention (teaching in this case) or other factors that might contribute to increased ESL reading abilities.

The third result means that there is no interaction between forms and test times. In other words, the results for forms and test times are clear and systematic. Hence, this non-significant result is good news because it means that we can make a straightforward interpretation of the first and second results just explained.

Based on our experiences, we have found that several factors must be kept in mind when performing intervention studies to support the validity of criterion-referenced tests:

1. It may be necessary and important to make sure that only the results of those students who took both the pre-test and post-test be used in the analysis for the intervention study.
2. It may be necessary and important to perform item analysis and compare the results for the reduced set of items to the results for the original versions.
3. In many cases, especially in ESL settings, it may be necessary to remember that the observed differences in such a study may be due to other factors like simultaneous exposure to English from other sources in daily life, other ESL courses being taken, or even other content area courses being taken elsewhere on campus.

It may also prove discouraging to realize that after 15 weeks of instruction and after all the work necessary to develop criterion-referenced tests, that gains of only 11.73% and 14.37% were realized. However, this represents the sort of gains that we have experienced in our real-world criterion-referenced testing situations. Language learning is not an all or nothing proposition like learning fractions; it is incremental, and at the upper levels like the ELI, small gains on the order of those reported here may be important. Also remember that the item analyses mentioned above (using the difference index) were attempts to make the tests better fit the curriculum and the learning going on it. Analysis of the results item by item can also be used the other way around: to make the curriculum better fit the tests. Changing the curriculum to better fit the tests can be accomplished by targeting those objectives that need better materials or need to be taught better. Thus, changes in the curriculum can also improve gains found in such an intervention study.

Differential-groups construct validity studies

Differential-groups studies involve first finding two groups of students: one group that possesses the construct in question (*masters*), and another group that lacks the construct (*non-masters*). Once the two groups have been identified, the test developer administers the test under investigation to both groups and analyzes the results. If the mean for the masters group is considerably higher than the mean for the non-masters, that constitutes support for the notion that the scores are related to the construct that differentiates the two groups, presumably the construct that the test was designed to measure. In other words, the difference in means supports the validity of the test for purposes of measuring the construct in question. However, the question of how large a difference is necessary to make a respectable validity argument has never been established. We feel, as noted above, that the difference between the two groups should at least be significant, that is, it should be established statistically that the difference is due to factors other than chance. Beyond that, we can only say that the larger the difference in means, the more convincing the validity argument will be.

Here, we will discuss two examples of differential-groups studies that take different approaches to building validity arguments for the tests involved. The first example uses what we call truly different groups; this example will be drawn from Brown 1984c, which used the differential-groups approach as one argument for the validity of a test of engineering-English reading ability. The second example creates master and non-master differential groups from the pilot data; this example will continue the discussion of the ELI intermediate reading course testing project mentioned above and reported in Brown (1993).

Using truly differential groups: engineering-English reading. *Truly differential groups* are groups that are different because one is made up of people who have the construct being tested and the other one is made up of people who do not have the construct. For example, Brown (1984c) describes a construct validity study that was conducted for the engineering-English testing project described in the section above under "content validity". Recall that the test included three passages on three different engineering topics: (a) "Mechanics of Deformable Bodies," (b) "Refactories," and (c) "Thermodynamic Analysis of Heat Pumps." Also recall that the test was made up of 20 items on each of three passages for a total of 60 items. In designing the test as we did, we had already begun our arguments for the validity by carefully planning with engineering professors and defining various theoretical categories of item types that we wanted to pilot. The next step was to administer the test and find out how well we had measured what we thought we were assessing.

The differential-groups study addressed the question of whether our test was valid for purposes of measuring engineering-English reading ability for international students studying or wanting to study in the United States. The participants in the differential-groups study were all graduate students. Half were Americans, and half were Chinese. The Americans were studying at UCLA, and the Chinese were students at Zhongshan University in the People's Republic of China (PRC). Thus two nationalities were tested to see if the test could differentiate on the basis of overall English proficiency. In addition, two academic majors, engineers and non-engineers, were also studied to determine the degree to which the test could differentiate on the basis of reading abilities that engineers have. Note that the non-engineers were all humanities students in the sense that they had varied backgrounds at the undergraduate level but were currently doing graduate work in TESL/TEFL. In this way, four groups were established for this differential-groups study based on their majors and nationalities: (a) American engineers, (b) American non-engineers, (c) Chinese engineers, and (d) Chinese non-engineers. There were 29 students in each of these groups.

After the test was administered to the four groups of students, test consistency was investigated from a criterion-referenced point of view using generalizability theory as explained in the previous chapter. Then, Brown calculated the descriptive statistics shown in Table 6.10. Clearly, the American engineers scored highest with a mean of 50.52 out of 60, and the Chinese non-engineers (TESL/TEFL) scored lowest with a mean of 27.38. Moreover, examining the descriptive statistics along the bottom of Table 6.10, all the engineers

Table 6.10. *Means and marginals for engineering-English reading test differential groups study*

		Engineer	Major Non-engineer	Total
Nationality	American	M = 50.52 S = 3.91 n = 29	M = 44.79 S = 6.94 n = 29	M = 47.66 S = 6.31 n = 58
	Chinese	M = 36.97 S = 8.22 n = 29	M = 27.38 S = 6.63 n = 29	M = 32.17 S = 8.92 n = 58
	Total	M = 43.74 S = 8.54 n = 58	M = 36.09 S = 6.97 n = 58	

(adapted from Brown, 1982)

taken together as a group clearly scored better with an overall mean of 43.74 than all the non-engineers taken together, who had an overall mean of 36.09. Thus, these results tend to support the validity of the test in that it is clearly assessing something related to engineering reading ability because people who have it score higher than people who do not. Since the focus of the test was on international students, the construct validity of the test was also supported by the fact that the Chinese engineers clearly outscored the Chinese non-engineers with means of 36.97 and 27.38, respectively.

To investigate the possibility that the observed differences were chance fluctuations, analysis of variance (ANOVA) procedures were used. As shown in Table 6.11, the mean differences between majors and nationalities both were found to be statistically significant at $p < .01$. Suffice it to say that the ANOVA procedures used here indicate that the test systematically differentiates between engineers and non-engineers, as well as between native and non-native speakers of English for other than chance reasons. Thus, this differential-groups study was appropriately used to argue for the construct validity of the engineering-English reading test.

Using master and non-master differential groups: ELI intermediate reading. One aspect of criterion-referenced testing that is particularly satisfying from a pedagogical standpoint is the fact that content and differential-groups approaches to validity are an integral part of item

Table 6.11. *Two-way ANOVA for engineering-English reading test differential groups study*

Source	SS	df	MS	F
Major	1699.45	1	1699.45	35.88*
Nationality	6951.76	1	6951.76	146.75*
Major × Nationality	108.14	1	108.14	2.28
Residual (error)	5305.65	112	47.37	
Total	14064.99	115	122.30	

* $p < .01$
(from Brown, 1982, 1984c)

writing and item analysis, that is, item selection and test revision are integrated right into the processes of analyzing and improving test validity. In a sense, the pass/fail decisions that are often made with criterion-referenced tests help us to set up differential groups: those who passed the test and those who failed. For instance, in the ELI intermediate reading course testing project discussed above, Brown (1993) addressed the differential-groups aspects of validity in two ways:

1. First, we have compared the scores of students who passed the courses (masters) with scores of students who failed (non-masters). Quite naturally, we found large differences between these two groups because passing or failing was partly determined by the test itself.
2. Second, we have examined the individual and mean item *f*, the *B*-index, and *A* estimates. These statistics indicated a fairly strong relationship between the accuracy of the students' answers on individual items, and whether or not they passed the course (i.e., whether they were masters or non-masters). (pp. 177–178)

Clearly then, differential-groups studies can be particularly valuable for investigating the fairness and validity of pass/fail decisions like that involved in the criterion-referenced project reported in Brown (1993).

Hierarchical-structure construct validity studies

Drawing once more from the task-based performance assessment project described above, we would like to illustrate one more approach to investigating and demonstrating the construct validity of a test. What we are calling the *hierarchical-structure approach* to construct validity involves showing that the subtests (or the items) on a test are in some sort of clear-cut hierarchical relationship that makes sense theoretically. In this case, we predicted on the basis of theory that the tasks on our task-based performance would vary systematically in terms of difficulty. That would mean that students who succeeded on the more difficult tasks should also succeed on those of intermediate, and low difficulty; those who did not succeed on the more difficult tasks, but succeeded on tasks of intermediate difficulty, should also succeed on tasks of low difficulty; and students who succeeded only on tasks of low difficulty, should not do so on any of the tasks of higher difficulty. In other words, the tasks should be in a hierarchical order of success matching the hierarchical order of theoretically predicted difficulty. We will show how a form of analysis called *implicational scaling* (Guttman, 1944, 1950; Dunn-Rankin, 1983, pp. 102–109) can be used to verify that a scale, or hierarchy, exists.

As part of our efforts to investigate the scalability of our tasks, we examined the performances of 19 students on seven of our tasks on what we called Form P. Table 6.12 shows the students' identification numbers down the left-hand side and columns for each task and the total labeled across the top. Inside of the table, a 1 indicates that the student got an average score of 60% or higher (across three raters) and therefore succeeded on that task, while a 0 indicates that the student got an average score of 59% or lower and therefore failed on that task.

Notice that the 1s for each row were totaled on the right and the 1s for each column were summed at the bottom. Then the rows were sorted from the highest total to the lowest – top to bottom – and the columns were sorted from the highest sum to the lowest, left to right. This sorting is necessary for the analyses that follow. Next a line was drawn to reflect as best we could the stepping of the hierarchy involved (see Table 6.12). Based on that line we then counted up the number of errors involved in the hierarchy, that is, the number of 0s in the area above and to the left of the line that should be 1s and the number of 1s in the area below and to the left of the line that should be 0s. These errors were counted up for each column, and the result is shown in the row labeled ERRORS.

A statistic called the coefficient of reproducibility can be calculated at this point by using the following formula:

$$CR = 1 - \frac{\Sigma E}{N(k)}$$

Table 6.12. *Example implicational scale – ALP, Form P*

Students IDs on Form P:	A20	B20	A18	C15	F7	E22	A9	TOTAL
9	1	1	1	1	1	1	1	7
19	1	1	1	1	1	1	1	7
11	1	1	0	1	1	1	1	6
16	1	1	1	1	1	0	1	6
18	1	1	1	1	1	1	0	6
36	1	1	1	1	1	1	0	6
41	1	1	1	1	1	1	0	6
10	1	1	1	0	1	1	0	5
14	1	0	1	1	1	0	0	4
21	1	1	1	0	0	0	0	3
24	1	1	0	1	0	0	0	3
12	1	0	1	0	0	0	0	2
23	1	0	1	0	0	0	0	2
28	1	0	1	0	0	0	0	2
31	1	0	0	1	0	0	0	2
25	0	1	0	0	0	0	0	1
32	0	1	0	0	0	0	0	1
38	0	0	0	1	0	0	0	1
39	0	0	0	0	0	0	0	0
SUM OF 1s	15	12	12	11	9	7	4	
ERRORS	0	3	5	4	0	1	0	13
DIFFICULTY	2	4	2	2	4	4	6	
CR	0.9023							
p	0.79*	0.63*	0.63*	0.58*	0.47	0.37	0.21	
q	0.21	0.37	0.37	0.42	0.53*	0.63*	0.79*	
MMR	0.6543							
PI	0.2566							
CS	0.7423							

* the higher value of p or q for each item

Where: CR = the coefficient of reproducibility
E = errors
N = number of people
k = number of items

Using the formula on the data in Table 6.12, we find that we need to know the total number of errors, 13 in this case, and total number of persons and items, $19 \times 7 = 133$ in this case. Applying the formula as follows, we find that the CR is .9023.

$$CR = 1 - \frac{\Sigma E}{N(k)} = 1 - \frac{13}{19(7)} = 1 - \frac{13}{133} = 1 - .0977 = .9023$$

Another statistic that we need to calculate is the coefficient of scalability. In order to get that statistic, we first need to calculate several intermediary statistics:

1. The proportion of 1s in each column (p) is calculated by dividing the number of 1s by the total number of numbers in the column. The proportion of 0s in each column (q) is calculated by dividing the number of 0s by the total number of numbers in the column.

2. Then, we need to calculate the *minimum marginal reproducibility* (*MMR*), which is the average of p or q, (whichever is larger in each case) divided by the number of items, k. Formulaically, that would be:

$$MMR = \frac{\Sigma p_{or} q}{k}$$

Where: MMR = minimum marginal reproducibility
$p_{or} q$ = whichever value of p or q is larger for each item
k = number of items

Using the formula on the data in Table 6.12, we find that we need to know whichever value of p or q is larger for each item, that is, the p or q values in Table 6.13 with the asterisks (i.e., .79, .63, .63, .58, .53, .63, and .79) and the number of items, which is 7 in this case. Then, we can calculate the MMR for these data as follows:

$$MMR = \frac{\Sigma p_{or} q}{k} = \frac{.79 + .63 + .63 + .58 + .53 + .63 + .79}{7} = \frac{4.58}{7} = .6543$$

3. Next, we need to calculate the *percentage of improvement* (*PI*) using the following formula:

$$PI = CR - MMR$$

Where all components are defined above.
For the data in Table 6.12, the *PI* would be calculated as follows:

$$PI = CR - MMR = .9023 - .6453 = .257$$

4. Finally, we need to calculate the *coefficient of scalability* (*CS*) using the following formula:

$$CS = \frac{PI}{1 - MMR}$$

Where all components are defined above.

For the data in Table 6.12, the *CS* would be calculated as follows:

$$CS = \frac{PI}{1 - MMR} = \frac{.257}{1 - .6543} = \frac{.257}{.3457} = .7434 \approx .74$$

Interpreting the two key statistics, *CR* and *CS*, can be done as follows: According to Guttman's original work a *CR* of .90 or greater is necessary for an adequate approximation to a scale; Dunn-Rankin (1983, p. 107) suggests that in addition to a CR of at least .90, a CS of at least .60 is necessary to claim that an adequate scale has been found.

In terms of validity, the results in Table 6.12 indicate that Form P (using a 60% cut-point for success or failure on each task) has a *CR* of about .90 and a *CS* of about .74. Consequently, the data in the table can be considered an implicational scale and hierarchical. Notice seven rows from the bottom of Table 6.12 that there are *difficulty* estimates. These numbers 2, 4, or 6 (for easy, intermediate, and difficult tasks, respectively) were assigned by us a priori (as described in the previous chapter) on the basis of theoretical considerations of what ought to constitute task difficulty (as described in detail in Norris, Brown, Hudson, & Yoshioka, 1998). With the exception of task B20, the task difficulty estimates are in exactly the same order as the implicational scale would predict. Thus, we need to take a look at B20 to figure out why it does not conform to our predictions, but otherwise, this implicational scaling analysis supports the hierarchical-structure and therefore the construct validity of our performance tests.

Further evidence was sought in additional analyses of Forms P, Q, and J at 40%, 60%, and 80% cut-points (as shown in Table 6.13). Examining the *CR* and *CS* statistics in Table 6.13, it quickly becomes clear that Forms P and J are scalable, while Form Q is not. Further analyses with larger sample sizes may confirm that Form Q is also scalable, but for the moment, these analyses only provide evidence for Forms P and J, which is certainly a good start.

Combining content and construct validity

The validity of a test is best understood and defended if a variety of validity arguments are combined. For instance, in a case like the engineering-English reading ability test, both content validity and differential groups arguments were combined to defend the construct validity of that test (as discussed above). However, further steps may be possible that combine the two approaches and thereby reveal

Table 6.13. *Implicational scale statistics: all forms*

FORM STATISTIC	CUT-POINT		
	40%	60%	80%
FORM P			
CR	0.9023	0.9023	0.9624
MMR	0.7143	0.6541	0.6767
%IMPROV	0.1880	0.2481	0.2857
CS	0.6579	0.7174	0.8837
FORM Q			
CR	0.8947	0.8872	0.8947
MMR	0.7444	0.6917	0.7218
%IMPROV	0.1504	0.1955	0.1729
CS	0.5882	0.6341	0.6216
FORM J			
CR	0.9714	0.9286	0.9857
MMR	0.8571	0.7857	0.9143
%IMPROV	0.1143	0.1429	0.0714
CS	0.8000	0.6667	0.8333

useful insights and information about different item types in a criterion-referenced test.

For example, consider once again the engineering-English reading test. Table 6.4 outlined the types of content systematically included in subtests on the total test (based on the best theoretical information available at that time in the English for science literature and from direct research with engineering professors); Table 6.10 revealed how American engineers outperformed American non-engineers, who outperformed Chinese engineers, who in turn outperformed Chinese non-engineers; and Table 6.11 showed ANOVA results which indicated that the differences between engineers and non-engineers as well as those between native and non-native speakers of English were statistically significant at $p < .01$ (that is, most probably due to other than chance fluctuations in means). The analysis shown in Table 6.14 combines the content validity arguments covered in Table 6.4 with the differential-groups construct validity arguments in a very criterion-referenced way. Table 6.14 shows percent scores for each of the groups (labeled across the top) and subtest by subtest for each of the item types (labeled in the left column). For example, in the first row of numbers (for the reference items under *Linguistic factors*) the

Table 6.14. *Performance of differential groups on each content type*

Item Type	Americans		Chinese	
	Engineers %	TESL %	Engineers %	TESL %
Linguistic factors				
Reference	82	67	60	52
Substitution	100	79	77	41
Lexical cohesion	94	64	63	55
Conjunction	85	80	66	65
Non-technical vocabulary	97	95	78	72
Engineering factors				
Fact	89	81	62	48
Inference	90	69	59	36
Subtechnical vocab.	71	65	59	28
Technical vocab.	80	52	42	21
Rhetorical functions	92	91	81	50

(from Brown, 1988b)

American engineers performed best with 82% correct on average, the American non-engineers performed second best with 67% correct, then the Chinese engineers with 60%, and Chinese non-engineers with 52%.

Clearly, the same pattern of percentage scores shows up throughout Table 6.14 that appeared in Table 6.10, which is to say, the American engineers performed best across the board, followed in order by the American non-engineers, Chinese engineers, and Chinese non-engineers. The pattern holds true for each and every subtest, further supporting both the content validity analysis and the differential construct validity argument.

Other things can be learned from such detailed analyses of test results. For instance, a quick glance at Table 6.14 will reveal that some subtests appear to be somewhat easier than others. In fact, the subtests labeled as *Linguistic factors* seem to be easier than those that are labeled *Engineering factors* for all groups included in this investigation. As Brown (1988b, p. 198) put it:

. . . the engineering items are more efficient than the linguistic ones. There are only 34 percentage points between high and low group scores (American engineers and Chinese TEFL) for the linguistic items, while the same figure for the engineering items is 49 points. Using only the engineering items might also be more justified, from a theoretical standpoint, as more "authentic" engineering tasks after Widdowson's (1978, p. 80) distinction between "genuine" and "authentic."

Such additional information can prove useful in further revising a test and improving its validity.

All in all, using a variety of approaches to investigate the validity of a criterion-referenced test and even combining those various approaches can lead to better understanding the degree to which a test is measuring the construct in question, how that construct works, and what types of content will most effectively measure the construct. In short, using a variety of validity approaches singly or combined should help test developers examine what it is they are measuring and how the construct should be defined in both practical and theoretical terms.

In the particular example here, combining several validity approaches helped us understand the degree to which the test was measuring the engineering-English reading ability construct (see Brown, 1984c), but also helped us to figure out which of the subtests might be most important to that measurement (see Brown, 1988b).

Expanded views of validity

In the last decade, a number of educational measurement specialists have wrestled with expanding our views of validity and what it ought to include. Primary movers in this area have been Messick and Cronbach. Basically, Messick (1988) suggested that we should be considering the evidential and consequential bases of test interpretation and use, and Cronbach (1988) pointed out that we need to be asking questions about the validity of our tests from functional, political, economic, and explanatory perspectives. Let's consider each of these sets of ideas separately.

Messick's ideas on validity

Messick (1988, 1989) lays out a unified theory of validity. Messick (1989) redefined validity as follows: "an integrated evaluative judgment of the degree to which empirical evidence and theoretical rationales support the adequacy and appropriateness of inferences and actions based on test scores or other modes of assessment" (p. 13). He basically viewed validity studies as serving much the same purpose as a lawyer's arguments for her or his client. Here, instead of conceptualizing validity as a test feature, validity is an argument, or more often a series of arguments, for the effectiveness of a test for a

	Test Interpretation	Test Use
Evidential Basis	Construct Validity	Construct Validity + Relevance/Utility
Consequential Basis	Value Implications	Social Consequences

Figure 6.1. Messick's (1989) facets of validity

particular purpose. It has been suggested that even this view of validation needs to be expanded to include not only a lawyer's argument for her or his client, but also to include the prosecutor's arguments against the defense, as well as arguments looking for alternative interpretations to score inferences. In such a view, the construct validity arguments go beyond simple advocacy for the validity of a particular test or set of tests. As noted above in the discussion of the performance testing project, Form Q did not demonstrate scalability. This should provoke some questions regarding just how categorical the + or − ratings in fact are. Additionally, it should lead to a questioning of how robust the three difficulty categories are, suggesting that there may be additional categories that are perhaps of variable importance depending upon the particular task and its context. Thus, while there is fairly strong support for the construct validity arguments behind the test approach that was adopted, much questioning is still in order.

According to Shepard, Messick (1989) served two purposes: "(a) It cements the consensus that construct validity is the one unifying conception of validity, and (b) it extends the boundaries of validity beyond test score meaning to include relevance and utility, value implications, and social consequences. While much of the discussion of Messick's ideas has focused on norm-referenced testing, we believe that his conceptualizations apply to criterion-referenced assessments just as much.

The facets of validity identified by Messick are shown in Figure 6.1. Notice that on the left side, he identifies two sources of justification for test validity: the evidential basis and consequential basis. The *evidential basis* focuses on justification for a test grounded in evidence in the form of empirical investigation of numerical data or other information. The *consequential basis* focuses on justification for a test in terms of the results or after effects of the test. Across the top of Figure 6.1, Messick labels two functions of testing: test interpretation and test use. *Test interpretation* focuses on the degree to which test interpretations are adequate and justified. In contrast, *test use* focuses on the degree to which actions based on the test are appropriate and justified.

We will now turn to a brief discussion of each of the cells in Figure 6.1. The upper-left cell is the evidential basis for test interpretation, which is the appraisal of empirical investigation of construct validity (which in turn involves the theoretical context of implied relationships to other constructs) of test interpretations. In contrast, the upper-right cell is the evidential basis for test use, which is the appraisal of empirical investigations of both construct validity and relevance/utility (that is, the theoretical contexts of implied relevance and utility) of test use. The lower-left cell is the consequential basis for test interpretation, which is the appraisal of the value implications (the contexts of implied relationships to good/bad, desirable/undesirable, etc.) of score interpretations. The value implications of test interpretation are the "more political and situational sources of social values bearing on testing" (Ibid., p. 42). Such value implications of test interpretation have traditionally been viewed as the ethical responsibility of the users of test scores because only the users know the special pedagogical and political circumstances in the particular context in which the test is being administered and in which the decisions are being made.

In contrast, the lower-right cell is the consequential basis for test use, which is the appraisal of the social consequences (that is, the value contexts of implied means and ends, or the consequences of a planned test use and the concrete after effects of actually applying a test) of test use. The social consequences of test use include "the appraisal of the potential social consequences of the proposed use and of the actual consequences when used" (p. 42). Such social consequences have also traditionally been viewed as primarily the responsibility of test users because only those score users know the social, political, or personal consequences of their decisions. More recently, however, that responsibility has shifted back to the test designer, who is responsible for predicting how the test will be used and misused and the social consequences of those uses, as well as obligated to follow through on the actual use of a test by studying the consequences of real-life decisions made with the test.

Since Messick clarified his facets of validity, considerable debate has issued from the general educational measurement community. For instance, Shepard (1997) argues the importance of consequential validity, as does Linn (1997), who argues that "Consequences of the uses and interpretations of test scores are central to an evaluation of those uses and interpretations. The evaluation of consequences rightly belongs in the domain of validity" (p. 16). In contrast, Popham (1997) counters that consequences are an important concern, but that it is a mistake to "tie social consequences into a validity framework" (p. 13). Mehrens (1997) argues very much the same thing.

The implementation of Messick's notions on the consequential basis of validity involves gathering evidence of various kinds on results or after effects of the test uses and interpretations. Lane, Parke, and Stone (1998) suggest investigating at least the intended effects and unintended effects of a test (or testing program) such that at least the issues that we have summarized in Table 6.15 are raised. Notice that we have reformulated the issues in Table 6.15 as yes/no questions. The questions might just as easily have been formulated as Wh-questions by using the phrase *To what degree is there* . . . instead of *Is there* . . . The overall goal of such an evaluation of the consequential basis of validity would be to determine whether the test (or testing program) is having the intended effects, and whether there are unintended effects that should be corrected.

Consonant with Messick's distinction between evidential basis and consequential basis of validity, Lane, Parke, and Stone (1998) further suggest using multiple sources of information (for example, students, teachers, and administrators) as well as multiple types of data gathering instruments (for instance, interviews, questionnaires, and classroom observations) in evaluating the consequential basis of the validity of test uses and interpretations. (For further recent discussions on implementing the consequential aspects of validity in general educational settings, see Green (1998); Linn (1998); Lane, Parke, & Stone (1998); Moss (1998); Reckase (1998); Taleporos (1998); and Yen (1998).)

Some of the considerable recent literature on the washback effect in language testing (for instance, see Alderson & Wall, 1993a, 1993b; Brown, 1997, 1998b; Gates, 1995; Alderson & Hamp-Lyons, 1996; Bailey, 1996; Messick, 1996; Shohamy, Donitsa-Schmidt, & Ferman, 1996; Wall, 1996; Wall & Alderson, 1996; and Watanabe, 1996), especially the literature on negative washback effect, is also directly related to the consequential basis of validity. For example, Brown (1997, 1998b, 1999) summarized and synthesized a number of the notions presented in Alderson & Hamp-Lyons (1996), Bailey (1996), and Shohamy et al (1996) to discuss many of the ways that tests can have a negative washback effect on (a) teaching, (b) course

Table 6.15. *Framework for evaluating consequences of assessment*

A. Intended effects
   1. Is there improvement in curriculum due to the testing?
   2. Is there upgrading of instructional strategies and content?
   3. Is there enhancement of format and content of classroom tests and quizzes?
   4. Is there increased motivation of students, teachers, and administrators?
   5. Is there improvement of learning for all students?
   6. Is there increased professional development and support?
   7. Is there enlargement of teachers' participation in the testing processes?
   8. Is there elevated awareness about testing (students, teachers, administrators, parents, etc.)?
   9. Is there enhanced awareness of criteria for judging performances (students, teachers, administrators, parents, etc.)?
  10. Is there increased awareness of the uses of test results (students, teachers, administrators, parents, etc.)?
  11. Is there awareness of the value and nature of test preparation materials (students, teachers, administrators, parents, etc.)?
B. Unintended effects
   1. Are there potential misuses of test results?
   2. Are there potential negative effects through the eyes of students, teachers, administrators, parents, etc.?
   3. Are there potential unintended effects related to intended effects (above) including (but not restricted to) the following:
     a. narrowing of curriculum and instruction?
     b. use of test preparation materials closely linked to the tests but not to the curriculum?
     c. use of unethical test preparation materials?
     d. differential performance on the test for subgroups?
     e. unfair and unethical uses of test scores (e.g., for judging teacher performance)?

(adapted from Lane, Parke, & Stone, 1998)

content, (c) class characteristicss, and (d) class time. We have reformulated these four sets of issues in Table 6.16 as questions that could be asked in evaluating the consequential basis of the validity of any test.

Generally, we take the stance that the consequences of test uses and interpretations are of primary importance, especially for criterion-referenced tests. Consider, for instance, item selection techniques like the *B*-index and validity arguments like the pass/fail differential-

Table 6.16. *Negative aspects of washback*

Teaching factors
1. Are the teachers narrowing the curriculum because of the test?
2. Have teachers stopped teaching new material and turned to reviewing test related materials?
3. Have teachers replaced class textbooks with worksheets similar to the tests?
4. Are the teachers teaching unnaturally?

Course content factors
1. Are students being taught "examination-ese"?
2. Are students practicing "testlike" items similar in format to those on the test?
3. Are students applying test-taking strategies in class?
4. Are students studying vocabulary and grammar rules (to the exclusion of other aspects of language)?

Course characteristic factors
1. Are students being taught inappropriate language-learning and language-using strategies?
2. Is there a reduced emphasis on skills that require complex thinking or problem-solving?
3. Are there courses that raise examination scores without providing students with the English they will need in language interaction or in the college or university courses they are entering'?
4. Is there a tense atmosphere in the class?

Class time factors
1. Are students enrolling in, requesting or demanding additional (unscheduled) test-preparation classes or tutorials (in addition to or in lieu of other language classes)?
2. Have review sessions been added to regular class hours?
3. Are students skipping language classes to study for the test?
4. Is there any lost instructional time due to the tests?

(adapted from Brown, 1997)

groups strategy. The *B*-index is clearly a technique for selecting the items on the basis of their consequences in decision making, and the pass/fail differential-groups approach to validity is similarly concerned with the consequences of decision making. Indeed, the consequences of test uses and interpretations are interwoven into the very nature of criterion-referenced tests. Hence, we feel that thinking about such consequences and the attendant values implications can only strengthen the validity of criterion-referenced tests.

Cronbach's perspectives on questions about validity

Cronbach (1988) summarized his thinking in four perspectives on the types of questions that we ought to be asking with regard to the validity of our tests: the functional, political, economic, and explanatory perspectives.

Functional perspectives. Cronbach (1988, pp. 5–6) begins by discussing the *functional perspectives*, which have to do with our views of what it means for a test to be valid. He points out that, historically, test validators have focused their studies on the content and truthfulness of interpretations in testing and that recently validators have turned more to examining the worth of score interpretations rather than the truthfulness of those interpretations. No doubt a stronger position on validity would include both the truth and worth of score interpretations though the two are not necessarily tightly linked:

1. For instance, the worth of a criterion-referenced test "lies in its contribution to the learning of students working up to the test, or to next year's quality of instruction" (Cronbach, 1988, p. 5).
2. At the same time, we must recognize that there is a built-in conservatism in tests in that constructs are defined at a specific period of time. Under these circumstances the notion of worth changes over time, when construct definitions change or when social norms change for definitions of constructs.
3. Therefore, validators are obliged to review the degree to which testing practices have appropriate consequences (after Messick, 1988) for the people and organizations involved.

This type of thinking naturally leads to conclusions like those of Messick summarized above.

Political perspectives. Cronbach's (1988, pp. 6–9) next set of perspectives involves the *political perspectives*, which have to do mostly with how people make decisions based on test scores as well as who will make those decisions. One important fact that we often forget is that all language testing decisions, indeed all language curriculum decisions, are essentially political. They may simply be political in the sense of local, within-institution politics, or if brought to the attention of politicians and the general public, they may become political in the more general sense of the word.

Unanimity of beliefs is not necessary for a political system to reach equilibrium as Cronbach (1988) points out. He further points out that:

Democracy is functioning well when every party learns how a pending decision would affect his or her interests, and feels that the decision process is being suitably sensitive to them. The investigator should canvass all types of stakeholders for candidate questions, then spread resources judiciously over inquiries likely to influence community judgments (Cronbach, 1982; Cronbach et al., 1980). Evaluators should resist pressure to concentrate on what persons in power have specified as *their* chief question [emphasis from the original]. (p. 7)

But, what is our responsibility as testers working within such a democratic framework?

As pointed out by Kleiman and Faley (1985), if expert test developers do not explain their testing practices clearly and adequately, the non-professionals (that is to say the politicians, the public, and so forth) will make the necessary decisions without the help of those experts. Generally, the degree to which examinees are being treated fairly and what the definition of "fairness" will be are both political decisions. However, we owe it to ourselves to shape those decisions by providing the best possible information to the decision makers.

Economic perspectives. Cronbach (1988, pp. 9–12) also discusses the *economic perspectives* of validity in terms of employment testing with a special emphasis on classification and the use of qualitative judgments in making actual decisions. We feel that we should also consider other economic aspects of validity including the costs of testing that we pass on to students and their parents, the costs of inappropriate testing in terms of bad decisions, inefficient learning processes, and so forth.

The costs of testing are imposed on students and parents in many ways, but most often in the form of test fees and the costs of test preparation courses. Other emotional and psychological costs are no doubt also levied on occasions, but here we are referring solely to the financial costs of tests to the test takers and their sponsors.

When we refer to the costs of inappropriate testing it is in terms of the costs of bad decisions and inefficient learning processes. These costs are also often borne by students and their parents as well. For example, students may incur costs in the form of extra tuition (and time) spent because of errors in admissions or placement decisions. All in all the financial perspectives on language test validity have been almost entirely overlooked in the literature to date.

Explanatory perspectives. *Explanatory perspectives* on test validity are the different approaches to doing the research necessary to support the construct validity and inferences drawn from a set of test scores. According to Cronbach (1988, pp. 12–14), such approaches can be broken into two categories: weak and strong approaches. *Weak explanatory approaches* consist of exploratory research that seeks to understand any observed relationships found in the data. Examples of the weak approach in language testing would include exploratory factor analyses used to cast about and hopefully understand the multi-factor nature of a test, exploratory talk-aloud protocols for test development, etc. *Strong explanatory approaches* involve clearly defining the theory underlying the construct or constructs being tested and then systematically challenging the theory empirically. This strong approach therefore necessitates envisioning plausible alternative explanations and examining them, and doing so before critics can mount them as an attack.

Making decisions with criterion-referenced tests

There is no question that one primary application for language tests is decision making. There is also no question that the validity of a test is, at least in part, directly linked to the degree to which the test scores are accurate and useful in making decisions. In Chapter 5, we discussed how the accuracy of a decision is related to criterion-referenced dependability and how that accuracy can be improved by using the confidence interval as part of the decision-making process – particularly for students whose scores are near any cut-points for decisions. However, the appropriateness of a particular cut-point as well as the pertinence of the resulting decisions is clearly a test validity issue. The discussion of how cut-points, standards, decision making, and validity are related will be organized around seven overall questions:

1. Are traditional cut-points and grading on a curve justified in classroom assessment?
2. Are cut-points necessarily arbitrary?
3. What is standards setting?
4. What are the alternatives in standards setting?
5. How can standards setting help with criterion-referenced decision making?
6. What is the relationship between standards and dependability?
7. How are validity and criterion-referenced decision making related?

Are traditional cut-points and grading on a curve justified?

Traditionally in North America, classroom teachers have usually decided that students must score at least 60% in order to pass the final examination for their course with a minimum grade of *D*. What is the justification for making 60% the cut-point? Is 60% always the same? Does 60% mean the students know the material? In short, what makes 60% cut-point decisions valid? Equally traditional is the notion that 60% to 69% gets a *D* grade (often including finer gradations for *D*−, D, and *D*+), 70% to 79% is some form of *C* grade (including *C*−, *C*, and *C*+), while 80% to 89% constitutes a *B* (including *B*−, *B*, and *B*+), and 90% to 100% is an *A* (including *A*−, *A*, and sometimes *A*+). What is the justification for any of these decisions? Can we simply say, "It's tradition" and leave it at that? What makes these decisions valid? Tradition?

In addition, what happens if the test is unusually easy or difficult? For instance, consider a situation in which the examination in a particular class is much more difficult for the students than previous tests the teacher has administered in other similar classes? How will the teacher deal with the fact that this particular administration will force him/her to fail many more students than usual? Will the teacher adjust by "grading on a curve" as is commonly done? And, why is the new cut-point any more valid than the original 60% decision point? These and other related issues will be answered in this section.

Generally speaking, the most arbitrary of systems for deciding cut-points are the traditional ones of setting a percentage cut-point of say 60% or grading on a curve. *Grading on a curve* essentially means using the concept of the normal distribution to assign grades. Figure 6.2 shows how grades of *A*, *B*, *C*, *D*, and *F* are assigned when people grade on a curve. Those students who fall within the area between one standard deviation below the mean and one standard deviation above the mean would be given grades of *C*. Above that, up to the second standard deviation above the mean would be a few *B*s, and above that yet another standard deviation would be a very few *A*s. Below the *C*s, down to the second standard deviation below the mean would be a few *D*s, and below that yet another standard deviation would be a very few *F*s. Language educators who espouse the grading-on-a-curve method of grading will often argue that it is necessary for *maintaining standards*. Unlike the *standards* used in the phrase *standards setting* (discussed elsewhere in this chapter), *maintaining standards* means upholding the reputation or relative standing of the institution, rather than setting some score point for decision making.

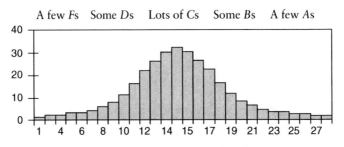

Figure 6.2. Grading on a curve and the normal distribution

Clearly, a main premise that underlies the idea of grading on a curve is that the normal distribution exists in classroom tests and classroom grades generally. Certainly the normal distribution does occur in language education. For instance, when large heterogeneous groups of students take norm-referenced tests, their scores are often normally distributed if the test is suitable for them. For example, hundreds of thousands of students ranging from virtually no English to native-speaker level take the TOEFL, a test of overall English proficiency, and to a large extent, the scores are normally distributed. Notice that the students are large in number and very heterogeneous. The same is true on large-scale norm-referenced ESL placement tests like the *English Language Institute Placement Test* (ELIPT) at UHM or the *English as a Second Language Placement Examination* (ESLPE) at UCLA. In both cases, hundreds of students take the test battery every year and they range considerably in ability levels. In large-scale norm-referenced testing with heterogeneous student abilities, the normal distribution not only exists, but serves as a powerful model for statistical analyses.

Unfortunately, the premise that underlies grading on a curve in classroom situations is fundamentally flawed, that is, the normal distribution probably does not exist in most classroom testing and grading situations. There are at least three reasons why the normal distribution is not an appropriate model for analyzing classroom testing and grading. First, it is unreasonable to expect a normal distribution of scores or grades in small groups. It simply does not happen very often. It would not happen with TOEFL scores either, not with small groups of students. Second, students in classrooms, because of placement procedures or personal choices (like wanting to be with a friend, or not liking morning or afternoon classes) tend to constitute relatively homogeneous groups with regard to language proficiency levels, language backgrounds, and other important variables. It is therefore unreasonable to expect normal distributions in such homogeneous groups; the students are just not spread out enough. Third, teachers teach students certain material and then test that material. To the degree that all the students actually learn the material, these acts of teaching and testing specific material will tend to make the group even more homogeneous on those tests. It is therefore unreasonable to expect normal distributions in such small and homogeneous groups.

Are cut-points necessarily arbitrary?

Language teachers must often make decisions about their students. Sometimes teachers must use testing to make program level admissions or placement decisions, though these types of decisions are commonly the responsibility of administrators. More often, teachers are directly involved in assessment for diagnosis, progress, or achievement decisions in their own classrooms.

At this point in the book, it should be abundantly clear that the first two types of decisions for admissions and placement decisions are best made using norm-referenced tests.[2] For admissions decisions and placement decisions, administrators need to categorize students in relationship to each other so they can be put into groups. For instance, in an admissions decision, administrators might use overall English proficiency scores on the TOEFL to decide whether students should be admitted or denied admissions to a particular university. In placement decisions, administrators might use a placement examination to decide whether students should be placed into the elementary, intermediate, or advanced level of study. In short, a norm-referenced test is administered, the students are spread out along a continuum of general abilities, and then actions are taken based on those test scores that will decide the fate of the students, at least in terms of which group they belong in. The question being addressed here is where the line should be drawn that separates the groups. For instance, at the University of Hawai'i in Manoa, undergraduates must have a 500 on the traditional paper-and-pencil TOEFL scale in order to be admitted. That is the standard for admissions at UHM. But why 500? The graduate school requires 600. Why 600? Why not 500? Other colleges and universities have set different standards – for example

---

[2] We make this statement in light of the present state of knowledge about how language is learned. However, if one day we come to understand clear-cut stages throughout the language learning process, and/or if a truly hierarchical curriculum is developed some day, there is no theoretical reason why we could not have a CRT placement test.

450 or 550, or even at 400 – depending on their needs and the types of students they want to admit. So why is UHM justified in setting its standard at 500? Isn't that arbitrary?

We have argued throughout this book that the second set of decisions mentioned above (diagnostic, progress, and achievement decisions) are better made with criterion-referenced assessments. Take, for instance, achievement decisions using a criterion-referenced achievement assessment. Typically a final examination achievement test is administered at the end of a course. The test is scored and the scores are converted into percentages. Then, as described in the previous section, students whose results are in the 60% to 69% range are assigned a grade of *D*, 70% to 79% get a *C*, 80% to 89% a *B*, and 90% to 100% an *A*. Perhaps more importantly, students with 60% or above pass the course, while those with 59% or lower fail. But what is the rationale for setting the standards for the various grades at 60%, 70%, 80%, and 90%? Aren't these criterion-referenced cut-points just as arbitrarily decided as the norm-referenced cut-points discussed in the previous chapter? The answer is a qualified *yes*. However, arbitrary or not, as long as language educators need to make admissions, placement, diagnosis, progress, and achievement decisions, standards will be necessary and appropriate, despite the fact that there are social and political aspects to making such decisions.

The idea that standards are arbitrary is far from a new idea. For instance, as far back as 1978, Glass pointed out that ". . . every attempt to derive a criterion score is either blatantly arbitrary or derives from a set of arbitrary premises" (p. 258). However, arbitrariness is not inevitably capricious, as pointed out by Popham (1978, p. 169):

To have someone snag a performance standard "off the wall", with little or no thinking involved, is truly arbitrary with all the negative connotations that the term deserves. To go about the task of standard setting seriously, relying on decent collateral data, wide-ranging input from concerned parties, and systematic efforts to make sense out of relevant performance and judgmental data is not capriciously arbitrary. Rather, it represents the efforts of human beings to bring their best analytic powers to bear on important decisions.

Clearly, standards are here to stay in language education. Because such decisions must be made and because they sometimes dramatically affect the lives of the language students involved, teachers/ testers must use the best available techniques to establish standards. In short, well-considered (though necessarily imperfect) standards must be used and generally, they will be better than no standards at all (Hambleton, 1978; Popham, 1978; and Scriven, 1978).

What is standards setting?

The general area of making the types of decisions discussed in the previous section is referred to as standards setting. *Standards setting* will be defined here as the process of determining where test score cut-points should be made for making logical and valid decisions about students' performances. To establish standards, teachers or administrators must decide the appropriate cut-point for a given set of test scores and a given decision. *Cut-point* will be formally defined here as whatever score is established as the point along the continuum of scores at or above which students will be categorized one way and below which they will be categorized otherwise. As discussed above, cut-points may divide students who will be admitted into an institution from those who will not, or separate students into different levels of study, or indicate the level at which students are considered to have mastered material or skills for diagnostic decisions, progress decisions, or achievement decisions. When we talk of setting a *standard*, we are referring to setting that cut-point. Thus one synonym for *standard* would be *cut-point*.

Standards setting has been a substantial issue for several decades in the general education field. (For overviews see Berk, 1986; Burton, 1978; Jaeger, 1989; Koffler, 1980; Livingston & Zieky, 1982; Popham, 1978; Shepard, 1984; Skakun & Kling, 1980; Impara & Plake, 1995, 1997. Glass, 1978, provides a negative, but reasonable, review; Rowley, 1982 provides a very light-hearted alternative view.) In language testing, the ideas involved in standards setting are not completely new either (for instance, Powers & Stansfield, 1982; Moy, unpublished ms.) and indeed, appear to be rising in prominence (see Alderson, 1993; Alderson & Buck, 1993). Unfortunately, standards are seldom discussed in language programs even though standards are often the basis for making important decisions that may dramatically affect our students financially, emotionally, and in terms of their future well-being.

What are the alternatives in standards setting?

The educational testing literature offers a wide variety of approaches for rationally setting standards. Brown, 1996, categorized these various approaches into state-mastery and continuum approaches, as well as test-centered approaches and student-centered approaches.

State-mastery approaches. Some of the first standards setting approaches would now be classified as state-mastery approaches (see Emrick, 1971; or Macready & Dayton, 1977 for further description). *State-mastery approaches* presuppose that the characteristic being assessed on a given test is dichotomous and absolute, for example with a criterion-referenced assessment, you can look at the results as though the students have either mastered the course material or not. Over the years heavy criticism has been leveled at state-mastery approaches (see Shepard, 1984; or Jaeger, 1989 for summaries). The most serious criticism is that state-mastery approaches implicitly presuppose that students will either be masters knowing 100% of the material, or be non-masters knowing zero% (Meskauskas, 1976).

For language teachers, the state-mastery approach may be especially questionable because so much of language learning is a matter of degrees rather than all-or-nothing in nature. In math, it may be reasonable to expect students to have mastered simple addition before moving on to subtraction, and simple subtraction before moving on to more complex addition and subtraction (though even that proposition is open to attack). But in language teaching, there is very little that we would expect students to learn with 100% accuracy before moving on to other topics. For example, the third person agreement grammatical structure in English (I run vs. he runs) is taught early in most ESL/EFL courses, yet this particular structure is one of the last grammatical points students master with 100% accuracy. Hence, it is absurd to expect students to have mastered that structure with 100% accuracy at any point in their language learning careers except at the very end when assessment is probably irrelevant. In short, state-mastery standards setting approaches may work for some very clearly defined subject matter areas, but they are probably not reasonable in most cases for assessing language learning and making decisions about language students. Typically, even in the education literature on standards setting (see Shepard, 1984; Jaeger, 1989), state-mastery approaches are only mentioned because they are interesting historically.

Some educational measurement specialists also found state-mastery approaches problematic in that they dichotomize learning into 0% and 100% mastery categories without taking into account the fact that these decisions are based on scores, which are continuous, not dichotomous, in nature. Such critics felt that standards setting approaches should be developed that account for the fact that most test scores locate students on a continuum of scores. The approaches that resulted from this kind of thinking have come to be known as continuum approaches. They will be briefly described next

Table 6.17. *Nedelsky's test-centered continuum approach to standards setting*

1. Sample from a population of appropriate judges
2. Have judges define and characterize a minimally competent student
3. Have judges predict which of the multiple-choice options on a test the minimally competent student would find implausible
4. Assume students guess randomly from among the remaining plausible options and calculate a minimum passing score for each item based on the predictions in step 3 by calculating the reciprocal of the number of plausible options as follows: 1/(# plausible − # implausible). For example, if one of four options is predicted to be implausible for a minimally competent student, the reciprocal of the plausible options would be $1/(4-1) = 1/3$
5. Calculate the standard for each judge by adding up the minimal pass levels for all items
6. Calculate the overall standard by averaging the individual judge's standards

in two main categories: test-centered continuum approaches and student-centered continuum approaches (after Jaeger's 1989 classification system).

Test-centered continuum approaches. Most approaches to standards setting require that experts (in whatever field is appropriate) make judgments. The primary differences between methods lie in what the experts are being asked to judge. For instance, in the *test-centered continuum approaches*, expert judgments are centered on the test content itself, while in the student-centered approaches the experts' judgments are concentrated on students' performances. The four test-centered continuum approaches most often encountered in the literature are Nedelsky's, Anghoff's, Ebel's, and Jaeger's.

Nedelsky's approach (Nedelsky, 1954) relied on expert judgments of the test design. Table 6.17 shows the steps involved in Nedelsky's approach.

Nedelsky's approach was criticized for the following reasons:

1. It is only appropriate for multiple-choice tests (which precludes using it for productive language tests).
2. Students do not always use a strategy of eliminating implausible options and guessing from among the remaining plausible ones (sometimes, they even know the answer).
3. The values resulting from this approach are systematically lower than the values arrived at through other test-centered continuum approaches.

Anghoff's approach (Anghoff, 1971) also relied on expert judg-

Table 6.18. *Anghoff's test-centered continuum approach to standards setting*

1. Sample from a population of appropriate judges
2. Have judges review the content that the test is designed to assess and have them estimate the performance level that separates competent students from those who are not
3. Have judges predict the probability that a minimally competent student will correctly answer each item (that is, the proportion of minimally competent students in a normal group)
4. The sum of the probability estimates (in step 3) then form the minimally acceptable score
5. Calculate the standard for each judge by adding up the probability estimate (in step 3) for all items
6. Calculate the overall standard by averaging the individual judge's standards

ments of test design quality by estimating the probability that competent students would correctly answer each question. However, this approach could be used for all kinds of tests because it was applicable to items in formats other than multiple-choice. Table 6.18 shows the steps involved in Anghoff's approach.

Anghoff's approach was criticized because it is only applicable to test items that are scored dichotomously (that is, either right or wrong). However, in all fairness, we must add that Anghoff's approach is relatively easy to use and it does summarize the judgments of those experts most qualified to make such judgments.

Recently, Impara and Plake (1997) suggested two modifications in Anghoff's approach. In the Anghoff approach, judges are asked to imagine hypothetical competent students and predict the proportion of competent students who would answer each item correctly. Impara and Plake suggested that judges be asked to imagine a real student who they would consider competent and answer yes/no to whether or not that student would be able to answer each item correctly. Those may seem like minor adjustments, but the results they obtained in the two studies reported in Impara and Plake (1997) suggest that those modifications may not only make the standards more valid but also easier to apply than the Anghoff method.

Ebel's approach (Ebel, 1979) relied on expert judges to evaluate the expected success of items in terms of their difficulty and relevance. Table 6.19 and Figure 6.3 show the steps involved in Ebel's approach. Unfortunately, according to Shepard (1984, p. 176), judges often have difficulty keeping the two dimensions (difficulty

Table 6.19. *Ebel's test-centered continuum approach to standards setting*

1. Sample from a population of appropriate judges
2. Create a two-way table of difficulty and relevance for use in judging test items, for instance (as shown in Figure 6.3), one dimension could be difficulty (with three levels: hard, medium, and easy), and the other could be relevance (with three levels: irrelevant, acceptable, and essential)
3. Assign each item of the tests' items to one cell of the two-way table (for example, write item numbers within the cells of Figure 6.3)
4. Have the judges decide the proportion of items in each cell a borderline passing student (that is, a student answering a large number of questions like those assigned to cells in the previous step) would correctly answer
5. Calculate the standard for each judge by multiplying the proportion suggested by each judge for each cell by the number of items in the cell and sum the results across all cells
6. Calculate the overall standard by averaging the individual judge's standards

RELEVANCE

		Irrelevant	Acceptable	Essential
	Hard			
DIFFICULTY	Medium			
	Easy			

Figure 6.3. Two-way table for Ebel's test-centered continuum approach

and relevance) separate in their minds. In some cases, this distinct disadvantage may be outweighed by the advantages accrued from having all judges working with a single scale that yields similar probability estimates.

Jaeger's approach (described in Jaeger, 1982, 1989) was far more complex than the other test-centered approaches we describe in that it advocated using an iterative process for developing a consensus among the expert judges. Table 6.20 shows the steps involved in Jaeger's approach.

Table 6.20. *Jaeger's test-centered continuum approach to standards setting*

---

1. Sample from all groups of judges with a legitimate interest in the testing outcomes
2. Have judges examine each item and answer *yes* or *no* to the question: Should students who pass the test be able to answer the item correctly?
3. Show judges data on real student performance on the test and the answers of the other judges
4. Have the judges re-examine each item and again answer *yes* or *no*
5. Calculate each judge's standard by summing the *yes* answers
6. Calculate the test standard for each group of judges by calculating the median across judges in the sample
7. Determine the overall test standard by examining the medians for all groups of judges and using the lowest as the passing standard

---

Table 6.21. *Borderline-group approach to standards setting*

---

1. Sample from a population of appropriate judges
2. Have the judges discuss and collectively define three categories of performance on the test in question: acceptable, borderline, and inadequate
3. Have the judges identify any students known to them based on information other than their test scores, who they consider borderline cases
4. Administer the test
5. Set the standard at the median of the performances of the borderline students identified by the judges in #3 above

---

Jaeger's approach was criticized for its complexity, and indeed, it would be relatively difficult to apply. However, that single disadvantage might be dwarfed by the political advantages gained by involving all relevant groups in examining, discussing, and judging individual test items.

Student-centered continuum approaches. Unlike test-centered continuum approaches, which are based on judgments of test content, *student-centered continuum approaches* require that expert judgments be focused on students' performances on the test. Two types of student-centered continuum approaches have been developed: the borderline-group approach and the contrasting-groups approach.

The *borderline-group approach* (after Zieky & Livingston, 1977) requires expert judges to decide who the borderline students are in a particular population and then establish what a representative bor-

Table 6.22. *Contrasting-groups approach to standard setting (original overlapping-groups strategies)*

1. Sample from a population of judges familiar with the students
2. Have the judges discuss and collectively define acceptable, borderline, and inadequate performance on the test
3. Use information other than the test scores and have the judges identify all students they know in each category: acceptable, borderline, or inadequate categories
4. Administer the test
5. Examine the distributions of the acceptable and inadequate groups (as identified by the judges)
6. Set the standard in one of four possible ways:
    a. Plot the two sets of scores in one graph allowing them to overlap and set the standard at the point where they cross (see Figure 6.4a)
    b. Calculate the percent of students who are acceptable at each test score and set the standard at that score where 50% are classified as acceptable (see Figure 6.4b)
    c. Plot the two sets of scores in one graph allowing them to overlap and set the standard at the point to the right of where they cross at the point where none of the inadequate students would be above the cut-point (see Figure 6.4c)
    d. Plot the two sets of scores in one graph allowing them to overlap and set the standard at the point to the left of where they cross where none of the acceptable students would be below the cut-point (see Figure 6.4d)

derline performance would be on each test question. Table 6.21 shows the steps involved in the borderline-group approach.

The primary advantage of the borderline-group approach is that, typically, teachers' classroom observations are used to establish the cut-point. Since teachers are the expert judges who know the students best, they can serve as an excellent source of information about students' performances, they can accurately decide who the borderline students are, and they can provide judgments that are both appropriate and relevant for any standard being set for achievement in their classes. Ironically, this advantage is also related to one disadvantage of the borderline-group approach: this approach can only be used for decisions where the teachers actually have classroom experience with the students and such experience may not necessarily be available if all teachers do not cooperate.

The *contrasting-groups approach* (also after Zieky & Livingston, 1977) is similar to the borderline-group approach, except that acceptable and inadequate groups are used as the basis for estab-

a. Original overlapping-groups strategy

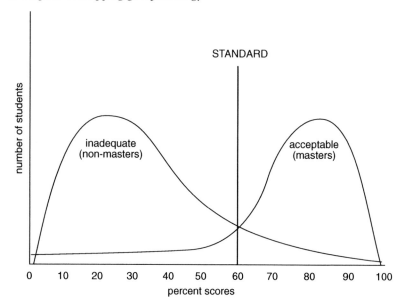

b. Percentage of acceptable performances

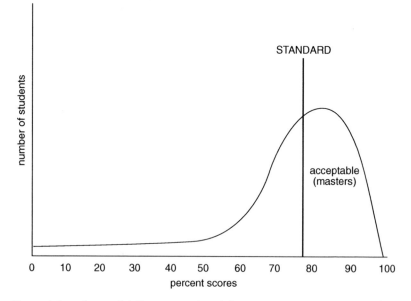

Figure 6.4. a, b, c and d. Four strategies of the contrasting-groups approach to standard setting

c. Protecting-the-institution strategy

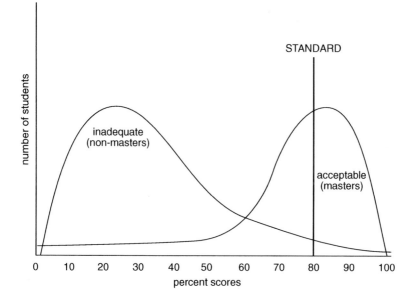

d. Protecting-the-students strategy

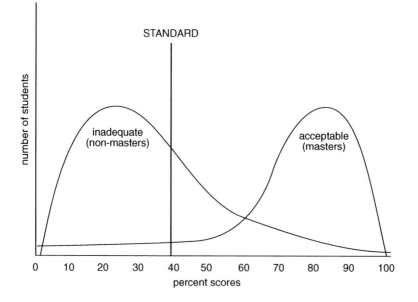

lishing the cut-point. Table 6.22 numbers 1–5 show the main steps involved in all the variants of the contrasting-groups approach.

Note that at least four main variant strategies can be used within the contrasting-groups approach depending on how the cut-point is determined. First, the *original overlapping-groups strategy* of the contrasting-groups approach uses steps 1 through 5 of Table 6.22, and step 6a for actually determining the standard. Step 6a requires plotting the two sets of scores in one graph so they overlap and setting the standard at the point where the two distributions cross (as shown in Figure 6.4a).

Second, the *percentage of acceptable performances strategy* of the contrasting-groups approach also uses steps 1 through 5 of Table 6.22, but then uses step 6b for actually determining the standard. Step 6b requires calculating the percent of students who are acceptable at each test score and setting the standard at that score where 50% are classified as acceptable (see Figure 6.4b).

Third, the *protecting-the-institution strategy* of the contrasting-groups approach also uses steps 1 through 5 of Table 6.22, but then uses step 6c for actually determining the standard. Step 6c requires plotting the two sets of scores in one graph so they overlap and setting the standard at the point to the right of where they cross at the point where none of the inadequate students would be above the cut-point (see Figure 6.4c). Such a cut-point would protect the institution from passing students who did not deserve to pass. Popham (1981, p. 389) called these *false positives*, that is, decisions that wrongly placed students on the *passing* side of the cut-point. The protecting-the-institution strategy might be appropriate for admissions decisions at an institution where there are many more students applying than positions available. In such a case, a conservative policy on admissions decisions could make sense because the responsible parties would want to mistakenly accept as few unqualified students as possible even at the cost of rejecting some qualified students. For CRT achievement testing, such an approach might be useful and prudent in setting the standards for high stakes decisions like advancing potential surgeons to full professional status. Wouldn't you want such a decision to err on the conservative side?

Fourth, the *protecting-the-students strategy* of the contrasting-groups approach also uses steps 1 through 5 of Table 6.22, but then uses step 6d for actually determining the standard. Step 6d requires plotting the two sets of scores in one graph so they overlap and setting the standard at the point to the left of where they cross at the point where none of the acceptable students would be below the cut-point (see Figure 6.4d). Such a cut-point would protect the students from failing who deserved to pass. Popham (1981, p. 389) called these *false negatives*, that is, decisions that wrongly placed students on the *failing* side of the cut-point. The protecting-the-students strategy could be appropriate in a final examination achievement decision where failed students would have to repeat the entire course. In such a case, the teachers might create a liberal policy on pass/fail decisions in order to make sure as few students as possible are mistakenly failed even if that means that a few weak students will be passed.

Which of the four strategies shown in Table 6.22 under steps 6a to d to use in a particular situation will depend on the type of decision being made, the importance of the decision, and the opinions of the teachers and administrators (and sometimes, students) involved in the decision. Regardless of which strategy is finally used, from a criterion-referenced assessment perspective, the general contrasting-groups approach for standards setting is very useful because it is closely related to the item analysis statistics of difference index and *B* index as well as to the intervention and differential-groups strategies for investigating construct validity. Hence, we find it reassuring that the use of the contrasting-groups standards setting approach is intimately related with the purpose of the test and in turn to its validity.

How can standards setting help with criterion-referenced decision making?

Given boundless time and resources, you could use all the standards setting approaches covered in the previous section to help you set the cut-points for decision making on one of your tests. One strategy you might want to try is to select a few of the approaches in the previous section. You could work with your colleagues to select those two or three approaches that make the most sense in your decision-making setting and then compare the results of the various approaches before deciding on a cut-point. We hope that it is clear from reading the previous section that all the standards setting approaches, in their own ways, are designed to be rational processes that focus the critical faculties of expert judges on test content or on student performances in order to decide what test performance levels will serve fairly and accurately as cut-points.

Naturally, you must also recognize that, even using the best of standards setting approaches, no standard will ever be perfect. But, how can you assess the effects of such imperfection on your decision making? You may find it useful to think about the effects of a particular cut-point on a specific assessment procedure in relation to both test dependability and validity.

What is the relationship between standards and dependability?

Standards are related to test dependability in that you can rely on the consistency of a decision based on a cut-point on a highly dependable test, but you should put much less confidence into any decision based on a cut-point on a test with low test dependability. The degree of confidence you can put in decisions based on a particular cut-point is directly related to the confidence interval (CI) discussed in the previous chapter. Recall that the CI can be interpreted as a band of confidence around a particular cut-point. At least in theory, such a band of scores is one within which the students' scores are likely to occur repeatedly if they were to take the test repeatedly. A test with high dependability will produce a CI band of scores above and below the cut-point which is relatively narrow; a test with low dependability will produce a CI band which is relatively wide.

For instance, consider two tests that are based on a 0% to 100% scale. If one of the tests is very dependable, it might have a CI of three percent, which would mean that you could reasonably expect students' scores to fluctuate plus or minus 3% for 68% of the time, plus or minus 6% for an additional 27% percent of the time, and even plus or minus 9% for a much smaller 3% of the time. In contrast, if the other test was much less dependable, it might have a much larger CI of say 15%. That would mean that you could reasonably expect students' scores to fluctuate plus or minus 15% about 68% of the time, plus or minus 30% an additional 27% percent of the time, and a whopping plus or minus 45% three percent of the time.

Typically, you will want to use the CI to limit *decision errors* by ascertaining which students would fall on the other side of a cut-point if they were to take the test again. In other words, students who score within one CI below a particular cut-point might fall above that cut-point if they were to take the test again or vice versa. Such a result would represent a decision error. Thus, you might want to gather additional information in making your decisions about such students. Using the CI in this way for decision making should improve the overall consistency and accuracy of those decisions. The steps involved in using the CI in decision-making should probably involve at least the following steps shown in Table 6.23.

Table 6.23. *Using the confidence interval in decision making*

1. Set the standard using whatever approach is deemed most appropriate in the particular language program
2. Calculate the CI, recognizing that it represents a band of possible decision errors that are normally distributed around the cut-point
3. Decide whether to consider errors that will work against the student, against the institution, or against both
4. Isolate those students who scored within one CI band (for 68% confidence) above and/or below the cut-point (depending on number 3 above). Gather additional information about these students and make decisions on the basis of all available information
5. At some point, use all available test dependability information, as well as the CI to inspect other possibilities and revise the cut-point for future use

How are validity and criterion-referenced decision making related?

Standards are directly related to the validity of criterion-referenced assessment procedures because the purposes of the test will usually determine to a large degree where the cut-point should be placed.

As mentioned above, test validity is closely related to the purposes of the test, and standards can affect the purpose(s). Thus standards can affect the degree to which a test is measuring what it is supposed to be measuring, and by extension, the degree to which a test is being used to make decisions in the way they were intended to be made. Thus testers should worry not only about the validity of their tests, but also about the *decision validity* of using the scores on those tests for making whatever decisions are involved.

For example, as described earlier, during our tenures as Directors of the ELI at the University of Hawai'i, we administered two forms of our criterion-referenced assessments at the beginning and end of each course for diagnostic and achievement purposes, respectively. These forms were administered in a counterbalanced manner with forms A and B each being administered to about half the students at the beginning of the course and the opposite forms being administered to the students at the end of the course. In this way, no student took exactly the same form two times.

At the beginning of the courses, the tests were administered in the first or second week for diagnostic purposes. In addition, we used the scores to decide which students, if any, had been misplaced by our placement examinations. In general, we set the cut-points for this decision at 90%. We considered such high cut-points to be valid because we wanted to identify only those students who had been placed below their actual level of proficiency. We felt that students who scored 90% or higher on the diagnostic criterion-referenced assessment procedure should quite reasonably be moved up to the next level of study or exempted from study in the skill area involved. For psychological and political reasons, we felt that we could not move students the other way, that is, we could not move students who had been placed above their actual levels of proficiency down to a lower level of study.

At the end of the courses, we administered the opposite forms of the tests for quite a different purpose, that is, whether each student should pass the course. Reasonably, the cut-point for this decision was set at a much lower level, typically at 60 or 70%, depending on the course. Teachers were also advised to use additional information about their students, particularly for any students who were at or close to the cut-point. More precisely, they were advised to gather further information on any students who scored within one confidence interval (CI) below the cut-point.

In short, our decisions to use cut-points of 90% for exemption on the diagnostic criterion-referenced pre-test in our academic reading courses and 60% for passing our courses on the achievement criterion-referenced post-test were based on the purposes involved. To reverse those cut-points would have been ill conceived: a 60% criterion for exempting students from the course on the diagnostic pre-test would have erroneously exempted students who needed instruction, and would have left us without many students. On the other hand, a 90% cut-point for passing the course on the achievement post-test would have led us to fail many students. Clearly then, none of the approaches discussed in the previous section will make any sense if the purposes for the test and the subsequent decisions are not already eminently clear.

Decision validity must also take into account Messick's (1988, 1989) notions of the value implications of test interpretation and the social consequences of test use (see discussion earlier in this chapter). Recall that the value implications of test interpretation involve factoring in any special political and pedagogical circumstances surrounding the particular context in which the test is to be used for decision making. The social consequences of test use include any social, political, or personal consequences of their decisions.

For example, for an achievement test at the end of a course, it might turn out that decision makers would set a cut-point at 80% based on the best available statistical and judgmental information.

Nevertheless, an 80% cut-point would probably create a political disaster among the teachers because it is "just too high." In such a case, the opinions of statisticians and other experts would become irrelevant if their views and conclusions caused the teachers and students to riot in the halls because the achievement decisions were perceived as unfair.

Thus, the consequences of decisions based on criterion-referenced tests must be viewed from a number of perspectives. Here we will discuss them in terms of the consequences of passing and the consequences of failing.

Consequences of passing. Test developers far too seldom think about the consequences of passing students based on the test scores they have helped to create. With regard specifically to criterion-referenced tests, they should be addressing at least the following questions related to passing:

1. What constitutes passing the test? In other words, what does it mean in real-world terms if a student passes the test?
2. What are the consequences for students if they are passed erroneously in terms of getting in over their heads in future courses, having to live up to the abilities implied in their passing the course, and so forth?
3. Should the passing scores be reported as a single total score for each student? Or, should subtest scores be reported along with descriptors of what each score means?
4. Should scores also be reported elsewhere? To the institution? To parents? etc.
5. Will anybody actually use the more detailed information provided by individual subtest scores? Or do the test developers need to educate those receiving the score reports so they can understand the value of what they are getting?

Consequences of failing. Test developers more often consider the consequences of deciding to fail students based on the test scores they have helped to create. With regard specifically to criterion-referenced tests, they should be addressing at least the following questions related to failing:

1. What constitutes failure? In other words, what does it mean in real-world terms if a student fails the test?
2. Should students fail if they score below the cut-point on any subtest? Or should the test developers average the subtest scores, and then make their decisions based on a single cut-point on the average scores?

3. What should decision makers do with students who fail? Should students who pass the whole test (based on average scores) be made to undergo remediation for those subtests they failed? Or should they just be moved on to the next level? Should their future teachers at the next level be told about their weaknesses (that is, the subtests which they failed)?

Standards setting and decision making with criterion-referenced tests can clearly be very difficult and political in nature. None the less, teachers and administrators are often faced with the need to set cut-points and make decisions about their students' lives. One thing we have learned in the process of making such decisions is that open, honest, and systematic standards setting is preferable to no standards setting. The alternative is to set no standards, which may mean that decisions will be made covertly, unsystematically, and possibly in an unfair and invalid manner.

See uk.cambridge.org/elt/crlt/ for chapter summary and exercises.

7 Administering, giving feedback, and reporting on criterion-referenced tests

Introduction

In this chapter, we would like to wrap up a number of loose ends that have not been covered in previous chapters and, at the same time, review some of the key concepts involved in criterion-referenced testing. To those ends, we will provide practical suggestions based on our experiences with real criterion-referenced testing projects in three major areas: developing criterion-referenced tests, giving criterion-referenced feedback, and reporting criterion-referenced results. In addition, we will also provide access to a sample report of a CRT project along with commentary with some suggestions on writing such reports.

Developing criterion-referenced tests

Most language teaching professionals have some experience developing and administering tests on their own for their own classes. In many cases, a number of teachers will be assigned different sections of the same course; at the end of the courses, the teachers develop separate tests for each of their classes. Especially if the course has common objectives across all of the sections, such test development practices seem to us to be duplicative, redundant, and inefficient. We will focus in this section on two sets of strategies that can be used to get teachers to work together on CRT projects. These strategies will be discussed in two main sections – one on fostering teacher cooperation and the other on marshaling adequate resources. We will also discuss the issues involved in developing multiple forms of a CRT so they can be administered in a counterbalanced manner. First, however, we look briefly at some of the roles that joint test development of CRTs can play.

Team development of CRTs

The idea that evaluation should be linked to explicit program goals may seem on the face of it to be a non-controversial issue. This is the basic step of operationalizing the attributes to be tested. However, the process of developing methods of evaluation linked to program goals will frequently bring to light disagreements and discrepancies among teachers which have not previously been noticed. For example, in specifying the test content, the following questions will have to be addressed directly by the teachers and administrators in the test writing process:

What actually is the curriculum? That is, in the process of constructing tests that are specific to the program, the nature of the curriculum and its goals will have to be made explicit and refined. If the course is an English for Special Purposes course, the characteristics that distinguish it from a General English Program will need to be specified. This process can have direct effects on curriculum development. There may be a general view that a particular program adheres to a communicative framework. However, how the individual teachers interpret that may be very different in practice.

How much of the syllabus actually gets covered in a term? It is frequently the case that a syllabus is overly optimistic. The teachers may make every effort to complete the materials, but not manage this or, for reasons of time pressure, go over some of the material in a cursory manner. Likewise, teachers may discover that they have covered the core syllabus in a relatively short amount of time and spent substantial time with auxiliary or supplemental material idiosyncratic to each course. Taking a realistic view of how much has been covered can help refine the syllabus for future terms and can help make the course goals more realistic and standardize what supplemental material is introduced into the course content.

How are the courses taught? Teachers will have to address the issue of teaching and testing match, that is, whether the particular classroom instructional techniques are consistent with the ways in which the material is to be tested. Adjustments will then either have to be made in how the material is taught or how it is tested. Although time consuming and occasionally frustrating, this process strengthens the program of instruction by affecting not only what the teachers teach, but also how they teach.

What can students in the particular course be expected to do? The level and type of performance expected of the students on the test must be defined. For example, if students have been taught a set of grammatical points during the first part of the course, will they be expected to identify those structures on a test or will they be expected to use those grammatical structures in a composition? If this is not specified prior to writing the examinations, the types of instruction can vary considerably.

What part of the curriculum is actually on the test? Language curricula often include enabling skills as well as end goals. For example, a reading syllabus may have both of the following as instructional goals:

1. Students will be able to outline an expository text of five paragraphs.
2. Students will determine if the generalization within the reading passage is fact or opinion.

Those who are writing the test will need to determine if the first goal is primarily an enabling skill, that is, a mechanism for getting to the second goal, or an important end goal that will be necessary for the next level of language courses. This will determine whether the first goal should be included in the final examination.

What material will actually be on the test? If the test is too long for the students it may introduce a fatigue factor into the score. Due to this time constraint not everything that was covered in the syllabus can be tested. The teachers must, therefore, determine how to weight the various parts of the curriculum by reaching a consensus on what are its most important components.

We now move to several practical matters in the development of CRTs. These address how to promote teacher cooperation and considerations in the actual administration of the tests within a program. Some might consider these issues to be mundane in scope. However, if they are not addressed in some way prior to the testing process they can negatively affect the test results and negate all of the issues raised in earlier chapters about test content, dependability, and validity.

Fostering teacher cooperation

No test development project can succeed without teacher cooperation. For that matter, the same is true for any curriculum development project. Anything that affects teachers' classrooms or students directly must have their approval and input, not only for political reasons, but also because teachers know a great deal about their students, the materials the students are studying, the organization of the lessons, the types of language teaching and practice that have gone on in the classrooms, and so forth.

Table 7.1. *Strategies for fostering teacher cooperation*

1. Provide coordination.
2. Make the testing useful to teachers.
3. Appeal to teachers' self-interest.
4. Appeal to teachers' professionalism.
5. Pay for their professionalism.
6. Make the testing less fearful.
7. Leave flexibility in the assessment.
8. Give other smaller incentives.

Because of the way CRTs are integral to the classroom teaching/learning processes, fostering teacher cooperation may be the most important part of any CRT project. Cooperation can be built through a number of strategies as shown in Table 7.1.

Provide coordination. In any CRT project that involves more than one teacher, the project will be much more likely to move forward and succeed if some identifiable individual takes responsibility for the project and answers to the rest of the group for the project's success or failure. This person may be an administrator, a lead teacher, or a single ambitious teacher who has the other teachers' respect. This testing coordinator will need to be good with people, and able to encourage them to do things well. Ultimately, they must find a way to get teachers to (a) review existing items; (b) revise test items; and/or (c) write new test items as necessary for the particular courses that they teach. At the beginning of the semester (diagnostic pre-test) and end of the semester (achievement post-test), the leader must also (d) get adequate photocopies of the tests made; (e) distribute the tests in a timely manner to the teachers for the classroom administrations; (f) collect the tests from the teachers after the administrations; (g) do, or at least organize and supervise the scoring of the tests; and (h) get the results back to the teachers in a timely manner.

Of course, steps (a) through (h) will require a great deal of time and effort on the part of the testing coordinator. What can be used to motivate a teacher to take on all those responsibilities? They will need to be encouraged and rewarded with additional pay, release time, being officially designated as the *Testing Coordinator*, or simply receiving praise and the good opinion of peers.

Make the testing useful to teachers. Teachers will also need to feel that cooperating in the testing project will be beneficial to them and their students. This feeling can be fostered by having the testing coordinator support the teachers by efficiently taking care of all the logistical steps discussed in the previous section. In particular, if photocopying, distributing, and collecting the tests, as well as getting feedback to the teachers and students, are all carried out in a timely manner, teachers are more likely to feel that their part in the process is respected and important, that they are being helped in doing their classroom testing, and that they should therefore support the testing program.

Appeal to teachers' self-interest. In addition to making the tests useful to teachers, any other available strategies that appeal to teachers' self-interest should be used. For instance, when teachers realize that writing a few test items will result in their getting back many more test items from their colleagues, they are more likely to be motivated to support the process. Of course, such a result presupposes that the items they get back are of good quality, that is, that all the teachers are taking the item writing process seriously. This type of motivation can also result if teachers understand that it is in their best interest to use tests that have been developed rationally along criterion-referenced lines and provide direct feedback on the learning going on in their particular courses.

Appeal to teachers' professionalism. In the best of all possible worlds, professional teachers do more than just teach; they also grade papers, advise students, set objectives, select materials, continue to grow professionally by reading journals and attending conferences, and so forth. Professional teachers also take care of the testing in their classes. Hence, it does not seem unreasonable to expect them to cooperate in a process of working with other teachers of the same course in developing tests that will ultimately make their job easier and more effective.

One reason teachers may choose to act in this professional manner is if cooperating in test development is written directly into their job description. It may also help if certain times are set aside in their work days or work weeks so they feel they are being paid to meet and work on such projects.

Pay for their professionalism. If teachers are in the classroom five, six, or seven hours per day, or are teaching on a part-time basis, they may feel it is unreasonable to ask them to do any extra work beyond the usual correcting of papers, grading, and other ordinary paper work. However, if the teachers are working on a full-time basis and teach a reasonable number of hours per day, they may consider that requiring them to work on the curriculum is fair. There is no reason to expect professional teachers to do extra work for nothing any more than any other profession. Yet, somehow, that belief seems to have infected many administrators in language teaching. In short, if administrators are going to expect language teachers to act like professionals, those administrators must also treat the teachers like professionals. Only then can the teachers be expected to respond positively to requests for work on curriculum development projects in general, and CRT projects in particular.

Make the testing less fearful. One of the issues that sometimes prevents teachers from cooperating with testing projects is fear. Close examination of the issue will often reveal that what they are concerned about is that the tests will introduce an element of accountability into the curriculum.

With the kind of criterion-referenced pre-test (diagnostic) and post-test (achievement) testing advocated in this book, the effectiveness of objectives and the teaching of those objectives can be compared. In addition, if the results are looked at from a different angle, the performances of different teachers' classes can be compared. Teachers often quite reasonably fear that such comparisons could make the students in their classes look bad with the consequence that they might be fired. Whether or not such a thing could happen depends on the administrator, not on the tests, though the tests do provide information that could be misused. Two possible strategies to assuage such fears are:

- teachers could be guaranteed that the tests will never be analyzed for class comparisons or in order to fire them; or
- teachers could be promised that such information would only be given to the individual teacher and would never be used as the sole reason for firing, but rather to give feedback so that such a firing would not be necessary.

Leave flexibility in the assessment. Another issue that prevents teachers from cooperating with testing projects is concern that those aspects of their class that are unique to their teaching style and their particular group of students will not be included on the test. In developing common tests across multiple sections of the same course, it is important to acknowledge that teachers function differently according to their personalities and training, and that different groups of students need to be handled differently. However, a common syllabus and set of objectives will make curriculum development in general and testing in particular much easier. Also, from the students' perspective, it will be comforting to know that there are similarities across sections of a particular course, that is, that students in other sections will not be getting something different or better just because they signed up for a different teacher.

This issue can be addressed by having the teachers work together on a common core testing procedure that assesses the common objectives but leaves flexibility in terms of time during the test for the teachers to assess any material that is unique to their particular class. Such an arrangement should quell any concerns about glossing over the unique aspects of individual teachers' classes.

Give other smaller incentives. There are also a number of other smaller incentives that may encourage teachers to cooperate and help with testing projects. For instance, the promise of strong recommendation letters when they leave the institution may encourage them to cooperate in the testing project, especially if they realize the letters will specifically mention their cooperation and good work on the testing project. Yearly letters of thank you for their work on testing (or other curriculum efforts) are also appreciated. Even just words of praise when meeting them in the hallway may help a great deal. Teachers are human and need to feel useful and important.

The important point overall is that the opinions and feelings of teachers must be considered and addressed in any testing project, but especially in any CRT project. Simply ordering teachers to cooperate and do criterion-referenced testing is likely to backfire.

Marshaling adequate resources

Too often, testing is just an afterthought. We know of at least one teacher who often treated tests like this. During the last week of classes, he suddenly realized that he had not written the final examination yet. So the night before the scheduled exam, he spread out all the materials for his course and adapted a little from here and a little from there to build a test that was as representative as possible of all the language points that he remembered teaching during the semester. He rushed to campus on the morning of the test only to find that the faculty copy room was already packed with other teachers running off their tests. Then, the copy machine broke down under the pressure. So he had to drive to the nearest commercial photocopying center and pay for the copies out of his own pocket. Having managed to collate and staple the copies just in time for class, he arrived with sweat on his brow, and told the students to clear their desks, move further apart, and get out a pencil or pen. He then passed out the tests, one to each student, and sat down at his desk to work out an answer key. When he got to question number 3, he discovered that there were two possible answers, so he interrupted the students to tell them that several possible answers would be accepted for number 3. Then, a hand in the back of the room went up. The student wanted to know if the word *asdfjkl* was a typo in question number 6. And so it went on throughout the testing period . . . At the end of the test, when the last student had finally left, he sighed in relief and swore that such a disaster would never happen again.

The next semester he taught the same course and was very proud of himself because he was not caught off guard this time. In fact, he ran off copies of the final examination a week ahead of time. This time he was relaxed, cool, and confident when he passed out the exams. Then, a hand in the back of the room went up. The student wanted to know if there were two possible answers for question 3; another student asked if the word *asdfjkl* in number 6 was a typo. And so it went on throughout the testing period . . .

We believe that testing is far too important to be treated in this way. In fact, as we argued in Chapter 2, testing should be at least as important as any other element of the curriculum and should therefore be included in systematic curriculum design right along with the course objectives, materials, and other aspects of the curriculum.

Our point is that criterion-referenced tests must be carefully and systematically planned, developed, administered, scored, analyzed, and reported as a matter of course in the curriculum development process. To do so, adequate time and resources must be allocated to testing. Like all other educational endeavors, the primary resource needed will be teachers' time. Teachers will be needed to do some or all of the following: (a) write test items; (b) review the test items of other teachers; (c) administer the tests; (d) score the tests; (e) understand and report the results to their students; (f) critique the quality of the test items; and (g) provide feedback on the test administration and scoring procedures.

In the best of all possible worlds, teachers should be paid extra money for such testing. Since it is most often not possible to pay teachers for testing, other alternative rewards should be considered especially for any lead teachers who take responsibility for organizing other teachers to do the job. Such rewards could take the form of a free institutional dinner to celebrate finishing the testing, or release time throughout the semester for testing and other curriculum development activities, recognition and expression of gratitude in public and private, or even making sure that research possibilities are opened up to teachers (after all, it was research possibilities that served as one motivation for both authors to do extra work as directors of the ELI at UHM).

Timing	Group 1	Group 2
End of Course	Form B	Form A
During Course	Teaching/ Learning	Teaching/ Learning
Beginning of Course	Form A	Form B

Figure 7.1. Counterbalancing with two forms for criterion-referenced diagnostic and achievement purposes

Counterbalancing criterion-referenced forms

As we pointed out in Chapter 2, it is usually a good idea to develop CRTs in at least two forms (preferably drawn from a larger item bank as discussed in Chapter 4) and administer them at the beginning and end of the course. To do so in such a way that none of the students take exactly the same test twice, counterbalancing will probably be advisable. *Counterbalancing* means administering multiple forms of a tests in a pre-test/post-test design such that no student takes exactly the same test twice. In situations where tests are to be used for assessing diagnosis at the beginning of the course and achievement at the end, two forms will suffice; let's say forms A and B. These tests should be administered so that half the students (preferably randomly selected from the class list) take each form at the beginning of the course for diagnostic purposes. The teaching and learning processes then take place for whatever amount of time is involved in the term, and then, at the end, the forms are switched so that all the students take the opposite form at the end of the course for achievement purposes. This type of counterbalancing is shown in Figure 7.1.

In situations where tests are to be used for diagnosis at the beginning of the course, progress in the middle of the course, and achievement at the end, three forms would be advisable, let's say forms A, B, and C. These tests should then be administered so that one-third of the students (preferably randomly selected from the class list) take each form at the beginning of the course for diagnostic purposes. The teaching and learning processes then take place for whatever amount of time is involved in the first half of the term; then, the forms are administered for progress purposes in such a way that all the students take a different form from the one they took at the beginning. The teaching and learning processes then continue for

Timing	Group 1	Group 2	Group 3
End of Course	Form C	Form A	Form B
2nd Half of Course	Teaching/ Learning	Teaching/ Learning	Teaching/ Learning
Middle of Course	Form B	Form C	Form A
1st Half of Course	Teaching/ Learning	Teaching/ Learning	Teaching/ Learning
Beginning of Course	Form A	Form B	Form C

Figure 7.2. Counterbalancing with three forms for criterion-referenced diagnostic, progress, and achievement purposes

whatever amount of time is involved in the last half of the term; then, the forms are administered for achievement purposes in such a way that the students take the one remaining form they have not previously seen. This type of counterbalancing is shown in Figure 7.2.

In practical testing situations, counterbalancing poses two problems which must be addressed: (a) making sure students get the right form at each administration and (b) insuring that test security is not a major issue.

In our experience, getting the right form to the right student is made easiest by planning in advance. Trying to sort out who takes which form on the spot at the beginning of a test will just cause confusion and should thus be avoided. The only alternative is to sit down with the blank tests including all forms involved and the class list and decide which students will take which test. Once those decisions are made, their names should be put on the tests that they will be taking so that when the test is administered, the tests can be passed out with a minimum of confusion. Preassigning forms in this manner will help with test security as well (although there is still the possibility that students will exchange information about the tests).

Giving criterion-referenced feedback

One of the most important lessons we have learned about CRTs is that feedback is crucial; this involves more than just feedback to the students, but also to teachers, administrators, parents, etc. In addition, we have come to realize that feedback should not just be top–down, but a two-way communication.

Who should get feedback?

In administering CRTs, we automatically think about giving feedback on the results of the tests to students. In fact, the possibility of giving feedback in detail by providing students with objective-by-objective subtest scores is one of the most attractive features of CRTs. Indeed, the feedback sheet shown in Figure 7.3a is for giving diagnostic feedback. Objective-by-objective feedback will be particularly helpful to students at the beginning of the course as diagnostic information (or during the course as information about the progress they are making) on which objectives are particularly weak and need additional work, or are particularly strong and need very little work. Such feedback can be given objective-by-objective even if different forms have been used within the same group of students, as long as those forms have been shown to be equivalent in difficulty and sensitivity to the curriculum using the item analysis statistics discussed in Chapter 5.

If they will see it, objective-by-objective achievement information (like that shown in Figure 7.3b) at the end of the course may also prove helpful for students. Notice that the feedback sheet shown in Figure 7.3b includes spaces for average scores pre (for the diagnostic test at the beginning of the course) and post (for the final achievement test at the end of the course) so students can see where they were when the course started and what they have achieved since then. In an ideal world, such an end-of-term score report would also help students understand what they have achieved in terms of the objectives and what still needs work after the course is finished.

Similar feedback will also be useful for teachers. Naturally, a set of individual students' score reports (as shown in Figures 7.3a and 7.3b) might prove useful for a conscientious teacher. However, teachers may also benefit from a class summary including average percent scores for each objective (as shown in Figure 7.4). Using averages is important so the teacher can easily see which objectives the class as a whole needs to focus on and which objectives are not so weak. Notice that the teacher feedback sheet in Figure 7.4 includes spaces for average scores pre (at the beginning for diagnostic purposes), mid (at the midpoint in the course for progress purposes), and post (at the end of the course as a final achievement test). Additional information on the variability of scores (for instance, the highest and lowest score

GELC READING COURSE, LEVEL C*
DIAGNOSTIC SCORE REPORT SHEET

STUDENT'S NAME: _____

OBJECTIVES   SCORES

1. Answer 5 multiple-choice questions about main topics   ____
   of a 1500-word science article in five minutes with 70%
   accuracy.
2. Answer 5 factual multiple-choice questions in 5 minutes on ____
   a 1500-word science article with accuracy.
3. Supply the word or phrase to which another word or phrase   ____
   refers, taken from a 1500-word science article, with 70%
   accuracy.
4. Match a passage with the rhetorical function it represents ____
   (definition, process description, physical description,
   classification, listing, cause and effect, or comparison and
   contrast) with 70% accuracy.
5. Fill in the correct signal words, from a given list, in a   ____
   passage taken from a 1500-word science article with 70%
   accuracy.
6. Decide whether inferences drawn from a 1500-word   ____
   science article are valid or invalid with 70% accuracy.
7. Answer multiple-choice vocabulary questions chosen from   ____
   a 1500-word science article with 70% accuracy.
8. Select the paraphrase which most nearly restates the meaning ____
   of the original sentence (taken from a science article) with
   70% accuracy.
9. Answer interpretive and inferential multiple-choice   ____
   questions about charts, tables, and graphs taken from a
   1500-word science article with 70% accuracy.
10. Summarize at least three main points of a 1500-word   ____
    science article in one paragraph with 70% accuracy.

* All reading passages will be at about grade 15, which is equal to third-year
  college in the United States, or approximately what you have read in *Scientific
  American.*

*Figure 7.3a. Diagnostic feedback sheet for students
(adapted from objectives reported in GELC, 1982)*

GELC READING COURSE, LEVEL C*
FINAL SCORE REPORT SHEET

*STUDENT'S NAME:*_____

OBJECTIVES	SCORES	
	Pre	Post

1. Answer 5 multiple-choice questions about main topics of a 1500-word science article in five minutes with 70% accuracy.   ____ ____

2. Answer 5 factual multiple-choice questions in 5 minutes on a 1500-word science article with accuracy.   ____ ____

3. Supply the word or phrase to which another word or phrase refers, taken from a 1500-word science article, with 70% accuracy.   ____ ____

4. Match a passage with the rhetorical function it represents (definition, process description, physical description, classification, listing, cause and effect, or comparison and contrast) with 70% accuracy.   ____ ____

5. Fill in the correct signal words, from a given list, in a passage taken from a 1500-word science article with 70% accuracy.   ____ ____

6. Decide whether inferences drawn from a 1500-word science article are valid or invalid with 70% accuracy.   ____ ____

7. Answer multiple-choice vocabulary questions chosen from a 1500-word science article with 70% accuracy.   ____ ____

8. Select the paraphrase which most nearly restates the meaning of the original sentence (taken from a science article) with 70% accuracy.   ____ ____

9. Answer interpretive and inferential multiple-choice questions about charts, tables, and graphs taken from a 1500-word science article with 70% accuracy.   ____ ____

10. Summarize at least three main points of a 1500-word science article in one paragraph with 70% accuracy.   ____ ____

* All reading passages will be at about grade 15, which is equal to third-year college in the United States, or approximately what you have read in *Scientific American*.

Figure 7.3b. Final feedback sheet for students
(adapted from objectives reported in GELC, 1982)

on each objective) or information about individuals who are particularly low or high on each objective might also prove useful. Pointing out the low students on each objective may help the teacher focus extra help or materials on those students in particular need of improvement on the objective. Pointing to students who are particularly high on an objective can also be useful so teachers can single them out to focus on other objectives (where they do need work), or to use them to help other weaker students work on the objective in question.

Administrators should also get feedback on the testing, especially if they are interested in curriculum development. In such cases, pre–post gain may be most interesting (objective-by-objective and total). A feedback sheet for administrators might simply provide average scores for each class at the end of the term and the beginning, with a subtraction that shows the average amount of gain across students for each objective. Figure 7.5 shows an example report sheet for giving overall performance feedback to administrators. Notice that it contains spaces for post, pre, and gain score percentages objective-by-objective. Note also that an overall average is presented at the bottom.

The type of information shown in Figure 7.5 might also be useful to distribute to teachers, especially when they are working on curriculum development. Naturally, there are many other possible permutations of these score report sheets and choosing which ones to use at a particular institution will depend on local conditions and constraints.

Other interested parties might also benefit from receiving feedback on students' performances. For instance, parents might appreciate getting feedback on their child's performance in the middle of the course (maybe at teacher/parent conferences) or at the end of the course as a more detailed than usual way of gauging what their son or daughter learned in the course. Of course, special report sheets could be designed for that purpose. The point is that feedback mechanisms must be thought through in terms of who should receive the feedback, what should be reported, and how the report form should look. Such feedback is a special characteristic of CRTs that is quite different from the more holistic and less personal score reports that usually accompany norm-referenced tests.

Feedback as two-way communication

We have found that feedback is not necessarily just a unidirectional top–down institution-to-concerned-parties procedure. Particularly where teachers are concerned, it may be crucial to involve them in

GELC READING COURSE, LEVEL C*
SCORE REPORT SHEET

TEACHER'S NAME: _____ *SECTION NUMBER:* _____

OBJECTIVES	*CLASS AVERAGES*		
	Pre	Mid	Post

1. Answer 5 multiple-choice questions about main topics of a 1500-word science article in 5 minutes with 70% accuracy. ____ ____ ____

2. Answer 5 factual multiple-choice questions in 5 minutes on a 1500-word science article with accuracy. ____ ____ ____

3. Supply the word or phrase to which another word or phrase refers, taken from a 1500-word science article, with 70% accuracy. ____ ____ ____

4. Match a passage with the rhetorical function it represents (definition, process description, physical description, classification, listing, cause and effect, or comparison and contrast) with 70% accuracy. ____ ____ ____

5. Fill in the correct signal words, from a given list, in a passage taken from a 1500-word science article with 70% accuracy. ____ ____ ____

6. Decide whether inferences drawn from a 1500-word science article are valid or invalid with 70% accuracy. ____ ____ ____

7. Answer multiple-choice vocabulary questions chosen from a 1500-word science article with 70% accuracy. ____ ____ ____

8. Select the paraphrase which most nearly restates the meaning of the original sentence (taken from a science article) with 70% accuracy. ____ ____ ____

9. Answer interpretive and inferential multiple-choice questions about charts, tables, and graphs taken from a 1500-word science article with 70% accuracy. ____ ____ ____

10. Summarize at least three main points of a 1500-word science article in one paragraph with 70% accuracy. ____ ____ ____

Overall average for your section: ____ ____ ____

* All reading passages will be at about grade 15, which is equal to third-year college in the United States, or approximately what you have read in *Scientific American*.

Figure 7.4. Feedback sheet for teachers
(adapted from objectives reported in GELC, 1982)

GELC READING COURSE, LEVEL C*
SCORE REPORT SHEET

TEACHER'S NAME: _____   *SECTION NUMBER:* _____

OBJECTIVES   *COURSE*
AVERAGES

Post - Pre = Gain

1. Answer 5 multiple-choice questions about main topics   ____ ____ ____
    of a 1500-word science article in 5 minutes with 70%
    accuracy.
2. Answer 5 factual multiple-choice questions in 5   ____ ____ ____
    minutes on a 1500-word science article with accuracy.
3. Supply the word or phrase to which another word or   ____ ____ ____
    phrase refers, taken from a 1500-word science article,
    with 70% accuracy.
4. Match a passage with the rhetorical function it   ____ ____ ____
    represents (definition, process description, physical
    description, classification, listing, cause and effect, or
    comparison and contrast) with 70% accuracy.
5. Fill in the correct signal words, from a given list, in a ____ ____ ____
    passage taken from a 1500-word science article with
    70% accuracy.
6. Decide whether inferences drawn from a 1500-word   ____ ____ ____
    science article are valid or invalid with 70% accuracy.
7. Answer multiple-choice vocabulary questions chosen   ____ ____ ____
    from a 1500-word science article with 70% accuracy.
8. Select the paraphrase which most nearly restates the   ____ ____ ____
    meaning of the original sentence (taken from a science
    article) with 70% accuracy.
9. Answer interpretive and inferential multiple-choice   ____ ____ ____
    questions about charts, tables, and graphs taken from
    a 1500-word science article with 70% accuracy.
10. Summarize at least three main points of a 1500-word   ____ ____ ____
    science article in one paragraph with 70% accuracy.

Overall average: ____ ____ ____

* All reading passages will be at about grade 15, which is equal to third-year
  college in the United States, or approximately what you have read in *Scientific
  American.*

*Figure 7.5. Performance feedback sheet for administrators
(adapted from objectives reported in GELC, 1982)*

the actual development processes including writing and evaluating items, planning and evaluating administration procedures, as well as interpreting and reporting the results.

Writing and evaluating items. From the most cynical point of view, involving teachers in the item writing process provides personnel to actually get the job done. As pointed out above, if the teachers all realize that they will benefit greatly from contributing their small share of items, they may be more willing to participate in the process. In addition, the teachers should be made aware that it is only through writing items that they maintain control of tests and how the tests will match the objectives of the courses.

Once the teachers are convinced that they should help write items, they need to be organized so that each can write 10–15 items or take charge of one subtest, or however the organization works best. Once the items or subtests are written, they can be assembled into rough drafts of the tests, and, at that point, the items should probably be reviewed for feedback by all of the teachers involved and then revised once again before administering even a first draft test.

If teachers are not involved in creating the curriculum tests, there is always the danger that item writers will write test items that do not match the ways that the objectives are being addressed by the teachers and practiced by the students. Therefore, whether or not the teachers actually write the items, they should play an important role in item evaluation. Any subsequent revisions of the tests should also be reviewed by the teachers. Even when the tests appear to be working reasonably well, the teachers should review them periodically in case the objectives themselves or the teaching of the objectives have changed in the intervening time. Naturally, any observed inconsistencies between the course objectives, teaching approaches, and the criterion-referenced tests should be resolved by revising the test items appropriately.

Planning and evaluating administration procedures. Before the tests are actually administered, teachers should be enlisted in the process of planning the administration procedures. At least four points of view can be taken on any test administration: those of the students, teachers, test coordinator, and administrators (others, such as parents, may also have views).

However, particularly in administering the objectives-referenced type of CRT, the teachers know best how the logistics will work, that is, how long it will take to administer each subtest and each item and what will be needed in terms of equipment and personnel in order to do so. Since, in most cases, the teachers will be the most appropriate people to actually administer the tests, it would be foolhardy indeed to fail to get their feedback on the steps they will have to do in the process. They must be clear about what each step entails and why it is being done. Then the test administration stands at least a chance of going relatively smoothly.

Certainly, soon after the test takes place, the test administration procedures should once again be reviewed by the teachers so those procedures can be fine-tuned to operate even better the next time the test is administered. Even when a test appears to be working reasonably well, the teachers should probably be recruited to review the administration procedures periodically in case the items, students, teaching, or other circumstances have changed in the intervening time.

Interpreting and reporting results. Certainly, one of the main purposes of any CRT is to give score feedback to the students on their performance either in terms of diagnosis, progress, or achievement. If that feedback is presented in terms of percent scores on individual objectives as shown in Figures 7.3a, 7.3b, and 7.4 for reporting results to students and teachers, respectively, those scores should prove maximally useful for those parties.

However, handing those score reports to the teachers and students should not be the end of the process. The views of students and teachers should be systematically gathered not only on what the scores mean personally to them and to the curriculum (as discussed in Chapter 2, but also on how the tests, administrations procedures, and score report strategies themselves can be improved. Gathering feedback from teachers and students in this way can prove informative, but also it may increase their motivation in the class and during the testing session.

Reporting criterion-referenced results

Throughout this book, we have shown the numerous ways in which CRTs differ from NRTs. However, there are some problems that happen when administering and reporting the results of CRTs that would not normally occur in norm-referenced testing. These include problems with students who want to fail; students who take only the pre-test; interpreting gain scores; the need for promoting criterion-referenced tests to colleagues; and difficulties in reporting criterion-referenced results. Each of these sets of special problems will be addressed in turn.

Students who want to fail

Normally, students are taking a test with the purpose of doing their best, whether it be a proficiency test for admissions to a university or the final exam in a course that they are taking. However, under certain conditions, some students may actually be motivated to fail or at least get a low score on a CRT. Cynical students may try to outsmart the criterion-referenced testing process when they understand what is going on. If they find themselves taking a test at the beginning of a course and are told by the teacher (or guess) that they will also be taking a test at the end of the course, they may further figure out that they will be graded, at least partly, on how much they improve in the course. If they start low by intentionally failing the pre-test, then even without learning much they will appear to have gained a great deal when they take the final test. Hence, in order to get a good grade, some students may actually be motivated to score low on the diagnostic test at the beginning of the course.

Unfortunately for the CRT processes described in this book, especially those in Chapter 4, such deliberate failure makes a mess of the item statistics and gain scores that are at the heart of all the statistical analyses. For this reason, strategies must be developed to counter the tendency of some students to intentionally fail pre-tests.

One strategy that has worked especially well in the ELI at UHM is to tell students that those who do well on the pre-test will be promoted out of the course to the next level, or exempted, as appropriate. Since many of our students are motivated to get out of the ELI as soon as possible, we find that most students, even those who really have no chance of being promoted, will take the test seriously and do their best to get a high score. Naturally, this strategy will only work if some students are actually promoted/exempted in this way. We chose to exempt/promote students who scored 90% or higher on the pre-test administrations of our CRT, as we felt that there was no reason to keep such students in the classes.

Students who take only the pre-test

One problem that may arise from promoting/exempting students on the basis of pre-test scores is what to do with those students who are promoted/exempted (or simply drop the course during the term) when doing item analyses and examining gain scores. In calculating and interpreting the *B*-index item statistic for the pre-test decision as to who should be promoted/exempted, it is crucial to include these promoted/exempted students. However, in calculating and interpreting the difference index, these promoted/exempted students should probably be eliminated from the pre-test results because they are not subject to the teaching/learning process and will not be included in the post-test results. If these students are not eliminated from the pre-test results, the difference indexes will tend to be depressed and will not represent the true state of affairs.

Interpreting gain scores

Percentage gains, or *gain scores*, are easy to calculate as shown in Figure 7.5. Each individual's gain score can be calculated by subtracting their pre-test score from their post-test score. For instance, if Xiao Wang scored 77% on the pre-test and 97% on the post-test, her gain score would be 97% − 77% = 20%. Similarly, the gain scores for a whole class or an entire organization can be calculated by using the averages across students. So if the average score on objective number 1 for a particular class was 53% on the pre-test and 87% on the post-test, the gain score for that objective would be 87% − 53% = 34%. In a like manner, the overall gain score for all objectives can be calculated by using the average scores for all students on all objectives. For example, if the average score in the reading class was 64% on the pre-test and 87% on the post-test, the overall gain score for the class would be 87% − 64% = 23%. Unfortunately, as we will explain next, interpreting such gain scores, while seemingly simple, is not always straightforward. In the process, it is necessary to temper interpretations of gain scores by considering all the possible sources of gains and by remembering that gain scores may tend to be unreliable/undependable.

Extraneous sources of gains. While any teacher would like to think that the gains they see in students' performances between the pre-test and post-test are entirely attributable to their teaching and the experiences the students had in their class, it is important to realize that such gains can be attributed to many other sources that are not directly related to the classroom.

One such source is the *practice effect*, that is, the consequences of having taken the test twice, even if it is a different form the second time. The simple fact of having taken a certain type of test, especially if it is a novel test type, can favorably affect students' performances on any subsequent administrations of the same type of test.

Since criterion-referenced tests may be task-based or take other forms novel to students, they may be learning through the very act of having taken the pre-test, such that they will perform better on the post-test, regardless of what they learn in the classroom.

The practice effect may be further complicated by the fact that certain of the classroom practice sessions and homework exercises may be very similar to the items on the test. Indeed, a CRT probably should reflect the kinds of learning experiences students have had in the classroom. Thus by the time the students take the final post-test, they may have practiced the material or skills necessary to perform well on the post-test in the pre-test, in their classroom practice sessions and in their homework, and of course, all this practice will hopefully have an effect. In short, the practice effect in many ways is what we are trying to increase in our teaching, and the fact that it is strong on the post-test may be good news. However, we must admit and think about the fact that the practice effect is a complicating factor in interpreting and making claims about the gains that we observe in any CRT project.

Teachers must also realize that, in addition to their class, the gain scores they observe in their class may be related to any or all of the following factors: (a) other language courses the students are taking at the same time; (b) other academic experiences the students are having with the language at the same time (for example, their content area courses, campus lectures, meetings, conferences with teachers, and so forth); and (c) other more general experiences the students are having with the language (watching TV, talking with friends, filling out forms, shopping, going to the health center, and so forth).

All in all, the gain scores that we examine so carefully in CRT projects must be interpreted with great caution as being the result of our teaching and all the other experiences the student may be having with the English language. In a sense, gain scores may be easier to interpret in a foreign language setting, where students do not get much extracurricular exposure to the language, than in a second language setting where all of the above listed complicating factors may be at play.

Gain score reliability/dependability. Gain scores have some serious problems with regard to reliability (Cronbach & Furby, 1970; Sax, 1980, pp. 278–280) – problems that apparently extend to criterion-referenced tests as well (see Ross & Hua, 1994). Naturally, if gain scores turn out to have low dependability, they should not be used. That does not obviate the possibility of examining and comparing pre-test and post-test results for purposes of item analysis or studying construct validity from an intervention study point of view. However, the gains themselves should only be used in grading (or research) with extreme care and only to the extent that is justified by their dependability.

Promoting criterion-referenced tests to colleagues

Despite the fact that criterion-referenced testing has been around for at least three decades in the general educational testing literature, it is relatively new in the language testing literature and therefore to many language teachers and administrators. As a result, there may be a need to convince colleagues that such tests are useful at all. Thus, ironically, it is sometimes necessary to promote CRTs to the very people who will benefit most from them.

One of the reasons for this phenomenon is that language teachers and administrators, particularly those trained in North America, are often steeped in the ideas of norm-referenced testing. They may have even taken a language testing course as part of their training, but unless that course was fairly recent, they probably were trained only in norm-referenced testing concepts, and if they remember anything at all from the course, it is the shape of the normal distribution, which was no doubt drawn on the board in almost every class session. This pattern appears to be changing and now criterion-referenced testing is becoming a part of language testing courses. Indeed, Bailey and Brown (1996), surveying about 400 language testing teachers, and getting responses from 84 of them (about 21%), reported that, on a scale of 0 to 5 (where 0 = no coverage and 1 to 5 indicate some coverage to extensive coverage), language testing course teachers reported covering criterion-referenced testing as follows: 0(none) = 0% 1(some) = 20.5%; 2 = 18.1%; 3 = 28.90; 4 = 21.7%; and 5 (extensive) = 10.8%. Since those are approximately the same percentages given for norm-referenced testing, it appears that both topics – norm-referenced and criterion-referenced testing – are now being covered at least to some degree in most language testing courses. Recent language testing textbooks have also begun to seriously discuss criterion-referenced testing (for instance, Alderson, Clapham, & Wall, 1995; Bachman, 1990; Bachman & Palmer, 1996; Bailey, 1998; Brown, 1996; Genessee & Upshur, 1996).

As we explained in the previous chapter, the long standing tradition of "grading on a curve", which permeates American educational institutions, does not make sense in classroom tests because (a) it is unreasonable to expect a normal distribution of scores or grades in small groups; (b) students in classrooms tend to form relatively homogeneous groups; and (c) teachers teaching and testing specific material will tend to make the group even more homogeneous on those tests. These and other arguments may have to be marshaled in the process of implementing CRTs in order to convince colleagues that the criterion-referenced testing models explained in this book (including non-normal distributions at both the beginning and end of a course) are more appropriate for assessing learning processes in small homogeneous groups of students.

Difficulties in reporting criterion-referenced results

One last problem that is peculiar to criterion-referenced testing is that many of the statistics associated with this form of testing will be new to language teaching professionals. The meaning of these statistics need to be explained with ample examples in order to make the concepts clear to local audiences, particularly the hard-working teachers and administrators who are involved in the project. In short, as with most writing, in explaining criterion-referenced statistics, it is important to keep your audience in mind.

See uk.cambridge.org/elt/crlt/ for chapter summary, exercises and a sample report. The report is aimed at readers with no prior knowledge of statistics.

References

Alderson, J. C. (1981). Reaction to Morrow paper. In J. C. Alderson & A. Hughes (Eds.), *Issues in language testing* (pp. 45–54). ELT Documents 111. London: The British Council.

Alderson, J. C. (1993). Judgments in language testing. In D. Douglas & C. Chapelle (Eds.) *A new decade of language testing: Collaboration and cooperation* (pp. 46–57). Ann Arbor, MI: University of Michigan.

Alderson, J. C., & Buck, G. (1993). Standards in testing: A survey of the practice of UK examination boards in EFL testing. *Language Testing, 10*(2), 1–26.

Alderson, J. C., Clapham, C., & Wall, D. (1995). *Language test construction and evaluation.* Cambridge: Cambridge University Press.

Alderson, J. C., & Hamp-Lyons, L. (1996). TOEFL preparation courses: A study of washback. *Language Testing, 13,* 280–297.

Alderson, J. C., & Hughes, A. (Eds.). (1981). *Issues in language testing.* ELT Documents 111. London: The British Council.

Alderson, J. C., & Wall, D. (1993a). Does washback exist? *Applied Linguistics, 14,* 115–129.

Alderson, J. C., & Wall, D. (1993b). Examining washback: The Sri Lankan impact study. *Language Testing, 10,* 41–69.

Allen, M. J., & Yen, W. M. (1979). *Introduction to measurement theory.* Monterey: Brooks/Cole.

American Council on the Teaching of Foreign Languages. (1986). *ACTFL proficiency guidelines.* Hastings-on-Hudson, NY: American Council on the Teaching of Foreign Languages.

American Council on the Teaching of Foreign Languages. (1987). ACTFL Japanese proficiency guidelines. *Foreign Language Annals, 20,* 589–603.

American Psychological Association. (1985). *Standards for educational and psychological testing.* Washington, DC: American Psychological Association.

American Psychological Association. (1994). *Publication manual of the American Psychological Association* (4th ed.). Washington, DC: American Psychological Association.

Anghoff, W. H. (1971). Scales, norms, and equivalent scores. In R. L.

Thorndike (Ed.), *Educational Measurement* (2nd ed.) (pp. 508–600). Washington, DC: American Council on Education.

Arter, J. A., & Spandel, V. (1992). Using portfolios of student work in instruction and assessment. *Educational Measurement: Issues and Practice*, *11*, 36–44.

Assessment Systems Corporation. (1996–1997). *User's manual for the XCALIBRE marginal maximum-likelihood estimation program*. St. Paul, MN: Assessment Systems Corporation.

Bachman, L. F. (1989). The development and use of criterion-referenced tests of language proficiency in language program evaluation. In K. Johnson (Ed.) *Program design and evaluation in language teaching* (pp. 242–258). London: Cambridge University Press.

Bachman, L. F. (1990). *Fundamental considerations in language testing*. Oxford: Oxford University Press.

Bachman, L. F., Lynch, B. K., & Mason, M. (1995). Investigating variability in tasks and rater judgments in a performance test of foreign language speaking. *Language Testing, 12*(2), 239–257.

Bachman, L. F., & Palmer, A. S. (1981). A multitrait-multimethod investigation into the construct validity of six tests of speaking and reading. In A. S. Palmer, P. J. M. Groot, & G. A. Trosper (Eds.) *The construct validation of tests of communicative competence* (pp. 149–165). Washington, DC: TESOL.

Bachman, L. F., & A. S. Palmer. (1982). The construct validation of some components of communicative proficiency. *TESOL Quarterly, 16*, 449–465.

Bachman, L. F., & Palmer, A. S. (1996). *Language testing in practice*. Oxford: Oxford University Press.

Bachman, L., & Savignon, S. (1986). The evaluation of communicative language proficiency: a critique of the ACTFL oral interview. *Modern Language Journal, 70*, 380–397.

Bailey, K. M. (1996). Working for washback: A review of the washback concept in language testing. *Language Testing, 13*, 257–279.

Bailey, K. M. (1998). *Learning about language assessment*. Boston: Newbury House Heinle & Heinle.

Bailey, K. M., & Brown, J. D. (1996). Language testing courses: What are they? In A. Cumming & R. Berwick (Eds.) *Validation in Language Testing* (pp. 236–256). Clevedon, England: Multilingual Matters.

Bergman, M. L., & Kasper, G. (1993). Perception and performance in native and nonnative apology. In G. Kasper & S. Blum-Kulka (Eds.), *Interlanguage pragmatics* (pp. 82–107). Oxford: Oxford University Press.

Berk, R. A. (1980a). *Criterion-referenced measurement: The state of the art*. Baltimore: Johns Hopkins University Press.

Berk, R. A. (1980b). Item analysis. In R. A. Berk (Ed.) *Criterion-referenced measurement: The state of the art* (pp. 49–79). Baltimore: Johns Hopkins University Press.

Berk, R. A. (1980c). A consumer's guide to criterion-referenced test reliability. *Journal of Educational Measurement, 17*, 186–223.

Berk, R. A. (1984). Selecting the index of reliability. In R. A. Berk (Ed.) *A guide to criterion-referenced test construction* (pp. 231–266). Baltimore: Johns Hopkins University Press.

Berk, R. A. (1986). A consumer's guide to setting performance standards on criterion-referenced tests. *Review of Educational Research, 56*, 137–172.

Bernknopf, S., & Bashaw, W. L. (1976). An investigation of criterion-referenced tests under different conditions of sample variability and item homogeneity. Paper presented at the Annual Meeting of the American Educational Research Association, San Francisco.

Birnbaum, A. (1968). Some latent trait models and their use in inferring an examinee's ability. In F. M. Lord & M. R. Novick (Eds.) *Statistical theories of mental test scores* (pp. 395–479). Reading, MA: Addison-Wesley.

Blanche, P. (1988). Self-assessment of foreign language skills: Implications for teachers and researchers. *RELC Journal, 19*, 75–96.

Blanche, P., & Merino, B. J. (1989). Self assessment of foreign-language skills: Implications for teachers and researchers. *Language Learning, 39*, 313–340.

Bock, R. D., Thissen, D., & Zimowski, M. F. (1997). IRT estimation of domain scores. *Journal of Educational Measurement, 34*, 197–211.

Bolus, R. E., Hinofotis, F. B., & Bailey, K. M. (1982). An introduction to generalizability theory in second language research. *Language Learning, 32*, 245–258.

Borland (1989). *QuattroPro*. Scotts Valley, CA: Borland International.

Brennan, R. L. (1972). A generalized upper-lower item discrimination index. *Educational and Psychological Measurement, 32*, 289–303.

Brennan, R. L. (1980). Reliability: Applications of generalizability theory. In R. A. Berk (Ed.) *Criterion-referenced measurement: The state of the art* (pp. 186–233). Baltimore, MD: Johns Hopkins University Press.

Brennan, R. L. (1983). *Elements of generalizability theory*. Iowa City, IA: American College Testing Program.

Brennan, R. L. (1984). Estimating the dependability of the scores. In R. A. Berk (Ed.) *A guide to criterion-referenced test construction* (pp. 292–334). Baltimore: Johns Hopkins University Press.

Brennan, R. L., & M. T. Kane. (1977). Signal/noise ratios for domain-referenced tests. *Psychometrika, 42*, 609–625.

Brown, J. D. (1980). Relative merits of four methods for scoring cloze tests. *Modern Language Journal, 64*, 311–317.

Brown, J. D. (1981). Newly placed versus continuing students: Comparing proficiency. In J. C. Fisher, M. A. Clarke, & J. Schachter (Eds.) *On TESOL '80 building bridges: research and practice in teaching English as a second language* (pp. 111–119). Washington, DC: TESOL.

Brown, J. D. (1982). *Testing EFL reading comprehension in engineering*

English. Unpublished doctoral dissertation, University of California at Los Angeles.

Brown, J. D. (1984a). Criterion-referenced language tests: What, how and why? *Gulf Area TESOL Bi-annual*, *1*, 32–34.

Brown, J. D. (1984b). A cloze is a cloze is a cloze? In J. Handscombe, R. A. Orem, & B. P. Taylor (Eds.) *On TESOL '83: the question of control* (pp. 109–119). Washington, DC: TESOL.

Brown, J. D. (1984c). A norm-referenced engineering reading test. In A. K. Pugh, & J. M. Ulijn (Eds.), *Reading for professional purposes: Studies and practices in native and foreign languages* (pp. 213–222). London: Heinemann Educational Books.

Brown, J. D. (1988a). *Understanding research in second language learning*. Cambridge: Cambridge University Press.

Brown, J.D. (1988b). Components of engineering-English reading ability. *System, 16*, 193–200.

Brown, J. D. (1989a). Improving ESL placement tests using two perspectives. *TESOL Quarterly, 23*, 65–83.

Brown, J. D. (1989b). Language program evaluation: A synthesis of existing possibilities. In K. Johnson (Ed.). *Program design and evaluation in language teaching* (pp. 222–241). London: Cambridge University Press.

Brown, J. D. (1990a) Short-cut estimates of criterion-referenced test consistency. *Language Testing, 7*(1), 77–97.

Brown, J. D. (1990b). Where do tests fit into language programs? *JALT Journal, 12*, 121–140.

Brown, J. D. (1992). Classroom-centered language testing. *TESOL Journal, 1*, 12–15.

Brown, J. D. (1993). A comprehensive criterion-referenced testing project. In D. Douglas & C. Chapelle (Eds.) *A new decade of language testing: collaboration and cooperation* (pp. 163–184). Ann Arbor, MI: University of Michigan.

Brown, J. D. (1995a). *The elements of language curriculum: A systematic approach to program development*. Boston, MA: Heinle & Heinle.

Brown, J. D. (1995b). Differences between norm-referenced and criterion-referenced tests. In J. D. Brown & S. O. Yamashita (Eds.), *Language testing in Japan* (pp. 12–19). Tokyo: Japanese Association for Language Teaching.

Brown, J. D. (1996). *Testing in language programs*. Upper Saddle River, NJ: Prentice-Hall.

Brown, J. D. (1997). Do tests washback on the language classroom? *TESOLANZ Journal, 5*, 63–80. [An earlier version appeared in 1997 under the title "The washback effect of language tests" in *University of Hawai'i Working Papers in ESL, 16*(1), 27–45.]

Brown, J. D. (Ed.). (1998a). *New ways of classroom assessment*. Washington, DC: Teachers of English to Speakers of Other Languages.

Brown, J. D. (1998b). University entrance examinations and their effect on English language teaching in Japan. In J. Kahny & M. James (Eds.) *Perspectives on Secondary School EFL: A publication in commemora-*

tion of the 30th anniversary of the Language Institute of Japan (pp. 20–27). Odawara, Japan: Language Institute of Japan.

Brown, J. D. (1999). Relative importance of persons, items, subtests and languages to TOEFL test variance. *Language Testing, 16*(2), 216–237.

Brown, J. D. (2001). *Using surveys in language programs.* Cambridge: Cambridge University Press.

Brown, J. D. (2001). Six types of pragmatics tests in two different contexts. In K. Rose & G. Kasper (Eds.), *Pragmatics in language teaching.* Cambridge: Cambridge University Press.

Brown, J. D., & Bailey, K. M. (1984). A categorical instrument for scoring second language writing skills. *Language Learning, 34*, 21–42.

Brown, J. D., Cook, H. G., Lockhart, C., & Ramos, T. (1991). Southeast Asian Languages Proficiency Examinations. In S. Anivan (Ed.) *Current Developments in Language Testing* (pp. 210–226). Singapore: SEAMEO Regional Language Centre.

Brown, J. D., & Hua, T-F. (1998). A review of the *Chinese Speaking Test.* In J. C. Conoley and J. I. Impara (Eds.) *The Thirteenth Mental Measurements Yearbook* (pp. 248–250). The Buros Institute of Mental Measurements, Lincoln, Nebraska: University of Nebraska Press.

Brown, J. D., & Hudson, T. (1998). The alternatives in language assessment. *TESOL Quarterly, 32*(4), 653–675.

Brown, J. D., Hudson, T., Norris, J. M., & Bonk, W. (2001). *Investigating second language performance assessments: Tasks, tests, and rating criteria.* Honolulu, HI: University of Hawai'i Press.

Brown, J. D., Norris, J. M. Hudson, T., & Yoshioka, J. K. (1998). *Designing performance assessments.* Honolulu, HI: University of Hawai'i Press.

Brown, J. D., Ramos, T., Cook, H. G. and Lockhart, C. (1990). *SEASSI Placement Examinations* (including Listening, Cloze, Dictation and Interview tests in Indonesian, Khmer, Tagalog, Thai and Vietnamese with user's manual, test booklets, answer sheets, answer keys and tapes). Honolulu, HI: Department of Indo-Pacific Languages, University of Hawai'i at Manoa.

Brown, J. D., & Ross, J. A. (1996). Decision dependability of item types, sections, tests, and the overall TOEFL test battery. In M. Milanovic & N. Saville (Eds.) *Performance Testing, Cognition and Assessment* (pp. 231–265). Cambridge: Cambridge University Press.

Brown, J. D., & Wolfe-Quintero, K. (1997). Teacher portfolios for evaluation: A great idea or waste of time? *The Language Teacher, 21*(1), 28–30.

Burton, N. W. (1978). Societal standards. *Journal of Educational Measurement, 15*, 263–271.

Camp, R. (1993). The place of portfolios in our changing views of writing assessment. In R. S. Bennett, & W. C. Ward (Eds.) *Construction versus choice in cognitive measurement: Issues in constructed response, performance testing and portfolio assessment* (pp. 183–212). Hillsdale, NJ: Lawrence Erlbaum.

Campbell, R., & Wales, R. (1970). The study of language acquisition. In J. Lyons (Ed.) *New horizons in linguistics*. Harmondsworth, England: Penguin Books.

Canale, M. (1983). On some dimensions of language proficiency. In J. W. Oller Jr. (Ed.) *Issues in language testing* (pp. 333–342). Cambridge, MA: Newbury House.

Canale, M., & M. Swain. (1979). Testing and communicative competence. Paper presented at the 13th annual TESOL Convention, Boston.

Canale, M., & Swain, M. (1980). Theoretical bases of communicative approaches to second language teaching and testing. *Applied Linguistics, 1*, 1–47.

Canale, M., & Swain, M. (1981). A theoretical framework for communicative competence. In A. S. Palmer, P. J. M. Groot, & G. A. Trosper (Eds.) *The construct validation of tests of communicative competence* (pp. 31–36). Washington, DC: TESOL.

Carroll, J. B. (1961). Fundamental considerations in testing for English language proficiency of foreign students. In H. B. Allen and R. N. Campbell (1972) *Teaching English as a second language: A book of readings*. (pp. 313–321). New York: McGraw-Hill.

Carson, J. G. (1993). Reading for writing: Cognitive perspectives. In J. G. Carson, & I. Leki (Eds.), *Reading in the composition classroom: Second language perspectives* (pp. 85–104). Boston: Heinle and Heinle Publishers.

Cartier, F. A. (1968). Criterion-referenced testing of language skills. *TESOL Quarterly, 1*, 27–32.

Center for Applied Linguistics. (1988). *Portuguese speaking test*. Washington, DC: Center for Applied Linguistics.

Center for Applied Linguistics. (1989). *Chinese speaking test*. Washington, DC: Center for Applied Linguistics.

Center for Applied Linguistics. (1996). *German speaking test*. Washington, DC: Center for Applied Linguistics.

Chittenden, E. (1991). Authentic assessment, evaluation, and documentation of student performance. In V. Perrone (Ed.) *Expanding student assessment* (pp. 22–31). Alexandria, VA: Association for Supervision and Curriculum Development.

Chomsky, N. (1965). *Aspects of the theory of syntax*. Cambridge, MA: MIT Press.

Clark, J. L. D., & Li, Y. C. (1986). *Development, validation, and dissemination of a proficiency-based test of speaking ability in Chinese and an associated assessment model for other less commonly taught languages*. Washington, DC: Center for Applied Linguistics.

Cohen, J. A. (1960). A coefficient of agreement for nominal scales. *Educational and Psychological Measurement, 20*, 37–46.

Cook, H. G. (1990). Tailoring ESL reading placement tests with criterion-referenced items. Unpublished MA thesis. Honolulu, HI: University of Hawai'i at Manoa.

Cowan, J. R. (1974). Lexical and syntactic research for the design of EFL materials. *TESOL Quarterly, 8,* 389–399.

Cronbach, L. J. (1951). Coefficient alpha and the internal structure of tests. *Psychometrika, 42,* 375–399.

Cronbach, L. J. (1982). *Designing evaluations of educational and social programs.* San Francisco: Jossey-Bass.

Cronbach, L. J., Ambron, S. R., Dornbusch, S. M., Hess, R. D., Hornik, R. C., Phillips, D. C., Walker, D. F., & Weiner, S. S. (1980). *Toward reform in program evaluation.* San Francisco: Jossey-Bass.

Cronbach, L. J. (1988). Five perspectives on validity argument. In H. Wainer & H. I. Braun (Eds.) *Test validity* (pp. 3–17). Hillsdale, NJ: Lawrence Erlbaum Associates.

Cronbach, L. J., & Furby, L. (1970). How we should measure "change" – or should we? *Psychological Bulletin, 74,* 68–80.

Cronbach, L. J., & Gleser, G. C. (1964). The signal/noise ration in the comparison of reliability coefficients. *Education and Psychological Measurement, 24,* 467–480.

Cronbach, L. J., Gleser, G. C., Nanda, H., & Rajaratnam, N. (1972). *The dependability of behavioral measurements.* New York: Wiley.

Cronbach, L. J., Rajaratnam, N., & Gleser, G. C. (1963). Theory of generalizability: A liberalization of reliability theory. *British Journal of Statistical Psychology, 16,* 137–163.

Cziko, G. A. (1982). Improving the psychometric, criterion-referenced, and practical qualities of integrative language tests. *TESOL Quarterly, 16,* 367–379.

Cziko, G. A. (1983). Psychometric and edumetric approaches to language testing. In J.W. Oller, Jr. (Ed.). *Issues in language testing research* (pp. 289–307). Rowley, MA: Newbury House.

Cziko, G. A. (1984). Some problems with empirically-based models of communicative competence. *Applied Linguistics, 5,* 23–38.

Dandinoli, P. (1987). ACTFL's current research in proficiency testing. In H. Byrnes, & M. Canale (Eds.), *Defining and developing proficiency: Guidelines, implementations and concepts.* (pp. 75–96). Lincolnwood, Il: National Textbook Company.

Davidson, F., & Henning, G. (1985). A self-rating scale of English difficulty. *Language Testing, 2,* 164–179.

Davidson, F., & Lynch, B. K. (2001). *A teacher's guide to writing and using language test specifications.* New Haven, CT: Yale University.

Davies, A. (1990) *Principles of language testing.* Oxford: Basil Blackwell.

Delamere, T. (1985). Notional-functional syllabi and criterion-referenced tests: The missing link. *System, 13,* 43–47.

Divgi, D. R. (1981). A nonparametric test for comparing goodness of fit in latent trait theory. Paper at the annual meeting of the American Educational Research Association, Boston.

Dunn-Rankin, P. (1983). *Scaling methods.* Hillsdale, NJ: Lawrence Erlbaum.

Ebel, R. L. (1979). *Essentials of educational measurement* (3rd ed.). Englewood Cliffs, NJ: Prentice-Hall.

Educational Testing Service. (1995). *Performance assessment: Different needs, difficult answers*. Princeton, NJ: Educational Testing Service.

Educational Testing Service. (2000a). *Graduate record examination*. Princeton, NJ: Educational Testing Service.

Educational Testing Service. (2000b). *Test of English as a foreign language*. Princeton, NJ: Educational Testing Service.

Embretson, S. E., & Reise, S. P. (2000). *Item response theory for psychologists*. Mahwah, NJ: Lawrence Erlbaum Associates.

Emrick, J. A. (1971). An evaluation model for mastery testing. *Journal of Educational Measurement, 8*, 321–326.

Erickson, M., & Molloy, J. (1982). ESP test development: Listening and reading comprehension for engineering students. In J. W. Oller, Jr. (Ed.), *Issues in Language Testing Research* (pp. 280–288). Rowley, MA: Newbury House.

Findley, C. A., & Nathan, L. A. (1980). Functional language objectives in a competency ESL curriculum. *TESOL Quarterly, 14*, 221–231.

Fry, E. B. (1985). Readability graph. In E. B. Fry, D. L. Fountoukidis, & J. K. Polk (Eds.) *The new reading teacher's book of lists* (pp. 273–274). Englewood Cliffs, NJ: Prentice-Hall.

Gardner, D. (1996). Self-assessment for self-access learners. *TESOL Journal, 5*, 18–23.

Gates, S. (1995). Exploiting washback from standardized tests. In J. D. Brown & S. O. Yamashita (Eds.) *Language testing in Japan* (pp. 101–106). Tokyo: Japanese Association for Language Teaching.

GELC (1982). Materials developed at the Guangzhou English Language Center, Zhongshan University, Guangzhou, Guangdong, People's Republic of China.

Genessee, F., & Upshur, J. (1996). *Classroom-based evaluation in second language education*. Cambridge: Cambridge University Press.

Glaser, R. (1963). Instructional technology and the measurement of learning outcomes: Some questions. *American Psychologist, 18*, 519–521.

Glaser, R. (1994). Critertion referenced tests: Part I. Origins. *Educational Measurement: Issues and Practice, 13*, 9–11.

Glaser, R., & Klaus, D. J. (1962). Proficiency measurement: Assessing human performance. In R. M. Gagné (Ed.) *Psychological principles in systems development* (pp. 419–474). New York: Holt, Rinehart, & Winston.

Glaser, R., & Nitko, A. J. (1971). Measurement in learning and instruction. In R. L. Thorndike (Ed.), *Educational measurement* (2nd ed.) (pp. 625–670). Washington, DC: American Council on Education.

Glass, G. V. (1978). Standards and criteria. *Journal of Educational Measurement, 15*, 237–261.

Glass, G. V., & Stanley, J. C. (1970). *Statistical Methods in Education and Psychology*. Englewood Cliffs, NJ: Prentice-Hall.

Green, D. R. (1998). Consequential aspects of the validity of achievement tests: A publisher's point of view. *Educational Measurement, 17*, 16–19, 34.

Griffee, D. T. (1995). Criterion-referenced test construction and evaluation.

In J. D. Brown & S. O. Yamashita (Eds.) *Language testing in Japan* (pp. 20–28). Tokyo: Japanese Association for Language Teaching.

Grice, H. P. (1975). Logic and conversation. In P. Cole & J. Morgan (Eds.) *Syntax and semantics 3: Speech acts* (pp. 41–58). New York: Academic Press.

Gronlund, N. E. (1988). *How to construct achievement tests* (4th ed.). Englewood Cliffs, NJ: Prentice Hall.

Guilford, J. P,. & Fruchter, B. (1973). *Fundamental statistics in psychology and education* (5th ed.). New York: McGraw-Hill.

Guttman, L. (1944). A basis for scaling qualitative data. *American Sociological Review, 9*, 139–150.

Guttman, L. (1950). The basis of scalogram analysis. In S. A. Stouffer (Ed.) *Measurement and prediction*. Princeton, NJ: Princeton University.

Haladyna, T. M. (1974). Effects of different samples on item and test characteristics of criterion-referenced tests. *Journal of Educational Measurement*, 11, 93–99.

Haladyna, T. M., & Downing, S. M. (1989). A taxonomy of multiple-choice item writing rules. *Applied Measurement in Education*, 2(1), 37–50.

Halliday, M. A. K., & Hasan, R. (1976). *Cohesion in English*. London: Longman.

Hambleton, R. K. (1979). Latent trait models and their applications. In R. Traub (Ed.) *Methodological developments: New directions for testing and measurement (No. 4)* (pp. 13–32). San Francisco, CA: Jossey-Bass.

Hambleton, R. K. (1982). Advances in item response theory and applications: An Introduction. *Applied Psychological Measurement*, 6, 373–378.

Hambleton, R. K. (1983). Applications of item response models to criterion-referenced assessment. *Applied Psychological Measurement*, 7, 33–44.

Hambleton, R. K. (1994). The rise and fall of criterion-referenced measurement?. *Educational Measurement: Issues and Practice*, 13, 21–26.

Hambleton, R. K., & Cook, L. L. (1977). Latent trait models and their use in the analysis of educational test data. *Journal of Educational Measurement*, 14, 75–96.

Hambleton, R. K., & de Gruijter, D. N. M. (1983). Application of item response models to criterion-referenced test item selection. *Journal of Educational Measurement*, 20, 355–367.

Hambleton, R. K., & Rovinelli, R. J. (1986). Assessing the dimensionality of a set of test items. *Applied Psychological Measurement*, 10, 287–302.

Hambleton, R. K., Swaminathan, H., Algina, J., & Coulson, D. B. (1978). Criterion-referenced testing and measurement: A review of technical issues and developments. *Review of Educational Research*, 48, 1–47.

Hambleton, R. K., & Swaminathan, H. (1985). *Item response theory: Principles and applications*. Hingham, MA: Kluwer Nijhoff.

Hambleton, R. K., Swaminathan, H., & Rogers, H. J. (1991). *Fundamentals of item response theory*. Newbury Park, CA: Sage.

Harris, C. W. (1972). An interpretation of Livingston's reliability coefficient for criterion-referenced tests. *Journal of Educational Measurement, 9*, 27–29.

Harris, C. W., & Subkoviak, M. J. (1986). Item analysis: A short-cut statistic for mastery tests. *Educational and Psychological Measurement. 46:* 495–507.

Hatch, E., & Lazaraton, A. (1990). *The research manual: Design and statistics for applied linguistics.* Cambridge, MA: Newbury House.

Hattie, J. (1985). Methodology review: Assessing unidimensionality of tests and items. *Applied Psychological Measurement, 9*, 139–164.

Heilenman, L. K. (1990). Self-assessment of second language ability: The role of response effects. *Language Testing, 7*, 174–201.

Henning, G. (1987). *A guide to language testing: Development, evaluation, research.* Cambridge, MA: Newbury House.

Henning, G. (1988). The influence of test and sample dimensionality on latent trait person ability and item difficulty calibrations. *Language Testing, 5*, 83–99.

Henning, G. (1992). Dimensionality and construct validity. *Language Testing, 9*, 1–11.

Hively, W. (1974). Introduction to domain-referenced testing. *Educational Technology, 14*, 5–10.

Hively, W., Patterson, H. L., & Page, S. A. (1968). A "universe-defined" system of arithmetic achievement tests. *Journal of Educational Measurement, 5*, 275–290.

Hudson, T. D. (1989a). Mastery decisions in program evaluation. In K. Johnson (Ed.) *Program design and evaluation in language teaching* (pp. 259–269). London: Cambridge University Press.

Hudson, T. D. (1989b). Measurement approaches in the development of functional ability level language tests: norm-referenced, criterion-referenced, and item response theory decisions. Unpublished PhD dissertation. University of California at Los Angeles.

Hudson, T., Detmer, E., & Brown, J. D. (1992). *A framework for testing cross-cultural pragmatics.* Honolulu, HI: University of Hawai'i Press.

Hudson, T., Detmer, E., & Brown, J. D. (1995). *Developing prototypic measures of cross-cultural pragmatics.* Honolulu, HI: University of Hawai'i Press.

Hudson, T., & Lynch, B. (1984). A criterion-referenced approach to ESL achievement testing. *Language Testing, 1*, 171–201.

Hughes, A., & Porter, D. (1983). *Current developments in language testing.* London: Academic Press.

Hulin, C. L., Drasgow, F., & Parsons, C. K. (1983). *Item response theory: Application to psychological measurement.* Homewood, IL: Dow Jones-Irwin.

Hulin, C. L., Lissik, R. I., & Drasgow, F. (1982). Recovery of two- and three-parameter logistic item characteristic curves: A Monte Carlo study. *Applied Psychological Measurement, 6*, 249–260.

Huynh, H. (1976). On the reliability of decisions in domain-referenced testing. *Journal of Educational Measurement, 13*, 253–264.

Huynh, H. (1978). Computation and inference for two reliability indices in mastery testing based on the beta-binomial model. Publication Series in Mastery Testing, Research Memorandum 78–1. Columbia, S.C. College of Education, University of South Carolina.

Hymes, D. H. (1972). On communicative competence. In J. B. Pride & J. Holmes (Eds.) *Sociolinguistics* (pp. 269–293). Harmondsworth, England: Penguin Books.

Impara, J. C., & Plake, B. S. (1995). Standard setting for complex performance tasks. *Applied Measurement in Education, 8,* 1–109.

Impara, J. C., & Plake, B. S. (1997). Standard setting: An alternative approach. *Journal of Educational Measurement, 34,* 353–366.

Inman, M. (1978). Lexical analysis of scientific and technical prose. In M. Todd-Trimble, L. Trimble & K. Drobnic (Eds.) *English for specific purposes sciences and technology* (pp. 242–256). Oregon: Oregon State University.

Jaeger, R. M. (1982). An iterative structured judgment process for establishing standards on competency tests: Theory and application. *Educational Evaluation and Policy Analysis, 4,* 461–476.

Jaeger, R. M. (1989). Certification of student competence. In R. L. Linn (Ed.) *Educational measurement* (3rd ed.) (pp. 485–514). New York: Macmillan.

Jones, R. L. (1985). Some basic considerations in testing oral proficiency. In Y. P. Lee, A. C. C. Y. Fok, R. Lord, & G. Low (Eds.) *New directions in language testing* (pp. 77–84). Oxford: Pergamon Press.

Kane, M. (1996). The precision of measurements. *Applied Measurement in Education, 9,* 355–379.

Keleiman, L. S., & Faley, R. H. (1985). The implications of professional and legal guidelines for court decisions involving criterion-related validity: A review and analysis. *Personal Psychology, 38,* 803–833.

Keller, E., & Warner, S. (1979). *Gambits conversational tools* (Books one, two, & three). Hull, Quebec: Canadian Government Printing Office.

Koffler, S. L. (1980). A comparison of approaches for setting proficiency standards. *Journal of Educational Measurement, 17,* 167–178.

Kreiter, C. D., & Frisbie, D. A. (1989). Effectiveness of multiple true-false items. *Applied Measurement in Education, 2,* 207–216.

Kunnan, A. J. (1992). An investigation of a criterion-referenced test using G-theory, and factor and cluster analysis. *Language Testing, 9*(1), 30–49.

Lackstrom, J. E., Selinker, L., & Trimble, L. (1973). Technical rhetorical principles and grammatical choice. *TESOL Quarterly, 7,* 127–136.

Lane, S., Parke, C. S., & Stone, C. A. (1998). A framework for evaluating the consequences of assessment programs. *Educational Measurement: Issues and Practice, 17*(2), 24–27.

LeBlanc, R., & Painchaud, G. (1985). Self-assessment as a second language placement instrument. *TESOL Quarterly, 19,* 673–687.

Lee, J. F. L., & Musumeci, D. (1988). On hierarchies of reading skills and text types. *The Modern Language Journal, 72,* 173–187.

Leki, I. (1993). Reciprocal themes in ESL reading and writing. In J. G. Carson, & I. Leki (Eds.) *Reading in the composition classroom: Second language perspectives* (pp.9–32). Boston: Heinle and Heinle Publishers.

LeMahieu, F. G., Eresh, J. T., & Wallace, R. C. Jr. (1992). Using student portfolios for a public accounting. *The School Administrator, 49,* 8–15.

Lennon, R. T. (1956). Assumptions underlying the use of content validity. *Educational and Psychological Measurement, 16,* 294–304.

Li, H., & Wainer, H. (1997). Toward a coherent view of reliability in test theory. *Journal of Educational Statistics, 22,* 478–484.

Li, M. F., & Olejnik, S. (1997). The power of Rasch person-fit statistics in detecting unusual response patterns. *Applied Psychological Measurement, 21,* 215–231.

Linacre, J. M. (1989–1996). *A user's guide to Facets: Rasch measurement computer program.* Chicago: Mesa Press.

Linacre, J. M. (1988). *Facets: A computer program for many-facet Rasch measurement.* Chicago: Mesa Press.

Linn, R. L. (1994). Criterion-referenced measurement: A valuable perspective clouded by surplus meaning. *Educational Measurement: Issues and Practice, 13,* 12–14.

Linn, R. L. (1997). Evaluating the validity of assessments: The consequences of use. *Educational Measurement, 16,* 14–16.

Linn, R. L. (1998). Partitioning responsibility for the evaluation of the consequences of assessment programs. *Educational Measurement, 17,* 28–30.

Liskin-Gasparro, J. (1987). *Testing and teaching for oral proficiency.* Boston, MA: Heinle & Heinle.

Livingston, S. A. (1972). Criterion-referenced applications of classical test theory. *Journal of Educational Measurement, 9,* 13–26.

Livingston, S. A., & Zieky, M. J. (1982). *Passing scores: A manual for setting standards of performance on educational and occupational tests.* Princeton, NJ: Educational Testing Service.

Lord, F. M. (1968). An analysis of the Verbal Scholastic Aptitude Test using Birnbaum's three-parameter logistic model. *Educational and Psychological Measurement, 28,* 989–1020.

Lord, F. M. (1977) Practical applications of item characteristic curve theory. *Journal of Educational Measurement, 14,* 117–138.

Lord, F. M. (1980). *Applications of item response theory to practical testing problems.* Hillsdale, NJ: Lawrence Erlbaum Associates.

Lowe, P. (1998). Keeping the optic constant: A framework of principles for writing and specifying the AEI definitions of language abilities. *Foreign Language Annals, 31,* 358–380.

Lynch, B. K., & Davidson, F. (1994). Criterion-referenced language test development: Linking curricula, teachers, and tests. *TESOL Quarterly, 28,* 727–743.

Lynch, B. K., & Davidson, F. (1997). Criterion referenced testing. In Clapham, C. and Corson, D. (Eds.) *Encyclopedia of language and education, Volume 7: Language testing and assessment.* Dordrecht: Kluwer. 263–273.

Macready, G. B., & Dayton, C. M. (1977). The use of probabilistic models in the assessment of mastery. *Journal of Educational Measurement, 14,* 99–120.

Mager, R. F. (1975). *Preparing instructional objectives.* Belmont, CA: Fearon-Pitman.

Magill, F. N. (Ed.) (1996). *International encyclopedia of psychology.* London: Fitzroy Dearborn Publishers.

McNamara, M. J., & Deane, D. (1995). Self-assessment activities: Toward autonomy in language learning. *TESOL Journal, 5,* 17–21.

McNamara, T. (1996). *Measuring second language performance.* London: Longman.

Mehrens, W. A. (1997). The consequences of consequential validity. *Educational Measurement, 16,* 16–18.

Meskauskas, J. A. (1976). Evaluation models for criterion-referenced testing: Views regarding mastery and standard-setting. *Review of Educational Research, 45,* 133–158.

Messick, S. (1988). The once and future issues of validity: Assessing the meaning and consequences of measurement. In H. Wainer & H. I. Braun (Eds.) *Test validity* (pp. 33–45). Hillsdale, NJ: Lawrence Erlbaum Associates.

Messick, S. (1989). Validity. In R. L. Linn (Ed.) *Educational measurement* (3rd ed.) (pp. 13–103). New York: Macmillan.

Messick, S. (1996). Validity and washback in language testing. *Language Testing, 13,* 241–256.

Millman, J. (1974). Criterion-referenced measurement. In W. J. Popham (Ed.) *Evaluation in education: Current applications* (pp. 311–397). Berkeley, CA: McCutchan.

Millman, J., & Greene, J. (1989). The specification and development of tests of achievement and ability. In R. Linn (Ed.) *Educational Measurement* (3rd ed. pp. 335–366). New York: American Council on Education/ Macmillan Publishing Company.

Mislevy, R. (1991). Toward a test theory for assessing student understanding. Plenary speech. 13th Annual Language Testing Research Colloquium. Princeton, NJ.

Mislevy, R., & Bock, R. D. (1982 & 1990). *BILOG: Maximum likelihood item analysis and test scoring with logistic models.* Mooresville, IN: Scientific Software.

Morrow, K. (1979). Communicative language testing: Revolution or evolution? In C. J. Brumfit & K. Johnson (Eds.) *The communicative approach to language teaching* (pp. 143–157). Oxford: Oxford University Press.

Moss, P. A. (1998). The role of consequences in validity theory. *Educational Measurement, 17,* 6–12.

Moy, R. H. (unpublished ms.) Proficiency standards and cut-scores for language proficiency tests. Los Angeles: University of California.

Nandakumar, R. (1994). Assessing dimensionality of a set of items: Comparison of different approaches. *Journal of Educational Measurement,* 21, 41–68.

Nandakumar, R., & Stout, W. F. (1993). Refinement of Stout's procedure for assessing latent trait dimensionality. *Journal of Educational Statistics, 18,* 41–68.

National Standards in Foreign Language Education Project. (1996). *Standards for foreign language learning: Preparing for the 21st century.* Lawrence, KS: Allen.

Nedelsky, L. (1954). Absolute grading standards for objective tests. *Educational and Psychological Measurement, 14,* 3–19.

Nitko, A. J. (1984). Review of the book *A technology for test-item writing. Journal of Educational Measurement, 21,* 201–212.

Norris, J. M., Brown, J. D., Hudson, T., & Yoshioka, J. (1998). *Designing second language performance assessments.* Honolulu, HI: University of Hawai'i Press.

North, B. (2000). *The development of a common framework scale of language proficiency.* New York: Peter Lang.

Nuttall, D., & Goldstein, G. (1986). Profiles and graded achievements: The technical issues. In P. Broadfoot (Ed.) *Profiles and records of achievement: a review of issues and practice* (pp. 183–202). London: Holt, Rinehart and Winston.

Oller, J. W. Jr. (1976). Evidence for a general language proficiency factor: An expectancy grammar. *Die Neuren Sprachen, 2m,* 165–174.

Oller, J. W. Jr. (1979). *Language tests at school.* London: Longman.

Osburn, H. G. (1968). Item sampling for achievement testing. *Educational and Psychological Measurement, 28,* 95–104.

Oscarson, M. (1989). Self-assessment of language proficiency: Rationale and applications. *Language Testing, 6,* 1–13.

Oskarsson [Oscarson], M. (1978). *Approaches to self-assessment in foreign language learning.* Oxford: Pergamon.

Osterlind, S. (1989). *Constructing test items.* Boston: Kluwer Academic Publishers.

Pedhazur, E. J., & Schmelkin, L. P. (1991). *Measurement, design, and analysis: An integrated approach.* Hillsdale, NJ: Lawrence Erlbaum Associates.

Popham, W. J. (1978). *Criterion-referenced measurement.* Englewood Cliffs, NJ: Prentice-Hall.

Popham, W. J. (1981). *Modern educational measurement.* Englewood Cliffs, NJ: Prentice-Hall.

Popham, W. J. (1990). *Modern educational measurement* (2nd ed.). Englewood Cliffs, NJ: Prentice-Hall.

Popham, W. J. (1993). *Educational evaluation* (3rd ed.), Needham Heights, MA: Allyn and Bacon.

Popham, W. J. (1994). The instructional consequences of criterion-referenced clarity. *Educational Measurement: Issues and Practice, 13,* 15–18, 30.

Popham, W. J. (1997). Consequential validity: Right concern – wrong concept. *Educational Measurement: Issues and Practice. 13*, 9–13.

Popham, W. J. (1999). *Classroom Assessment: What teachers need to know.* Needham Heights, MA: Allyn & Bacon.

Popham, W. J. (2000). *Modern educational measurement.* (3ʳᵈ ed.). Englewood Cliffs, NJ: Prentice-Hall.

Popham, W. J., & Husek, T. R. (1969). Implications of criterion-referenced measurement. *Journal of Educational Measurement, 6*, 1–9.

Powers, D. E., & Stansfield, C. S. (1982). *Towards standards of proficiency on the Test of Spoken English. TOEFL Final Report.* Princeton, NJ: Educational Testing Service.

Prator, C. H. Jr., & Robinett, B. W. (1985). *Manual of American English pronunciation.* New York: Holt, Rinehart, & Winston.

Reckase, M. D. (1998). Consequential validity from the test developer's perspective. *Educational Measurement, 17*, 13–16.

Reise, S. P. (1990). A comparison of item- and person-fit methods of assessing model-data fit in IRT. *Applied Psychological Measurement. 14*, 127–138.

Rentz, R. R., & Rentz, C. C. (1978). *Does the Rasch model really work? A discussion for practitioners. Technical Memorandum (No. 67).* Princeton, NJ: ERIC Clearinghouse on Tests and Measurement and Evaluation, Educational Testing Service.

Richards, J. C., Platt, J., & Weber, H. (1985). *Longman dictionary of applied linguistics.* London: Longman.

Roid, G. H., & Haladyna, T. M. (1982). *A technology for item writing.* New York: Academic Press.

Ross, S., & Hua, T.-F. (1994). An approach to gain score dependability and validity for criterion-referenced tests. *University of Hawai'i Working Papers in English as a Second Language, 12*, 119–139.

Rowley, G. L. (1982). Historical antecedents of the standard-setting debate: An inside account of the minimal-beardness controversy. *Journal of Educational Measurement, 19* (2), 87–95.

Salvia, J., & Ysseldyke, J. E. (1991). *Assessment* (5th ed.), Boston: Houghton Mifflin Company.

Savignon, S. (1985). Evaluation of communicative competence: The ACTFL provisional proficiency guidelines. *Modern Language Journal, 69*, 129–142.

Sax, G. (1980). *Principles of educational and psychological measurement and evaluation* (2nd ed.). Belmont, CA: Wadsworth.

Scriven, M. (1978). How to anchor standards. *Journal of Educational Measurement, 15*, 273–275.

Selinker, L., Todd-Trimble, R. M., & Trimble, L. (1976). Presuppositional rhetorical information in EST discourse. *TESOL Quarterly, 10*, 281–290.

Selinker, L., Todd-Trimble, R. M., & Trimble, L. (1978). Rhetorical function shifts in EST discourse. *TESOL Quarterly, 12*, 311–320.

Shaklee, B. D., & Viechnicki, K. J. (1995). A qualitative approach to portfolios: The early assessment for exceptional potential model. *Journal for the Education of the Gifted, 18*, 156–170.

Shannon, G. A., & Cliver, B. A. (1987). An application of item response theory in the comparison of four conventional item discrimination indices for criterion-referenced tests. *Journal of Educational Measurement, 24*, 347–356.

Shavelson, R. J., Block, J. H., & Ravitch, M. M. (1972). Criterion-referenced testing: Comments on reliability. *Journal of Educational Measurement, 9*, 133–137.

Shavelson, R. J., & Webb, N. M. (1981). Generalizability theory: 1973–1980. *British Journal of Mathematical and Statistical Psychology, 34*, 133–169.

Shavelson, R. J., & Webb, N. M. (1991). *Generalizability theory: A primer.* Newbury Park, CA: Sage.

Shepard, L. A. (1984). Setting performance standards. In R. A. Berk (Ed.), *A guide to criterion-referenced test construction* (pp. 169–198). Baltimore: Johns Hopkins University Press.

Shepard, L. A. (1997). The centrality of test use and consequences of test validity. *Educational Measurement, 16*, 5–8, 13, 24.

Shimamura, K. (1993). Judgment of request strategies and contextual factors by Americans and Japanese EFL learners. Unpublished MA thesis, University of Hawai'i at Manoa.

Shohamy, E. (1995). Performance assessment in language testing. *Annual Review of Applied Linguistics, 15*, 188–211.

Shohamy, E., Donitsa-Schmidt, S., & Ferman, I. (1996). Test impact revisited: Washback effect over time. *Language Testing, 13*, 298–317.

Skakun, E. N., & Kling, S. (1980). Comparability of methods for setting standards. *Journal of Educational Measurement, 17*, 229–235.

Skehan, P. (1996). A framework for the implementation of task-based instruction. *Applied Linguistics, 17*(1), 38–62.

Smit, D., Kolonosky, P., & Seltzer, K. (1991). Implementing a portfolio system. In P. Melanoff & M. Dickson (Eds.) *Portfolios: Process and product* (pp. 46–56). Portsmouth, NH: Boynton/Cook Heinemann.

Spolsky, B. (1985). What does it mean to know how to use a language? An essay on the theoretical basis of language testing. *Language Testing, 2*, 180–191.

Stansfield, C. W., & Kenyon, D. M. (1992). Research of the comparability of the oral proficiency interview and the simulated oral proficiency interview. *System, 20*, 347–364.

Stout, W. (1987). A nonparametric approach for assessing latent trait unidimensionality, *Psychometrika, 52*, 589–617.

Stout, W. (1990). A new item response theory modeling approach with applications to unidimensional assessment and ability estimation. *Psychometrika, 55*, 293–326.

Subkoviak, M. J. (1980). Reliability: Decision-consistency approaches. In R. A. Berk, (Ed.), *Criterion-referenced measurement: the state of the art* (pp. 129–185). Baltimore: Johns Hopkins University Press.

Subkoviak, M. J. (1988). A practitioner's guide to computation and interpretation of reliability indices for mastery tests. *Journal of Educational Measurement, 25*, 47–55.

Suen, H. K. (1990). *Principles of test theories.* Hillsdale, NJ: Lawrence Erlbaum Associates.

SYSTAT (1987). *TESTAT.* Evanston, IL: SYSTAT.

Taleporos, E. (1998). Consequential validity: A practitioner's perspective. *Educational Measurement, 17*, 20–23, 34.

Tall, G. (1981). The possible dangers of applying the Rasch Model to school examinations and standardized tests. In Lacey, C. & Lawton, D. (Eds.) *Issues in evaluation and accountability* (pp. 189–203). London: Methuen.

Tumposky, N. R. (1984). Behavioral objectives, the cult of efficiency and foreign language learning: Are they compatible? *TESOL Quarterly, 18*, 295–310.

Valdman, A. (1975). On the specification of performance objectives in individualized foreign language instruction. *Modern Language Journal, 59*, 353–360.

Valencia, S. (1990). A portfolio approach to classroom assessment: The whys, whats, and hows. *The Reading Teacher, 1*, 338–340.

Valencia, S. W., & Calfee, R. (1991). The development and use of literacy portfolios for students, classes, and teachers. *Applied Measurement in Education, 4*, 333–345.

Valette, R., & Disick, R. S. (1972). *Modern language performance objectives and individualization: A handbook.* New York: Harcourt, Brace, Jovanovich.

van Ek, J. A., & Alexander, L. G. (1980). *Threshold level English.* Oxford: Pergamon.

Wainer, H., & Kiely, G. L. (1987). Item clusters and computer adaptive testing. A case for testlets. *Journal of Educational Measurement, 30*, 187–213.

Wall, D. (1996). Introducing new tests into traditional systems: Insights from general education and from innovation theory. *Language Testing, 13*, 234–354.

Wall, D., & Alderson, J. C. (1996). Examining washback: The Sri Lankan impact study. In A. Cumming & R. Berwick (Eds.), *Validation in language testing* (pp. 194–221). Clevedon, UK: Multilingual Matters.

Watanabe, Y. (1996). Does grammar translation come from the entrance examination? Preliminary findings from classroom-based research. *Language Testing, 13*, 318–333.

Wesche, M. (1992). Work-related second language assessment. In E. Shohamy & R. Walton (Eds.) *Language assessment for feedback: Testing and other strategies* (pp. 103–122). Dubuque: National Foreign Language Center, Kendall/Hunt.

Widdowson, H. G. (1978). *Teaching language as communication.* Oxford: Oxford University Press.

Wiggins, G. (1989). A true test: Toward more authentic and equitable assessment. *Phi Delta Kappan, 70*, 703–713.

Williams, P. L., & Slawski, E. J. (1980). Applications of the Rasch Model for the development of equivalent forms of criterion-referenced tests. Paper presented at the Annual Meeting of the American Educational Research Association. Boston, MA.

Wolf, D. P. (1989). Portfolio assessment: Sampling student work. *Educational Leadership, 46*, 35–39.

Wolfe-Quintero, K., & Brown, J. D. (1998). Teacher portfolios. *TESOL Journal, 7*(6), 24–27.

Wright, B. D. (1999). Fundamental measurement for psychology. In S. Embretson & S. L. Hershberger (Eds.) *The new rules of measurement: What every psychologist and educator should know* (pp. 65–101). Mahwah, NJ: Lawrence Erlbaum Associates.

Wright, B. D., & Masters, G. N. (1982). Rating scale analysis: Rasch measurement. Chicago: Mesa Press.

Wright, B. D., & Linacre, J. M. (1984). *Microscale manual*. Black Rock, CT: Mediax Interactive Technologies.

Wright, B. D., Mead, R. J., & Bell, S. R. (1979). BICAL: Calibrating items with the Rasch model (Research Report 23–B). Chicago, IL: University of Chicago, Department of Education. Statistical Laboratory.

Wright, B. D., & Panchapakesan, N. (1969) A procedure for sample-free item analysis, *Educational and Psychological Measurement, 29*, 23–48.

Wright, B. D., & Stone, M. H. (1979). *Best test design: Rasch measurement*. Chicago: MESA Press.

Yamashita, S. O. (1996). *Six measures of JSL pragmatics*. Honolulu, HI: University of Hawai'i Press.

Yen, W. M. (1984). Effects of local item dependence on the fit and equating performance of the three-parameter logistic model. *Applied Psychological Measurement, 8*, 125–145.

Yen, W. M. (1993). Scaling performance assessments: Strategies for managing local item dependence. *Journal of Educational Measurement, 30*, 187–213.

Yen, W. M. (1998). Investigating the consequential aspects of validity: Who is responsible and what should they do? *Educational Measurement, 17*, 5.

Zieky, M. J. & Livingston, S. A. (1977). *Manual for setting standards on the basic skills assessment tests*. Princeton, NJ: Educational Testing Service.

Index

9 780521 000833